SAP PRESS e-books

Print or e-book, Kindle or iPad, workplace or airplane: Choose where and how to read your SAP PRESS books! You can now get all our titles as e-books, too:

- By download and online access
- For all popular devices
- And, of course, DRM-free

Convinced? Then go to www.sap-press.com and get your e-book today.

SAP® Billing and Revenue Innovation Management

 **PRESS**

SAP PRESS is a joint initiative of SAP and Rheinwerk Publishing. The know-how offered by SAP specialists combined with the expertise of Rheinwerk Publishing offers the reader expert books in the field. SAP PRESS features first-hand information and expert advice, and provides useful skills for professional decision-making.

SAP PRESS offers a variety of books on technical and business-related topics for the SAP user. For further information, please visit our website: *www.sap-press.com*.

Singh, Messinger-Michaels, Feurer, Vetter
SAP C/4HANA: An Introduction (2nd Edition)
2019, 383 pages, hardcover and e-book
www.sap-press.com/4852

Sanjjeev K. Singh, Karan Sood
SAP Sales Cloud: Sales Force Automation with SAP C/4HANA
2018, 512 pages, hardcover and e-book
www.sap-press.com/4372

Vishnoi, Verhoog, Messinger-Michaels
SAP Commerce Cloud: Commerce with SAP C/4HANA
2019, 531 pages, hardcover and e-book
www.sap-press.com/4621

Chandrakant Agarwal
SAP CRM: Business Processes and Configuration
2015, 737 pages, hardcover and e-book
www.sap-press.com/3648

Maniprakash Balasubramanian, Chaitanaya Desai, Sheikna Kulam, Chun Wei Ooi, Rakesh Rajgopal, Clement Sanjivi, and Andreas Tan

SAP® Billing and Revenue Innovation Management

Functionality and Configuration

Rheinwerk
Publishing

Editor Will Jobst
Acquisitions Editor Emily Nicholls
Copyeditor Melinda Rankin
Cover Design Graham Geary
Photo Credit Shutterstock.com/124029454/© Brian A Jackson
Layout Design Vera Brauner
Production Graham Geary
Typesetting SatzPro, Krefeld (Germany)
Printed and bound in the United States of America, on paper from sustainable sources

ISBN 978-1-4932-1883-7
© 2020 by Rheinwerk Publishing, Inc., Boston (MA)
1st edition 2020

Library of Congress Cataloging-in-Publication Data
Names: Desai, Chaitanaya, author.
Title: SAP billing and revenue innovation management : functionality and
   configuration / Chaitanaya Desai, Sheikna Kulam, Chun Wei Ooi, Clement
   Sanjivi, Andreas Tan.
Description: 1st edition. | Bonn ; Boston : Rheinwerk Publishing, 2019. |
   Includes index.
Identifiers: LCCN 2019039199 (print) | LCCN 2019039200 (ebook) | ISBN
   9781493218837 (hardcover) | ISBN 9781493218844 (ebook)
Subjects: LCSH: Collecting of accounts--Data processing. | Collecting of
   accounts--Electronic resources. | Electronic invoices. | Electronic
   funds transfers.
Classification: LCC HG3752.5 .D467 2019 (print) | LCC HG3752.5 (ebook) |
   DDC 658.8/8--dc23
LC record available at https://lccn.loc.gov/2019039199
LC ebook record available at https://lccn.loc.gov/2019039200

Contents at a Glance

Dear Reader,

There are some things you simply can't leave to chance. With customer expectations evolving faster than you can say "SAP Billing and Revenue Innovation Management," it's particularly important that you find good information fast to get your SAP BRIM system up and running. (Woe to the team that derails business model expansion through trial-and-error system setup!)

To help steer your project, we've assembled a team of SAP BRIM experts from Deloitte to guide first your implementation and then ongoing operations. Forget a make-it-up-as-you-go mentality; fifteen authors and contributors offer decades of cumulative experience structuring SAP billing systems around specialized customer requirements and processes. When project deadlines or financial close milestones are approaching but detailed documentation and hands-on experience are in short supply, this book is the end-to-end SAP BRIM guide for you.

What did you think about *SAP Billing and Revenue Innovation Management: Functionality and Configuration*? Your comments and suggestions are the most useful tools to help us make our books the best they can be. Please feel free to contact me and share any praise or criticism you may have.

Thank you for purchasing a book from SAP PRESS!

Will Jobst
Editor, SAP PRESS

willj@rheinwerk-publishing.com
www.sap-press.com
Rheinwerk Publishing · Boston, MA

Contents

3   Charging

6   Integration with Other Solutions   369

7   First Steps to SAP BRIM

Foreword

CEOs and board rooms are driving major transformations of their businesses by moving from discrete product sales to recurring revenue business models. These business transformations are primarily based on subscription and consumption-based offers and solutions. Wall Street values recurring revenue streams significantly higher, as much as 10-12x more than discrete product sales, driving up market caps of these companies and increasing shareholder returns. The fundamental reason of this substantial valuation difference is rooted in the fact that recurring revenue businesses have lower operational costs and higher profit margins. For example, renewing an existing customer's contract or upselling and cross-selling to that customer costs less than acquiring a new customer.

There are numerous examples of recurring revenue models evolving in the market: software companies moving from shrink-wrapped or perpetual license software to subscription services; manufacturing companies bundling their products with warranty and repair services into subscriptions; printer companies selling by the printed page and consumables instead of solely selling printer machines; medical device companies selling equipment based on dosage, procedures, or test kits; technology and media companies selling cloud, digital content, and streaming subscription services; automotive companies moving into mobility and ride share businesses; cities integrating mobility-as-a-service across various transportation modes; and product companies launching Internet of Things solutions, among many others.

Many leading enterprises have successfully transformed their businesses to recurring revenue models with the help of agile and flexible software application platforms. There are several key characteristics to consider in such a software platform. First and foremost, the data model should be flexible to support monetization of any service, in any industry, and therefore should easily and quickly adapt via configuration to market changes and evolving customer needs. Recurring revenues business generates a massive volume of transactions and therefore requires a high-performing and scalable global solution. Product orders become evergreen subscription contracts, which require full lifecycle management capabilities such as free trials, renewals, addition and co-terming of new services, upgrades and downgrades from one plan to the next, frequent pricing and term changes, and so on. Large enterprise and B2B sales require a master agreement construct in which global terms and conditions are negotiated once and are then inherited with minor tweaks by subsidiaries for their own subscription orders.

Recurring revenue business models require a variety of dynamic pricing and charge calculations from flat fees to tiered and overage charges, from bundled offers to complex promotions and discounts, from pro-rated terms to shared allowances and pooled subscriptions, and from balance management to pre-paid, post-paid, and hybrid payment models. Once charges are calculated, the software solution must support converged invoicing of products, subscriptions, and services on a single invoice, aggregated and non-aggregated, with granular transaction-level details from the billing period. To successfully scale up the recurring revenue business at highest operating efficiencies requires lights-out automation of billing and revenue management processes. The majority of the revenue management processes—receivables, disputes, collections, credit management, revenue recognition, and financial postings—must be designed and implemented with principles of high automation and management by exception. Lastly, from a CFO and controller perspective, the solution should provide an end-to-end transaction integrity, traceability, and auditability for the entire order-to-cash process.

SAP Billing and Revenue Innovation Management (BRIM) offers a comprehensive, next-generation order-to-cash solution to support subscription and consumption-based recurring revenue business models. It is a highly integrated platform that can be implemented in a modular manner, depending on the priority and needs of the business. SAP BRIM supports all the key characteristics of the agile, flexible, scalable, and global multi-currency revenue management platform just described. In addition to supporting B2B, direct, and indirect business models, SAP BRIM also provides a high-volume revenue management platform for B2C commerce and retail POS transactions. Customers often use SAP Convergent Mediation for high-volume transaction data transformation, error/duplication check, and ingestion to support SAP BRIM processes like charging, billing, financial reconciliation, and revenue management.

One innovation of the recurring revenue model is the *multi-sided business model*, in which partners or third-party service providers are part of the monetization process, and money needs to be shared and paid out for every customer subscription or charge billed. Due to its application architecture and data model, SAP BRIM has the unique advantage of being able to support both customer receivable processes and partner payable processes in a single platform on the same instance. Hence a single customer event or transaction can also result in a partner revenue share and payment in SAP BRIM. With this payables capability, customers are also deploying SAP BRIM to support partner and multi-tier channel reimbursements use cases.

To grow customer lifetime value, businesses have been launching rewards and loyalty programs. SAP BRIM supports the calculation and tracking of rewards and loyalty points based on customer transactions, facilitating customer payments and redemption and fulfilling financial liability and reporting processes.

Many large enterprises operate multiple lines of businesses that have grown in a siloed manner with a myriad of systems. To truly enable a great customer experience, drive growth, and reduce operating costs, companies must have an integrated back-end revenue management process across all their business segments. SAP BRIM enables a single revenue management platform across all lines of business, and delivers a single 360-degree financial view of each customer's billing and revenue transactions across the company. Many companies have also leveraged SAP BRIM to integrate acquisitions and consolidate multiple revenue streams from acquired companies into a single revenue management system, thereby enabling comprehensive analytics and reporting and faster financial close.

I am both happy and excited about the publication of this book written by our partner Deloitte. It provides a detailed understanding of the breadth and depth of SAP BRIM's capabilities for the various use cases I have described. It will be a highly valuable resource for new and existing SAP BRIM customers, and will help you gain more insights about ways to leverage its rich functionality and maximize the value of your investment. Besides providing key instructions for IT and technical implementation teams, this book is equally useful for functional teams, such as product management, sales operations, finance, and revenue operations. You will learn how to design and implement SAP BRIM to achieve increased business agility, flexibility, and faster time to market with new offers and new services.

Congratulations and special thanks to the Deloitte team for launching this valuable resource for the SAP BRIM customers and community!

Alkesh "Al" Patel
Head of SAP BRIM Americas
SAP America, Palo Alto, CA

Preface

Flexible consumption business models have existed for long time, especially in the utilities industry, but in recent years there has been a major shift in other industries to adopt them. One of the key drivers for this shift is the customer desire for pay-per-use or service-based models. Today we can buy a service that allows us to stream videos, read a best-selling author, or listen to a favorite artist with a single subscription. In the telecommunications industry, we can choose data volume, voice services, and text services, or even share with a group of additional users. In the automotive industry, we can rent cars, scooters, or bikes on a time-based or time and mileage basis, and we can even charge our cars at charging station or get paid to charge scooters at home. In the software industry, we can choose to use a single application or a suite of applications for single monthly or annual price, and can store our photos and videos in the cloud with flexible payment options based on usage. There are many more relevant examples across all industries.

The adoption and demand for flexible consumption models across industries is driving change in how businesses operate today and how they need to be ready to operate tomorrow. Selecting the right platform is key to a successful organizational transformation. With the introduction on SAP Billing and Revenue Innovation Management (BRIM), enterprises are staying ahead of the changing industry and customer demands. SAP BRIM allows them to enable various flexible consumption models such as consumption-based, subscription-based, usage-based, or event-based business. It reduces time-to-market metrics for new products and services, and provides greater transparency and traceability of data in the offer-to-cash process, including usage data. Because SAP BRIM sits on SAP S/4HANA, it manages high-volume transactions efficiently and systematically. It helps reduce operating costs and increases customer experience in the new digital age.

Objective of This Book

Deloitte has been in the forefront of implementing SAP BRIM globally across all industries. Deloitte brings the ability to help businesses move to an everything-as-a-service (XaaS) model, by providing end-to-end capabilities from operating model change to enabling new models in SAP BRIM. This is an extension of business transformation, rather than just a technical deployment of a solution. To enable an XaaS model, one must consider the process enablement focusing on people, technology, information management, and controls. As we continue our dialogue with various businesses and executives, we realized that there are several questions that clients and organizations would like to address:

- How can SAP BRIM help enable flexible consumption models?
- What is changing with SAP BRIM on SAP S/4HANA?
- How does SAP BRIM fit into the SAP ecosystem?
- And finally, where's the practical, step-by-step instructions for project teams and system integrators?

This book represents our efforts to help business experts and technology enthusiasts understand the scope of SAP BRIM and how its capabilities can help realize relevant business scenarios. With this book, we'll help you understand the different types of business models supported by SAP BRIM, the different components of SAP BRIM, how to set up and configure SAP BRIM to meet the business scenarios outlined in the case study, and the step-by-step instructions for using SAP BRIM. Finally, we will discuss how SAP BRIM integrates with other complementary solutions such as SAP Convergent Mediation, SAP Revenue Accounting and Reporting, SAP C/4HANA, entitlement management systems, tax engines, and payment gateways.

Who Should Read This Book?

This book is intended for anyone that has a desire to learn more about flexible consumption models and how they can be enabled with SAP BRIM and its ancillary applications as part of the business and IT transformation and implementation. Our target group includes IT executives, managers, consultants, power users, business process owners, and subject matter experts involved in the definition, planning, design, implementation, and adoption of SAP BRIM.

What Will Be Covered?

We begin in **Chapter 1, Introduction to SAP BRIM,** which discusses the primary business drivers that lead businesses to select a new platform for their order-to-cash processes. It will introduce the key components that make up the SAP BRIM platform and its supporting add-ons. It will also introduce our fictitious case study (Martex Corp.), which will serve as a baseline for master data setup and configurations for the subsequent chapters.

Chapter 2, Subscription Order Management, explores how to set up and use SAP BRIM, subscription order management, including the configuration steps to build the use case and the integration with SAP Convergent Charging and SAP Convergent Invoicing.

Chapter 3, Charging, explores how to set up and use SAP Convergent Charging and its modeling process based on our case study. We'll go through the charge creation process by explaining the core tool, the charge types (recurring, one time, usage), and interface objects such as chargeable item classes and charged item classes.

Chapter 4, Invoicing, explores how to set up and use SAP Convergent Invoicing, which resides within SAP S/4HANA, in conjunction with the setup performed in Chapter 2 and 3. We'll discuss billable items, consumption items, rating, billing, invoicing, and partner settlement, as well as some of the standard out-of-the-box reporting capabilities that SAP Convergent Invoicing offers.

Chapter 5, Contract Accounts Receivable and Payable, explores how to set up and use Contract Accounts Receivable and Payable (FI-CA), along with key concepts like account determination, open item management, account balance display, and integration with the general ledger, as well as some of the standard out-of-the-box reporting capabilities and relevant transaction codes for FI-CA.

Chapter 6, Integration with Other Solutions, explores how SAP BRIM is implemented in a heterogenous CRM landscape and with other ancillary systems such as SAP Convergent Mediation by DigitalRoute, SAP Revenue Accounting and Reporting, SAP C/4HANA, CFM, entitlement management systems, tax engines, and payment gateways.

Chapter 7, First Steps to SAP BRIM, explores leading practices for planning, evaluating, and considering SAP BRIM as a solution for the future. This chapter offers best practices for planning and considering SAP BRIM as a solution. You will learn how to avoid common pitfalls and gain insights into key decision points.

Finally, we will close the book with a **Conclusion** discussing the changing business models and need to organization to evolve the business processes.

Acknowledgments

We would like to thank our families for their love, patience, and continuous support; this effort required countless hours spent after work, and we are very grateful for their understanding.

A very special thanks to our Deloitte subject matter experts who are the key authors and contributors for this book. They have brought the best of their experience in the field and we are very grateful for all the time they contributed to write, review, and bring this book to life. We would like to extend our sincere thanks to Derek Maak and Amit Agrawal, Deloitte SAP BRIM practice leads who were pivotal in making this project a reality and providing the resources required to complete this book.

We would also like to thank our partners at SAP: Al Patel, Richard Chen, Karthikeyan Krishnamoorthy, and Arun Govindaraja, they have been a crucial part of our journey for this book and the BRIM practice at large.

Finally, we are very grateful to the SAP PRESS team for their trust, support, and time invested in this book. We extend special thanks to Emily Nicholls and Will Jobst for their guidance during the editorial process.

Chapter 1
Introduction to SAP BRIM

This chapter highlights the shift in how institutions sell and deliver their products and services. It discusses key concepts, such as the definition of flexible consumption, the driving factors behind the shift, and the SAP BRIM solution that can help business adopt this new trend. This chapter also provides an introduction to all SAP BRIM solution components and a case study that will be the main point of discussion for the following chapters.

Technology is advancing at an unprecedented rate, driving a whole new age of digital transformation and innovation. To stay ahead of these technology disruptions and to gain competitive advantages in the new economy, many companies are undergoing major revolutions. These revolutions will profoundly change their business strategies. Among these is the switch to a new billing and revenue management solution: flexible consumption. Companies that can shift to the flexible consumption model will reap great benefits—from a predictable revenue stream with higher profit margins to higher customer loyalty, resulting from the on-going customer relationship—along with higher cost of switching.

This first chapter begins by discussing the concept of flexible consumption and the factors driving companies to adopt this new business model, especially in the technology, media, and telecommunication (TMT) industry. We'll also take a quick look at SAP Billing and Revenue Innovation Management (BRIM, previously SAP Hybris Billing) along with other peripheral solutions. Finally, the chapter closes with a case study. This case study is about a fictitious company, Martex Corp., and it serves as the main baseline for the following chapters in terms of how to enable and utilize the SAP BRIM solution (configurations, master data setup, etc.).

1.1 Flexible Consumption, the Subscription Economy, and Business Model Transformation

Let's begin by examining some of the key terminology that will be used throughout the book:

- **Cloud computing**
  The delivery of on-demand computing resources and hosted services—everything from applications to data centers, including the storage and access of data—over the internet.

- **Infrastructure as a service (IaaS)**
  Providers supply a virtual server instance and various storage capacities via IaaS services. Depending on customer needs, there is a specific allocation of storage capacity and access to particular virtual machine (VM) configurations. IaaS providers can offer instances in all sizes and customizations as needed.

- **Platform as a service (PaaS)**
  Providers host development tools on their hardware and infrastructure. Web portals, gateway software, or APIs are used to access the tools. These services are generally leveraged for software development.

- **Software as a service (SaaS)**
  Software applications are made available on the internet for users in this distribution model. These are also commonly known as web services. These services are also mobile-friendly and can be accessed from any computer or device with an internet connection.

- **Flexible consumption**
  This new business model is enabled by new trends in technology. This model affords customers flexibility in how they consume and pay based on their needs and usage. In essence, flexible consumption transforms a company's existing products or services by packaging them into different layers of use and selling these packages to the end consumer, then, depending on the amount of service consumption, customers are billed accordingly. The switch to this new business model is the main driving force behind companies seeking out a new billing solution that can support complex billing processes.

- **Subscription and subscription economy**
  A *subscription* is a business model in which customers pay a recurring fee at a regular interval to use a product or services. The *subscription economy* refers to the many companies offering subscriptions to customers and how customers consume these subscriptions.

  If you have ever used any of the following products or services, you are a participant in the subscription economy:

  - Netflix
  - Dollar Shave Club
  - Blue Apron
  - Spotify
  - Amazon products or services, such as Amazon Prime or Amazon Web Services

  By participating in this new business model, companies and customers enter into a more long-term and intimate relationship, which requires the companies to better manage this relationship through various channels. The subscription economy pushes these companies to refocus and redesign their products/service portfolios to fit this demand, as well as the consumption style of the customers. As a result, many companies must reinvent both their offerings and their enterprise infrastructure, which in turn gives rise to the demand for the SAP BRIM solution.

- **Business model transformation**
  Business model transformation, in this context, describes the process in which companies develop a business case for the shift to an *everything-as-a-service* (Xaas) model and offer constructs and use cases to explain what is sold to whom and provide a clear articulation of a strategic vision and value proposition. The transformation journey is grounded in customer experience and business simplification, as well as upgrading the billing solution. In addition, a new go-to market and new buying models also are developed to fit the redesigned business architecture and business requirements. All these activities are carried out with a focus on delivering the desired experience and on lead to cash, operational capabilities, and processes.

Now that you have an understanding of the key concepts for the chapter, let's dive into the next section and explore the business drivers that fuel the growth of SAP BRIM.

1.2   Business Drivers for SAP BRIM

Let's take a detailed look at why there is such a strong demand for the switch to SAP BRIM by going through the key business drivers. First, we'll explore the business model changes and the benefits brought about by pursuing these changes for many companies. Then, we'll provide an overview of the three main business models that are utilized by companies in their journey to reinvent themselves in this new subscription economy.

1.2.1   Business Model Changes: From Products to Subscriptions

In a time of constant technological and model disruption, there is a fundamental shift to flexible consumption across multiple industries. Flexible consumption is not a new idea. Traditionally, this model is offered by firms that are part of the utilities industry. However, it is now expanding to businesses in a wide range of industries, creating value for both customers and the companies that adopt them (as seen in Figure 1.1). For example, Amazon primarily used to sell books, but now it offers the Prime Reading subscription membership, via which subscribers can have unlimited access to books.

Benefits of flexible consumption for the consumer include the following:

- Flexibility to scale
- Asset-light model
- Lower initial investment

Benefits of flexible consumption for companies include the following:

- Predictable revenue stream
- Deeper customer engagement
- Lower unit costs from aggregation

Increasing demand for consumption flexibility is allowing companies to shift the dial on multiple internal levels.

The technology, media, and telecom (TMT) industry may be the one that experiences the strongest impact with regard to the shift to new model based on consumption.

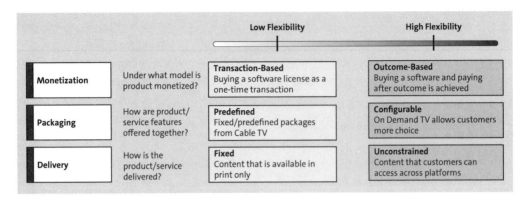

Figure 1.1 Traditional versus Flexible Model

Table 1.1 provides a list of flexible consumption models offered by many TMT companies as part of the effort to diversify their products.

Consumption model	Description	Examples
Subscription (Unlimited)	Access to unlimited quantity or features for a predefined period	Kindle Unlimited Netflix Amazon Prime
Subscription (Predefined)	Access to a predefined quantity or features for a predefined period, generally with a minimum commitment	Salesforce *The Economist*
Freemium	Access to basic services for free while charging a premium for advanced or special features	*The New York Times* Box LinkedIn
Subscription and Overage	Subscription offering with additional overage charges based on actual usage	HP Ink Cisco Webex
Pay per Use	Access on a pay-per-use basis, generally without a minimum commitment	Amazon Web Service Twilio

Table 1.1 Flexible Consumption Models

Consumption model	Description	Examples
Outcome-based	Monetization based on the value delivered to the customer, measured as a quantifiable outcome	Xerox

Table 1.1 Flexible Consumption Models (Cont.)

There are many trends that fuel the demand for a flexible consumption model. Some of the main ones are as follows:

- The rise in cloud product offerings
- The growth of mobile devices
- The increase in social networking access
- Big data
- The Internet of Things

By taking advantage of the advances in cloud-based computing, many IT companies have increased their offerings in a more flexible model based on shared hosted solutions. These solutions can range from SaaS to PaaS to IaaS, and even to "everything" as a service (XaaS). In addition, the exponential growth in mobile device usage and the expansion of broadband and Wi-Fi access points have created an expectation that customers should be able to conduct business from anywhere, at any time, from any device.

The next sections provide an overview of the three main models for flexible consumption: the consumption-based model, subscription-based model, and event-based model. These are not exclusive and can be combined to create an even more flexible model to accommodate business needs

1.2.2   Consumption-Based Model

The consumption-based model, also known as the usage-based model, is built on the idea that customers will pay accordingly for the amount of services or products that they consume. The philosophy for this model is pretty straightforward: First, the business will quantify the services that it provides and determine a pricing model based on actual usage. Then, at the end of every billing cycle, the customer is billed according to what it used. In one example of such a model, many network providers offer out-of-country roaming plans to their customers and charge them based on the number of messages sent or received. Another good example is many internet café in developing countries, which charge per minute or hour for the use of their computers or for internet access.

As shown in Figure 1.2, the invoice amount billed to customers depends on the customer usage. For example, during the first period, the customer consumes the most compared to the second and third periods. As a result, billing event 1 has the highest amount (amount 1) billed.

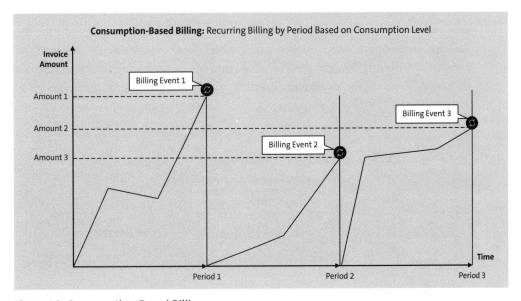

Figure 1.2 Consumption-Based Billing

Besides being simple, another advantage of this model is that it offers a linkage between the amount the customers have to pay and the actual usage and value delivered to the customers. If for whatever reason the customers deem that the services or products don't offer the expected return on investment, they can stop using them and are not liable for the bill. Nonetheless, a potential drawback to this model is that there can be surprises for the customer at the end of the billing cycle. Consider again the network roaming model. The use of out-of-country roaming can be reckless, and if not monitored properly, this behavior can run up an outrageous bill. An additional downside can be the effect of seasonality on the revenue stream.

1.2.3 Subscription-Based Model

In contrast to the consumption-based model, companies that employ a subscription-based model offer access to their products and services for a fixed fee, and this fee is billed periodically (weekly, monthly, quarterly, annually, etc.). This model was first presented by many publishers of books and magazines. However, almost any company can adopt this model today.

Figure 1.3 provides a simple diagram of the subscription-based model. Looking at the diagram, the reader can see that the customer's consumption levels are not considered. Unlike the consumption-based model, subscription-based model billable amounts and functionalities depend on subscription levels. For example, during the first and second period, the customer subscribed to the basic subscription level; as a result, the amounts charged are the same (amount 1 = amount 2). Then, during the third period, the customer decided to switch to a higher subscription level. This led to an increase in the amount billed (amount 3) and accessible functionalities for the customer.

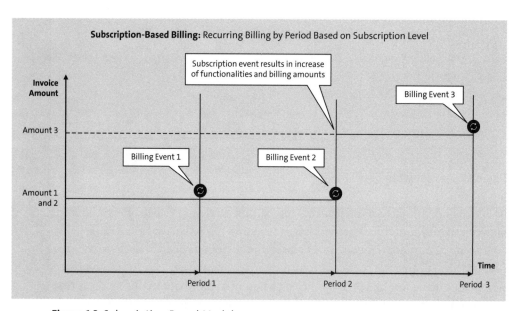

Figure 1.3 Subscription-Based Model

The key difference between consumption-based and subscription-based models is that with a subscription, customers need only to pay a fee and have virtually unlimited access to services (although limitations can sometimes apply depending on how the tier pricing is structured). In the flexible consumption economy, this model has become common thanks to the rise of companies like Netflix, Shopify, and Dollar Shave Club. The subscription model is a win/win for customers and businesses. For businesses, this model is the nearest the business can get to having a crystal ball: the revenue stream is recurrent, predictable, and often not subject to aspects such as seasonality.

The following are some of the most popular ways for companies to implement this model:

- **Unlimited subscription**
  Customers have access to products and services without any limitation for a predefined period.

- **Predefined subscription**
  Customers have access to up to a specific quantity or amount of products and services for a predefined period.

- **Subscription plus coverage**
  Customers have access to up to a specific quantity or amount of products and services for a predefined period. Any additional usage that goes beyond this limit will be billed based on actual usage.

- **Freemium**
  Customers have access to the most basic features of the products and services for free. If customers want access to the premium functionalities, they will have to pay more for these features.

1.2.4   Event-Based Model

The event-based model is a hybrid model that uses the consumption-based model as the starting point and adds different events, which influence the lifecycle of the products, to charge customers. These events can range from simple events, such as the activation/deactivation of the service/device, to more complex events, such as suspension of the device usage and charging customers a prorated rate.

Figure 1.4 provides a diagram of a simple event-based model. Unlike a subscription- or consumption-based model, which has billing events triggered at regular intervals, event-based model billing events are triggered based on events (or milestones). These events are typically decided as part of the contract and will be configured into the system. These events can be automatically triggered based on the lifecycle or manually triggered by either the customer or the company. As a result, as soon as the contract reaches a certain milestone of its lifecycle, the billing event will trigger.

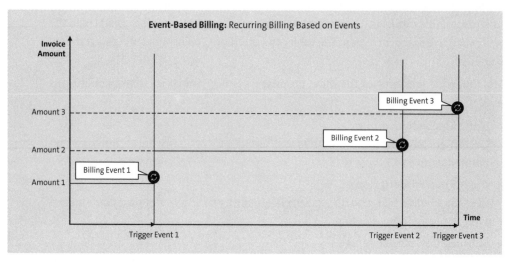

Figure 1.4 Event-Based Billing

With all that said, you might think that switching to this new model is a no-brainer and that many companies should already be getting onboard with this business model transformation.

Table 1.2 lists some of the key companies that were initially created with a flexible consumption model in mind and some of the key players that are trying to transition their current models to flexible consumption models.

	Consumer and Enterprise Software (Saas)	Cloud Computing Services (Iaas/PaaS)	Streaming Audiovisual Content	Other Products and Services
Born Flexible Consumption Model	■ Salesforce ■ Workday ■ Box	■ Amazon Web Services ■ Microsoft Azure	■ Netflix ■ Spotify	■ Dollar Shave Club ■ Birchbox

Table 1.2 Companies Originating with or Transitioning to Flexible Consumption Models

	Consumer and Enterprise Software (Saas)	Cloud Computing Services (Iaas/PaaS)	Streaming Audiovisual Content	Other Products and Services
Transitioning to Functional Consumption Model	▪ Adobe ▪ Intuit	▪ VMware vCloud Air	▪ Electronic Arts (EA) ▪ Home Box Office (HBO)	▪ Amazon Prime ▪ Toyota ▪ General Electric

Table 1.2 Companies Originating with or Transitioning to Flexible Consumption Models (Cont.)

Note that most of the companies that are in the transition process are big and established companies; not many are small or midsized.

However, this transition is easier said than done and involves many challenges. A successful transformation to a flexible consumption model requires strategic thinking and high levels of organizational coordination and alignment and is driven by visionary leadership. For instance, current organizational capabilities (e.g., billing and support) may not support the new model, or risk-averse stakeholders may be resistant to the change. Furthermore, the short-term impact on financial performance may have significant implications, both internally and externally.

The following are some of the challenges involved that act as deterrents when a company considers implementing an SAP BRIM solution:

- *The stakes are high and rising.* With traditional business models under threat, the pressure to offer flexibility in consumption is rising.
- *The challenge is complex.* The scope of disruption requires a complete reconsideration, recalibration, and redefinition of operations.
- *There is little room for error.* Failure to act, execute, and transform in a timely manner may threaten the viability of the business.

To solve these challenges, SAP offers businesses SAP BRIM. SAP BRIM is an end-to-end cross-industry solution that comprises SAP Billing and Revenue Innovation Management, subscription order management; SAP Convergent Charging; SAP Convergent Invoicing; and Contract Accounts Receivable and Payable (FI-CA). In the next few sections, we'll take a quick look at each of these solutions individually.

1.3   SAP BRIM Components

SAP BRIM, previously known as SAP Hybris Billing, is a comprehensive solution for high-volume consumption businesses. SAP BRIM enables the various flexible consumption models that we discussed in Section 1.2. It is a modular solution designed to optimize the business lifecycle processes of design, sales, delivery, and billing, as depicted in Figure 1.5 which illustrates the lifecycle of the SAP BRIM solution based on its business benefits.

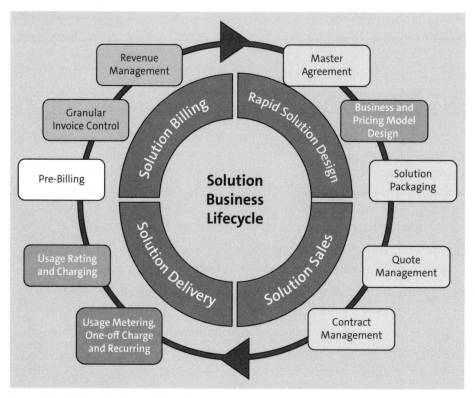

Figure 1.5 Solution Business Lifecycle

The first phase is design, in which SAP BRIM assists with the creation of a uniform design for a business and pricing model, along with the master agreement that will be used as the base for other downstream processes.

Once this is done, the next phase, solution sales, kicks in. In this phase, companies define how they will sell their products with the assistance of the contract management and/or quote management functionalities offered by SAP BRIM.

The third phase is solution delivery. In this phase, companies define the charging methodology for their portfolios. In other words, this is when the companies decide how and how much their customers will be charged based on the business models they pursue. For example, if a company follows an event-based model, it will define the business/transaction events that trigger charges for customers. If a company chooses a consumption-based model, it will calculate the tiers of consumption in which customers will be charged.

The final phase is solution billing. In this phase, SAP BRIM lets companies manage their billing and invoicing mechanisms for consumers based on what has been finalized in previous phases. Furthermore, SAP BRIM aids in the management of revenue recognition and management with various tools for revenue analysis.

The solution comprises four core components:

- SAP BRIM, subscription order management
- SAP Convergent Charging
- SAP Convergent Invoicing
- Contract Accounts Receivable and Payable

Together these components help in the management of business model design; perform order management; track usage metering and transaction pricing, billing, and invoice processing; manage receivables and payables, royalties, and commissions; and provide support for financial customer care (Figure 1.6 and Figure 1.7).

SAP BRIM also offers peripheral solutions such as SAP Convergent Mediation by DigitalRoute, SAP Flexible Solution Billing, SAP Revenue Accounting and Reporting, and SAP Entitlement Management, which are implemented as needed per business requirements and complement the core SAP BRIM solution. Table 1.3 shows a breakdown of the SAP BRIM components.

Core Components	SAP Customer Relationship Management (SAP CRM)	■ Manages product catalogs, including bundles of services and physical goods ■ Manages contract lifecycles
	SAP Convergent Charging	■ One-time, recurring, and usage-based pricing can all be integrated together ■ Pricing rate changes can be easily applied with increased flexibility
	SAP Convergent Invoicing	■ Consolidates multiple billing sources into a single, simplified invoice from multiple sources ■ Supports high volumes, custom pricing, and third-party revenue sharing and partner settlement
	Contract Accounts Receivable and Payable	■ Posts financial documents and receives/makes payments ■ Manages disputes, credits, and collections
Peripheral Solutions	SAP Flexible Solution Billing	■ Integrates easily with existing SD and FI-AR ■ Billing customizability decreases customer inquiries and reduces time to payment ■ Consolidated invoice
	SAP Convergent Mediation	■ Flexible online and batch mediation tool ■ Aggregation, filtration, and data enrichment

Table 1.3 SAP BRIM Core Components and Peripheral Solutions

SAP BRIM solution components reside both as areas within SAP S/4HANA and as standalone modules that integrate with SAP S/4HANA. Figure 1.6 illustrates how each core component of SAP BRIM resides within the end-to-end solution landscape. SAP BRIM, subscription order management and SAP Convergent Charging reside in different instances because they are standalone applications. This is denoted by ❶ for SAP BRIM, subscription order management and ❷ for SAP Convergent Charging. On the other hand, SAP Convergent Invoicing and FI-CA are part of the SAP S/4HANA solution and come out of the box with SAP S/4HANA. This is denoted in the diagram with ❸, used for SAP S/4HANA, FI-CA, and SAP Convergent Invoicing.

As part of the new architecture of SAP S/4HANA 1909, subscription order management is now part of the SAP S/4HANA solution, as seen in Figure 1.7. This significantly reduces the complexity in the implementation and integration when companies implement SAP BRIM solution.

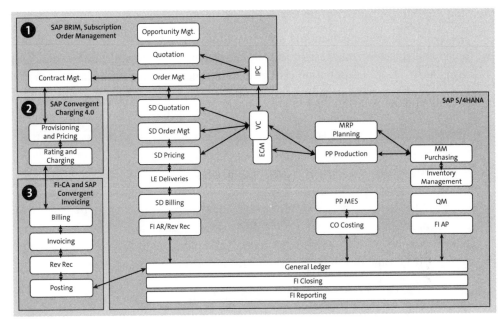

Figure 1.6 SAP BRIM Solution Landscape

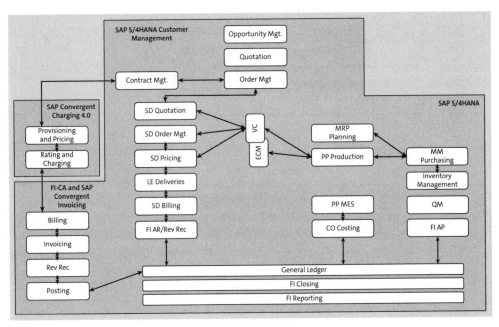

Figure 1.7 SAP BRIM Solution Landscape as of SAP S/4HANA 1909

1.3.1   SAP BRIM, Subscription Order Management

SAP BRIM, subscription order management is an integral part of the end-to-end SAP BRIM solution. It is a business process developed in SAP for the purposes of addressing generation of fees for periodic usage of rights and the consumption of fees for the actual amount of measurable usage. It is built as an additional function relying on the SAP CRM backbone. As of SAP S/4HANA 1909, it has been folded into SAP S/4HANA.

Before 1909, SAP CRM acted as the frontend for companies to connect with their customers for the purpose of product/service selection. SAP CRM and SAP BRIM, subscription order management are the starting point for SAP BRIM as it manages contract lifecycles and product catalogs, including bundles of services and physical goods. Once these activities are done, SAP BRIM, subscription order management creates orders that are then fulfilled by the core SAP ERP system. The order information is then passed to the next component, SAP Convergent Charging, for charging/rating defining and processing (as shown in Figure 1.8).

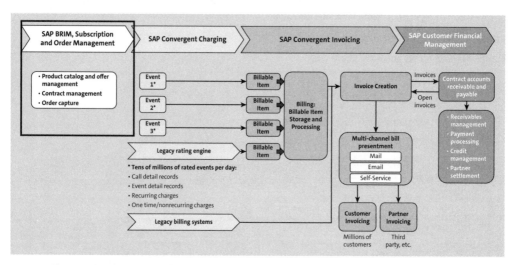

Figure 1.8 SAP BRIM, Subscription Order Management

Equipped with the following specialized features, SAP BRIM, subscription order management allows a company to effectively manage its customers by creating flexible ways to meet its customers' needs:

- Product catalog and offer management
- Order capture

- Order distribution
- Contract management
- Customer care

Chapter 2 will cover these features in depth.

1.3.2   SAP Convergent Charging

SAP Convergent Charging is designed to deliver pricing flexibility when charging customers. In SAP Convergent Charging, a *charge* is a price generated from a rating and charging event that is charged to the customer (or subscriber). In other words, SAP Convergent Charging is a calculation engine tool used to determine the type of charges, such as recurring, one-time, and usage-based charges.

Figure 1.9 illustrates how SAP Convergent Charging fits into the SAP BRIM solution. There are two main components in SAP Convergent Charging: charging and rating. Charging is how SAP Convergent Charging determines which exact customer account will be charged against for a specific customer. On the other hand, rating focuses on the calculation mechanism that derives the total amount to be charged in the billing document.

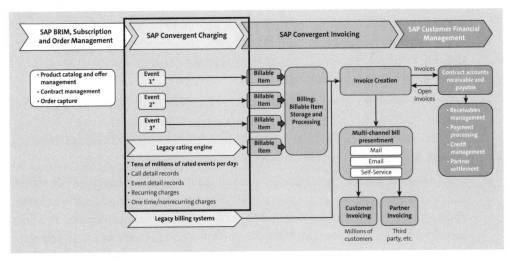

Figure 1.9 SAP Convergent Charging in SAP BRIM

As part of the SAP BRIM solution, SAP Convergent Charging comes with an intuitive graphical user interface, which allows for visual programming (Figure 1.10). This, in turn, virtually eliminates functional and technical limitations to developing pricing offers and revenue sharing plans for different types of services.

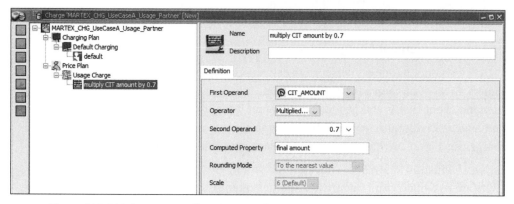

Figure 1.10 SAP Convergent Charging Interface

1.3.3   SAP Convergent Invoicing

SAP Convergent Invoicing's role in SAP BRIM is to consume the billable items once they are passed down from SAP Convergent Charging. Once these items reach SAP Convergent Invoicing, the application will handle the process of uploading consumption detail records, storage of billable items, aggregation of billable items, invoice creation, and invoicing the customer.

SAP Convergent Invoicing stores and manages rated consumption data records from the SAP Convergent Charging system (as shown in Figure 1.11). The rated consumption data records are also known as billable items and undergo a billing and invoicing process as part of posting of receivables in FI-CA.

Unlike SAP BRIM, subscription order management and SAP Convergent Charging, which come as separate applications, SAP Convergent Invoicing is not a separate application and is a part of Contract Accounts Receivable and Payable, which is included as part of the core SAP S/4HANA portfolio. This means that SAP Convergent Invoicing is natively integrated with all SAP S/4HANA areas out of the box, especially SAP S/4HANA Cloud for contract accounting and invoicing.

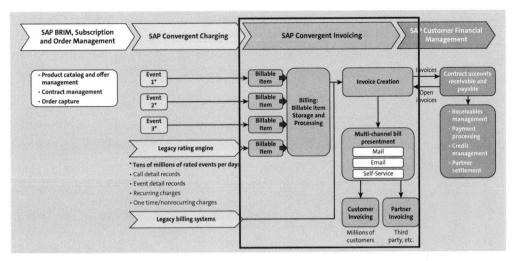

Figure 1.11 SAP Convergent Invoicing in SAP BRIM

1.3.4   Contract Accounts Receivables and Payables

Contract Accounts Receivable and Payable (FI-CA) is the last component of SAP BRIM. It is the financial backend that provides subledger accounting postings tailored to accommodate the requirements of industry sectors in which companies must interact with multiple customers (in this case, subscribers) and a large number of transactions.

As the financial backend of a robust solution in a dynamic business model, FI-CA also offers a wide range of functionalities. As shown in Figure 1.12, FI-CA offers taxation, tax calculations, and country-specific processes, such as accounting principles, payment processing, collection management, partner settlement, and so on. Because of these requirements, FI-CA is highly automated after its initial setup and requires little intervention.

To summarize at a high level, we create orders in SAP BRIM, subscription order management, perform calculations in SAP Convergent Charging for an order based on usage, and get the final charge amounts in SAP Convergent Charging. Bills and invoices are sent to the customer using SAP Convergent Invoicing. Finally, in FI-CA we post the financial documents and receive/make payments. We also use FI-CA for dispute management, credit management, and collections.

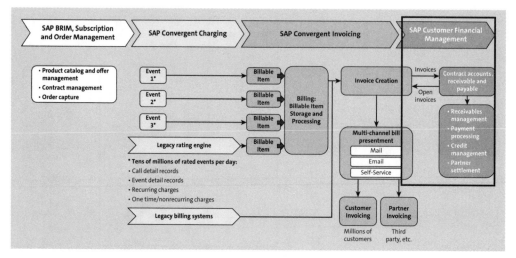

Figure 1.12 Contract Accounts Receivable and Payable in SAP BRIM

1.3.5 Peripheral Solutions

For the most part, SAP BRIM's four core components within the core SAP ERP system is well-suited to meet most business requirements. However, in certain cases, companies have the option to create even more robust and flexible solutions by integrating with other peripheral solutions offered on the market. In the following sections, we discuss some of more popular peripheral solutions that can complement SAP BRIM.

SAP Convergent Mediation by DigitalRoute

SAP Convergent Mediation is an SAP partner product developed by DigitalRoute. Its role is to enable a standardized approach to data mediation. This means this solution first gathers data from multiple sources, then the data is then filtered and converted into a format that can be consumed by other SAP BRIM components. The advantage of SAP Convergent Mediation is that even though it is developed by another party, it is preintegrated into SAP BRIM and can be deployed quickly. The benefits that come with this solution include the reduction of multiple integration points required to manage data, reduction in infrastructure costs, and increased efficiency in data processing, which leads to higher scalability.

OpenText

OpenText is developed by the company of the same name. OpenText complements the SAP BRIM solution by extending the document management capabilities of all SAP modules. It enables businesses to have a comprehensive view of all scanned business documents and all related data across systems and applications. OpenText's advantage lays in its preintegration with SAP modules and its ability to optimize and standardize document management through automation to ensure productivity and compliance.

Payment Gateways

Payment gateways is a generic term that refers to a set of applications offered by many vendors to provide portals for payment processing. These applications typically offer functionality for secured payment processing through major financial methods (credit cards, PayPal, checks, etc.), payment and personal data tokenization, and fraud monitoring,

SAP Customer Financial Management

SAP Customer Financial Management is a set of solutions created to streamline analyzing and optimizing financial processes. They provide solutions for cash management, investment and debt management, and financial risk management. In most cases, SAP Customer Financial Management is used in conjunction with SAP BRIM to measure, analyze, and control the risk of a business partner defaulting on financial obligations.

SAP Revenue Accounting and Reporting

SAP Revenue Accounting and Reporting (SAP RAR) lets businesses manage their revenue and income recognition cycles in compliance with various accounting policies. The solution comes with many accounting standards and rules preconfigured and automated (e.g., ASC 606 or IFRS 15). In addition, SAP RAR also provides a wide range of configurable reporting capabilities for cases in which the standard reports cannot meet a company's requirements.

SAP Entitlement Management

SAP Entitlement Management streamlines and automates the process of entitlement management for companies. The solution manages the entitlement lifecycle (i.e., manages what the customer is entitled to). This ensures transparency into what customers are entitled to for both the customer and the sales rep (alerts, reminders, etc.). This, in turn, increases customer satisfaction and provides more opportunities for upselling or cross-selling.

1.4   Case Study: Martex Corp

Now that you have a basic understanding of SAP BRIM, its driving force, and its components, let's look at our case study. At this point, you should have a high-level understanding of the benefits SAP BRIM offers and the role of each SAP BRIM component in an end-to-end solution. Moreover, you've also learned about the auxiliary solutions that can enhance the SAP BRIM functionalities so that the entire solution can meet your needs and deliver the best performance.

The next several chapters will take deep dives into each component of SAP BRIM to further explain its features and the configurations to enable them. However, as mentioned previously, SAP BRIM is very comprehensive and highly configurable, which means that if we jump directly into the master data and the setup of the components, it will be near impossible to explore all possibilities. With this in mind, similar to many other projects and applications, SAP BRIM works best when it is tailored to specific use cases—like the one in our case study. We will examine a fictional company call Martex and its requirements to transform its business model to a flexible consumption model. This case study will play a vital role in the rest of the book and will be the focal point for all the master data and configuration setup.

1.4.1   Background

Martex Corp. is a distribution company that distributes an office software product, Martex Workplace Solution (MWS). MWS is a suite of workplace productivity software that includes an office suite, along with other specific applications aimed toward the content-development market. Martex doesn't develop MWS from scratch but instead purchases/licenses the rights to the MWS applications from its vendors, then bundles them together and resells the suite. The company has been operating under the traditional model, in which customers purchase a license key or a physical copy (compact disk [CD]) of the MWS software. Martex Corp. generates revenue from the margin between the purchase price from the vendors and the selling price for its customers.

1.4.2   Concerns

Recently, Martex has been experiencing a decline in its sales numbers; growth has been disappointing. Sales have stagnated: many of the company's clients' laptops no longer have CD drives. The drop in the number of laptops with CD drives hammers the company's ability to sell physical copies of its software. Furthermore, the license key distribution model is falling short because the price is fixed, whereas many competitors can now offer more flexible functionalities and pricing.

After thorough reviews of its business model and customers' survey feedback, Martex's leadership realize that they have to change their business model to a new flexible consumption model to survive. Martex will provide its MWS product as a SaaS offering through the cloud and provide hosting services for files created from the MWS suite.

1.4.3   New Business Model

Martex Corp. will transform itself into a distribution company with IaaS and SaaS offerings. Under its new strategy, it obtains products from multiple different vendors and sells them to its customers on behalf of those vendors. Each product is sold via different models, such as recurring, usage consumption, one-off, and pay-per-use models.

Based on the business model offered by Martex Corp., the following use case leverage SAP BRIM functions to process the company's end-to-end billing requirements.

1.4.4   Use Case

The purpose of this use case is to help Martex offer its customers the ability to combine charges (hence the name *combo charge*). In this use case, we will look at service A and service B, and each has a different chargeable rate based on whether the customer opts for a reserved instance. In the cloud computing world, a reserved instance is an option provided to customers in which they pay an upfront recurring charge in exchange for lower usage rates.

X is a monthly recurring reserved instance membership charge of $100.00 per month to customer. Customers with membership X can purchase additional services at lower prices, as follows:

- Service A
  - $300/GB without a reserved instance
  - $250/GB with a reserved instance
- Service B
  - $20/hour without a reserved instance
  - $10/hour with a reserved instance

Customers can also terminate their contracts after 30 days, which will result in a pro-rated refund of the upfront charge.

The first month of the subscription is regarded as a trial period:

- If a customer chooses to suspend their contract in the first month, there should be no charge.
- If a customer suspends and resumes their contract in the first month, they should be charged the full price of $100.00.

After the first month, a customer will only be charged based on days when contracts are not in a suspended state.

Vendor A does not sell its software directly to customers, but rather through multiple distributors in different regions. Distributors acquire and invoice customers on behalf of vendor A. In return, vendor A provides 10 percent off the MSRP cost to all distributors.

In summary, let's briefly revisit the background of Martex Corp. As sales struggle, the company is trying to bring about a new business model to replace its old one. The company wants to switch the current distribution and billing model from physical distribution and one-time payments to a SaaS distribution model and subscription-based billing. There can be many different use cases to consider, depending on the specific requirements from Martex drawn from its pain points and vision. However, this won't be the focus of the next several chapters. The combo charge and prorated charge use cases are just two examples of the most common use cases in which SAP BRIM can help Martex revamp its business model.

1.5   Summary

This chapter focused on introducing and familiarizing readers with SAP BRIM. We first discussed the key terminology frequently used and the business drivers that lead the transformation from product-based to subscription-based business models. Then we talked about each of the core SAP BRIM components at a high level, in addition to the peripheral applications that enhance SAP BRIM functionalities. Finally, we created a case study with a fictious company, Martex Corp., with two use cases to act the baseline for all the master data and configuration in coming chapters.

Now that you have a grasp of the basics, it's time to take a closer look at the core components of SAP BRIM. We will start with Chapter 2, in which we will begin our discussion with SAP BRIM, subscription order management.

Chapter 2
Subscription Order Management

In this chapter, we will introduce SAP BRIM, subscription order management and its functions. Then we will describe and execute the necessary configuration steps to build the use case and the integration with SAP Convergent Charging and SAP Convergent Invoicing.

SAP BRIM, subscription order management is a business process developed in SAP solely for the purposes of addressing the subscription model businesses that are prevailing today, in which products are not sold outright; the right to use them is sold instead.

This process utilizes the backbone of SAP CRM. As of SAP S/4HANA 1909, subscription order management resides in SAP S/4HANA. This is analogous to the business process in the telecom industry in which a consumer is charged a monthly fee for the right to use a telephone service for a month, regardless of the number of calls or amount of data used during that month. This fee is usually charged in advance. In addition, the actual usage—that is, calls, SMS, and data—are measured and billed in the next billing cycle in arrears. This same business and billing model can be leveraged for other industries that employ this concept.

SAP BRIM, subscription order management utilizes SAP CRM as its frontend system to connect customers with services they buy and consume. SAP CRM is strictly utilized for customer/service linkage. Although SAP CRM provides several standard out-of-the-box functionalities, they are not part of SAP BRIM, subscription order management and will not be discussed in detail. SAP BRIM, subscription order management uses the one-order framework that is available in SAP CRM, so it will follow a standard sales order process in which all the necessary configurations needed for a sales process will be maintained in SAP BRIM, subscription order management to varying degrees.

In this chapter, we will guide you through how to configure SAP BRIM, subscription order management from beginning to end. We'll begin with setting up the required master data, such as business partners, business agreements, and products.

Then we will continue with the configurations of the various transaction types and item categories, required profiles within transaction types, item category determination, and document distribution steps.

2.1   Master Data

Master data in SAP CRM is any data that plays an anchoring role in any of the business process in SAP CRM, and mainly in SAP BRIM, subscription order management. It includes data about customers, vendors, contact persons, and products that do not change across any given business process. The main benefit of master data is that you do not have to enter all the relevant information because it will be copied over into transactions seamlessly.

We will discuss setting up the following master data in detail in the context of SAP BRIM, subscription order management:

- Business partner
- Business agreement
- Products

2.1.1   Business Partner

In this section, we will discuss the business partner concept and describe the configuration steps to set up a business partner.

A *business partner* is an entity that is the focus of any interaction within SAP CRM. It can play a role depending on the context of the business process. It can play the part of a customer, vendor, contact person, organization unit, employee, and more. In addition, one business partner can play different roles. To facilitate this, the business role concept was introduced.

Business role is a technical term that defines a set of characteristics and attributes maintained for a business partner to enable certain functions—for example:

- The *sold-to party*, the customer for whom a transaction is maintained for
- A *vendor* who supplies a company
- The *organization*, a structure within a company for hierarchical distribution
- An *employee*, a person involved with a company that drives the transactions

For business transactions to function, a business partner needs to maintain the role of the sold-to party. This is analogous to a customer in SAP ERP. A sold-to party will have three main areas to hold basic data, organizational data, and company code data. Basic data will be maintained for the business partner general role; the organization and company will be maintained in the **Sales Area** tab.

Before we begin the configuration of business partners, you need to understand business roles. Business roles provide a contextual view of business-partner-related information that is necessary for a business function. We do not need to configure any business roles because we will be using SAP-provided standard roles. To view standard roles or define new roles, follow menu path **Cross-Application Components · SAP Business Partner · Business Partner · Basic Settings · Business Partner Roles · Define BP Role.**

Figure 2.1 shows the various business partner roles defined in the system, which correspond to the different role categories.

BP Role	Title	Description
CRM000	Sold-To Party	Sold-To Party
CRM002	Ship-To Party	Ship-To Party
CRM003	Payer	Payer
CRM004	Bill-To Party	Bill-To Party
CRM005	Competitor	Competitor
CRM006	Consumer	Consumer
CRM007	Supplier	Supplier
CRM008	Marketplace Customer	Marketplace Customer
CRM010	Forwarding Agent	Forwarding Agent
CRM012	Consolidator	Consolidating Plant
CRM013	Remanufacturer	Remanufacturer
CRM014	MRP Area	MRP Area
CRM015	Loyalty Partner	Loyalty Partner
CRMACC	Account	Account
CRMICM		
FS0000	Financial Services BP	Financial Services Business Partner
FS0001	FS Max. No.	FS - Maximum Number of Characteristic Values

Figure 2.1 Define Business Partner Roles

To use business partner functions, you first need to activate them. These settings activate required fields in the business partner views. These specific functions activate the time dependencies for the business-partner-related objects, thus providing start and end dates.

To activate business partner functions, follow menu path **Cross-Application Components • SAP Business Partner • Activation Switch for Functions.**

Click the checkbox in the **Active** column next to a function to activate it. For our example, check the boxes shown in Figure 2.2. There are other functions you do not need to activate for our use case.

Activation Status for Functions			⚙
Development	Active	Description	
☐ BUT000	☐	Time Dependency BP Central Data (Table BUT000)	
☐ BUT020	☑	Time Dependency BP Addresses	
☐ BUT0BK	☑	Time Dependency BP Bank Data	
☐ BUT100	☑	Time Dependency BP Roles	
☐ CRMACELAT_	☐	Time Dependency BP Roles	
☐ CRM_ES_AC_	☐	Use Enterprise Search in account search	
☐ CRM_ES_CO_	☐	Use Enterprise Search in contact search	
☐ CRM_NO_DU_	☐	No Check for Duplicates in Business Partner Maintenance	

Figure 2.2 Activation Status for Functions

The next step is to configure the number range and groupings for the business partner. Every business partner needs a unique value that allows it to be easily identified in the system. The number range is defined as a numerical or alphanumerical limit that provides the flexibility to maintain different groups of business partners. This range can be set internally or externally if business partners are created from an external system.

Business partners can be maintained in different groups that are assigned to a number range, which allows the business partners within that group to inherit that specific number range. These number ranges help keep the different business partner groups separated.

To create a number range, follow menu path **Cross-Application Components • SAP Business Partner • Business Partner • Basic Settings • Number Ranges And Groupings • Define Number Ranges**. Click the **Define Number Ranges** link, click the **Change Interval** button, click the **+** button, and create the entries as shown in Figure 2.3.

No	From No.	To Number	NR Status	Ext	⚙
☐ p1	0000013000	0000199999	0	☑	˄ ˅
☐ 02	0002000000	0002999999	2000029	☐	
☐ T1	Tw40000499	Tw40001000	0	☑	
☐ X1	1100000000	1100000031	1100000029	☐	
☐ X2	1200000000	1299999999	0	☑	
☐ X3	1300000000	1399999999	1300000049	☐	
☐ XN	1800000000	1899999999	1800000149	☐	
☐ Z0	8000000000	8004999999	0	☐	
☐ ZN	1100000032	1199999999	1100000431	☐	

Figure 2.3 Define Number Range

The defined fields are as follows:

- **No.**
  Two-character number to define a range

- **From No.**
  Lower limit of the number range

- **To Number**
  Higher limit of the number range

- **NR status**
  Indicates the current state of the number that was last used

- **Ext**
  Indicates if the number used will be internal or external

Next, let's define the groupings and perform the number range assignment. *Grouping* is a concept in which you organize different sets of business partners and align them to follow a specific number allocation assignment.

To create a number range, follow menu path **Cross-Application Components · SAP Business Partner · Business Partner · Basic Settings · Number Ranges And Groupings · Define Groupings And Assign Number Ranges**. Click the **Define Groupings and Assign Number Ranges** link, click the **New Entries** button, and create an entry along with the description.

Next, assign the number range to the newly created group or groups. The business partners created under this group will inherit the number range during business partner creation.

Figure 2.4 shows the groupings that are created and the number range assignment for the ones created in Figure 2.3.

Grouping	Short name	Description	Number ran...	External	Int.Std.Grping	Ext.Std Grping
TWPU	S4H -> CRM (TW)	S4H -> CRM (TW)	T1	✓		○
XN	Org. BP	Org. BP	XN	☐	○	
YN01	CRM -> S4H	CRM -> S4H	ZN	☐	◉	
YN02	S4H -> CRM	S4H -> CRM	X2	✓		○
YN03	Employee	Employee	02	☐	○	

Figure 2.4 Grouping and Assignment of Number Range

The defined fields are as follows:

- **Grouping**
  Four-character grouping name to identify the group.
- **Short Name**
  Short text to define the grouping.
- **Description**
  Descriptive text for the grouping.
- **Number Range**
  Indicates the number range assigned to the group. Here a specific number range can be assigned to many groups, thus allowing the sharing of the number range.
- **Ext**
  Indicates if the number used will be internal or external and is inherited from the number range.
- **Int Std Grouping**
  Indicates the internal number range will be used as the standard if no specific number range is used.
- **Ext Std Grouping**
  Indicates the external number used will be used as the standard if no specific number range is used.

2.1.2   Business Agreement

A *business agreement* is an object that is always linked and created for a business partner functioning in the role of sold-to party. This object contains some of the necessary financial data that is required to process incoming and outgoing financial transactions. A business agreement in SAP BRIM, subscription order management cannot perform any business functions alone. It is always tied to a master data object called a contract account in SAP S/4HANA. A contract account is the main object that is called upon during billing and invoicing, from which financial details are pulled. A contract account has an exhaustive set of data fields utilized for contract accounting processes. The contract account object will be discussed in detail in subsequent chapters.

To configure the business agreement, proceed as follows. First, you need to maintain the number range. The number range can be numerical or alphanumerical in nature and will be defined as internal or external. This setting is critical because the business agreement will be utilized across the SAP BRIM, subscription order management and SAP Convergent Invoicing systems. This number range and the assignment to a class is essential in driving the business agreement replication across both systems.

The number range is defined via the following menu path: **Customer Relationship Management · Master Data · Business Partner · Business Agreement · Define Number Ranges for Business Agreement**. Click the **Define Number Range for Business Agreement** link, click the **Change Interval** button, click the **+** button, and create the entries as shown in Figure 2.5. Here you also define the internal and external range assignment.

No	From No.	To Number	NR Status	Ext	
X1	110000000000	119999999999	110000000239	☐	
X2	120000000000	129999999999	0	☑	
X3	130000000000	139999999999	130000000009	☐	
X4	140000000000	149999999999	0	☑	
X5	210000000000	219999999999	210000000059	☐	
X6	220000000000	229999999999	0	☑	

Figure 2.5 Business Agreement Number Range

The defined fields are as follows:

- **No.**
  Two-character number to define a range

- **From No.**
  Lower limit of the number range

- **To Number**
  Higher limit of the number range

- **NR status**
  Indicates the current state of the number that was last used

- **Ext**
  Indicates if the number used will be internal or external

Next, let's define the business agreement class. A *business agreement class* determines a collection of predefined values that can be set during replication as a contract account. Because a business agreement has a limited number of fields compared to a contract account, the class determines via a setting maintained in Convergent Invoicing for Template Contract Account from which it derives its values. The correct maintenance of internal and external number range assignments in the class helps in the determination of the correct contract account category during replication. This class is maintained to differentiate various types of business agreements/contract accounts for various business purposes, such as maintaining customer business agreements for incoming payments and vendor business agreements for outgoing payments. However, business agreements can be used for both incoming and outgoing payments.

The business agreement class will be defined in the following menu path: **Customer Relationship Management · Master Data · Business Partner · Business Agreement · Define Business Agreement Class**. Click the **Define Business Agreement** link, click the **New Entries** button, and create the entries as shown in Figure 2.6.

Business Agreement Class							⚙
	Bus. Agreem...	Text	Ctr	Int	Ext	BA	No Replica...
☐	YN001	O2C Bus. Agreement Customer	US	X1	X2	☐	☐
☐	YN003	O2C Bus. Agreement Vendor	US	X5	X6	☐	☐
☐	YN004	O2C Bus. Agreement Prelim. Inv.	US	X1	X2	☐	☐
☐	YNCB	O2C Collective Bus. Agreement	US	X3	X4	✓	☐

Figure 2.6 Business Agreement Class

The defined fields are as follows:

- **Business Agreement Class**
  Defines the name of the class

- **Text**
  Description of the business agreement class

- **Ctr**
  Setting where you define the country for which this process is set up
- **Int**
  Indicates the internal number range assigned to this class
- **Ext**
  Indicates the external number range assigned to this class
- **BA**
  Indicates the definition if the class is set to a collective business agreement
- **No Replication**
  Indicates if the business agreement is blocked for replication to an SAP ERP or SAP S/4HANA system

It is essential to decide which method of open item accounting will be active in the system, and you can choose **FI-AR**, **FI-CA**, **Mixed**, or undefined. Because we are utilizing business agreements here, FI-CA will be set as active.

The business agreement activation indicator can be set in the following menu path: **Customer Relationship Management · Master Data · Business Partner · Business Agreement · Define Basic Settings**. Click the **Define Basic Settings** link, click the **New Entries** button, and create the entries as shown in Figure 2.7 shows the business agreement activation indicator.

Business Agreement - Active Indicator	
Text	FI-CA Active
Active Account.	2 FI-CA Active
Ship.Cntr.Act.	0 Address Determined via Correspondence Variant
Max. Number of BAs	
☐ No Default Business Agreement	
☐ DD Limit Active	

Figure 2.7 Business Agreement—Active Indicator

The defined fields are as follows:

- **Text**
  Description of the business agreement active indicator
- **Active Account**
  Dropdown values providing the options for active accounts

- **Ship Contrl Active**
  Dropdown values providing options for shipping address derivation

- **Max Number of BAs**
  Defines the maximum number of business agreements displayed in a table

- **No Default Business Agreement**
  Defines if the default business agreement indicator is displayed or not in the interaction center UI

- **DD Limit Active**
  Defines if the direct debit limit is active in the business agreement

Next, let's define the correspondence variant. The *correspondence variant* is a value that defines the types that contain the control parameters, such as execution intervals and the charges schema. The functions of the correspondence variant are primarily used in SAP Convergent Invoicing. You maintain the corresponding values in SAP BRIM, subscription order management as defined in SAP Convergent Invoicing. You need to set this value so the replication of the contract accounts from SAP Convergent Invoicing will not fail.

The correspondence variant can be set in the following menu path: **Customer Relationship Management · Master Data · Business Partner · Business Agreement · Define Parameters for Business Agreement · Define Correspondence Variant**. Click the **Define Correspondence Variant** link, click the **New Entries** button, and create the entries as shown in Figure 2.8.

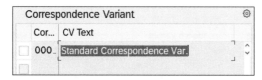

Figure 2.8 Correspondence Variant

The defined fields are as follows:

- **Correspondence Var**
  Defines the value for the correspondence variant

- **CV Text**
  Description of the correspondence variant

Next, let's define the payment method. The *payment method* is a value that defines the types of payment methods allowed for incoming and outgoing payments for each country. These values are used during the creation of business agreements. These values need to be aligned with corresponding values defined in SAP Convergent Invoicing.

Payment methods can be set in the following menu path: **Customer Relationship Management · Master Data · Business Partner · Business Agreement · Define Parameters for Business Agreement · Define Payment Methods**. Click the **Define Payment Methods** link, click the **New Entries** button, and create the entries as shown in Figure 2.9.

PayMeth	Ctr	Text- Payment Method	Usage	Bank/Card	ActAddr	Origin
1	DE	Debit Memo Procedure	Incoming Payment Method	X Bank Details Necessary		Manually Created in CRM (P.
1	EN	Debit Memo Procedure	Incoming Payment Method	X Bank Details Necessary		Manually Created in CRM (P.
1	FR		Incoming Payment Method	Bank Connection / Payment		A Automatically Created wit.
1	US	Debit Memo Procedure	Incoming Payment Method	X Bank Details Necessary		Manually Created in CRM (P.
2	DE		Incoming Payment Method	Bank Connection / Payment		A Automatically Created wit.
2	DK		Incoming Payment Method	Bank Connection / Payment		A Automatically Created wit.
2	FR		Incoming Payment Method	Bank Connection / Payment		A Automatically Created wit.
2	US	Check-Prenum/Remit Overflow	Incoming Payment Method	Bank Connection / Payment		A Automatically Created wit.
3	DE	Automatic Debit	Incoming Payment Method	X Bank Details Necessary		Manually Created in CRM (P.
3	EN	Automatic Debit	Incoming Payment Method	X Bank Details Necessary		Manually Created in CRM (P.
3	FR		Incoming Payment Method	Bank Connection / Payment		A Automatically Created wit.
3	US	Automatic Debit	Incoming Payment Method	X Bank Details Necessary		Manually Created in CRM (P.
4	DE	Check	A Outgoing Payment Method	Bank Connection / Payment	✓	Manually Created in CRM (P.
4	DK		Incoming Payment Method	Bank Connection / Payment		A Automatically Created wit.
4	EN	Check	A Outgoing Payment Method	Bank Connection / Payment	✓	Manually Created in CRM (P.
4	US	Check	A Outgoing Payment Method	Bank Connection / Payment	✓	Manually Created in CRM (P.
5	DE	Bank Transfer	A Outgoing Payment Method	X Bank Details Necessary		Manually Created in CRM (P.

Figure 2.9 Payment Methods

The defined fields are as follows:

- **Paymeth**
  Defines the key value for the payment method

- **Ctr**
  Country definition for which this value is valid

- **Text: Payment Method**
  Description of the payment method

- **Usage**
  Dropdown value defining the direction of the payment method (incoming or outgoing)

- **Bank/Card**
  Defines if the payment is via a bank or a credit card and if either is mandatory

- **ActAdd**
  Mandates if the actual address needs to be present in the business partner master record to use the payment method
- **Origin**
  Dropdown value determining the origination of the values; created in SAP CRM or replicated from SAP ERP

2.1.3   Product

The product master contains all the necessary information about the service being sold in the transaction to enable the subscription selling process. It is still modeled as a material, utilizing the material master concepts from materials management. Products/materials can be tangible, like hardware goods, or intangible, like services or software goods. Subscription orders can handle both hardware and software goods for sales and service. In the context of this book, we'll focus on software goods, which will be modeled as services. Service goods are not deliverable and hence do not require delivery processing to complete billing. The typical service process requires service confirmation to trigger the billing process. In SAP BRIM, subscription order management, there is not a confirmation involved. Although service goods are used, they are only to be offered as a subscription service to a customer to fulfill the sales order process in SAP BRIM, subscription order management.

Products can originate either in SAP BRIM, subscription order management or in SAP S/4HANA and then be replicated in the other. The best practice is to create hardware goods in SAP S/4HANA with all their attributes and replicate them to SAP BRIM, subscription order management, and to create subscription (service goods) in SAP BRIM, subscription order management and replicate them to SAP S/4HANA as type material DIEN. If during project implementation there is master data governance that requires that all materials must be created in SAP S/4HANA, then both hardware and subscription goods can be created there, replicated to SAP BRIM, subscription order management, and utilized in subscription process with no issues. This topic will not be addressed in the context of this book. The following sections will address the configuration of subscription goods in detail.

Product Hierarchy and Category

The best practice for the hierarchical organization of products is to match how materials are created in SAP S/4HANA. The hierarchies and categories can be either replicated from SAP S/4HANA or manually created with the corresponding values in SAP

BRIM, subscription order management. For our example, we'll follow the latter process.

A *hierarchy* is the highest level of the hierarchical structure under which the product attributes can be maintained. The next lowest structure level is the *category*. Several categories can be grouped under one hierarchy. The categories will be assigned a set type and attributes as part of maintenance. You can define your own set types and attributes if needed. For our example, we will use the set types and attributes that are predefined in the system.

Hierarchies and categories can be set in the following menu path: **Cross-application Components** · **SAP Product** · **Product without Customizing Transfer from Backend Systems** · **Maintain Categories/Hierarchies**. Click the **Product without Customizing Transfer from Backend systems** link, then click **Maintain Categories/Hierarchies**. For our purposes, create the R3PRODSTYP hierarchy as shown in Figure 2.10.

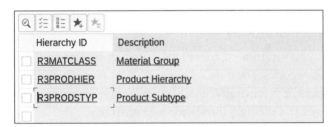

Figure 2.10 Hierarchies

The defined fields are as follows:

- **Hierarchy ID**
  Defines the key value for the hierarchy

- **Description**
  Description of the hierarchy

Next, double-click the R3PRODSTYP hierarchy to navigate to the categories setup screen. Click the **New Category** button to create a new category. This is a root category and is just a skeleton. It does not have any attributes behind it. Leave the name as a blank value to indicate that it is a root category, as shown in Figure 2.11.

The **Hierarchy ID** is autopopulated as R3PRODSTYP. You can create multiple subcategories to suit your business requirements. For this book, we'll focus only on the SRV_ subcategory.

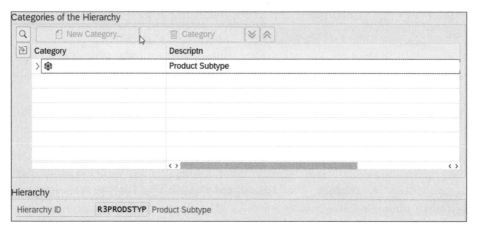

Figure 2.11 Root Category

A subcategory can also be called a category in a broader sense as well, and going forward we will use these terms interchangeably.

Based on the level of hierarchical assignment, these SRV_ category set types will be inherited by the lower level categories. The detailed concept of set type assignment will not be discussed in this book. It is imperative that required set types are assigned correctly so that they communicate the right information downstream.

Set types are groups of attributes that are used to describe products. The attributes are data fields stored in database tables. Therefore, set types, along with attributes, enable groups of fields to be available in a product. They cannot be assigned to a product directly. They are assigned to categories to which products are assigned, so they are inherited by a product via its category assignment.

Next select the root category and click the **New Category** button to create a subcategory. Create the subcategory SRV_, as shown in Figure 2.12.

Next, click the **Set Types** tab and assign the set types. Click the **+** button to add the following predefined set types. These set types are common to all the subcategories created under the SRV_ category.

Figure 2.13 shows the assignment of set types to the SRV_ category.

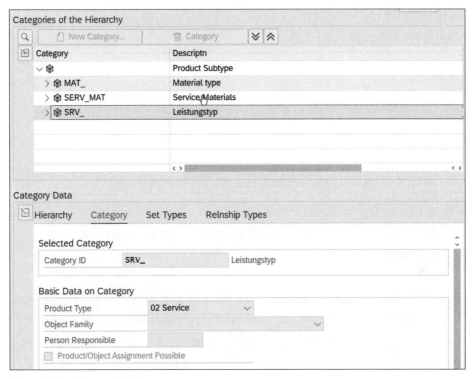

Figure 2.12 Category SRV_

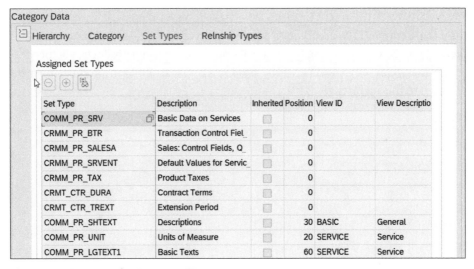

Figure 2.13 Set Types for Category SRV_

The defined fields are as follows:

- **Set Type**
  Define the user and predefined set types existing in the system

- **Description**
  Description of the set type

- **Inherited**
  Flag indicating if the set type is inherited from a higher-level category

- **Position**
  Numerical assignment defining the arrangement of the set types in a sequential order

- **View ID**
  Defines the view screen under which the set type is to be displayed

- **View Description**
  Description of the view

Next, select category SRV_ and create a new category called O2C_RATE_SER. This sub-category will have the same product type as SRV_, which is *service*.

Next, click the **Set Types** tab and assign the set types. Click the **+** button to add the set types. While doing so, some of the set types that were created in the previous step are already displayed due to inheritance from the higher-level category.

Figure 2.14 and Figure 2.15 show the assignment of set types to subcategory O2C_RATE_SER.

After the hierarchy is created, you need to assign it to an application. This enables the hierarchy to be used as a base hierarchy. Because we are using products, you need to assign hierarchy R3PRODSTYP to the products application. Each product must be assigned to this hierarchy.

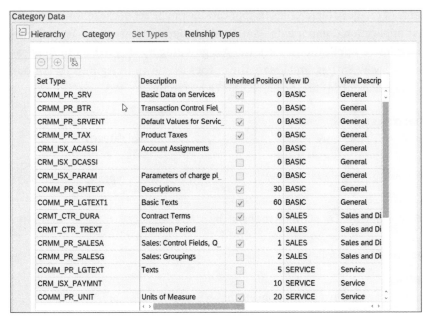

Figure 2.14 Set Types for Subcategory O2C_RATE_SER

Set Type	Description	Inherited	Position	View ID	View Descrip
COMM_PR_SRV	Basic Data on Services	☑	0	BASIC	General
CRMM_PR_BTR	Transaction Control Fiel_	☑	0	BASIC	General
CRMM_PR_SRVENT	Default Values for Servic_	☑	0	BASIC	General
CRMM_PR_TAX	Product Taxes	☑	0	BASIC	General
CRM_ISX_ACASSI	Account Assignments	☐	0	BASIC	General
CRM_ISX_DCASSI		☐	0	BASIC	General
CRM_ISX_PARAM	Parameters of charge pl_	☐	0	BASIC	General
COMM_PR_SHTEXT	Descriptions	☑	30	BASIC	General
COMM_PR_LGTEXT1	Basic Texts	☑	60	BASIC	General
CRMT_CTR_DURA	Contract Terms	☑	0	SALES	Sales and Di
CRMT_CTR_TREXT	Extension Period	☑	0	SALES	Sales and Di
CRMM_PR_SALESA	Sales: Control Fields, Q_	☑	1	SALES	Sales and Di
CRMM_PR_SALESG	Sales: Groupings	☐	2	SALES	Sales and Di
COMM_PR_LGTEXT	Texts	☐	5	SERVICE	Service
CRM_ISX_PAYMNT		☐	10	SERVICE	Service
COMM_PR_UNIT	Units of Measure	☑	20	SERVICE	Service

Figure 2.15 Set Types for Subcategory O2C_RATE_SER

Set Type	Description	Inherited	Position	View ID	View Descrip
CRMT_CTR_DURA	Contract Terms	☑	0	SALES	Sales and Di
CRMT_CTR_TREXT	Extension Period	☑	0	SALES	Sales and Di
CRMM_PR_SALESA	Sales: Control Fields, Q_	☑	1	SALES	Sales and Di
CRMM_PR_SALESG	Sales: Groupings	☐	2	SALES	Sales and Di
COMM_PR_LGTEXT	Texts	☐	5	SERVICE	Service
CRM_ISX_PAYMNT		☐	10	SERVICE	Service
COMM_PR_UNIT	Units of Measure	☑	20	SERVICE	Service
CRM_ISX_COUNTR	Counter sharing	☐	0	PSOB	Contract Obj
CRM_ISX_CPASSI	Charge plan assignment	☐	0	PSOB	Contract Obj
CRM_ISX_CPASST	Charge Plan Assignment_	☐	0	PSOB	Contract Obj
CRM_ISX_SERVIC	Service technical identifi_	☐	0	PSOB	Contract Obj
CRM_ISX_TECRES	Technical Resources	☐	0	PSOB	Contract Obj
CRM_ISX_VERSN	Versions of cross catalog_	☐	0	PSOB	Contract Obj
CRM_ISX_VERSNT	Cross catalog mapping v_	☐	0	PSOB	Contract Obj
TCTR_RESOURCES	TC: Resource assignmen_	☐	0	PSOB	Contract Obj

Assignments of category hierarchies to applications can be set in the following menu path: **Cross-application Components · SAP Product · Product Category · Assign Category Hierarchies to Applications**. Click the **Assign Category Hierarchies to Applications** link, click **New Entries**, and create the entries as shown in Figure 2.16. For our example, you make entries for the R3PRODSTYP hierarchy.

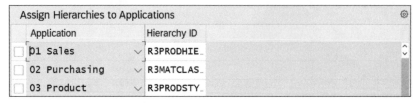

Figure 2.16 Assignment of Application to Hierarchy

The defined fields are as follows:

- **Application**
  Dropdown list of the available applications

- **Hierarchy ID**
  Dropdown list of the created hierarchies for which assignments are made

- **Purpose**
  Dropdown list of predefined values defining the product purpose

Next, you define the length of the product ID. It is mandatory to set the maximum length. The product ID length can be set in the following menu path: **Cross-application Components · SAP Product · Product without Customizing Transfer from Backend Systems · Define Output Display and save Type of Product ID**. Click the **Define Output Display and Save Type of Product ID** link and create the entries as shown in Figure 2.17.

Figure 2.17 Product ID Length

Define Assignment Schema for Technical Resources

The technical resources assignment is a step in which the subscription transactions receive key values that make them unique across the SAP BRIM, subscription order management system. This uniqueness is optional; the transactions can be made non-unique based on business needs. The schema defines the numbering scheme and the properties assigned to it, then this schema is assigned to the relevant product later to allow the product to hold the technical resource ID.

Schema assignment for technical resources can be set in the following menu path: **Customer Relationship Management · Cross-Industry Functions · Provider Order and Contract Management · Transactions · Technical Resources · Define Assignment Schema for Technical Resources**. Click **Define Assignment schema for Technical Resources**, then under the **Resource Type** area, create the entries as shown in Figure 2.18.

Resource Type			⚙
Type	Description	Category	
☐ AR	I	1 Local	
☐ BK	Airline Code	1 Local	
☐ CN	Customer ID	1 Local	
☐ EQ	Equipment ID	1 Local	
☐ MN	Membership ID	1 Local	
☐ PN	Phone number	1 Local	

Figure 2.18 Resource Types

The defined fields are as follows:

- **Type**
  Defines the values for the resource type

- **Description**
  Description of the resource type

- **Category**
  Dropdown list of predefined values defining the usage category

- **Unique**
  Checkbox that defines if the resource ID should be unique at any point in time

- **Time**
  Dropdown list options denoting when the ID uniqueness is checked

Under the dialog structure, double-click the **Assignment** schema and create the entries shown in Figure 2.19.

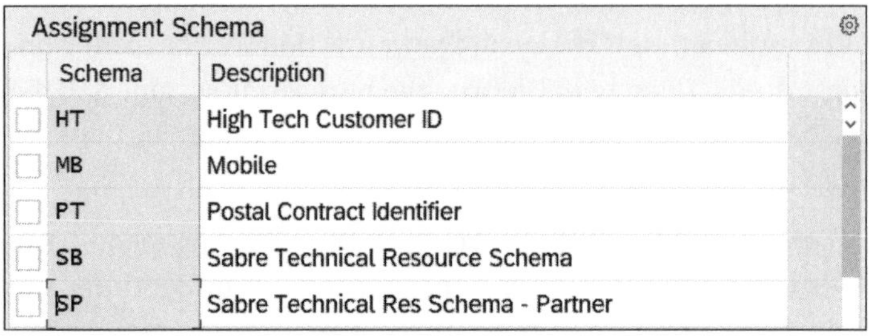

	Assignment Schema	⚙
	Schema	Description
☐	HT	High Tech Customer ID
☐	MB	Mobile
☐	PT	Postal Contract Identifier
☐	SB	Sabre Technical Resource Schema
☐	SP	Sabre Technical Res Schema - Partner

Figure 2.19 Assignment Schema

Click to select the **HT** schema, then click **Schema Details** to access the screen shown in Figure 2.20.

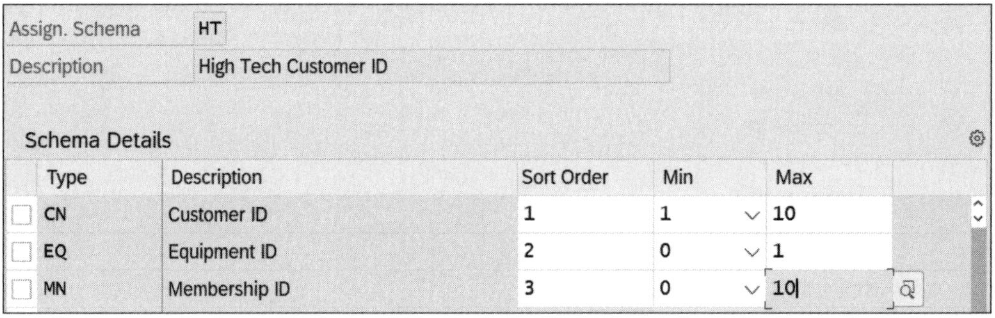

Assign. Schema	HT					
Description	High Tech Customer ID					

Schema Details   ⚙

	Type	Description	Sort Order	Min	Max	
☐	CN	Customer ID	1	1	10	
☐	EQ	Equipment ID	2	0	1	
☐	MN	Membership ID	3	0	10	🔍

Figure 2.20 Assignment Schema Details

Defined fields are as follows:

- **Type**
  Defines the values for the resource type.

- **Description**
  Description of the resource type.

- **Sort Order**
  The order in which the types of ID are displayed during order creation.

- **Min**
  Defines the minimum number of IDs required in the order. The value of 0 defines an ID type as not required.

- **Max**
  Defines the maximum number of IDs that are allowed in the order.

Product Purpose and Classification

Subscription products need to be classified according to business puposes. This supports the use of the products in a provider order, master agreement, or partner provider order. The system validates the purpose of the product in the transaction in which it is used. For example, a standard product cannot be used in a partner provider order and a revenue sharing product cannot be used in a provder order or master agreeement. Because transaction types are designed to drive different purposes, the product purpose needs to be aligned with those puposes.

Standard products are used in provider orders and provider contracts. If an explicit definition is not made, then the products take the standard product as the default assignment. However, this cannot be used in master agreement, revenue sharing or sharing purposes.

Revenue sharing products are used in partner provider orders and partner agreements, which are associated with vendors or partners. These cannot be used in other scenarios.

Master agreement products are used in master agreements or in provider orders and provider contracts. They can be used so long as the provider order is created from a master agreement or references the master agreement.

Sharing products are used in provider orders that used for sharing a single provider contract. These cannot be used in master agreement or revenue sharing scenarios.

Settings for product categories can be set in the following menu path: **Customer Relationship Management · Cross Industry Functions · Master Data · Products · Define Settings for Product Categories**. Click the **Define Settings for Product Categories** link, click the **New Entries** button, and create the entries as shown in Figure 2.21.

Cross-Billing Product Category Customizing			
Hierarchy	Category ID	Purpose	
R3PRODSTY_	O2C_PARTNER	B Revenue Sharing Product	∨
R3PRODSTY_	O2C_RATE_SER	Standard Product	∨
R3PRODSTY_	O2C_SHARING	P Sharing Product	∨

Figure 2.21 Setting for Categories for Product Purposes

The defined fields are as follows:

- **Hierarchy**
  Dropdown list of the created hierarchies
- **Category ID**
  Dropdown list of the created categories for which definition is to be made
- **Purpose**
  Dropdown list of predefined values defining the product purpose

Next, you need to define if any of the product types can be set as configurable. Configurable products can hold various parameters to suit business needs. Even if the product type is configurable, a product can be set as configurable or nonconfigurable during creation to suit business needs.

Settings for making product types configurable can be found in the following menu path: **Customer Relationship Management · Master Data · Products · Settings for Configurable Products · Allow Configurable Products for a Product Type**. Click the **Allow Configurable Product for Product Type** link, click the **New Entries** button, and create the entries as shown in Figure 2.22. Product 01 is a material and product 02 is a service. For our purposes, maintain product 02.

Product Type-Specific Settings for Configuration	
Prod. Type	Allow Configurable Products
01	☐
02	☑
03	☐
04	☐

Figure 2.22 Settings to Alow Configurable Products

The defined fields are as follows:

- **Product Type**
  The numbers to which the product types are assigned
- **Allow Configurable Products**
  Checkbox assignment to indicate if the product type is set to be configurable

Next, assign category O2C_RATE_SER to the right product role so the system can determine the right information for the product in the transaction.

There are three types of product roles:

- Sales package
- Rate plan
- Combined rate plan

A *sales package* is a structure that allows you to combine a hardware product, service, and rate plan in one offering, which allows you to provide a variety of services to a customer. In our example, we will focus on rate plan products.

Category assignment to a product role can be set in the following menu path: **Customer Relationship Management · Master Data · Products · Settings for Packages · Assign Product Roles to Categories**. Click the **Assign Product Roles to Categories** link, click the **New Entries** button, and create the entries shown in Figure 2.23. For our example, create the settings for the O2C_RATE_SER category.

Maintenance assignment of product roles to categories			⚙
Hierarchy	Category ID	Product Role	
☐ R3PRODSTY_	O2C_PARTNER	R Rate Plan	∨
☐ R3PRODSTY_	O2C_RATE_SER	R Rate Plan	∨
☐ R3PRODSTY_	O2C_SHARING	R Rate Plan	∨
☐ R3PRODSTY_	SRV_ALL	S Sales Package	∨

Figure 2.23 Settings for Product Role Assignment to Categories

The defined fields are as follows:

- **Hierarchy**
  Dropdown list of the created hierarchies
- **Category ID**
  Dropdown list of the created categories for which definitions are made
- **Product Role**
  Dropdown list of predefined values for the product role

2.2   Configuring Subscription Order Management

In the following sections, we will discuss the various steps for configuring the system as needed for our example scenario. These steps range from setting up the products to adopt and the relevant transaction types to processing the relevant orders.

2.2.1   Product Modeling

Because SAP BRIM, subscription order management uses the existing sales order framework to process customer order information, the subscription information needs to be adopted to mimic a line item in the sales order. Hence typical products are used in the line items to hold subscription information. Most often, the products in SAP CRM need to hold and pass multiple values for various purposes to downstream systems like SAP Convergent Charging and SAP Convergent Invoicing. To facilitate this, products can be set as configurable, which allows multiple values to be added to the product during order creation. For a configurable product to function correctly, a product model needs to be built and associated with the product.

There multiple ways to achieve product modeling. SAP has a mature application called the Variant Configuration Engine in SAP ERP and SAP S/4HANA that can be used to create product models. The product contains classes, characteristics, and values that can be built as a knowledge base, associated with the product, and sent to SAP CRM to be used with its Internet Pricing and Configurator application.

SAP CRM also has product modeling capabilities of its own. Although not as advanced as SAP ERP/SAP S/4HANA's variant configuration, SAP CRM's capabilities are sufficient for subscription business processes.

The following section on simplified configuration is solely for informational purposes. We will not discuss it in detail because we will be focusing on the Internet Pricing and Configurator-based product modeling.

2.2.2   Simplified Configuration

You can use simplified configuration to assign attributes to product models instead of using the Internet Pricing and Configurator. To use the Internet Pricing and Configurator, a Java application called VMC needs to be running, which requires additional resources.

Simplified configuration can address simple product modeling scenarios. For complex scenarios, Internet Pricing and Configurator-based product modeling will be used.

The ultimate purpose of product modeling is to link a product with configurations in SAP Convergent charging. This process is called *cross-catalog mapping* and will be explained in future chapters.

Simplified configuration uses attributes instead of characteristics (as in the Internet Pricing and Configurator) and can function with native SAP CRM applications. Products that employ simplified configuration can be used in cross-catalog mapping, master agreement provider order, contract distribution, discount setting, and payment setting.

A product can only use one type of modeling: simplified or Internet Pricing and Configurator. The two options cannot be combined in a single product.

Attributes

Attributes are similar to characteristics in the Internet Pricing and Configurator and allow you to add a value to a product during order capture. You define the attributes that can be assigned to a product.

Simplified configuration attributes can be set in the following menu path: **Customer Relationship Management • Cross-Industry Functions • Master Data • Products • Simplified Configuration • Maintain Simplified Configuration Attributes**. Click the **Maintain Simplified Configuration Attributes** link and create the entries as shown in Figure 2.24.

Available Fields										
Business Tran. Com...	Field Name	Data element	Visibility	Changeab.	Generic Display	View ID	Require...	Tra...	Multi-Select	Obsolete
ISUSEC	A5SEC_AMOUN		Always	B Changeab.	A Only Dis.				0 No	
ISUSEC	A5SEC_CURR		Always	B Changeab.	A Only Dis.				0 No	
ISUSEC	A5SEC_REASN		Always	B Changeab.	A Only Dis.				0 No	
ISUSEC	A5SEC_WAIVR		Always	B Changeab.	A Only Dis.				0 No	

Figure 2.24 Available Fields for Configuration Attributes

Attribute Groups

An attribute group is a grouping structure to present the attributes in a meaningful manner during order capture. The groups appear in the product views.

Product views can be set in the following menu: **Customer Relationship Management • Cross-Industry Functions • Master Data • Products • Simplified Configuration • Define Views**. Click the **Define Views** link and create the entries as shown in Figure 2.25.

Product Maintenance Definition Views

View	View	Position
BASIC	General	10
CONDITIONS	Conditions	40
CONFIG	Configuration	50
CONFIG_VAR	Product Variants	51
CONTENT_MGMNT	Documents	60
DR		200
FINANCE	Financing	22
FIN_OPTION	Financing Option	23
FS_001	Term and Interest	33
FS_002	Payment Structure	34
ISU_EXTENSION	Contract Extension	23
MATERIAL	Material	20
PSOB	Contract Object Data	20
PURCHASING	Purchasing	70
RE_DETAILS	Real Estate Data	110
SALES	Sales and Distribution	30
SALES_FIN	Sales: Financing (1)	31

Figure 2.25 Product Views and Their Positions

BRFplus Rules

BRFplus functions are built to drive dynamic value determination, dynamic value help, and help text/checks. You can build your own custom functions to drive the desired results.

BRFplus settings can be set in the following menu path: **Customer Relationship Management • Cross-Industry Functions • Master Data • Products • Simplified Configuration • Maintain BRFplus Applications**. Click the **Maintain BRFplus Applications** link and create the entries as shown in Figure 2.26.

BRFplus Application Name	Application Description	Usage	Usage Description	Storage	Locked	Generation	Workbench
ISU_PROD_COND_GEN		CS	Simple Condition (Deprecated)				
ISU_PROD_COND_MAN		CC	Component Conditions				
ISU_PROD_VALIDITY		PV	Product Eligibilty and Compatibility				

Figure 2.26 BRFplus Application Settings

Product Configuration Using the Internet Pricing and Configurator

Next we will be discussing product modeling using the Internet Pricing and Configurator, which we will return to in the following chapters. For a product to be configurable, you create it under a category that you assigned to be configurable. Once the product is created as configurable, the product model assignment block is visible in the SAP CRM web UI for that specific product. Here you can create the model for the product manually.

The model consists of products and components, classes, tables, functions and UI models. In the following sections, we discuss products and components, classes, and functions.

Under **Product and Components** you include the products or components within a product that is configurable. Multiple products or components can share one model. However, one product cannot be assigned to multiple models concurrently.

Classes are hierarchical structures in which to build characteristics and values that can be assigned to a single product or group of products. Classes can be superordinate or subordinate, with subclasses grouped under superordinate classes. Characteristics are the field definitions of values, in which field properties are maintained. Values are assigned to characteristics and can be set as options in a dropdown menu or as user-enterable.

Functions are similar to macros that can be defined to autopopulate characteristic values based on defined conditions. They utilize formulas along with conditions to execute the necessary functions.

To use product modeling, first you create a product. For our example, proceed as follows:

1. Log into the SAP CRM web UI using Transaction WUI_SSO or the SAP BRIM, simplified order management URL if one has been provided by your system administrator.
2. Select the **PROV-SALES** role.
3. Click **Sales Operations** in the left pane.
4. Click the **Products** link and then the **Product** button.
5. Enter a product ID and name for the product as follows:
   - **Product ID**: enter "MRTX_USG"
   - **Product Name**: enter "Martex Usage"
6. Select the **Base Category** and enter the **Base Unit**.
7. Enter the **Item Category Group**.
8. Check the **Configurable** checkbox.
9. Maintain the **Sales Organization** and **Distribution Channel**.
10. Enter the **Assignment Schema**.

Figure 2.27 shows the product details after completing these entries.

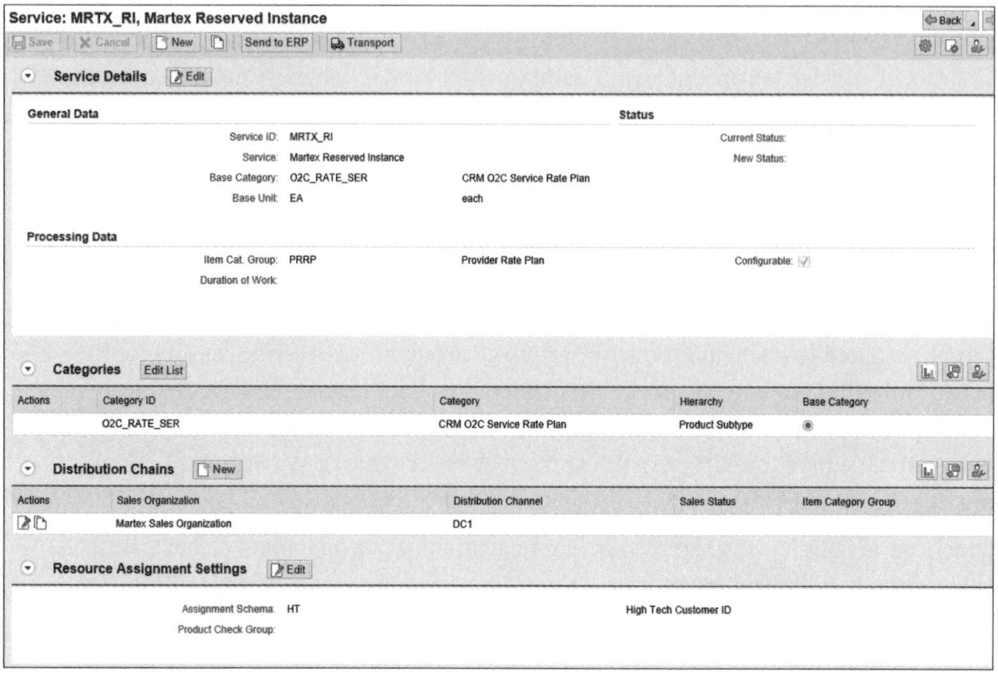

Figure 2.27 Product Setup Details

Product Modeling

To set up product modeling, proceed as follows:

1. In the product models view, click the **Edit List** button.

2. Click the **Create** button to create a new model. This will open a product model application screen. (Figure 2.28 shows the product model hierarchy.)

3. Enter "MARTEX_MODEL 001" for the model, and the system automatically assigns version 001. Because the model is created within the product screen, the **MRTX_USG** product is available under the **Products & Components** node in the tree view.

4. Click **Classes** to create a new class called MRTX_CLASS. Enter the description and long text in the right-hand windowpane.

5. Select the newly created **MRTX_CLASS** and click the **New** button.

6. A popup window will appear, asking you to select **Subclass** or **Characteristic**. Select **Characteristic** in this example to create a new characteristic.

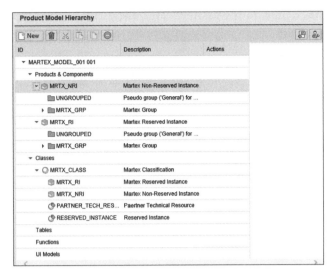

Figure 2.28 Product Model Hierarchy

7. Create new characteristic with the values as shown in Figure 2.29:
    - **ID:** PARTNER_TECH_RESOURCE
    - **Description:** Partner Technical Resource
    - **Reference Characteristic: 0**
    - **Data Type:** String

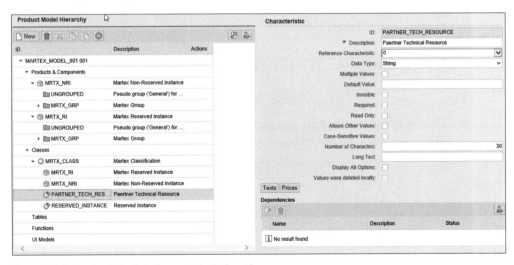

Figure 2.29 Product Model Characteristic Creation

77

Next, you assign product MRTX_USG to the newly created class. This enables the characteristics to be available as dropdown values during runtime for the product in the order. Proceed as follows:

1. Select the **MRTX_CLASS** radio button, then click the **New** button.

2. In the following popup window, select **Product** as the option.

3. In the right-hand window pane, in the **Product** field, select the dropdown and choose the **MRTX_USG** product. Now this product will be assigned under MRTX_ CLASS.

4. Select **MRTX_USG** the product under the **Products & Components** node.

The purpose of the following activity is to organize the characteristics in a meaningful manner:

1. Click the **New** button. In the following popup window, select **Characteristics Group**.

2. Enter the name and description for the characteristic group in the right-hand window pane (as in Figure 2.30).

3. Click the **Move Characteristics** button. In the following popup window, select the characteristics you want to move to the newly created characteristic group. Figure 2.30 shows the available characteristics from MARTEX_CLASS.

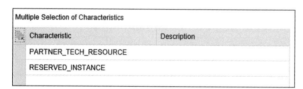

Figure 2.30 Available Characteristics in Class

4. Once complete, click **Save and Test**.

5. Click the **Simulation** button. The product model runtime screen shown in Figure 2.31 appears, showing the successful setup.

6. Product modeling is now complete, and you can use this product in your orders.

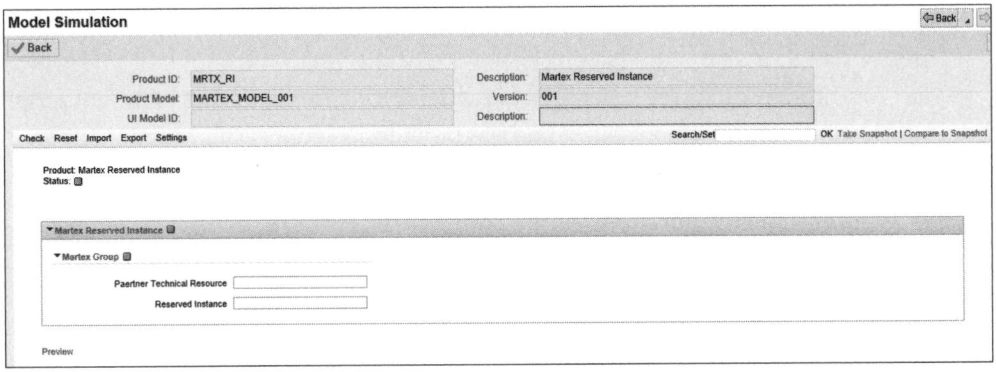

Figure 2.31 Product Model Simulation

2.2.3   Cross-Catalog Mapping

Cross-catalog mapping is a master data function that sets the key linkages between ChargePlan objects in SAP Convergent Charging (see Chapter 3 for more details) and the product setup in SAP CRM. This lets you sell subscriptions via SAP CRM. Charge-Plans are grouped under file folders called catalogs in SAP Convergent Charging, and this linking operation allows you to link one or many ChargePlans to a product in SAP CRM. To use cross-catalog mapping in SAP CRM, you need to assign mandatory set types to the product category. Based on the scenario requirements you many need to add additional set types. These set types enable the necessary assignment blocks in cross-catalog mapping assignment block in CRM product maintenance (within SAP CRM web UI. The assignment blocks are the individual views in the product screen.

Make sure the following set types are assigned for the category of the current product:

- CRM_ISX_VERSN (cross-catalog mapping version)
- CRM_ISX_VERSNT (cross-catalog mapping version description)
- CRM_ISX_CPASSI (charge plan assignment)
- CRM_ISX_CPASST (charge plan assignment description)
- CRM_ISX_PARAM (charge plan parameters)
- CRM_ISX_ACASSI (account assignments)
- CRM_ISX_TECRES (technical data)
- CRM_ISX_SERVIC (service IDs)

To use product modeling, you must first create a product. For our example, create the product as follows:

1. Log into SAP CRM web UI using Transaction WUI_SSO or the SAP BRIM, subscription order management URL if one was provided by your system administrator.

2. Select the **PROV-SALES** role.

3. Click **Sales Operations** from the left pane.

4. Click the **Products** link, then click the **Product** button.

5. Enter a product ID and name for the product and press ⌷Enter⌷:
   - **Product ID**: enter "MRTX_USG"
   - **Product Name**: enter "Martex Usage"

6. You are now in the product screen. Go to the **Cross Catalog Mapping** assignment block.

7. Click the **Edit List** button and the system will automatically generate version 001.

Mapping versions help to identify the mapping rules that are/were set forth during the life of the product with their own validity dates. Only the mapping versions are visible in the cross-catalog mapping assignment block. You can click a specific version to view the mapping details.

Mapping version IDs are internally assigned and cannot be changed.

The numbering starts with 0001 and is ascending. Unless they are released, they can be changed or deleted. If deleted, the numbering starts with the next version after the released one or the one in processing. You can maintain multiple released versions: the system selects the version that is applicable for a specific validity period. It is recommended to maintain only one released version for the product to avoid validity issues. Only released versions are used in the provider order and provider contract. Versions that are not applicable are set to obsolete and cannot be changed or used in a transaction. When creating a new mapping version, the system copies the recent version and sets the highest version number in processing status.

You can also copy the mapping version from another product and adjust if necessary to suit your business needs. To do so, proceed as follows:

1. Click the **001** hyperlink and you will be taken to the mapping version 001 screen. The is where the mapping process begins.

2. Enter the mapping version name and validity date, and set the status as open.

3. Under **Charge Plan Assignments**, click the **Add** button. In the popup window, search for the charge plan you want to assign.

4. Select the charge plan and click **Choose**. Now the charge plan is assigned. Figure 2.32 shows the charge plan selection window. You can assign multiple charge plans to a product, but for our example, you will select one charge plan. Figure 2.33 shows the mapping version screen for product MRTX_USG.

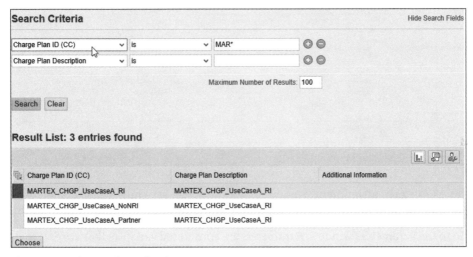

Figure 2.32 Charge Plan Selection

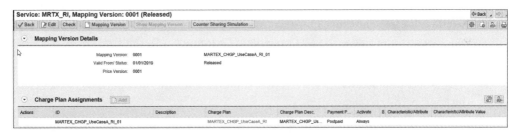

Figure 2.33 Mapping Version

Click the **MARTEX_CHGP_UseCaseA_RI** hyperlink under the charge plan. You will be taken to an expanded mapping screen in which you will set up the mapping process.

Figure 2.34 shows the expanded mapping version screen for the MRTX_USG product. Here you can see the assignment blocks that relate to the assigned set types.

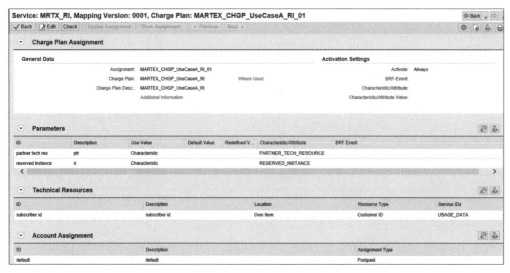

Figure 2.34 Expanded Mapping Version

The charge plan assignment window shows the actual assignment, the charge plan assigned, the charge plan description, and the active status.

Go to the **Parameters** window. *Parameters* are considered variables that are external, which are used to carry values from outside systems to SAP Convergent Charging. These parameters are used flexibly to inherit default values, redefined values, characteristics/attributes, or BRF events. Only external variables are exposed to SAP CRM. Parameters can be internal, in which case they are not exposed to SAP CRM and thus will not carry any values to SAP Convergent Charging.

The parameter ID and the description are autopopulated. Under the **Use Value** column, select **Characteristic**. Then under the **Characteristic/Attribute** column, select the appropriate characteristic.

Figure 2.35 shows the linked values of the parameters from SAP Convergent Charging, the type of linkage, and the associated characteristic.

⊙ Parameters						
ID	Description	Use Value	Default Value	Redefined V...	Characteristic/Attribute	BRF Event
partner tech res	ptr	Characteristic			PARTNER_TECH_RESOURCE	
reserved instance	ri	Characteristic			RESERVED_INSTANCE	

Figure 2.35 Parameter Assignment

Parameters you define in the charge plan in SAP Convergent Charging are exposed in this step. Because you defined them as external, they are visible in SAP BRIM, subscription order management (as shown in Figure 2.36).

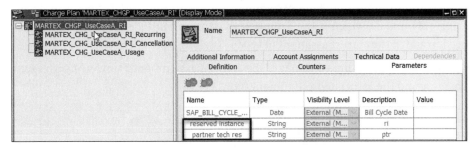

Figure 2.36 Parameters in SAP Convergent Charging Charge Plan

Now, go to the Technical Resources window. **Technical Resource** is a key field that helps to link the provider contract within the SAP BRIM landscape that is applicable in the billing context (as shown in Figure 2.37). It can be a customer ID, phone number, equipment ID, device serial number, or so on. You can make this value unique or nonunique, and your business requirements will drive this decision.

ID	Description	Location	Resource Type	Service IDs
subscriber id	subscriber id	Own Item	Customer ID	USAGE_DATA

Figure 2.37 Technical Resources Assignment

The ID and the description are autopopulated. Under the **Location** column, select **Own Item**. Then under the Resource Type column, select **Customer ID**. The **Service ID** is inherited from the charge plan in SAP Convergent Charging.

Figure 2.38 shows the linked values of the technical resources from SAP Convergent Charging, the type of linkage, and the associated resource type from SAP CRM.

Figure 2.38 Service Identifier and Technical Identifier

Now, go to the **Account Assignment** tab. Account assignment helps to link the accounts such as bank accounts, credit cards, and payment terms. These values are indirectly inherited from the business agreement assigned in the order.

The **ID**, the **Description**, and the **Assignment Type** are autopopulated because we are using only one ID, which is the default. If there were multiple IDs, then you would need to assign the correct assignment type.

Figure 2.39 shows the linked values of the account assignment from SAP Convergent Charging and the associated assignment type.

Account Assignment		
ID	Description	Assignment Type
default	default	Postpaid

Figure 2.39 Account Assignment

2.2.4   Extended Configuration Management

For the product model to work during runtime, you mark the product as configurable to make the product configuration active.

The product model we refer to in this section runs on the Internet Pricing and Configurator. For the Internet Pricing and Configurator to function, it needs to be running on an SAP CRM Java server. The Internet Pricing and Configurator engine is configured via the Extended Configuration Management UI. Configurations are set in both SAP CRM and Extended Configuration Management.

Internet Pricing and Configurator and SAP CRM Configuration

The SAP CRM Java server must be connected to the SAP CRM ABAP server for the Internet Pricing and Configurator to run; otherwise, it will fail to load during runtime. An SAP CRM ABAP user needs to be set up with admin rights to log into the Java server. Using the user management engine in the SAP CRM Java server is optional. There are multiple ways to achieve this setup. The process varies by customer project landscape and security rules. Because the Internet Pricing and Configurator is a complex application, we suggest working with SAP Basis resources to ensure that it functions properly. You do not set up Extended Configuration Management yourself, however. For this reason, its detailed configuration is out of the scope of this book.

2.2.5   One Order Objects

The transaction types utilized in SAP BRIM follow the one order object framework that exists in SAP CRM, which means the transactions use the same set of order tables to populate the header and item data from created transactions. It also uses the same set of function modules to create and modify transactional data.

The following are the different transaction types that are utilized in SAP BRIM scenarios:

- Provider order/provider contract
- Provider partner order/provider partner agreement
- Provider master agreement
- Solution quotation/solution contract

In the following sections, we will describe the detailed configuration steps that you need to follow.

Provider Order/Provider Contract

This is a type of sales order that is used only in SAP BRIM scenarios in which physical goods and services are bundled together as products. The services are usually for subscription products. This order type can also support one-time fees, which can include installation fees, activation fees, cancellation fees, and so on.

When the provider order is completed and then submitted, a linked new document called the provider contract is created. This document serves to hold and maintain long-term agreements that are made between the service provider and the end customer. This provider contract is system-generated and cannot be made manually by the user. When the contract change is required, a linked provider order called a change order is created. You can make necessary changes to this order. When this order is submitted, the existing contract will be changed and the changes logged in the contract. Any transactions or orders that are you create in the system have to be assigned a number from the set number range. Similar to business partners and business agreements, you define the number range at menu path **Customer Relationship Management • Transactions • Settings for Provider Contracts • Define Number Range for Provider Contracts**.

Figure 2.40 shows the number range assignment for provider contracts.

No	From No.	To Number	NR Status	Ext
		Maintain Intervals: Provider Contract		
01	000000000000000000001	000000000000000009999	350	☐
02	000000000000000010000	000000009999999999999	10329	☐

Figure 2.40 Define Number Ranges for Provider Contracts

By now, you should be familiar with the meaning of the required fields in this setup. For a quick refresher, see the number range for business partners.

Transaction Types

Next, you assign transaction types. A *transaction type* defines the characteristics and features of a business transaction. Examples include the provider order, provider contract, sales order, service request, activity, and more. All transaction types are associated with certain control attributes, like the partner determination procedure, text determination procedure, status profile, organization data profile, and so on. The transaction type controls business transaction processing.

SAP has provided a standard transaction type for provider orders: PRVO. In an SAP BRIM implementation, you copy this standard transaction type provided by SAP to create your own custom transaction types. For this example, copy PRVO to YPVO.

You can define the transaction type via menu path **Customer Relationship Management • Transactions • Basic Settings • Define Transaction Types**. On the change view definition of transaction types overview screen, select **PRVO** for the **Transaction Type**, then choose **Copy As to YPVO**.

Figure 2.41 shows the newly created transaction type copied from the standard provider order transaction.

In Figure 2.42, you can see that most of the control attributes are also copied over from the standard transaction type. If you want to maintain your own control attributes, like text determination procedure, partner determination procedure, and so on, you can copy the standard ones and assign the custom control attributes to the custom provider order transaction type.

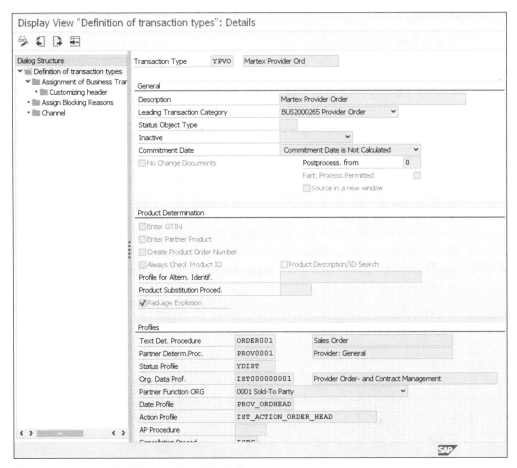

Figure 2.41 Transaction Type for Provider Order

Status Profile	Text	Lang.	⚙
YDIST	NO Distribute to S4H	EN	
YONEOFF	One off charges	EN	
ZUCQUOTE	SRVX Quote Copy	EN	

Figure 2.42 Status Profile Setting

The defined fields are as follows:

- **Status Profile**

  SAP has provided the flexibility to create and use your own statuses along with the system statuses. These statuses can be used for accommodating additional information. You can create any number of statuses according to your requirements by following menu path **Customer Relationship Management · Transactions · Basic Settings · Status Management · Define Status Profile For User Status**.

- **Partner Determination Procedure**

  This is a set of rules that you define to determine how business partners are assigned during transaction processing (see Figure 2.43). The system automatically determines the business partners involved in a business transaction. Partner determination procedure can be assigned to a transaction type or item category. You define this procedure by following menu path **Customer Relationship Management · Basic Functions · Partner Processing · Define Partner Determination Procedure**.

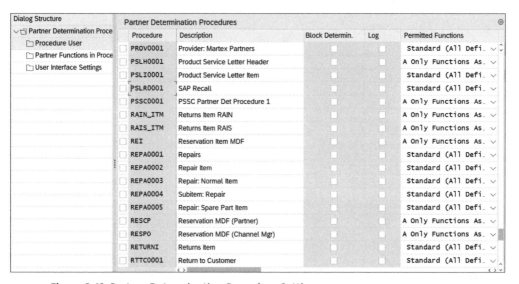

Figure 2.43 Partner Determination Procedure Setting

- **Date Profile**

  For every business transaction, there is a set of date types with its own set of rules to determine the dates (see Figure 2.44). These date types and the rules to determine the dates are defined in the date profile. The date profile is important and required for defining the validity of a transaction. SAP has provided different date profiles, and you can define a date profile by following menu path **Customer Relationship Management • Basic Functions • Date Management • Define Date Profile**.

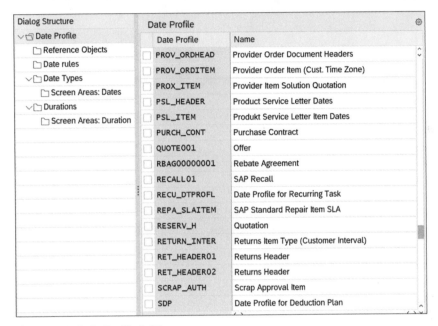

Figure 2.44 Date Profile Setting

- **Action Profiles**

  SAP has provided an option to trigger the subsequent events of a transaction using actions (see Figure 2.45). Actions can automatically trigger output, follow-up activities, or workflows and can be triggered with the help of user-definable conditions in transactions. You define action profiles by following menu path **Customer Relationship Management • Basic Functions • Actions • Actions In Transaction • Create Actions with Wizard**.

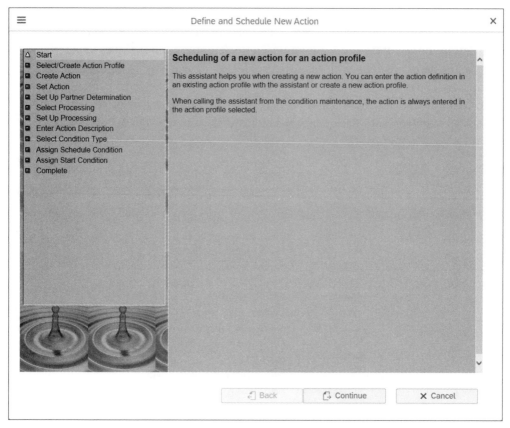

Figure 2.45 Action Profile Wizard

- **Text Determination Procedure**

  For every business transaction, there is a set of text types with their own sets of rules to determine the text (see Figure 2.46). These text types and the rules to determine the texts are defined in the text determination profile. Text types are optional in any transaction. You define a date profile by following menu path **Customer Relationship Management · Basic Functions · Date Management · Text Management · Text Determination Procedure**.

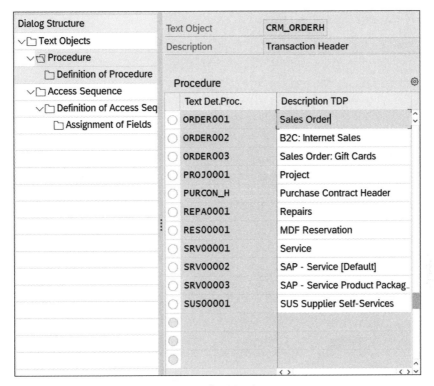

Figure 2.46 Text Determination Procedure Setting

Similarly, you create a provider contract transaction type by copying it from the standard transaction type provided by SAP, PRVC. Follow all the same steps you followed for provider order, YPVO. Figure 2.47 shows the newly created transaction type for a provider contract.

You define additional settings for provider contract transaction types to enable the proper distribution of the provider contracts into SAP Convergent Invoicing and SAP Convergent Charging. While submitting the provider order, a provider contract needs to be created asynchronously. You can make these settings at the following menu path: **Customer Relationship Management · Cross Industry Functions · Provider Order And Contract Management · Transactions · Define Settings For Transaction Types**.

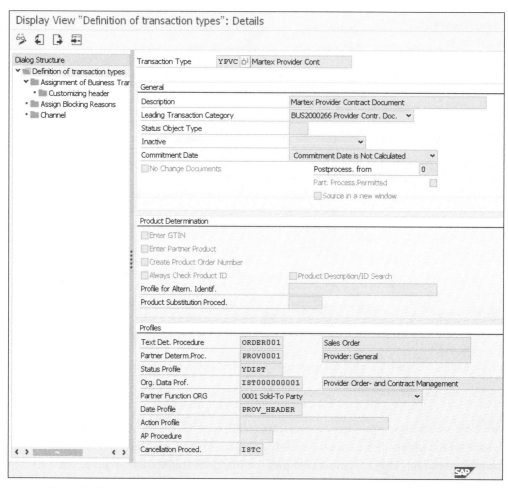

Figure 2.47 Transaction Type for Provider Contract

Figure 2.48 shows the configuration for asynchronous creation of a provider contract while submitting the provider order.

Display View "Provider Order settings": Overview

Provider Order settings

Trans.Type	Short Description	Asynchron.	BusAgAssgn	CurrTmeSts	CurrTmeChg		Template	DocPurpose		Ref. to MA	Objects		No Tgt Trans. Type	Subitems
PRCO	Ch'ing Contract		✓	✓	C Set Current Time Stamp an.. ∨			P Sharing Order	∨		□	□	02 PRCO	
PRCO	Sharing Order		✓	✓		∨	□	P Sharing Order	∨		✓			□
PRLO	Provider Order Lean	✓	□			∨		Standard Provider Order	∨		□			□
PRLR	Prov. Part. Ord Lean	✓	□			∨		Standard Provider Order	∨		□			□
PRPA	Prov. Partner Agmt	□	✓	✓		∨		B Revenue Sharing Order	∨		□		02	□
PRPO	Prov. Prov Part Ord	□	✓	✓		∨	□	B Revenue Sharing Order	∨		□			□
PRVC	Provider Contract	□	□	✓		∨		Standard Provider Order	∨		□		02 PRVO	□
PRVO	Provider Order	□	□	✓		∨		Standard Provider Order	∨		□		PRVC	□
PRVR	Provider Partner Ord	✓	□	□		∨		Standard Provider Order	∨		□			□
SRVX	Solution Quotation	□	✓	✓		∨		C Package Quotation	∨		✓		PRVC	□
YPVC	Martex Provider Cont	□	✓	✓	C Set Current Time Stamp an.. ∨			Standard Provider Order	∨		✓		02 YPVO	✓
YPVO	Martex Provider Ord	□	✓	✓	C Set Current Time Stamp an.. ∨		✓	Standard Provider Order	∨		✓	✓	YPVC	✓
YRPA	Martex Partner Agmt	□	✓	✓	C Set Current Time Stamp an.. ∨			B Revenue Sharing Order	∨		□		02 YRPO	□
YRPO	Martex Prov Part Ord	✓	✓	✓	C Set Current Time Stamp an.. ∨			B Revenue Sharing Order	∨		□		02 YRPA	□

Figure 2.48 Settings for Asynchronous Creation of Provider Contract

Item Category Group

Next, make the settings for the item category group. Products are viewed from a business view with the help of the item category group. This is an arbitrary setting to make the product adaptable for subscription processes. You can make the settings via the following menu path: **Customer Relationship Management · Transactions · Basic Settings · Define Item Category Group** (as shown in Figure 2.49).

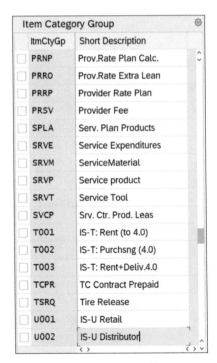

Item Category Group	⚙
ItmCtyGp	**Short Description**
☐ PRNP	Prov.Rate Plan Calc.
☐ PRRO	Prov.Rate Extra Lean
☐ PRRP	Provider Rate Plan
☐ PRSV	Provider Fee
☐ SPLA	Serv. Plan Products
☐ SRVE	Service Expenditures
☐ SRVM	ServiceMaterial
☐ SRVP	Service product
☐ SRVT	Service Tool
☐ SVCP	Srv. Ctr. Prod. Leas
☐ T001	IS-T: Rent (to 4.0)
☐ T002	IS-T: Purchsng (4.0)
☐ T003	IS-T: Rent+Deliv.4.0
☐ TCPR	TC Contract Prepaid
☐ TSRQ	Tire Release
☐ U001	IS-U Retail
☐ U002	IS-U Distributor

Figure 2.49 Item Category Group

SAP has provided the item category groups for SAP BRIM implementations listed in Table 2.1. You can create your own item category groups by copying these standard ones.

Item Category Group	Description
PRRP	Provider Rate Plan
PRNP	Prov. Rate Plan Calc.
PRRO	Prov. Rate Extra Lean

Table 2.1 Item Category Groups

Next, you define item categories. Item categories are settings in the system the enable the line items in transactions to behave in a certain way. You can make the settings for item categories for business transactions via menu path **Customer Relationship Management · Transactions · Basic Settings · Define Item Categories** (as shown in Figure 2.50).

SAP has provided item categories for provider order and contract (as listed in Table 2.2). You can create custom item categories by copying these standard ones.

Item Category	Description
PRCL	Provider Contract Item Lean
PRCN	Provider Contract Item, No Charge
PRCO	Provider Contract Item Extra Lean
PRCP	Provider Contract Item
PRMP	Provider Master Agreement Item
PRON	Provider Order Item, No Charge
PROP	Provider Order Item
PROX	Provider Order Package
PRPL	Provider Order Item Lean
PRPO	Provider Order Item Extra Lean

Table 2.2 Item Categories for Provider Order and Contract Categories

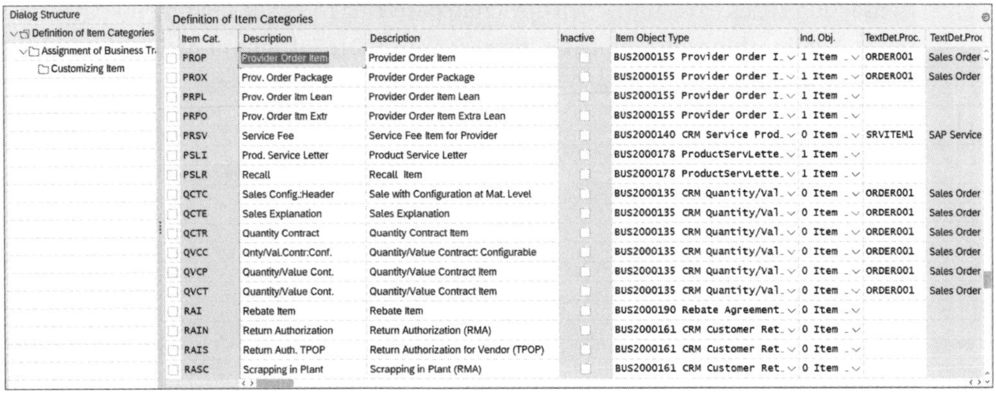

Dialog Structure	Definition of Item Categories

Figure 2.50 Item Categories

Next, you define the item category determination rules. This setting enables the system to determine the correct item category for the line item automatically based on the combination of certain parameters. This helps you avoid manually assigning the line item processing rules.

The item category is determined using the following parameters:

- Transaction type
- Item category group (product master)
- Item category usage
- Main item category

You make the settings for the item category determination by following menu path **Customer Relationship Management · Transactions · Basic Settings · Define Item Category Determination**.

Figure 2.51 shows the item category determination for the standard provider order transaction type, PRVO.

Next, you define the copy control for transaction types. Copy control enables the system to copy details from the source transaction to the target transaction. You define rules to determine what details are copied and how they are copied.

To create the provider contract while submitting the provider order, the copy control configuration needs to be maintained for the provider order and provider contract transaction types. You make the copy control settings by following menu path **Customer Relationship Management · Transactions · Basic Settings · Copying Control for Business Transactions · Define Copy Control for Transaction Types**.

Display View "Item Category Determination": Overview

Item Category Determination

Trans.type	Desc.TransTyp	ItmCtyGrp	Item usage	MainItmCty	Desc. itm cat.	Item Cat.	Desc.ItmCty
PRVO	vider Order	0002 Config.at Mat.Level				TAN	Sales Item
PRVO	Provider Order	0002 Config.at Mat.Level		PRON	Prov.Ord.Item_	TAN	Sales Item
PRVO	Provider Order	0002 Config.at Mat.Level		PROP	Provider Order _	TAN	Sales Item
PRVO	Provider Order	0002 Config.at Mat.Level		TAP	Pric.at Item Le_	TAN	Sales Item
PRVO	Provider Order	LUMF Structure Below				TAP	Pric.at Item L
PRVO	Provider Order	NORM Sales Item				TAN	Sales Item
PRVO	Provider Order	NORM Sales Item		PRON	Prov.Ord.Item_	TAN	Sales Item
PRVO	Provider Order	NORM Sales Item		PROP	Provider Order _	TAN	Sales Item
PRVO	Provider Order	NORM Sales Item		TAP	Pric.at Item Le_	TAN	Sales Item
PRVO	Provider Order	PRNP Prov.Rate Plan Calc.				PRON	Prov.Ord.Iter
PRVO	Provider Order	PRNP Prov.Rate Plan Calc.		PRON	Prov.Ord.Item_	PRON	Prov.Ord.Iter
PRVO	Provider Order	PRNP Prov.Rate Plan Calc.		PROP	Provider Order _	PRON	Prov.Ord.Iter
PRVO	Provider Order	PRNP Prov.Rate Plan Calc.		TAP	Pric.at Item Le_	PRON	Prov.Ord.Iter
PRVO	Provider Order	PRRO Prov.Rate Extra Lean				PRPO	Prov. Order I
PRVO	Provider Order	PRRO Prov.Rate Extra Lean		PRON	Prov.Ord.Item_	PRPO	Prov. Order I
PRVO	Provider Order	PRRO Prov.Rate Extra Lean		PROP	Provider Order _	PRPO	Prov. Order I
PRVO	Provider Order	PRRO Prov.Rate Extra Lean		PRPO	Prov. Order It_	PRPO	Prov. Order I
PRVO	Provider Order	PRRO Prov.Rate Extra Lean		TAP	Pric.at Item Le_	PRPO	Prov. Order I
PRVO	Provider Order	PRRP Provider Rate Plan				PROP	Provider Orde
PRVO	Provider Order	PRRP Provider Rate Plan		PRON	Prov.Ord.Item_	PROP	Provider Orde
PRVO	Provider Order	PRRP Provider Rate Plan		PROP	Provider Order _	PROP	Provider Orde
PRVO	Provider Order	PRRP Provider Rate Plan		TAP	Pric.at Item Le_	PROP	Provider Orde
PRVO	Provider Order	PRSV Provider Fee				PRSV	Service Fee
PRVO	Provider Order	PRSV Provider Fee		PRON	Prov.Ord.Item_	PRSV	Service Fee
PRVO	Provider Order	PRSV Provider Fee		PROP	Provider Order _	PRSV	Service Fee

Figure 2.51 Item Category Determination

Figure 2.52 shows the copy control configurations maintained for the standard provider order and contract transaction types.

All steps mentioned thus far need to be repeated to maintain the configurations for the provider contract. SAP has provided the standard transaction type PRVC for the provider contract, and you can refer to this transaction type and copy it to create your own custom provider contract transaction.

Display View "Copy Transaction Types - General Control Data": Overview

% 🛠 📑 📑 📑

Copy Transaction Types - General Control Data

Srce Trans. Type	Tgt Trans. Type	Short Description	Copy item no.	ComplRef	Copying routine	
PRLO	PRLC	Provider Contr. Lean	☐	☐		⌃
PRLR	PRLC	Provider Contr. Lean	☐	☐		⌄
PRPA	PRPO	Prov. Prov Part Ord	☐	☐		
PRPO	PRPA	Prov. Partner Agmt	☐	☐		
PRVC	PRVO	Provider Order	☐	☐		
PRVC	SRVX	Solution Quotation	☐	☐		
PRVO	PRVC	Provider Contract	☐	☐		
PRVR	PRVC	Provider Contract	☐	☐		
PRVR	YPVC	Martex Provider Cont	☐	☐		

Figure 2.52 Copying Control Configuration for Transaction Types

Partner Provider Order and Partner Agreement

Provider orders and provider contacts are used for handling accounts receivable in a subscription-based business model, but in a typical SAP BRIM implementation, you need to manage accounts payable as well. SAP has provided the partner provider order and partner agreement for handling this task. A partner provider order is equivalent to a provider order, and a partner agreement is similar to a provider contract for calculating the payout to vendors.

Once a partner provider order is submitted and released, it will be replicated to SAP Convergent Invoicing and SAP Convergent Charging via order distribution infrastructure (ODI), similar to the replication of provider contracts while submitting provider orders. SAP has provided the standard transaction types listed in Table 2.3 for partner provider orders and partner agreements.

Transaction Type	Description
PRPO	Partner Provider Order
PRPA	Partner Agreement

Table 2.3 Partner Provider Order and Partner Agreement Transactions

All the configurations mentioned in this section for provider orders and provider contracts need to be maintained for the partner provider order and partner agreement transaction types. You create custom transaction types by copying the PRPO (Partner Provider Order) and PRPA (Partner Agreement) transaction types.

Master Agreement

A *master agreement* is an agreement between your company and your customer that you sell subscription services to. This serves as a template agreement from which you create provider orders. You define the authorized groups, products, configurations, and prices/discounts with set validity periods. The validity periods define the periods for which agreements are valid. You can only use valid master agreements from which you can create provider orders. *Authorized groups* are customers that are allowed to use the agreement as a template and inherit the agreed-upon products and values in a provider order. The system performs this validation in the background. This agreement can contain many products, each with its own set of agreed-upon values. You can import all the products or choose the ones that are relevant to the current order. A master agreement can be saved with its line items in an in processing or released status. The master agreement has to be in a released status to be used in the provider order. After you set the values for the product during configuration, you can set this configuration as fixed or not fixed. Leaving it in a not fixed state enables the product configuration to be changed in the provider order. The fixed state locks the product for configuration in the order. The recommended option is to leave it in a not fixed state. The benefit of utilizing a master agreement is that it reduces the workload of repetitive data entry during provider order creation.

You define a master agreement in a similar manner as you defined the provider order and provider contract. Because you create provider orders from a master agreement, you set the copy controls to enable copying from master agreement to provider order only. For our example, we do not use a master agreement, and the detailed configurations are not in scope for this chapter.

Change Process

If you want to make further changes on an active provider contract and partner agreement, SAP has provided the change process framework to accomplish this. You either need to use a standard or a custom maintenance framework for business transactions (BTMF) change process to modify the contract line item. When a change process is executed, the system copies the latest technically active contract line item to a change order. According to the configuration, you can modify the change order and submit. Once the change order is submitted and released, it will be copied back to the provider contract as a new technically active line item. The previous line item status will be changed to technically inactive. This framework helps to maintain the change history of the provider contracts and partner agreements.

SAP has provided process types for executing the change processes on the provider contract (see Table 2.4).

Process Type	Description
ISTA	Contract Change
ISTB	Change Technical Data
ISTC	Lock/Unlock
ISTF	Change without Order
ISTG	Create Repair Order

Table 2.4 Process Types

Next, you define the change processes. Figure 2.53 shows the standard change processes provided by SAP.

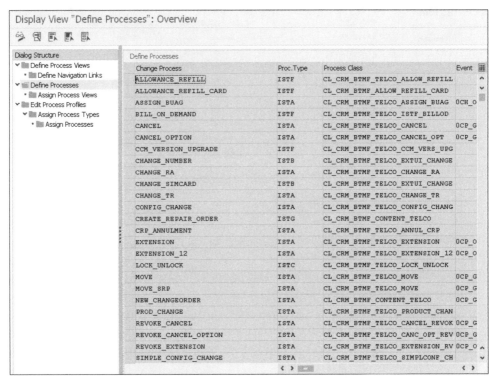

Figure 2.53 Define Change Processes

You can define the change processes via menu path **Customer Relationship Management · Cross-Industry Functions · Provider Order and Contract Management · Transactions · Define Provider-Contract-Specific Process Profiles**.

Every change process will be associated with a process type and a process class. You assign each of the change process to a process view and define the business server page application view name that can be assigned to the change processes. Once the view is assigned, while executing the change process on a provider contract, the corresponding view will be loaded, which gives you an option to make changes on the contract. You can maintain the configuration using the same menu path mentioned in the previous step.

Figure 2.54 shows the view configuration provided by SAP.

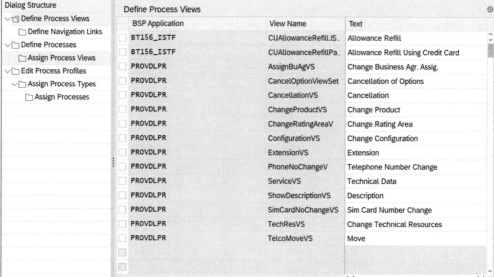

Figure 2.54 Defining Process Views

Next, you define the process profile. This profile contains a list of the allowed change process that are applicable for provider contracts. You make the settings for the process profile via menu path **Customer Relationship Management · Cross-Industry Functions · Provider Order and Contract Management · Transactions · Define Provider-Contract-Specific Process Profiles · Edit Process Profiles** (see Figure 2.55).

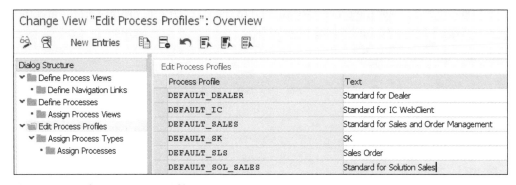

Figure 2.55 Defining Process Profiles

Next, you assign a process type to a process profile. Process types are predefined in the system because they follow certain rules. You assign process types to process profiles via menu path **Customer Relationship Management · Cross-Industry Functions · Provider Order and Contract Management · Transactions · Define Provider-Contract-Specific Process Profiles · Edit Process Profiles · Assign Process Types**.

Figure 2.56 shows the process types assigned to the DEFAULT_IC process profile. Similarly, you can select the process profile you created and assign the relevant process types.

Change View "Assign Process Types": Overview

Dialog Structure	Profile	DEFAULT_IC	
⌄ ▓ Define Process Views			
• ▓ Define Navigation Links			
⌄ ▓ Define Processes	Assign Process Types		
• ▓ Assign Process Views	Pro... Text		Pr.Ty.Pos.
⌄ ▓ Edit Process Profiles	ISTA Contract Change		10
⌄ ▓ Assign Process Types	ISTB Change Technical Data		20
• ▓ Assign Processes	ISTC Lock/Unlock		30
	ISTF Change without Order		40
	ISTG Create Repair Order		50

Figure 2.56 Assign Process Types to Process Profile

Next, you assign processes to the process types. You do so via menu path **Customer Relationship Management · Cross-Industry Functions · Provider Order and Contract Management · Transactions · Define Provider-Contract-Specific Process Profiles · Edit Process Profiles · Assign Process Types · Assign Processes**.

Figure 2.57 shows the processes assigned to the DEFAULT_IC process profile and the ISTB—Change Technical Data process type.

Figure 2.57 Assign Process to Process Profile and Process Type

Next, you assign the process profile to a business role. Because users are assigned to business roles through the organizational structure assignment, this process will be inherited for the business role. You make this setting in the following menu path: **Customer Relationship Management · UI Framework · Business Roles · Define Business Role** (as in Figure 2.58).

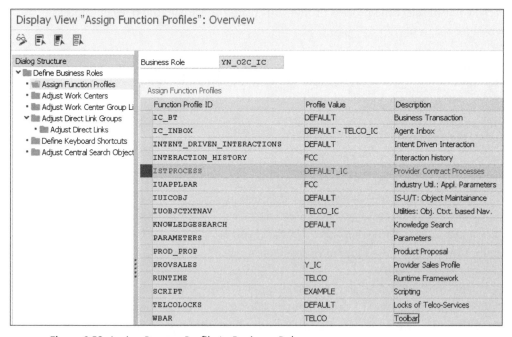

Figure 2.58 Assign Process Profile to Business Role

Select the business role and click **Assign Functional Profiles** in the left navigation bar. Search for the "ISTPROCESS" function profile ID, and assign the DEFAULT_IC process profile, as shown in Figure 2.58.

2.2.6   Order Distribution Infrastructure

The Order Distribution Infrastructure in SAP CRM is an order/document distribution framework utilized in the SAP BRIM processes to distribute provider contracts for SAP CRM to SAP S/4HANA. It is highly customizable and uses the actions framework to fulfill services that are part of the provider order and provider contract. It can be set up as synchronous or asynchronous.

Based on your business requirements, you can adopt multiple steps during the distribution. Provider orders are not distributed to SAP Convergent Invoicing as a standard practice. It can be designed to replicate a sales order if this contains a sales item. Only the sales item is replicated as the sales order in SAP S/4HANA.

The main elements are as follows:

- Document distribution categories
- Document distribution step type
- Document distribution schema
- Document distribution schema determination

The implementation class controls the behavior of each of the elements. These classes can be adopted to meet customer-specific requirements. It is essential that you create the main element settings in the correct sequence to set up the correct distribution method.

First, you create the settings for the document distribution categories. These are the ABAP class methods that are called during runtime to execute the distribution. Although you can flexibly create your own categories, it is mandatory that you maintain the six categories listed in Table 2.5. You can make the settings for the Order Distribution Infrastructure via the following menu path: **Customer Relationship Management · Cross-Industry Functions · Provider Order and Contract Management · Transactions · Document Distribution · Define Settings for Document Distribution**.

Step Category	Purpose of Category
C1	Update provider contract without using a change order
O1	Activate provider order until a required step is completed, such as an external provisioning step
P0	Wait for activation if the contract start date is in the future
P1	Activate provider contract if contract start date is immediate or in the past
P5	Wait for deactivation if the contract end date is in the future
P6	Deactivate provider contract if the contract end date is immediate

Table 2.5 Settings for Document Distribution Categories

Figure 2.59 shows the step categories and the respective implementation classes assigned to them. Each step performs a specific function.

Dialog Structure	Step Categories			
Step Categories	Category	Distribution Step Category	Distribution Step Category Class	Show Imple...
Step Types	C1	Provider Contract Update	CL_CRM_ISX_ORDER_MD_CAT_PRV_C1	Show
Schema Definition	O1	Order Distribution	CL_CRM_ISX_ORDER_MD_CAT_PRV_O1	Show
Schema Steps	P0	Provider Contract waits for activation	CL_CRM_ISX_ORDER_MD_CAT_PRV_P0	Show
Schema Determination	P1	Provider Contract Activation	CL_CRM_ISX_ORDER_MD_CAT_PRV_P1	Show
Schema Assignment	P5	Provider Contract waits for deactivation	CL_CRM_ISX_ORDER_MD_CAT_PRV_P5	Show
Schema Steps	P6	Provider Contract Deactivation	CL_CRM_ISX_ORDER_MD_CAT_PRV_P6	Show

Figure 2.59 Document Distributions: Step Categories

Next, you define the step type. The step type defines a single step in the entire document distribution. This is driven by the combination of the distribution category and document distribution step type class. This class determines how the distribution category is executed.

Figure 2.60 shows the step type settings that define the document category and the step type class.

Dialog Structure
- Step Categories
- Step Types
- Schema Definition
  - Schema Steps
- Schema Determination
  - Schema Assignment
    - Schema Steps

Step Types

Step Type	Document Distribution Step Type	Category	Batch	Document Distribution Step Type Class	Show Imple...
0011	Always true activation	P1		CL_CRM_ISX_MD_EXAMPLE_TRUE	Show
0012	Always true deactivation	P6		CL_CRM_ISX_MD_EXAMPLE_TRUE	Show
ALLW	Call Message for Allowance Creation	P1		CL_CRM_ISX_ORDER_MD_ALLOW	Show
CCMU	Step for Contract Update	C1		CL_CRM_ISX_ORDER_MD_ERP	Show
OTRC	Checks for Technical Resources	O1		CL_CRM_ISX_MD_TECH_RES_CHECKS	Show
PCEA	Call ERP Message contract activation	P1		CL_CRM_ISX_ORDER_MD_ERP	Show
PCED	Call ERP Message contract deactivation	P6		CL_CRM_ISX_ORDER_MD_ERP	Show
PCMA	Call ERP Message contract activation MCC	P1		CL_CRM_ISX_ORDER_MD_ERP_MCC	Show
PCMD	Call ERP MessageContractDeactivation MCC	P6		CL_CRM_ISX_ORDER_MD_ERP_MCC	Show
PCWA	Wait for activation	P0	✓	CL_CRM_ISX_ORDER_MD_WAIT_P0	Show
PCWD	Wait for deactivation	P5	✓	CL_CRM_ISX_ORDER_MD_WAIT_P5	Show
PCXD	Telco Service Message for deactivation	P6		CL_CRM_ISX_ORDER_MD_XI_MSG	Show
PCXI	Telco Service Message for activation	P1		CL_CRM_ISX_ORDER_MD_XI_MSG	Show
YCCA	Activate SAP CC Charging Contract	P1		CL_CRM_ISX_MD_CCONTR_ACTIVATE	Show
YOOC	Send one-offs as BIT to ERP	P1		CL_CRM_ISX_MD_EXAMPLE_ONEOFF	Show
YOOD	Direct deactivation for one-offs	P6		CL_CRM_ISX_MD_EXAMPLE_ONEOFF	Show
YPWA	Wait for activation (non-batch)	P0		CL_CRM_ISX_ORDER_MD_WAIT_P0	Show

Figure 2.60 Document Distributions: Step Types

Next, you define the distribution schema. The schema contains the distribution steps that are assigned to it. When this schema is called during runtime, it executes the steps within it. The schema is executed as a distribution schema class, which is an ABAP function.

Figure 2.61 shows the distribution schema definition that has the class assigned.

Dialog Structure
- Step Categories
- Step Types
- Schema Definition
  - Schema Steps
- Schema Determination
  - Schema Assignment
    - Schema Steps

Schema Definition

Schema	Document Distribution Schema	Document Distribution Schema Class	Show Imple...
0001	Direct activation	CL_CRM_ISX_ORDER_MD_SCH_PROV	Show
PC01	Provider Contract	CL_CRM_ISX_ORDER_MD_SCH_PROV	Show
PERP	Provider Contract to ERP	CL_CRM_ISX_ORDER_MD_SCH_PROV	Show
YPC	Provider Contract to SAPCC	CL_CRM_ISX_ORDER_MD_SCH_PROV	Show
YPM	Provider Contract to MCC	CL_CRM_ISX_ORDER_MD_SCH_PROV	Show

Figure 2.61 Document Distributions: Schema Definition

Next, you assign the previously defined step types to the schema definition. Here you assign the ones that are relevant for your distribution schema. Select the schema and add the step types.

Figure 2.62 shows the schema definition with the assigned step types.

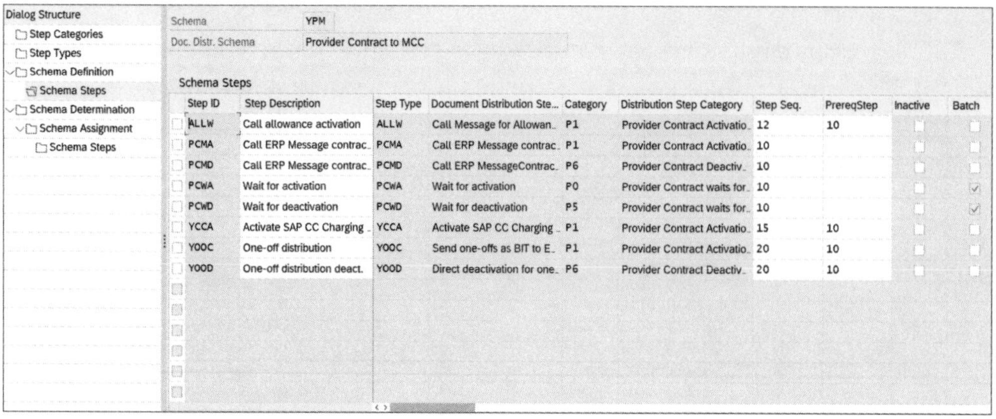

Figure 2.62 Document Distributions: Schema Definition with Step Types

Next, you define the schema determination. The culmination of creating the previous steps is to assign the schema to the contract distribution. The schema determination drives the step types for the transaction type and item category combination. Here we define the schema determination for YPVC (Martex Provider Contract) and the item category combinations (PRCN, PRCO, and PRCP).

Figure 2.63 shows the schema determination for YPVC.

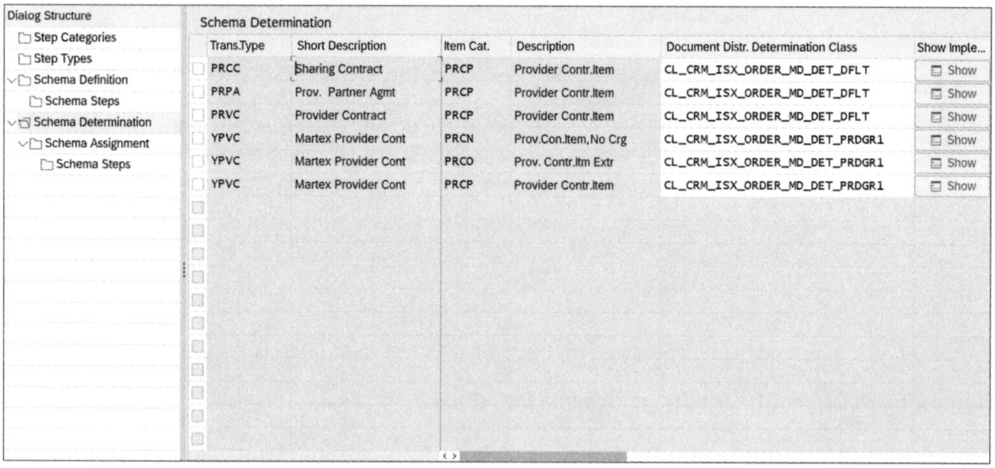

Figure 2.63 Document Distributions: Schema Determination

Next, you assign the schemas to the schema determination. Select the **YPVC/PRCP** combination, then double-click **Schema Assignent**. You can assign multiple schemas to one schema determination. Assign the **Default** flag to the schema you want to be the default during runtime.

Figure 2.64 shows the assigned schema for the schema determination for the YPVC/PRCP combination.

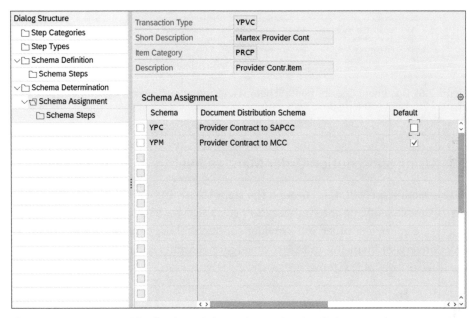

Figure 2.64 Document Distributions: Schema Determination/Schema Assignment

Next, select **YPM** and double-click **Schema Steps**. You can see that the steps assigned for this schema are automatically derived for the schema determination.

Figure 2.65 shows the assigned schema steps for the schema determination for the YPVC/PRCP/YPM combination.

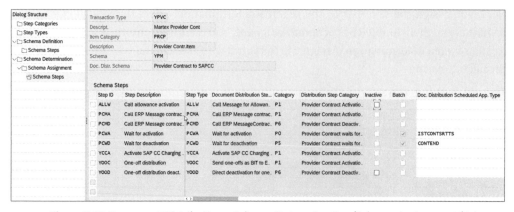

Figure 2.65 Document Distributions: Schema Determination/Schema Assignment/Schema Steps

2.3   Using Subscription Order Management

In this section, we will walk through the steps to use SAP BRIM, subscription order management. Utilizing the configuration steps that we have completed so far, you can create a provider order and provider contracts. These contracts will replicate to SAP Convergent Invoicing and SAP Convergent Charging and thus be in sync across the three distributed systems.

2.3.1   Creating Master Data

As preliminary step, create the following master data objects:

- Organizational structure
- Business partner
- Business agreement
- Product

Creating Organizational Structure

The organizational unit is a hierarchical structure within an organization set up with different levels, each with its own functionality. As a preliminary step to create any transactions, it is mandatory that the organizational units are created in SAP CRM.

They can be replicated from SAP S/4HANA so that they are in sync or can be created manually and aligned to each other as a post activity.

For our example, we will create an organizational structure manually and align it to the organization unit in SAP S/4HANA.

First, create the root organization directly in the SAP CRM web UI. You can add additional organizational units as needed. Proceed as follows:

1. Log into the SAP CRM web UI via Transaction WUI_SSO or via the SAP BRIM, subscription order management URL if one is provided by your system administrator.

2. Select the **PROV-SALES** role.

3. Click **Sales Operations** in the left pane.

4. Click the **Organizational Model** link, then click **Root Organizational Unit**.

5. Enter the name of the root organizational unit and the following details (as shown in Figure 2.66):
   - **General Data**
   - **Address**
   - **Valid From** and **To**

   Because this is a root organization, leave the functions unassigned.

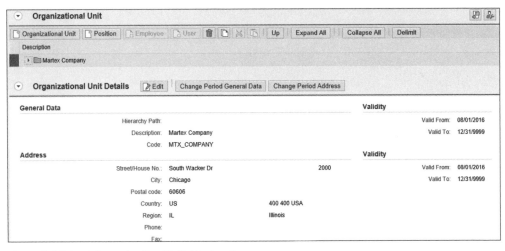

Figure 2.66 Root Organization Unit:Martex Company

6. Select the newly created root organizational unit, then click **Organizational Unit** to create a new organizational unit.

7. Enter the name of the root organizational unit and the following details and save; this will add a subordinate organization to the root organization (as shown in Figure 2.67):

   – **General Data**

   – **Address**

   – **Valid From** and **To**

   – **Functions**

   – **Attributes**

The function activation ensures the type of organization this unit is set to function as. For this example, set the type as a sales organization.

The attributes define the specific values that this sales organization will possess during run time.

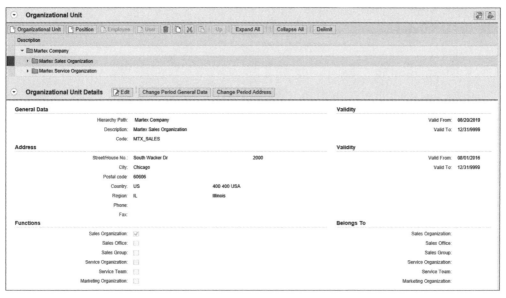

Figure 2.67 Martex Sales Organization

8. Enter the attributes for the sales organization as shown in Figure 2.68.

Actions	Scenario	Attribute Description	Value	Value to	Excluded
🗑	Sales	Tupel (distribution channel, division)	1010		☐
🗑	Sales	Country	US		☐
🗑	Sales	Local Currency	USD		☐
🗑	Sales	Ref. currency for document	USD		☐
🗑	Sales	Division	10		☐
🗑	Sales	Distribution Channel	10		☐
🗑	Sales	Correspondence Language	EN		☐
🗑	Sales	Partner number	*		☐
🗑	Sales	Transaction Type	PRPO		☐
🗑	Sales	Transaction Type	YPVO		☐

Figure 2.68 Martex Sales Organization Attributes

9. Assign the Martex Sales Organization to the SAP S/4HANA Sales Organization. This can be done by entering Transaction PPOMA_CRM in the SAP GUI.

10. Select the Martex Sales Organization and select the **Function** tab (as shown in Figure 2.69). Here you assign the sales organizations replicated from SAP S/4HANA.

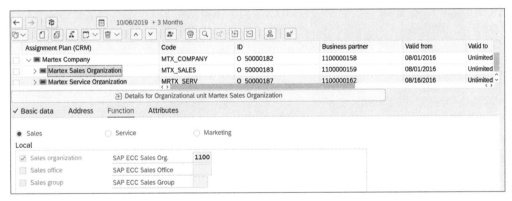

Figure 2.69 Martex Sales Organization with SAP ERP Sales Org Assignment

Creating Business Partner

In this section, you will create two business partners to serve as your end customer and your vendor:

- McFarland Systems will be your customer (sold-to party), a consumer of services from Martex.

- Loren Systems will be the partner/vendor that supplies services to Martex, which in turn sells those services to McFarland Systems.

You create business partners directly in the SAP CRM web UI (as shown in Figure 2.70 and Figure 2.71). Proceed as follows:

1. Log into the SAP CRM web UI using Transaction WUI_SSO or the SAP BRIM, subscription order management URL if one is provided by your system administrator.
2. Select the **PROV-SALES** role.
3. Click **Account Management** in the left pane.
4. Click **Create Corporate Account** under the **Create** menu.
5. Enter all the necessary details as shown in Figure 2.71 and save.
6. Perform the same steps to create Loren Systems (see Figure 2.72 and Figure 2.73).

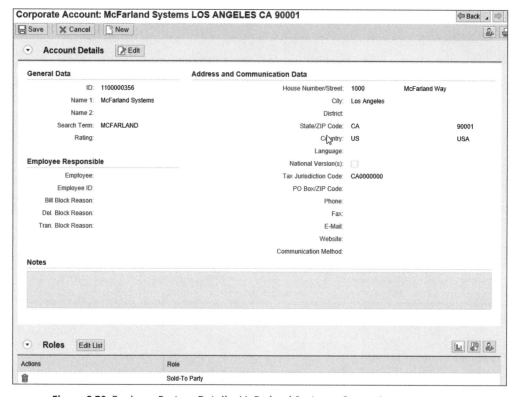

Figure 2.70 Business Partner Details: McFarland Systems, Screen 1

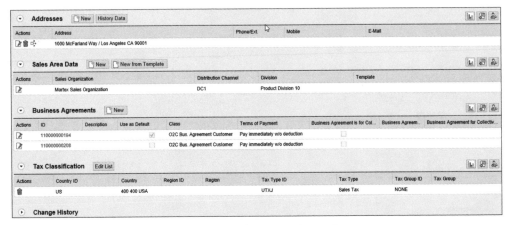

Figure 2.71 Business Partner Details: McFarland Systems, Screen 2

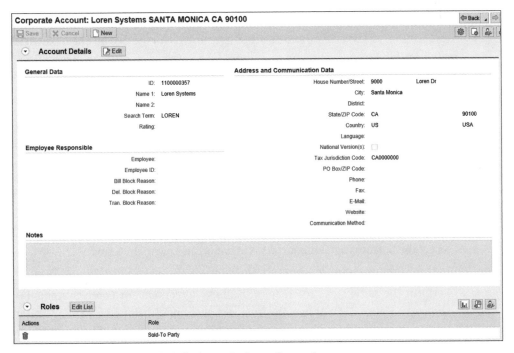

Figure 2.72 Business Partner Details: Loren Systems, Screen 1

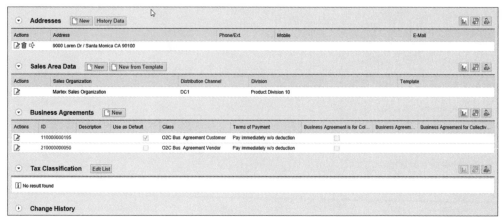

Figure 2.73 Business Partner Details: Loren Systems, Screen 2

Creating Business Agreements

In this section, you will create two business agreements for the two business partners created earlier. Business agreements cannot be created as standalone objects; they are always created for a business partner.

You create business agreements directly in the SAP CRM web UI, as follows:

1. Log into the SAP CRM web UI using Transaction WUI_SSO or the SAP BRIM, subscription order management URL if one is provided by your system administrator.

2. Select the **PROV-SALES** role.

3. Click **Account Management** in the left pane.

4. Click **Create Business Agreement** under the **Create** menu.

5. Select the **McFarland Systems** business partner.

6. Select the business agreement class (**Customer**) and payment terms.

7. Enter all the necessary details as shown in Figure 2.74 and save.

8. Perform the same steps to create a business agreement for Loren Systems (as shown in Figure 2.75). Assign the business agreement belonging to the **Vendor** business agreement class.

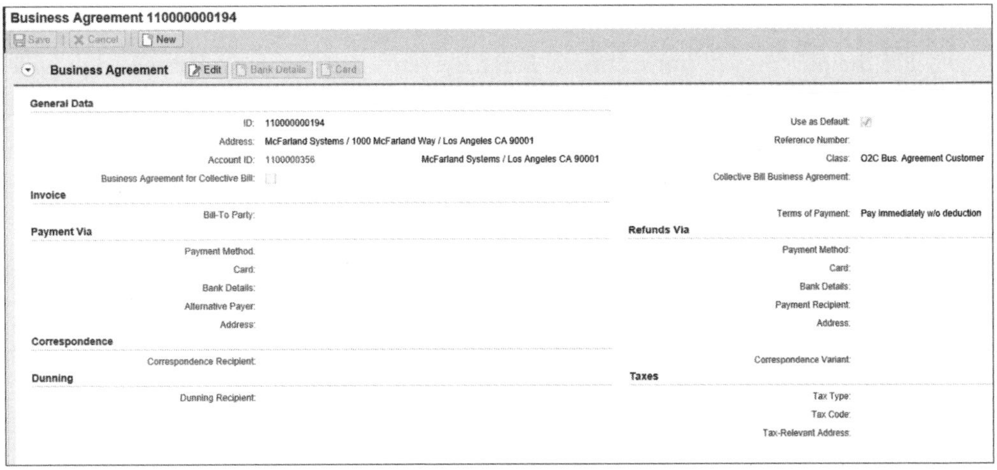

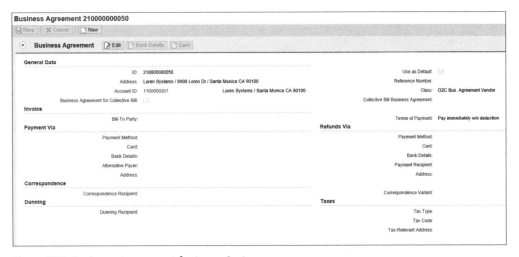

Figure 2.74 Business Agreement for McFarland Systems

Figure 2.75 Business Agreement for Loren Systems

2.3.2   Creating and Mapping Products

A product is considered master data. You use it in the line item in the order, and it behaves similarly to a regular sales and distribution or SAP CRM sales order. Although your product creation follows a standard process, you adapt it to function as a subscription product. This adaption is crucial to how this product will work. This step was detailed in Section 2.2.3.

2.3.3   Managing Provider Orders and Provider Contracts

For the purposes of our example, Loren Systems partners with Martex to provide Saas and Iass services for a cost.

Martex resells these services to McFarland Systems and generates revenue based on the services utilized. Martex pays a portion of the revenue to Loren. For this scenario to function, Martex first creates a provider partner agreement detailing the revenue-sharing conditions.

In this section, you will create a partner provider order and customer provider order. They both function similarly, but a partner provider order is linked to the partner/vendor and a customer provider order is linked to the customer.

You create provider orders directly in the SAP CRM web UI as follows:

1. Log into the SAP CRM web UI using Transaction WUI_SSO or the SAP BRIM, subscription order management URL if one is provided by the system administrator.
2. Select the **PROV-SALES** role.
3. Click **Provider Contract Management** in the left pane (see Figure 2.76).

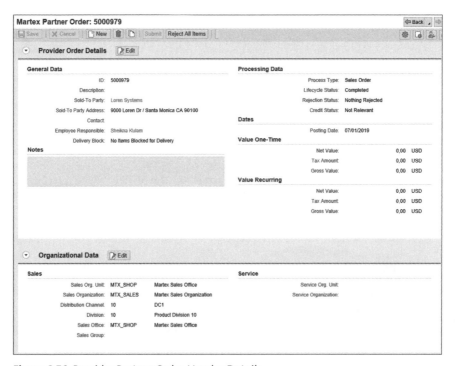

Figure 2.76 Provider Partner Order Header Details

4. Click **Provider Order** under the **Create** window.

5. In the popup window, select **YRPO.**

6. Enter the following details:
   - **Sold-To Party**: Loren Systems
   - **Employee Responsible**: Automatically identified
   - **Organizational Data**: Martex Sales Organization

7. In the **Items** section, enter MRTX_PRTNR for the product (see Figure 2.77).

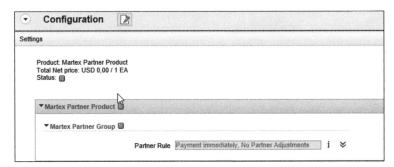

Figure 2.77 Provider Partner Order Item

8. Click the **Edit** button 📝 in line item 10.

9. Open the **Configuration** block and click the **Edit** button 📝 (see Figure 2.78).

10. Select the **Payment Rule** and close the configuration.

Configuration 📝

Settings

Product: Martex Partner Product
Total Net price: USD 0,00 / 1 EA
Status:

▼ Martex Partner Product

   ▼ Martex Partner Group

      Partner Rule   Payment immediately, No Partner Adjustments   i ⊻

Figure 2.78 Partner Rule Configuration Value

11. Open the **Technical Resources** block and click the **Edit** button 📝.

12. Under the **ID** column, enter a unique identifying value and close the window (see Figure 2.79).

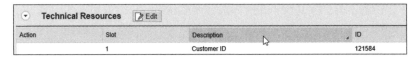

Figure 2.79 Technical Resource ID Value

Open Business Agreement Block

The business agreement assigned to the business partner is derived by default. If no business agreement is set as default, you can assign one by clicking the **Assign** button (shown in Figure 2.80).

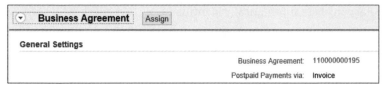

Figure 2.80 Business Agreement

1. Click **Back** to return to the provider order screen.
2. Click the **Save and Submit** button.
3. After clicking the **Save and Submit** button, the provider partner agreement is created. The agreement is available in the **Items** block as a contract.
4. Click the contract number hyperlink, and you will be taken to the partner agreement screen (Figure 2.81).

   The partner agreement is a secondary linked document created by the system. It can contain many vendor provider contracts.

Figure 2.81 Partner Agreement

5. Click the **Martex Partner Agreement** and you will be taken to the expanded details window (Figure 2.82).
6. Here, you can view details about the vendor, vendor product, contract start and end dates, and the distribution status.

The fulfillment status provides the status of the individual distribution steps. If the status is set to **Technically Active**, the contract is successfully distributed in SAP Convergent Invoicing and SAP Convergent Charging.

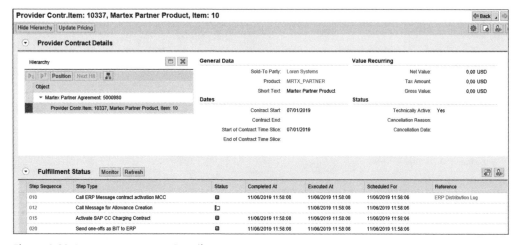

Figure 2.82 Partner Agreement Details

Next, you create the customer Provider Order and Provider Contract for McFarland Systems by following the above sequence of steps. Use **YPVO** instead of **YRPO**, and use the MRTX_USG product instead of MRTX_PRTNR. Figure 2.83 and Figure 2.84 show the provider order and provider contract that are created.

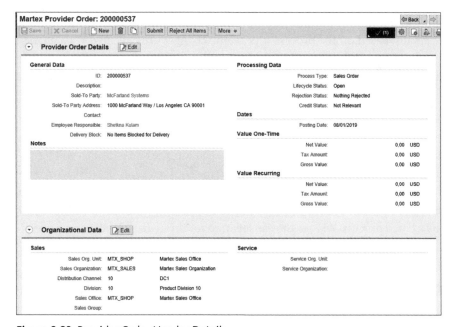

Figure 2.83 Provider Order Header Details

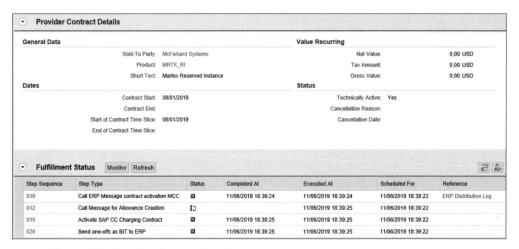

Figure 2.84 Provider Contract Details

2.3.4   Modifying Provider Contracts

A provider contract or a partner agreement cannot be changed directly. This functionality is restricted to protect the data integrity across the entire system landscape. Any change has to be made via a standard or custom maintenance framework for business transactions (BTMF) change process. Refer to the change process section for further details. Based on the process type, some changes are executed via a change order. Depending to the type of change, most of the changes are captured as time slices in the contract. All the changes are captured as various time slices with the effected change.

In our use case, you execute the cancellation process. In this example, the provider contract does not have an end date. This is considered an evergreen contract. It has a start date displayed; if the contract has a valid end date, the end date also will be displayed. Regardless of the end date's availability, the contract cancellation can be executed immediately or scheduled in the future. Immediate execution will happen without any delays. Cancellation in the future will be captured in the system and executed by a batch process. You set the cancellation for immediate processing here.

To set the cancellation for immediate processing, proceed as follows:

1. Log into the SAP CRM web UI using Transaction WUI_SSO or the SAP BRIM, subscription order management URL if one is provided by your system administrator.

2. Select the **PROV-SALES** role.

3. Click **Provider Contract Management** in the left pane.

4. Click **Provider Contract** under the **Search** window. Enter the provider contract number that you want to change.

5. Click the **Provider Contract** number hyperlink in the **Results** window. You will be navigated to the provider contract details screen.

6. Select line item 10 in the contract hierarchy. You will see the contract dates.

   Figure 2.85 and Figure 2.86 show the details of the contract, including the header item details, fulfillment status, a list of applicable change processes, and more.

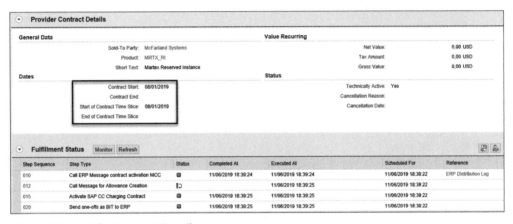

Figure 2.85 Provider Contract Details

Actions	Description	Process Type	Change Process
Execute	Trigger Bill-on-Demand Process in SAP ERP	ISTF	BILL_ON_DEMAND
Execute	Contract Extension	ISTA	EXTENSION
Execute	Product Change	ISTA	PROD_CHANGE
Execute	Change Technical Resources	ISTA	CHANGE_TR
Execute	Lock and Unlock Contracts	ISTC	LOCK_UNLOCK
Execute	Cancellation	ISTA	CANCEL

Figure 2.86 List of Change Processes

7. Click **Execute** in the row for the **CANCEL** change process. A new popup window opens. Figure 2.87 shows the details of the change process entry fields.

Figure 2.87 Cancellation Process Field Entries

The **Activation Date** and time is the actual date/time the contract is slated for cancellation. **Requested Cancellation Date/Requested Cancellation Time** can be the same as or after the **Activation Date** and time.

8. Enter the applicable date and time and click **Apply**, and you will be taken to the newly created change order.

As mentioned in Section 2.2.5, Change Process, the change order is automatically created with reference to the provider contract that is being changed.

9. Click the **Submit** button at the top of the screen to execute the change (as in Figure 2.88).

10. Click the contract number to view the changed contract (Figure 2.89).

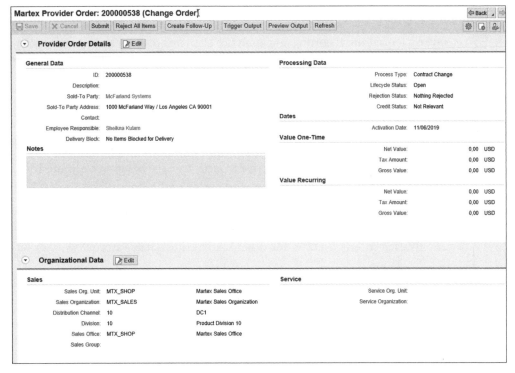

Figure 2.88 Cancellation Change Order

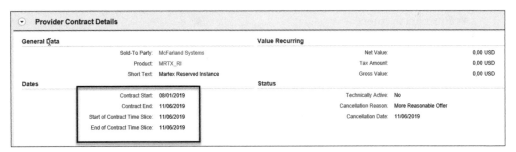

Figure 2.89 Provider Contract with Cancellation Date Updated

Note that the contract history is created with time slices. The contract status in **Technically Active** has changed to **No**, indicating the contract has ended.

2.4   Reporting and Analytics

Let's take a look at the reporting and analytics elements of subscription order management with SAP BRIM. We'll start by exploring SAP CRM, then we'll move on to the ODI distribution monitor and the middleware monitor.

2.4.1   SAP CRM

SAP CRM has the capability to create ad hoc reports without using an SAP BW system. This type of report, often called interactive reports, are used to report on limited data volumes very quickly. Setting up these reports is out of the scope of this book.

There are different ways to search with the help of multiple search and filter criteria. The search windows for different objects already come with a limited number of commonly used criteria. You can add other search criteria fields as well.

The following objects are commonly searched for in the scope of SAP BRIM, subscription order management:

- Provider orders
- Partner provider orders
- Provider contracts
- Partner agreements
- Master agreements
- Business partners
- Business agreements
- Products
- Mass runs
- Products
- SAP Convergent Charging tables

For our example, you will search for a list of Martex provider orders for McFarland Systems, as follows:

1. Log into the SAP CRM web UI using Transaction WUI_SSO or the SAP BRIM, subscription order management URL if one is provided by your system administrator.
2. Select the **PROV-SALES** role.
3. Click **Provider Contract Management** in the left pane.
4. Click **Provider Order** under the Search window. Enter "1100000356" for the **Sold-To Party** number and Martex Provider order for the **Transaction Type**.
5. Click the **Search** button and the results will be displayed in the **Results** window in a tabular form (see Figure 2.90).

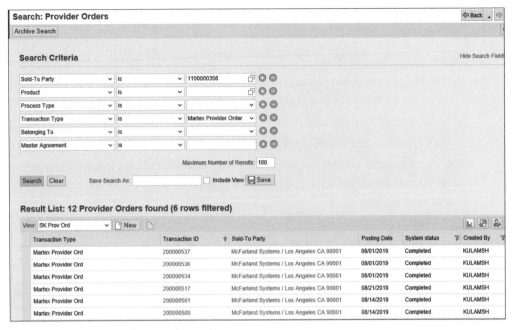

Figure 2.90 Provider Order Search Results

You can search for other objects in a similar way, adapting the filters as needed.

2.4.2   ODI Distribution Monitor

One of the essential tasks for following up on the creation of provider contracts or partner agreements is to confirm the status of the replication of these objects into SAP Convergent Invoicing and SAP Convergent Charging. If the replication is not successful, you cannot use these contracts for billing and invoicing in the downstream processes. You can view and analyze the status in the **Fulfillment** status block. You can reach this window in three ways:

1. When you are in the provider contract line item screen, open the **Fulfillment** status block and you can view the status. If the status is successful, the distribution steps are assigned a green light. Otherwise, the system provides error messages so that you can resolve the error, in which case the light is either yellow or red. With this option, you are limited to analyzing the particular contract you are working on.

2. Alternately, enter Transaction CRM_ISX_DMON in the SAP GUI menu window. This allows you to analyze the status of any contract.

3. Finally, you can get here from the SAP CRM web UI. Similar to option 2, you can analyze any contract from here.

For our example, proceed as follows:

1. Log into the SAP CRM web UI using Transaction WUI_SSO or the SAP BRIM, subscription order management URL if one is provided by your system administrator.
2. Select the **PROV-SALES** role.
3. Click **Provider Contract Management** in the left pane.
4. Click **Distribution Monitor** under the **Search** window and you will be taken to the fulfillment messages window. Enter the contract number you are searching for and click **Search**.
5. The **Results** window displays the status of each line item in the contract.
6. Click each line item, 10 and 20, to view the statuses. Figure 2.91 shows the overall status of each of the line items.

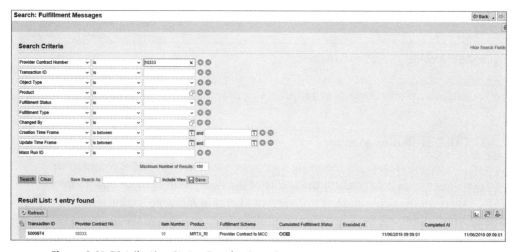

Figure 2.91 Distribution Status Results Overview

Figure 2.92 and Figure 2.93 show the detailed statuses of each of the distribution steps, along with the distribution messages.

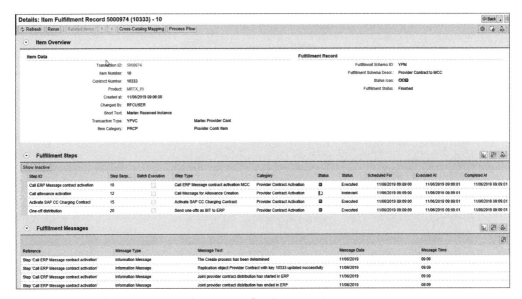

Figure 2.92 Distribution Status and Messages for Line Item 10

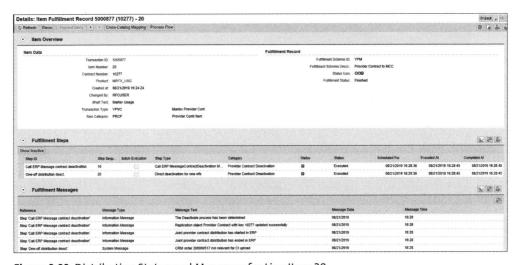

Figure 2.93 Distribution Status and Messages for Line Item 20

2.4.3   Middleware Monitor

SAP CRM uses middleware to replicate master data object like business partners, business agreements, and products, as well as transactional data. Configuration objects from SAP ERP or SAP S/4HANA can be replicated into SAP CRM via middle-ware as well based on the project system landscape. The scope of the middleware setup and the replication details are out of scope of this chapter. To view the monitor, in the SAP Menu follow menu path **Architecture and Technology · Middleware · Mon-itoring · Message Flow · SMW01**.

Alternately, execute Transaction SMW01.

Figure 2.94 shows the screen where you can enter multiple sets of values to run the status of the middleware objects. The result of this search will display the results of the business documents that are replicated between SAP ERP and SAP CRM.

Figure 2.94 Business Documents Monitor Selection Screen

To see the business documents errors, proceed as follows:

1. Select the checkboxes for **Errors** and **Date**, and press ⌞F8⌟ to execute. Figure 2.95 show the results, listing the business documents in an error status.

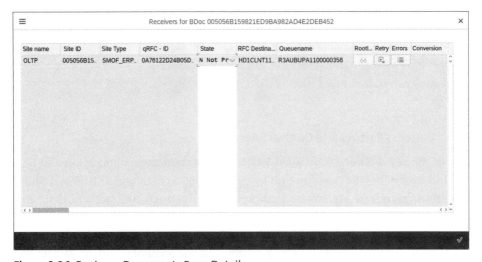

Figure 2.95 Business Documents in Error

2. Select a BDoc and click the ☐ button to view the errors.

3. Another window (Figure 2.96) pops up to display the error details.

Figure 2.96 Business Documents Error Details

You can now analyze the errors and resolve the issues.

2.5   Subscription Order Management in SAP S/4HANA

So far in this chapter, we have discussed in detail how subscription order management can be configured as part of SAP CRM to enable customers to sell their goods and services in a flexible consumption model.

However, with the release of SAP S/4HANA 1809 FSP 01 in March 2019, subscription order management functionality also became available as part of an add-on called SAP S/4HANA for customer management. Beginning in SAP S/4HANA 1909, released in September 2019, this has now been renamed as SAP S/4HANA Service. SAP BRIM customers can now choose whether to license subscription order management as part of SAP CRM or as part of SAP S/4HANA, which we will now cover.

To a large extent, most of these subscription order management configurations also apply to SAP S/4HANA, so we'll now highlight the key master data and configuration elements that are different for subscription order management on SAP S/4HANA. These changes are made to fully leverage the power of the SAP HANA-based system while maintaining the key frameworks built over the years as part of SAP CRM. They also enable an easier path to migration for customers who have been using SAP CRM over the years.

> **User Interface**
>
> SAP S/4HANA continues to support the traditional web user interface that users might have used as part of SAP CRM. It also supports several SAP Fiori apps that are delivered as part of the subscription order management functionality.

2.5.1   Business Partner and Contract Accounts

One of the key differences between SAP CRM as a standalone application and SAP S/4HANA Service is that users are no longer required to maintain SAP CRM middleware settings to replicate objects such as business partner, contract accounts, and products into the SAP S/4HANA system. Since SAP S/4HANA Service and SAP Convergent Invoicing share the same application, business partners are created in SAP S/4HANA directly and used in both. Similarly, contract accounts used in SAP Convergent Invoicing are extended to SAP S/4HANA Service as well. The core functionality of these two objects remain the same and are configured the same way as explained earlier in this chapter.

2.5.2   Product Setup

To support the use of subscription products, two new material types—subscription product (SUBS) used for subscription purposes, and subscription partner product (SUBP) used in the partner settlement process —have been introduced. Both these material types can be created using an SAP Fiori app called Manage Product Master Data. These products can be assigned with the following key attributes in the Manage Product Master Data app directly:

- Billing cycle
- Contract terms

- Extension periods
- Assignment schema for the technical resource

Additional attributes specific to the subscription model can be assigned to the product using an SAP Fiori app, Manage Subscription Product-Specific Data, shown in Figure 2.97. To access this app, a user should be assigned the role *SAP_BR_PROD_CONF_MODELR_SOM*. Key attributes maintained in this app include the following:

- Maintain cross-catalog mapping for the charge plans created in SAP Convergent Charging
- Maintain rules for discounts and charges defined in SAP Convergent Invoicing

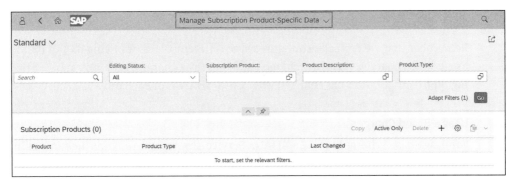

Figure 2.97 Maintain Subscription Product-Specific Data with SAP Fiori App

There are no changes in the way cross-catalog mapping is created and maintained in SAP S/4HANA. The charge plans created in SAP Convergent Charging are available to be maintained using the SAP Fiori app shown in Figure 2.98. However certain aspects that are supported for subscription order management in SAP CRM, like price key and price table functionality, are not supported in SAP S/4HANA.

Figure 2.98 Maintain Cross-Catalog Mapping

Customers can also create *product bundles*, which potentially include a combination of different material types (such as hardware, software, and service).

> **Note**
>
> As subscription order management is part of the SAP S/4HANA Service, it is no longer required to configure SAP CRM middleware for replication of customer, business agreement, and product information with SAP Convergent Invoicing, which is also part of SAP S/4HANA. However, existing data replication models between SAP Convergent Invoicing and SAP Convergent Charging will be leveraged for these objects.

2.5.3   Pricing

Remember that we typically configure three different types of pricing in SAP BRIM: usage-based charges, recurring charges, and one-time charges. Let's look at how pricing type configuration has changed with SAP S/4HANA for each one.

Usage-Based Charges

For usage-based charges in SAP S/4HANA Service, the process remains the same as in SAP CRM. The link between the charge plans created in SAP Convergent Charging and the products created in SAP S/4HANA Service is created through the cross-catalog mapping in Figure 2.99 using a new SAP Fiori app, Manage Subscription Product-Specific Data. As of SAP S/4HANA 1909, users can also trigger different charge plan setups in SAP Convergent Charging based on product parameters modeled in SAP S/4HANA Service.

Figure 2.99 Cross-Catalog Mapping for Usage-Based Charges

Product Configuration

As discussed previously in the chapter, product configuration enables customers to set different characteristics and parameters during order processing to drive variant-specific pricing calculations in subscription order management and in SAP Convergent Charging through cross-catalog mapping. As of SAP S/4HANA 1909, product configuration is now supported for subscription order management using advanced variant configuration functionality. Customers can create the product model using standard SAP S/4HANA variant configuration functionality. This replaces the SAP IPC-based product configuration supported in SAP CRM.

Recurring Charges

Recurring charges are applied in SAP S/4HANA subscription order management using billing plans/cycles. Billing cycles are generally defined in SAP Convergent Invoicing and are available for assignment when creating a subscription product. The following items can be specified at the time of subscription order creation:

- First date of billing cycle
- Last date of billing cycle
- Duration/periods

Recurring charge values are maintained using standard SAP S/4HANA pricing condition types and records. To support subscription order management with SAP S/4HANA, special condition types for monthly and annual recurring charges are pre-delivered with special calculation formulas. The calculation types shown in Figure 2.100 have been introduced in SAP S/4HANA 1809 to support this use case:

- Monthly price (M)
- Year price (N)
- Daily price (O)
- Weekly price (P)

An access sequence for Monthly Subscription Price (PSMB) has also been introduced, as shown in Figure 2.101.

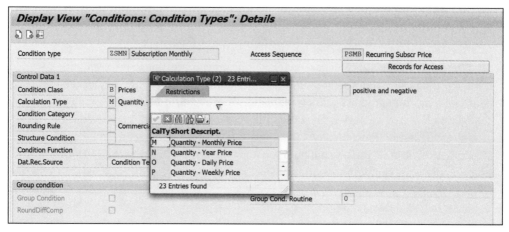

Figure 2.100 SAP S/4HANA Calculation Types

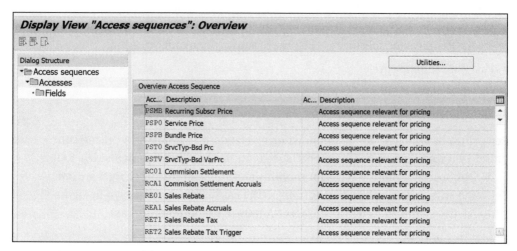

Figure 2.101 Monthly Subscription Price Access Sequence

The billing cycles maintained in SAP Convergent Invoicing are mapped to the billing cycles available for usage in SAP S/4HANA Service, as shown in Figure 2.102. It can be accessed through the menu path **IMG · Service · Transactions · Settings for Subscription Transactions · Recurring Fees · Define Billing Cycle Determination Rules**.

Figure 2.102 Maintain Billing Cycle Determination Rules

These can be leveraged and modified as per the customer requirement. Please note that in SAP S/4HANA 1909, it is possible to assign mapping tables created in SAP Convergent Charging to maintain recurring values using SAP S/4HANA Service.

One-Time Charges

One-time charges are applied by distributing these charges directly from subscription order management in SAP S/4HANA to SAP Convergent Invoicing. These leverage existing capabilities from SAP CRM. We will not go into the details of this, as it has been covered in the previous sections.

2.5.4   Subscription Orders and Contracts

The terms *provider order* and *provider contract* in SAP CRM have been replaced by *subscription order* and *subscription contract* in SAP S/4HANA. SAP S/4HANA Service supports the creation of different order types including:

- Subscription order
- Solution quotation
- Master agreement
- Subscription contract

Most of the functionalities and configuration from SAP CRM have been ported over to SAP S/4HANA Service with respect to master agreements and solution quotations, so in this section we will focus on subscription orders and subscription contracts.

The distribution of these orders and contracts leverages the standard document distribution framework Order Distribution Infrastructure (ODI), as shown in Figure 2.103. Subscription orders and contracts that are created in SAP S/4HANA are distributed to SAP Convergent Charging and Convergent Invoicing.

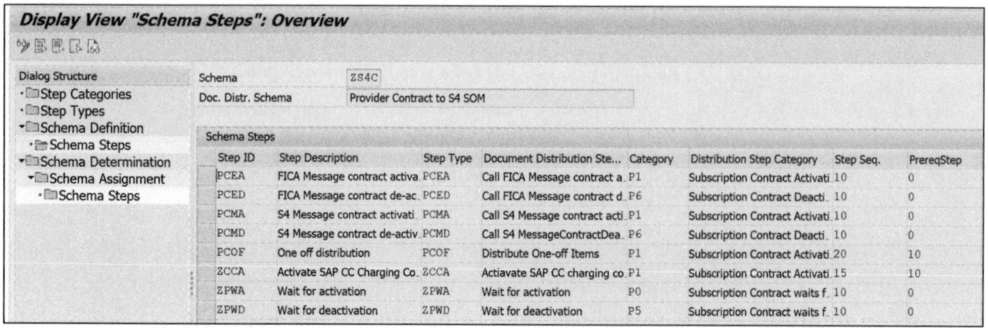

Figure 2.103 Maintain Settings for Document Distribution

For a subscription order that contains both hardware and subscription line items, the hardware line item is triggered as a sales order and distributed to SAP S/4HANA Sales. The subscription products are created as subscription contracts, and are distributed to SAP Convergent Invoicing and SAP Convergent Charging.

As of SAP S/4HANA 1909, most of the standard contract change processes available in the standalone SAP CRM system have been made available, including but not limited to the following:

- Product change
- Contract cancellation
- Contract extension
- Contract account assignment
- Change technical resource
- Upgrade CCM version
- Change of configuration using advanced variant configuration
- Change of quantity
- Allowance refill

The settings for the contract change processes shown in Figure 2.104 can be accessed via the file path **IMG · Service · Transactions · Settings for Subscription Transactions · Contract Changes · Settings for the Maintenance Framework (BTMF)**.

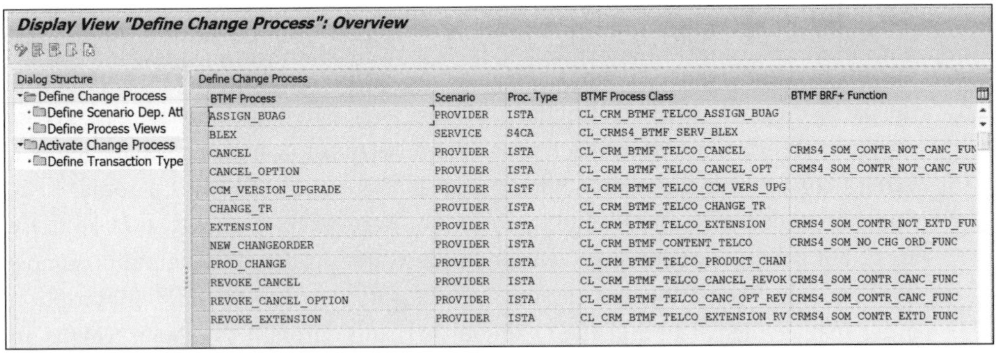

Figure 2.104 Define and Maintain Contract Change Process

2.5.5   Subscription Item Quantity

To support the use of quantities in subscription orders and subscription contracts, a new item category group (PRSR) and the following item categories have been introduced in SAP S/4HANA Service:

- PROR in subscription order
- PRQR in solution quotation
- PRCR in subscription contract
- PRQF for subscription one-off items

These item categories are delivered as part of standard, out-of-the-box SAP S/4HANA functionality. Additional customizations as required can be maintained using the following configuration file paths:

- **IMG · Service · Transactions · Basic Settings · Define Item Categories**
- **IMG · Service · Transactions · Basic Settings · Define Item Category Group**
- **IMG · Service · Transactions · Basic Settings · Define Item Category Determination**

Once these configurations are in place, you'll need to enable these item categories for the subscription items using the file path **IMG · Service · Transactions · Settings for Subscription Transactions · Define Settings for Item Categories**.

The quantity entered in the order is also available to be changed in a subscription contract as part of the standard contract change process, as outlined in Section 2.5.4.

2.6   Summary

By now, you know that SAP BRIM, subscription order management uses SAP CRM as the backbone upon which its functionalities are built. Often, the functionalities cross over into other SAP modules, such as sales and distribution, materials management, variant configuration, Internet Pricing and Configurator, and SAP Customer Relationship Management (SAP CRM). You do not need to have expertise in all these areas, but having functional knowledge in these areas is certainly helpful. You now have enough information to complete the necessary steps in SAP BRIM, subscription order management to build the example that runs through this book. This is an extensive chapter to cover in its entirety. As you gain more knowledge by building more scenarios, you will master the functionalities in SAP BRIM, subscription order management.

You have learned to set up and create all the necessary master data objects and all the necessary transactional data and you understand the purpose and functions of these objects and how they play their part in this process.

SAP BRIM is an integrated solution. We therefore recommend working through the other chapters in this book as well, which may prove helpful for reaching your goals.

Chapter 3
Charging

This chapter first explains charging master data and tables, then gives step-by-step instructions for configuring the SAP Convergent Charging charge creation process by explaining the core tool, the charge types (recurring, one time, usage), and interface objects such as chargeable item classes and charged item classes.

This chapter explains how to set up the SAP Convergent Charging modeling process using the case study established in Chapter 1. Modeling in SAP Convergent Charging is typically performed using the SAP Convergent Charging core tool. The core tool is a graphical user interface that allows you to create and maintain different types of objects such as provider contract, subscriber account, pricing, charge plan, charge, and more. The tool provides predefined components and functions to build the objects; no coding is required.

SAP Convergent Charging is an extremely robust and versatile system, the sole purpose of which is to rate, charge, and generate rated transactions. A rated (calculated) transaction generated out of convergent charging is called billable item. It is used to bill a customer. In SAP Convergent Charging, a customer is called a *subscriber account*. In Contract Accounts Receivable and Payable (FI-CA), a customer is known as a *business partner*.

SAP Convergent Charging provides three types of charges; one-time, recurring, and usage. For one-time charge, the charge is triggered based on an external event, such as contract activation or termination. For recurring charge, SAP Convergent Charging generates the charges based on internal scheduling determined during the build. For usage charge, the consumption data records originating from the multiple source systems or network elements are used to perform rating and charging by SAP Convergent Charging.

For example, in the telecommunications industry, a one-time charge can be an activation charge and a recurring charge can be a fixed monthly fee, such as unlimited voice and text messages. For usage charge, it can be data plan where consumption data records are generated based on customers consumptions. In an integrated environment, consumption data records are sent from multiple sources and directed to SAP Convergent charging to perform rating and charging. SAP Convergent Charging then generates billable items in FI-CA for further billing and invoice processing. We'll talk more about billable items in later chapters.

When first deployed, SAP Convergent Charging is an empty box offering a variety of creative solutioning possibilities, and a customer has the capability to create his own unique rating and charging requirements. Unlike other traditional suites of SAP products, SAP Convergent Charging doesn't have many custom objects; the only one is the interface design, which receives usage information.

SAP Convergent Charging integrates with SAP BRIM, subscription order management and FI-CA systems via web services. It also has the ability to integrate with non-SAP systems using either web services or Java APIs for rating usage events. To configure the SAP Convergent Charging system, you follow a define, assign, apply, and process (DAAP) methodology.

SAP Convergent Charging takes a decision tree approach to perform rating and charging of subscribers. There are many configuration elements provided to carry out the rating and charge tasks, each of which will be discussed with examples in further chapters, but in a nutshell they are rates, comparators, splitters, operators, and functions.

> **Note**
>
> The chapter does not include any instruction sections because SAP Convergent Charging is a pricing/rating engine that does not require user involvement in day-to-day operation once it has been set up.

3.1   Master Data

In most OLTP systems, data is separated into two main categories: master data and transactional data. Any data generated out of a transaction is transactional data (e.g., quotations, orders, contracts); everything else is master data (e.g., business partners). In SAP Convergent Charging terms, a provider contract is a type of transactional data, and subscriber accounts, external accounts, and charge objects are examples of master data.

Before rating and charging can be carried out in SAP Convergent Charging, master data elements need to be set up/configured in the way required by the use case. We will discuss key master data elements such as subscriber accounts, external accounts, range tables, subscriber range tables, mapping tables, and translation tables within the SAP Convergent Charging system in detail, and we will explain how they can be defined and created.

To access SAP Convergent Charging, first the core tool needs to be installed. The core tool is the user interface to perform charge modeling using visual programming in the form of a decision tree. The core tool is provided in the installation file of SAP Convergent Charging, which can be found at the SAP Support Launchpad (*https://authn.hana.ondemand.com/saml2/sp/mds*) under the **Software Downloads** section, as shown in Figure 3.1.

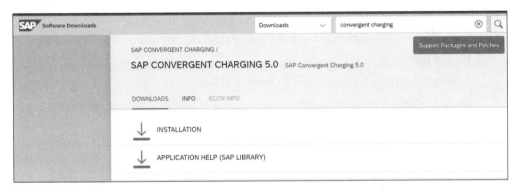

Figure 3.1 SAP Software Download Center

The core tool is a Java-based tool and will execute when the correct version of Java Virtual Machine is installed on the computer.

The core tool is available as part of the installation ZIP file and is in the *DATA_UNITS/ CCXX_TOOLS_CONTENT_UC_OSIND/core_tool.zip* archive. After extracting the files in *core_tool.zip*, execute either *core_tool.bat* or *core_tool.sh*, depending on your operating system.

On the login screen, provide the username and password created by your system administrator and the dispatcher URL (see Figure 3.2).

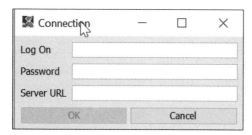

Figure 3.2 Core Tool Login Screen

3.1.1   Catalog

A catalog is a placeholder for all configuration objects. This is like the concept of pack-ages in other programming languages. In an integration scenario for SAP BRIM, it is best practice to only have one catalog per landscape to simplify integration. How-ever, it is not uncommon to see multiple catalogs created in lower environments for testing purposes.

To create a catalog, navigate to **File · New · Catalog**.

Once a catalog is created, you are shown a series of folders. All these folders are types of development objects for SAP Convergent Charging. As objects are created in SAP Convergent Charging, they will be displayed in their respective folders, as shown in Figure 3.3.

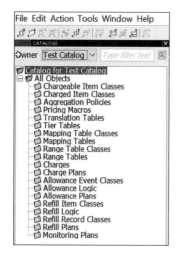

Figure 3.3 Object Categories with Catalog

3.1.2   Subscriber Account and External Account

A subscriber account within SAP Convergent Charging is a unique identifier for the end customer of the service user. Subscriber accounts can have one or many external accounts assigned to them, as shown in Figure 3.4.

In an integrated SAP BRIM scenario, a subscriber account is automatically created in SAP Convergent Charging via replication of a business partner from SAP Convergent Invoicing. Any change to the subscriber account should be initiated from the provisioning system for it to be consistent across all SAP BRIM systems.

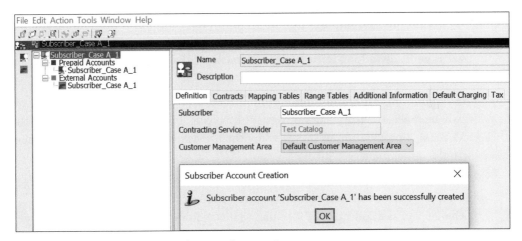

Figure 3.4 Subscriber Account and External Account

A subscriber account contains the prepaid account and external account subobjects. An external account is also called a postpaid account. The concept of a prepaid subscriber account is analogous to a prepaid customer in the telecommunications industry, in which a pay-as-you-go charging model is used. The postpaid subscriber account is similar most subscription models today that have different flavors such as advanced charging or arrears charging.

In SAP Convergent Charging, information about subscriber accounts is lean: although they represent a customer, they often only present an ID. Information such as names and addresses is typically stored in other SAP BRIM areas.

Subscriber accounts and external accounts are terms used exclusively in SAP Convergent Charging and are often referred to with other terminology in different SAP BRIM modules. Table 3.1 shows these differences in terminology.

SAP Convergent Charging	SAP BRIM, Subscription Order Management	Contract Accounts Receivable and Payable
Subscriber account	Business partner	Business partner
External account	Business agreement	Contract account

Table 3.1 Subsciber Account and External Account Terminology in Other Systems

3.1.3   Provider Contract

In SAP Convergent Charging, a provider contract represents a business arrangement between the provider of a service and the consumer of that service. A provider contract is generally a long-term business agreement that establishes certain agreed-upon terms and conditions.

We do not need to manually create a provider contract in SAP Convergent Charging; it will be replicated from SAP Convergent Invoicing. In an integrated scenario with SAP BRIM, a provider order is created by the provisioning system (SAP BRIM, subscription order management).

A provider contract usually comprises a subscriber, external account, and charge plan. Charge plans will be covered extensively in section Section 3.2. For now, think of a charge plan as a collection of formulas that is required to calculate what to charge customers. An example of a provider contract is shown in Figure 3.5.

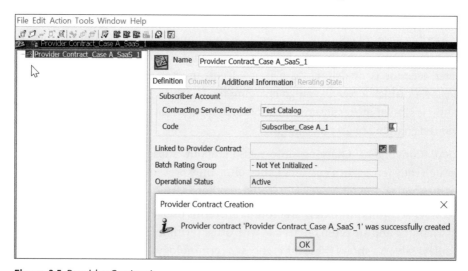

Figure 3.5 Provider Contract

In an integrated scenario, SAP BRIM, subscription order management can be used to update the provider contract through change processes; whenever that happens, a new version of the provider contract will be created in SAP Convergent Charging.

3.1.4   Tables

Tables are dynamic data structures within SAP Convergent Charging used to store information inside or outside the SAP Convergent Charging system. This information is later used for designing charge logic. This section describes the various tables available in SAP Convergent Charging, and subsequent chapters show how tables can be incorporated within charge logic.

Tier Table

A tier table is a type of table used internally within SAP Convergent Charging to calculate pricing requriements that involved tiers.

To create a tier table, proceed as follows:

1. Navigate to **File · New · Tier Table**, as shown in Figure 3.6.

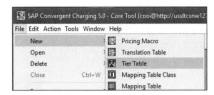

Figure 3.6 Tier Table

2. In the tier table definition window, click the **Table Schema** tab (as shown in Figure 3.7), then enter the **Name** and **Description**.

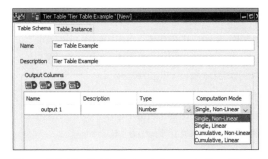

Figure 3.7 Tier Table Output Computation Modes

Then you must define an output column. There are four computation mode to pick from depending on your business requirements:

- **Single, Nonlinear**
- **Single, Linear**
- **Cumulative, Nonlinear**
- **Cumulative, Linear**

Now that you've configured the table schema, let's maintain the ranges and their corresponding output values in the **Table Instance** tab. In the tier table definition window, click the **Table Instance** tab, shown in Figure 3.8.

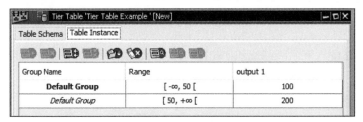

Figure 3.8 Tier Table Table Instance Definition

To save the tier table, follow menu path **File · Save · In the Database**. Once saved, the tier table is ready to be used in charge logic, which will be covered in Section 3.2.

Translation Table

A translation table is used internally within SAP Convergent Charging as a lookup table, in which a set of keys is passed in as input columns and a set of values is returned as output columns.

To create a translation table, proceed as follows:

1. Navigate to **File · New · Translation Table**.
2. Select the **Table Schema** tab. Here, specify a set of input columns by clicking the ⊞ in the **Input Columns** area and a set of corresponding output columns by clicking the ⊞ in the **Output Columns** area, as shown in Figure 3.9.
3. Next, select the **Table Instance** tab. Here, row values for input columns and their corresponding output columns can be specified depending on your business requirements by clicking the ⊞ button, as shown in Figure 3.10.

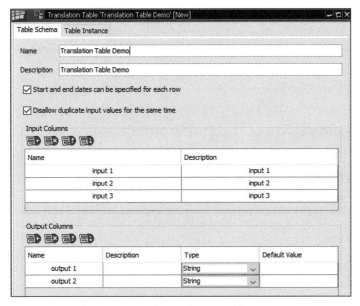

Figure 3.9 Definition View of Translation Table

input 1	input 2	input 3	Start Date	End Date	output 1	output 2
abc	def	ghi	August 1, 2019 ...	August 11, 201...	123	123
Any	*Any*	*Any*	August 1, 2019 ...	August 31, 201...	456	456

Figure 3.10 Values in Transation Table

To save the translation table, follow menuk path **File · Save · In the Database**. Once saved, the Translation Table is now ready to be used in charge logic, which will be covered in Section 3.2.

Mapping Table

A mapping table is used to build and store business data by validity for rating and charging purposes. Unlike their counterpart translation tables, mapping tables can be defined internally within SAP Convergent Charging or externally redefined with the help of a provisioning system contract. Because they can be redefined from a provisioning system, it is possible to have contract-specific and subscriber-specific mapping table data. Mapping tables can support up to 20 input and 30 output columns.

To define values in the mapping table, first create a mapping table class object at menu path **File · New · Mapping Table Class**. The next step is to define input and output columns and their respective data type: string or number.

In Figure 3.11, we have set **Membership Level** and **Service Option** as input columns and **Price** as an output column, all three with **String** as the **Type**.

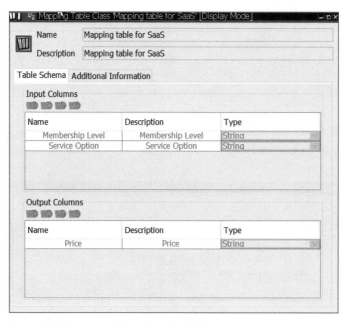

Figure 3.11 Mapping Table Class Definition

The mapping table class can be saved via the **File · Save** shortcut. Next, create a mapping table based on the mapping table class via **File · New · Mapping Table**, as shown in Figure 3.12.

To save the mapping table, follow menu path **File · Save · In the Database**. Once saved, the mapping table is ready to be used in charge logic, which will be covered in Section 3.2.

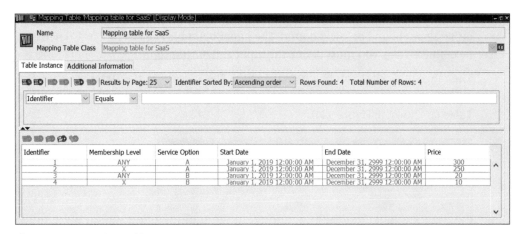

Figure 3.12 Mapping Table

Range Table

The range table is like the tier table, but with one main difference. In addition to internal SAP Convergent Charging maintenance, a range table can also be maintained via web services or direct from SAP BRIM, subscription order management. To create a range table, a range table class needs to be created first via menu path **File · New · Range Table Class** (as shown in Figure 3.13).

Figure 3.13 Range Table Class

When defining a range table class, the upper bound range needs to be defined as either upper bound or lower bound. The upper bound of the last range also needs to be defined. Then, you must define the input and output columns.

The range table class can be saved using the **File · Save · In the Database** shortcut. Next, create a range table based on the mapping table class via **File · New · Range Table** (as shown in Figure 3.14).

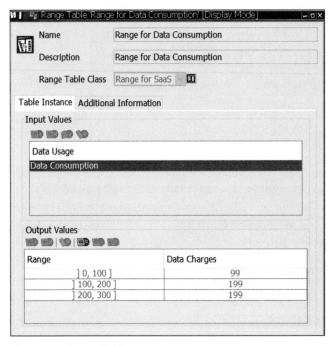

Figure 3.14 Range Table

To save the range table, follow menu path **File · Save · In the Database**. Once saved, the range table is ready to be used in charge logic, which will be covered in Section 3.2.

In this section we have seen the building blocks of convergent charging, In the next sections we will explore how all these building blocks can be weaved together to design charging logic.

3.2 Configuring SAP Convergent Charging

Now let's look at the technical aspects of product modeling and how to configure SAP Convergent Charging using the core tool. This is arguably the most important area of SAP BRIM because SAP Convergent Charging plays the role of the rating and pricing engine. We will continue to build on the Martex Corp. example to show how you can we can translate business requirements into SAP Convergent Charging objects.

3.2.1 Chargeable Item Class

A chargeable item class defines the structure or format of how usage charges are passed into SAP Convergent Charging. Usage charges could be measured by, say, the number of songs downloaded, the amount of computation power consumed, or the gigabytes of disk space used.

A chargeable item class can be created in two different ways:

- Manual definition using the core tool
- Consumption item mapping

Let's begin by looking at manual definition with the core tool. The manual definition option is commonly used when SAP Convergent Charging is being used as a standalone solution. Figure 3.15 shows how the chargeable item class can be defined using the core tool.

Proceed as follows:

1. Navigate to **File · New · Chargeable Item Class**.
2. During the definition of a chargeable item class, custom fields of type date, number, and string can be defined in addition to the three mandatory fields required by SAP Convergent Charging (**Consumption Date, User Identifier**, and **Service Identifier**), as shown in Figure 3.15.

Additional user property fields can be added by clicking the 🔲 button. The data type of the field can be changed by clicking the type column of the corresponding row. Subsequently, fill in the name and description and save using the following navigation path: **File · Save · In the Database** (see Figure 3.16).

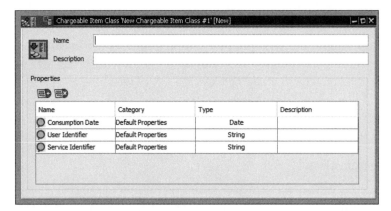

Figure 3.15 Defining Chargeable Item Class

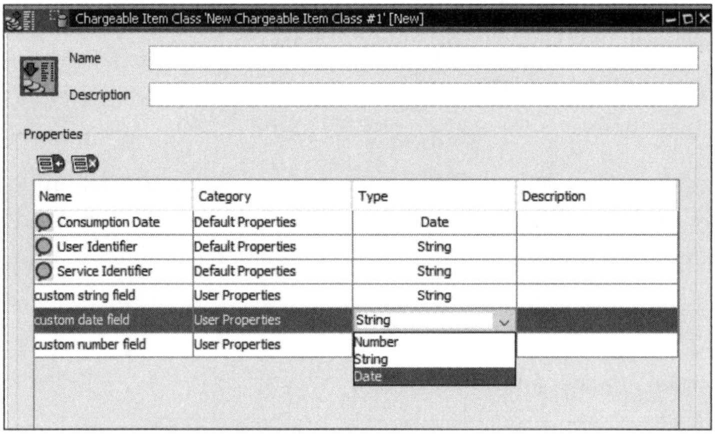

Figure 3.16 Custom Attributes in Chargable Item Class

Consumption item mapping is used to define chargeable item classes in an integration scenario with SAP Convergent Invoicing. Because the objective of this book is to cover SAP BRIM as an end-to-end solution, future chargeable item class examples in will be created using the consumption item mapping approach. To create a chargeable item class using the consumption item mapping approach, navigate to **File · New · Consumption Item Mapping.**

As shown in Figure 3.17, the consumption item mappings of types **HCOS** and **REVE** are predefined in SAP Convergent Invoicing as consumption item classes. The purpose of having separate COST and REVE consumption item classes is to distinguish between consumption items for revenue (customer) and cost (vendor).

The steps and configuration to define consumption item classes in SAP Convergent Invoicing will be covered in Chapter 4.

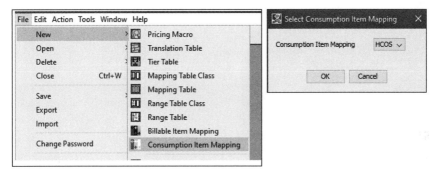

Figure 3.17 Consumption Item Mapping

The creation of consumption mapping will automatically create chargeable item class in the background. Figure 3.18 shows the consumption item mapping class created on the left and the corresponding chargeable item class COST created together. Note that all the fields of both objects are the same, except that the chargeable item class has a consumption date, user identifier, and service identifier.

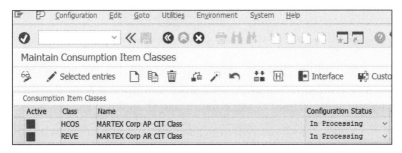

Figure 3.18 Maintain Consumption Item Classes

Figure 3.19 shows the steps to create COST consumption item mapping; the same steps apply when creating REVE consumption item mapping.

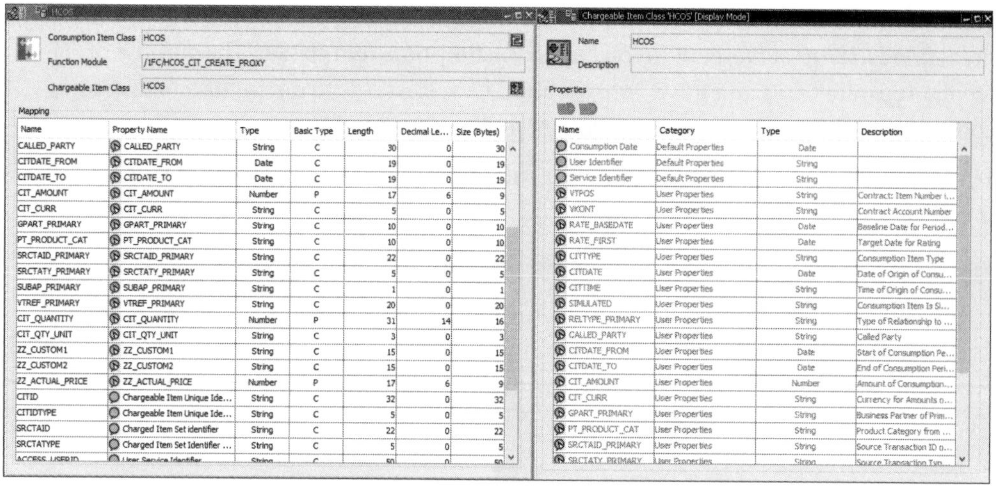

Figure 3.19 HCOS Consumption Item Mapping

3.2.2   Charged Item Class

Whereas chargeable item classes handle how usage charges are passed into SAP Convergent Charging, charged item classes handle how results from rating and charging generated by SAP Convergent Charging for usage-based or recurring subscriptions are passed from SAP Convergent Charging into subsequent systems for billing and invoicing.

A charged item class can also be created in two different ways:

- Manual definition using the core tool
- Billable item mapping

Let's begin with manual definition. The manual definition option is commonly used when SAP Convergent Charging is not being integrated with SAP Convergent Invoicing. To begin, navigate to **File · New · Charged Item Class**, as shown in Figure 3.20.

SAP Convergent Charging supports four different date types for charged items (number, string, date, and Boolean). To define a charged item class, select elements with the respective data type. ⬓ denotes string, ⬓ denotes number, ⬓ denotes date, and ⬓ denotes boolean (as shown in Figure 3.21).

Figure 3.20 Defining Charged Item Class

Figure 3.21 Adding Fields in Chargable Item Class

In an integrated scenario with SAP Convergent Invoicing, creation of a charged item class will be done using billable item mapping. The prerequisite for billable item mapping is to first create a billable item class in SAP Convergent Invoicing. This step will be covered in detail in Chapter 4. Figure 3.22 shows a sample of billable item classes HCOS and REVE in SAP Convergent Invoicing. The purpose of having separate HCOS and REVE billable item classes is to distinguish between billable items for revenue (customer) and costs (vendor).

Figure 3.22 Billable Item Classes

To create billable item mapping, use navigation path **File · New · Billable Item Mapping**. The creation of billable mapping will automatically create a charged item class in the background. Figure 3.23 shows the billable item mapping created on the left and the corresponding charged item class COST created together.

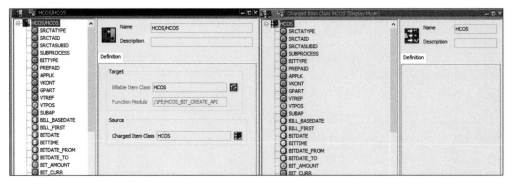

Figure 3.23 HCOS Billable Item Mapping

Now that you have defined the input/output formats for SAP Convergent Charging, the next step is to create charges that hold all the calculation logic that needs to be performed.

3.2.3   Creating Charges

In SAP Convergent Charging, the charge object contains all the rating and pricing logic that is triggered during the rating process. Charges are configured using the core tool in a decision tree structure. A charge consists of a charging plan and a price plan. The charging plan handles the determination of which reference account to charge, and the pricing plan contains the pricing and rating logic.

In this section, we will walk through how the charges in the Martex Corp. example are being created step by step from scratch.

Our example describes a few business requirements, a recurring membership cost, and usage charges for service A and service B. When performing charge modeling in SAP Convergent Charging, it is important to be able to decipher the number of charges needed by reading the business requirements. As a rule of thumb, this is usually determined by billing frequency (one time, usage-based, or recurring).

Modelling the Monthly Recurring Charge

The first charge to model is the recurring monthly cost of $100 every month, and the first step will be defining the charge attributes. For now, the default will be used, where **Type of Charge** is set to **Master** and **Fixed Currency** is set to **USD**. The other tabs—**Parameters**, **Persistent Counter**, and **Legal Text**—will be updated as needed per business requirements. To start, navigate to **File · New · Charge** and fill in the **Name** field, as shown in Figure 3.24.

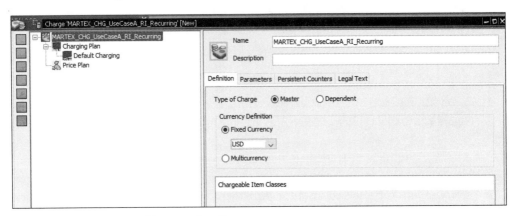

Figure 3.24 Defining Monthly Recurring Charge

The next step is to define the charge object for the example, MARTEX_CHG_UseCaseA_RI_Recurring. Our business requirements do not prompt a need for different charging references, so default charging will be used. Figure 3.25 shows the three steps required to create default charging reference. In the **Charging Plan** node of the tree, add a new charging reference called "default" with the **Type** set as **Postpaid** by using the ⊞ button (see Figure 3.26).

Next, in the **Default Charging** node, right-click and select **Add Component · References · Internal Reference** from the context menu. Next, set the name to "default" and select **default** from the **Internal Reference** dropdown list, as shown in Figure 3.26.

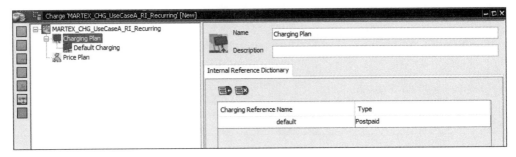

Figure 3.25 Adding Default Charging Reference in Account

Figure 3.26 Defining Internal References in Charging Plan

After a charging plan is defined, the second component of the charge, price plan, needs to be defined according to the business requirement to generate a $100 charge every month for reserved instance enrollment. In the **Pricing Plan** node, right-click and select **Add Component · Rates · Recurring Rate**. Next, in the **Recurring** node, set the **Name** and **Description** fields to "Monthly Charge". **Reference Date** should be set to **Charge Effective Date**, and set **Recurring Rate** to be triggered every **Month**, as shown in Figure 3.27.

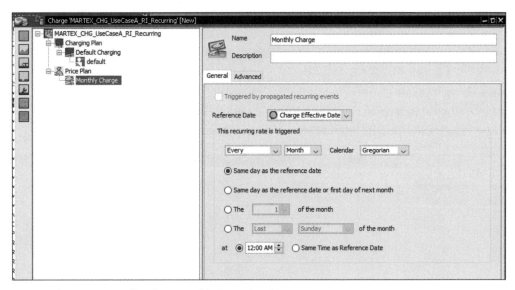

Figure 3.27 Configuring Monthly Recurring Rate

After the recurring rate component is defined, the next step is to create the charging logic beneath it. As a rule of thumb, all paths in the charging logic tree need to end with a function. Based on the example requirements so far, the charge only needs to return a flat fee amount of $100. At the **Monthly Charge** node, right-click, select **Add Component • Function • Flat**, and enter a fixed amount of $100, as shown in Figure 3.28.

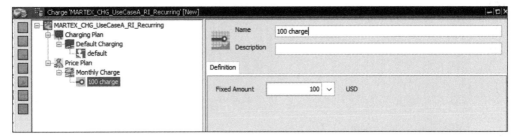

Figure 3.28 Configuring Fixed Flat Fee Charge of $100

The charge is now configured to be $100 every month. However, there are additional rules for Martex Corp. A Martex Corp. customer will be refunded the entire up-front fee if the contract is cancelled within the first month. To enable this requirement, add a persistent counter to the recurring reserved instance charge that will increment every time the charge is triggered. The purpose of the counter is to keep track of the current month of the contract. Figure 3.29 shows how a month counter is added. In the **Recurring Reserved Instance** node, select the **Persistent Counter** tab and click **Add Counter**.

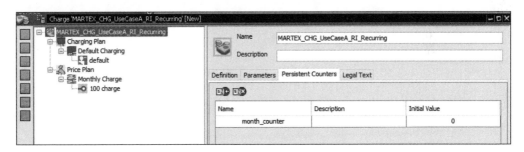

Figure 3.29 Defining Persistent Counters

To increment the counter, in the **Monthly Charge** node, right-click and select **Add Component • Operators • Update Counter**. The update counter operator is configured to add the value of 1 to the month counter every time the month counter is triggered, as shown in Figure 3.30.

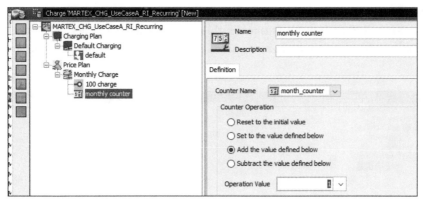

Figure 3.30 Update Monthly Counter

Finally, save the monthly charge by following menu path **File · Save · In the Database**.

Modeling the Cancellation Charge

Now that there is a way to track the current contract month, the next step is to create another charge called MARTEX_CHG_UseCaseA_RI_ Cancellation to calculate the cancellation fee. With exception of the price plan, other attributes of the charge remain the same as the recurring charge, as shown in Figure 3.31.

Figure 3.31 Cancellation Reserved Instance

First, add a rate component of the one-shot rate type by right-clicking the price plan, selecting **Add Component · Rates · Recurring Rate**, and setting the **Event Name** to **Suspension**. This indicates that the rating will only happen during cancellation, as shown in Figure 3.32.

Figure 3.32 Configuring Event Type for One Time Charge

The next step is to add special logic for first-month cancellation by right-clicking the **Cancellation Charge** node and selecting **Add Component · Comparator · Numbers**. Because the comparator object behaves as an `if` function, adding the comparator object to check for a month counter value of 1 will trigger a fork in the tree where the month counter equals 1 and the month counter does not equal 1, as shown in Figure 3.33.

From here on, the logic for a condition month counter equal 1 is to return -$100 as a refund to the customer. This step is the same as adding a flat free charge earlier, as shown in Figure 3.34.

Figure 3.33 Using Numbers Comparator in Charge Logic

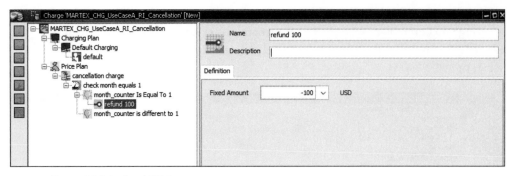

Figure 3.34 Refund $100

If the contract is past the trial period, the month counter will have a value greater than 1. Based on our example business requirements, only the value of the unused period will be refunded to the customer. The prorata operator can be used to calculate the value to be returned to the customer.

The prorata operator has several mandatory values to be populated, like the recurring rate component. One of the properties is the **Property to Prorate** field needs to be populated by a number type parameter. This can be added using the **Property Introducer** operator from context menu path, **Add Component • Operators • Property Introducer**. The next step is to add a prorata operator by right-clicking the **month_counter is different to 1** node and select **Add Component • Operators • Prorata**.

Figure 3.35 shows the values that need to be populated. To obtain the remaining unused portion to refund, select the Fraction from Prorata Date radio button and the result of the calculation will be stored in a variable called prorated_amount, as shown in Figure 3.36.

The prorated amount will be refunded by using the flat fee function, as shown in Figure 3.37.

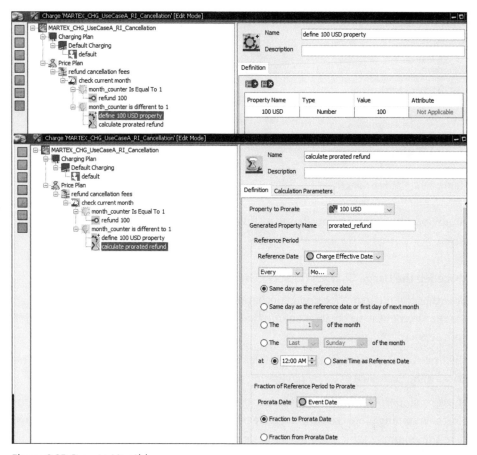

Figure 3.35 Prorate Monthly

Figure 3.36 Arithmetic Computation to Negate prorated_amount via Multiplication with -1

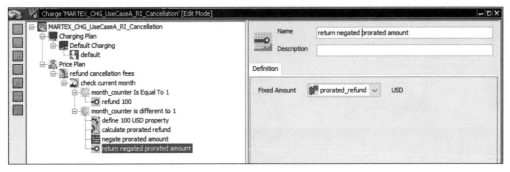

Figure 3.37 Flat Fee Function

Finally, save the cancellation charge by following menu path **File · Save · In the Database**.

Modeling the Usage Charges for Service A and Service B

Now that the recurring fee and cancellation fee have been created, the next part of the requirement is to create a charge that will support incoming usage charges for both services.

The first step is to create a mapping table class structure that can be used to store the prices of both service SKUs by navigating to **File · New · Mapping Table Class**.

The next step will be to define the structure of the mapping table class. For our example, the mapping table class should have one input column and two output columns. Save the mapping table class in the same catalog as all the other objects. The input column consists of microservice SKU IDs, and the output columns contain the regular amount and the reserved instance amount, as shown in Figure 3.38.

Once the mapping table class has been created, the next step is to create the mapping table for the mapping table class. Prices of service SKUs are stored in the mapping table. Navigate to **File · New · Mapping Table**.

For the next steps, enter the name of the mapping table in the **Name** field and pick the mapping table class created from the previous step. After that, manually insert two entries into the mapping table by using the ▤➍ button, as shown in Figure 3.39. Mapping table can be populated in different ways. For example, in an SAP BRIM integration scenario, the mapping table can be populated from the SAP BRIM, subscription order management component via web services.

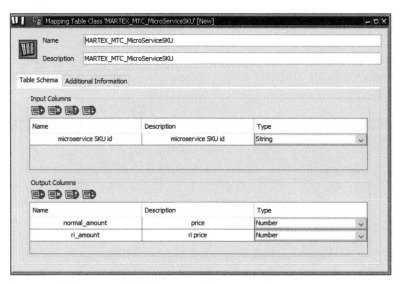

Figure 3.38 Mapping Table Class for Microservice SKU

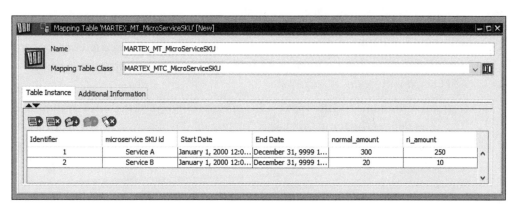

Figure 3.39 Martex_MT_MicroServiceSKU Mapping Table Defined

Finally, save the mapping table by following navigation path **File · Save · In the Database**.

Once the pricing master data for the services has been created in SAP Convergent Charging, the usage charge can be created. Based on our requirements, the price that needs to be charged when a customer is on a reserved instance is $250 for service A and $10 for service B, respectively, instead of the regular rates. To create a usage charge, proceed with the steps shown in Figure 3.40; most of the steps are similar to those for creating the usage and recurring charge earlier. Navigate to the following path in the cre tool: **File · New · Charge**.

With exception of the price plan, other attributes of the charge remain the same as the recurring charge. Provide MARTEX_CHG_UseCaseA_Usage as the name for the charge, as shown in Figure 3.40.

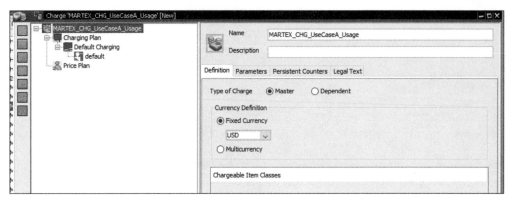

Figure 3.40 Creating Usage Type Charge Plan

Because the scenario is based on usage comsumption, a usage-based rate component needs to be added to the price plan. To create the usage rate component, navigate to **Add Component · Rates · Usage Rate**.

Next, fill in the name and description and select a chargable item class. The chargable item class defines the format that SAP Convergent Charging will be expecting as an input for the charge. Pick the consumption item item class REVE that you created earlier, as shown in Figure 3.41.

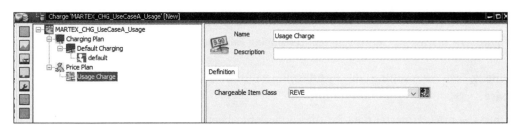

Figure 3.41 Define Usage Rate

After the usage rate component is created, an indicator is needed to let the system know that a reserved instance charge is being used. To do that, a parameter needs to be defined at the charge level: this denotes that an indicator will be passed to the charge from an external system. Right-click in the topmost level of the charge tree and select the **Parameters** tab, then add a new parameter using the 🔧 button as shown in Figure 3.42.

Figure 3.42 Define Parameters for Usage Charge

The next step is to read the mapping table created earlier using information from the chargable item and reserved instance parameter. The mapping table introducer comparator will be used to read the mapping table via menu path **Add Component · Comparator · Mapping Table Introducer**. After the mapping table introducer component is added, set the mapping table class, mapping table, reference date to MARTEX_ MTC_ MicroServiceSKU, MARTEX_MT_MicroService SKU and consumption date respectively as shown in Figure 3.43.

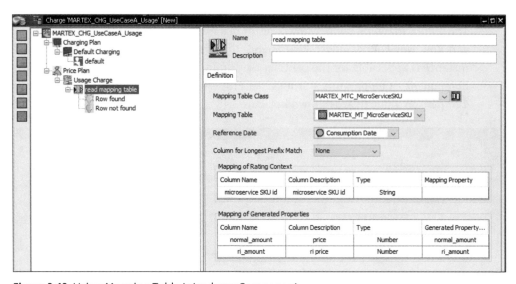

Figure 3.43 Using Mapping Table Introducer Component

In the same component, set the **microservice SKU id** mapping property column to the **ZZ_SRVCE_SKU** field from the chargeable item class REVE, as shown in Figure 3.44. By performing these settings, the charge logic will read the mapping table based on the service sku of the chargeable item and store the output results in the normal_amount and ri_amount variables, as shown in Figure 3.44.

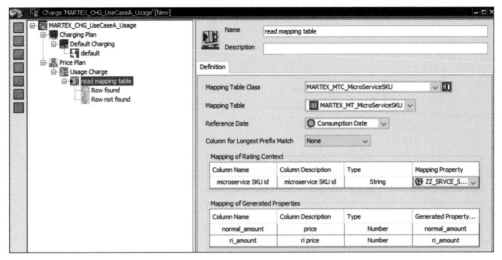

Figure 3.44 Set Mapping Property in Mapping Table Introducer

The output mapping table read will result in a fork in the logic tree, with **Row Found** and **Row Not Found**. Under **Row Found**, the first step is to check if the reserved instance is applicable for the contract by using the string comparator found at **Add Component · Comparators · Strings**. Set **Property Name** to **isReservedInstance** and **Comparison Value** to **X**, as shown in Figure 3.45.

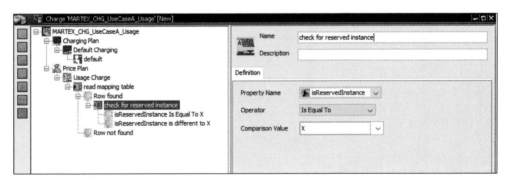

Figure 3.45 Using String Comparators

Under the **isReservedInstance Is Equal To X** node, add arithmetic operations from navigation path **Add Component · Operators · Arithmetic Computation** to perform multiplication of **ri_amount** and **CIT_QUANTITY**. Return a final amount as a result using the flat fee component found at **Add Component · Function · Flat**, as shown in Figure 3.46.

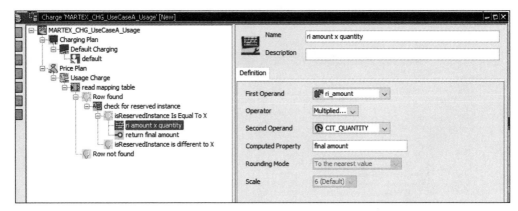

Figure 3.46 Using Arithmetic Computation Operator to Calculate Reserved Instance

Under the **isReservedInstance is different to X** node, add arithmetic operations from navigation path **Add Component · Operators · Arithmetic Computation** to perform multiplication of **normal_amount** and **CIT_QUANTITY**. Return a final amount as a result using a flat fee component found at **Add Component · Function · Flat**, as shown in Figure 3.47.

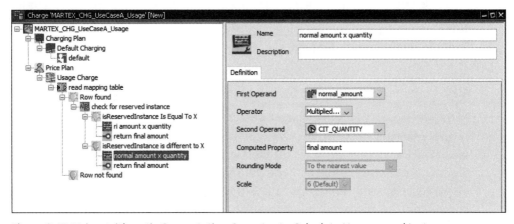

Figure 3.47 Using Arithmetic Computation Operator to Calculate Nonreserved Instance

Next, the **Row not Found** logic branch needs to be completed to handle exceptions in the event that a corresponding row is not found. In SAP Convergent Charging, the *no access* function is used to throw exceptions. To add the no access component, navigate to **Add Component · Functions · No Access**.

The purpose of the no access function is to generate exceptions in the log files. The message in the log file can be configured during the the creation of the object, as shown in Figure 3.48.

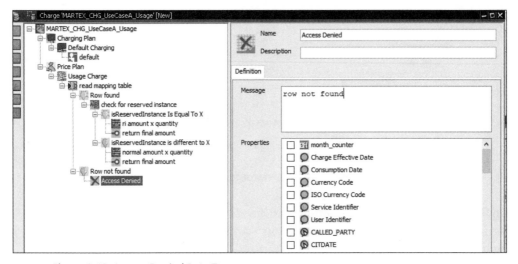

Figure 3.48 Access Denied Rate Type

Finally, save the mapping table by following menu path **File · Save · In the Database**.

Now that the required charges are created, the next step is to combine these separate logic elements into a charge plan.

3.2.4   Creating a Charge Plan (Reserved Instance)

In the previous section, three charges were created to meet the needs of our example: recurring charges, cancellation charges, and usage charges. Because charges are internal to SAP Convergent Charging, the next step is to group and expose the charges as an interface to other components of the SAP BRIM system. The component that is responsible for performing this task is the charge plan. In addition to exposing charges to external systems, the charge plan also allows for counter-sharing across all charges.

In this section, two charge plans will be created from the three charges, one for a reserved instance, which provides a cheaper consumption rate with additional recurring charges, and another for regular usage, which charges for consumption at the normal rate. Let's start by creating the reserved instance charge plan:

1. Navigate to **File · New · Charge Plan**.

2. Select the catalog and provide a name and description for the charge plan, as shown in Figure 3.49.

Figure 3.49 Creating Charge Plan

3. Right-click the **Charge Plan** object in the tree structure on the left and select **Add Item** from the context menu, as shown in Figure 3.50. This enables the association betweeen charges and the charge plan.

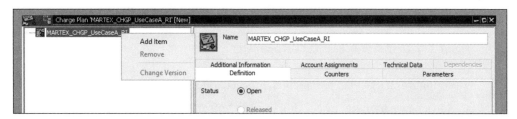

Figure 3.50 Adding Charges to Charge Plan

4. Add all the previously defined charges to the charge plan by repeating steps 1–3 three times. When you are finished, three charges will be assigned to the charge plan, as shown in Figure 3.51.

Once that is completed, the parameters of the charge plan need to be defined.

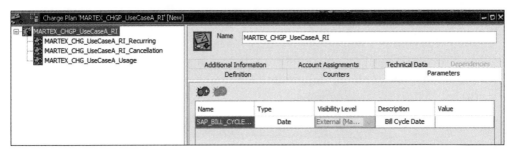

Figure 3.51 Charge Plan with Three Charges Added

Configuring Charge Plan Parameters

The purpose of the parameters is to receive input values from order provisioning or other SAP CRM systems. In an integrated system, the order provisioning system would be SAP BRIM, subscription order management.

For our example, parameter that is required is a reserved instance flag. To add that, click the **Parameters** tab in the charge plan.

In an integrated SAP BRIM scenario, a default SAP_BILL_CYCLE parameter is added by default, as shown in Figure 3.52. Because we do not need it for our example, we will ignore this field.

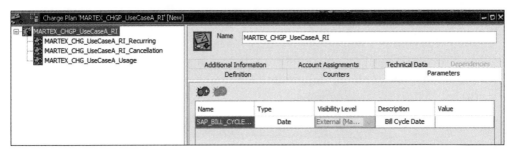

Figure 3.52 Default SAP_BILL_CYCLE Parameter

To configure charge plan parameters, proceed as follows:

1. Add a new parameter by clicking the 🔘 button, as shown in Figure 3.53.

Note

A parameter with the internal visiblity level is added because the charge plan is specifically designed for a reserved instance, so external input is not required.

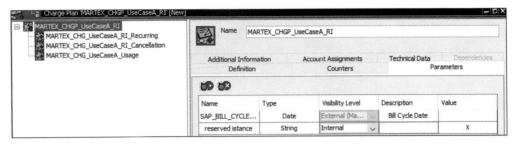

Figure 3.53 Adding Parameters to Charge Plan

2. Map the parameter defined to the specific charges that require its value; in this case, that would be the usage charge plan. To do so, select the charge in the tree navigation on the left and the select the **Parameters** tab, as shown in Figure 3.54.

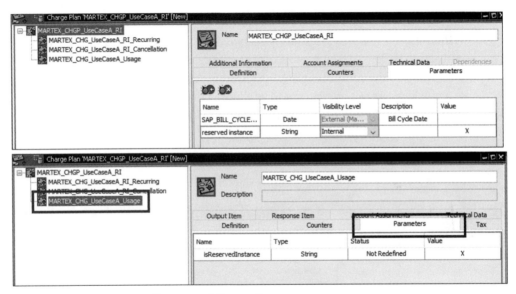

Figure 3.54 Parameters on Charges and Charge Plan

3. Change the the isReservedInstance parameter from **Not Redefined** to **Linked** and the **Value** to **Reserved Instance**. The purpose of this action is to link the parameter from the charge plan to the charge level (as shown in Figure 3.55).

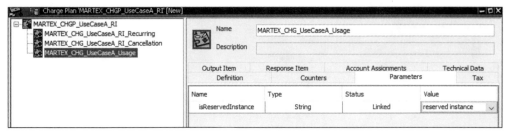

Figure 3.55 Linking Charge Parameter to Charge Plan

In summary, we have grouped all the charges that were defined seperately in the previous section within a single charge plan that will be exposed to the provisioning system.

Configuring Technical Data

Whenever a charge with a usage rate is defined, SAP Convergent Charging requires technical data to be defined. The purpose of the technical data is to uniquely identify combinations of provider contracts and charges. During implementations, it is very common for a provider contract number not to be exposed to the external system. For example, a technical ID in the telecommunications industry is normally a phone number.

To configure technical data, proceed as follows:

1. To configure the technical data, first navigate to the charge plan level via the tree in the left panel and select the **Technical Data** tab, as shown in Figure 3.56.

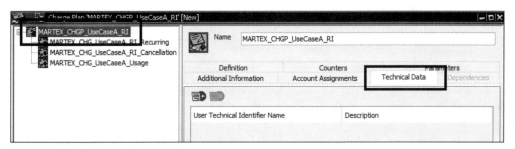

Figure 3.56 Configuring Technical Data

2. Add a new user technical identifier called "subscriber id" by clicking the 📑 button, as shown in Figure 3.57.

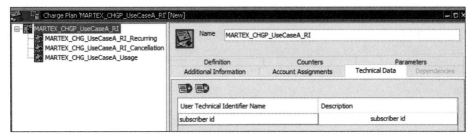

Figure 3.57 Adding New User Technical Identifiers

Once the user technical identifier has been defined, the next step is to define a service identifier. The purpose of the service identifier is determine the type of service that is consumed. For example, in the telecommunications industry, service identifiers could include data, voice, and message, which are calculated differently. However, in our example, a generic service identifier will be used.

To set up a service identifier, proceed as follows:

1. Select the usage charge using the tree in the left panel, then select the **Technical Data** tab (as shown in Figure 3.58).

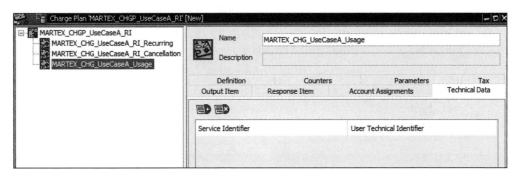

Figure 3.58 Technical Data

2. Add a new service identifier called "USAGE_DATA" by clicking the ⊞ button. For the corresponding user technical identifier, SAP Convergent Charging will provide a dropdown with the user technical identifier defined in the charge plan.

Now that you have defined the technical data, the next step is to configure the account assignment.

Configuring Account Assignment

To determine which external account to use for a contract, account assignment needs to be setup during charge plan creation. However, our example requires only one default postpaid account.

To configure account assignment, proceed as follows:

1. To set up account assignment, select the change plan using the tree in the left panel. Select the **Account Assignments** tab (as seen in Figure 3.59).

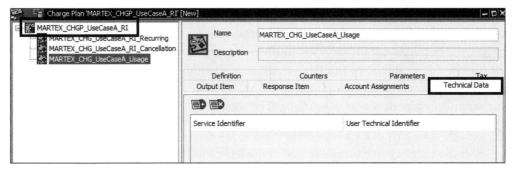

Figure 3.59 Account Assignements Tab

2. Insert a new entry by clicking the ▣ button. Use "default" for the name and description and set the type to **Postpaid**.

3. Account assignment needs to be performed at each individual charge level. To do that, select each charge at the charge level and navigate to each one's **Account Assignment** tab.

4. Select the **default** value from the **Linked Value** column, as shown in Figure 3.60.

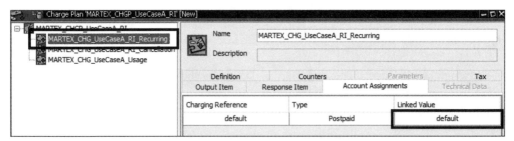

Figure 3.60 Linking Account Assignments between Charge and Charge Plan

After repeating the steps for each charge, the account assignment is considered completed. The next step is to configure the charge plan counter.

Configuring the Charge Plan Counter

When creating charges, a month counter was defined at the charge level for the recurring and cancellation charges. Assignment of the charges to the charge plan does not automatically link the counter. This has to be done explicitly at the charge plan level.

The first step is to navigate to the charge plan level by selecting the charge plan from the tree in the left panel and then select the **Counters** tab, as shown in Figure 3.61.

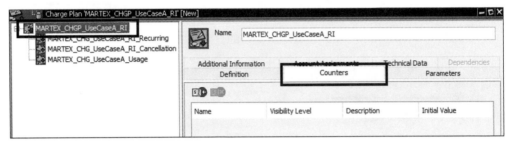

Figure 3.61 Adding Counters on Charge Plan

To configure the charge plan counter, proceed as follows:

1. Create a new counter by clicking the 🔘 button.
2. Enter "month counter" for a name and description and set the **Visibility Level** to **Internal**, as shown in Figure 3.62.

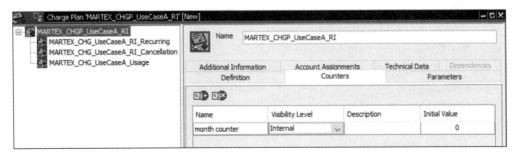

Figure 3.62 Adding Counter in Charge Plan

The next step is to link the counters at the charge level to the charge plan level. To do so, select the the cancellation and recurring charges from the tree in the left panel, then select the **Counter** tab and perform linking as shown in Figure 3.63 and Figure 3.64.

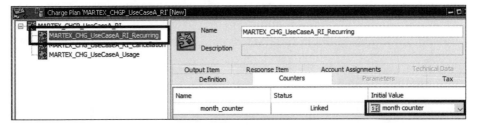

Figure 3.63 Linking Charge Counter and Charge Plan Counter for Recurring Charge

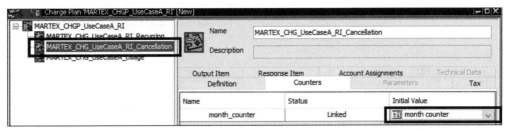

Figure 3.64 Linking Charge Counter and Charge Plan Counter for Cancellation Charge

This step allows for month counter values to be shared across both recurring and cancellation charges.

Disabling Tax on Charge Plan

SAP Convergent Charging supports tax calculations. However, in an SAP BRIM end-to-end integration scenario, tax calculations usually are deferred to the time of invoicing and performed by the SAP Convergent Invoicing module. To disable tax on charge plan, proceed as follows:

1. To disable tax calculations in SAP Convergent Charging, navigate to each charge and select the **Tax** tab.

2. Set the **Tax System** value to **Disabled**, as shown in Figure 3.65.

Now that we have disabled tax configuration on the charge level of the charge plan, let's continue with the charge plan creation by configuring output items.

Figure 3.65 Disable Tax Configuration in Charge Plan

Configuring Output Items

The charge plan is also responsible for how charging results are conveyed to external systems. In the Section 3.2.1, billable item mapping has already been completed, resulting in the creation of charged item classes REVE and COST.

The next step is to configure the charges for output item REVE. This action can be performed by clicking the **Output Item** tab, as shown in Figure 3.66.

When the REVE charged item class is picked, a list of of fields belonging to the item class will be populated. In an SAP BRIM integrated scenario, the fields BITTYPE and SUBPROCESS are mandatory. Fields PT_USERID_REF and PT_USERID_REFTY are applicable if partner settlement scenarios are populated. The values that need to be populated in the BITTYPE and SUBPROCESS fields will be communicated by the SAP Convergent Invoicing team because it will drive billing behavior.

Figure 3.66 Configuring Charged Item Class on Charges

For our example scenario, the values defined in the SAP Convergent Invoicing chapter need to be populated for each charge, as seen in Table 3.2.

MARTEX_CHG_UseCaseA_RI_Recurring	
BITTYPE	ZBT2
SUBPROCESS	ZHR1
BIT_QTY_UNIT	EA
BIT_QTY_QUANTITY	1
MARTEX_CHG_UseCaseA_RI_Cancellation	
BITTYPE	ZBT6
SUBPROCESS	ZHR1
BIT_QTY_UNIT	EA
BIT_QTY_QUANTITY	1`

Table 3.2 Convergent invoicing Martex Values

MARTEX_CHG_UseCaseA_RI_Usage	
BITTYPE	ZBT3
SUBPROCESS	ZHR1
PS_CAT	RVHV
BIT_QTY_UNIT	EA
BIT_QTY_QUANTITY	CIT_QUANTITY
PT_USERID_REF	I
PT_USERID_REFTY	partner tech_res

Table 3.2 Convergent invoicing Martex Values (Cont.)

After the output values for SAP Convergent Invoicing have been defined for each charge, the next step is to release the charge plan.

Releasing the Charge Plan

The release status of a charge plan enables it to be used by external provisioning systems such as SAP BRIM, subscription order management. By default, when a charge plan is created, it will be in an open status, as shown in Figure 3.67.

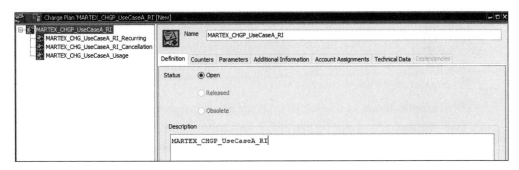

Figure 3.67 Charge Plan Status

To enable the **Released** status radio button, first save the charge plan using menu path **File · Save · In the Database** (as shown in Figure 3.68).

SAP Convergent Charging will display a prompt for catalog selection and subsequently save the charge plan in go into display mode. Next, toggle to edit mode and select the **Released** radio button by using menu path **File · Edit Mode** and then save again.

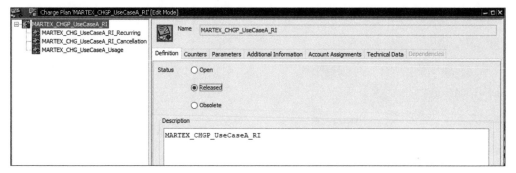

Figure 3.68 Releasing Charge Plan

The charge plan for a reserved instanced is now created, so the next step is to create the charge plan for a nonreserved instance for those customers who did not pick the reserved instance option.

3.2.5   Creating Charge Plan (Nonreserved Instance)

Another business requirement for Martex Corp. is to support customers who do not susbscribe to a reserved instance. These non-reserved-instance customers will be charged higher rates whenever they consume service A or service B. In return, they do not have to pay a monthly recurring fee of $100. As a result of that, cancellation fees are not applicable either.

The customer choice of a reserved instance or a nonreserved instance is captured in order management systems like SAP BRIM, subscription order management in an integrated scenario. Based on the customer decision, SAP BRIM, subscription order management will inform SAP Convergent Charging how to create the corresponding provider contract.

Because the nonreserved instances have the same usage charging behavior as their reserved instance counterparts, the same charge will be reused. When desiging charges for SAP Convergent Charging, it is good practice to encapsulate charging logic for reuse. To create a charge plan, proceed as follows:

1. To create the nonreserved instance charge plan, first make a copy of the existing charge plan. To access the catalog, follow menu path **Window · View Catalog**. In the catalog, locate the change plan, right-click it, and select **Open as Copy**.

2. Remove the both the recurring charge and cancellation charge from the copied charge plan by using the **Remove** option in the context menu of each respective charge, as shown in Figure 3.69. You want to remove these options because they are not applicable to a nonreserved instance scenario.

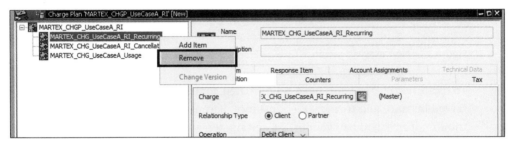

Figure 3.69 Removing Recurring and Cancellation Charge Plan

3. Counters also should be deleted as they are irrelevant in a nonreserved instance charge plan. Select the month counter and click the [icon] button (shown in Figure 3.70).

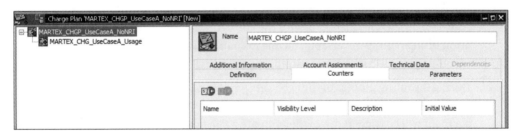

Figure 3.70 Removing All Counters for Nonreserved Instance Charge Plan

4. Finally, change the name and description to "Nonreserved Instance" in the **Name** and **Description** fields and save the charge plan via **File · Save · In the Database**, as shown in Figure 3.71. To release the charge plan, select **File · Edit Mode** to enter edit mode, then select the **Released** radio button.

Figure 3.71 Nonreserved Instance Charge Plan Open Status

To recap, two charge plans have been created, for customers subscribing to a nonreserved instance and to a reserved instance. Because Martex Corp. is a software distributor, it needs to pay vendor X a certain percentage of what it receives from its customers. In SAP BRIM, this can be accomplished using the partner settlement functionality, which is covered in detailed in Chapter 4.

The next section of this chapter explains the setup that is required in SAP Convergent Charging to support partner settlement capabilities.

Creating Partner Charges

As we will discuss in Chapter 4, with the configuration of partner settlement, the creation of an accounts receivable billable item in the system leads to the creation of an accounts payable consumption item.

During the rating process of the accounts payable consumption item, the charge plan associated with the partner agreement created in SAP BRIM, subscription order management will be triggered. Now, let's create a partner-related charge and charge plan:

1. Follow menu path **File · New · Charge** and define the charging plan for the MARTEX_CHG_UseCaseA_Usage_Partner charge. For our example, we do not need to have different charging references, so default charging will be used, as shown in Figure 3.72.

2. Figure 3.73 shows the three steps required to create a default charging reference. In the **Charging Plan** node of the tree, add a new charging reference name of "default" with the **Type** set as **Postpaid** by using the 🔲➕ button.

Figure 3.72 Creating Partner Charges

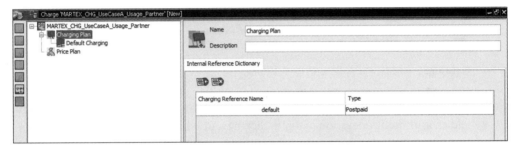

Figure 3.73 Add Charging Reference to Partner Charge

3. In the **Default Charging** node, right-click to launch the context menu and add **Internal Reference**. Set the name to "default" and select **Default** from the **Internal References** dropdown list, as shown in Figure 3.74.

Figure 3.74 Add Default Internal Reference to Partner Charge

The next step is to model the price plan. For our example scenario, Martex Corp. needs to pay vendor X 70% of each transaction. This includes any usage for service A or service B, recurring reserved instance charges, and cancellation charges.

Partner settlement is based on usage consumption, so a usage-based rate component needs to be added to the price plan by right-clicking and selecting **Add Component · Rates · Usage Rate**.

Next, fill in the name and description and select a chargable item class. The chargable item class defines the format that SAP Convergent Charging will be expecting as an input to the charge. Pick the consumption item class HCOS that you created earlier, as shown in Figure 3.75.

Figure 3.75 Add Usage Rate to Partner Charge

Because Martex Corp. needs to pay 70% of its revenue back to vendor X, we need to add an arithmetic operation by right-clicking and selecting **Add Component · Operators · Arithmetic Computation**, as shown in Figure 3.76.

Figure 3.76 Calculating Partner Charges

Next, use a flat function to return the final amount variable by right-clicking and selecting **Add Component · Function · Flat**, as shown in Figure 3.77.

To save the charge, use menu path **File · Save · In the Database**.

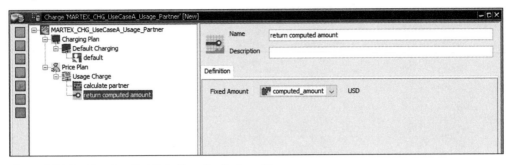

Figure 3.77 Configuring Flat Rate Item for Partner Charge

Creating Partner Charge Plans

After the charge is created, the next step is to create a charge plan for SAP BRIM, subscription order management to perform cross-catalog mapping. The steps to create a partner charge plan are the same as for the customer charge plan, so only the final output for each tab will be shown. Proceed as follows:

1. Navigate to **File · New · Charge Plan** and provide "MARTEX_CHGP_UseCaseA_Partner" for the name and description, as shown in Figure 3.78.

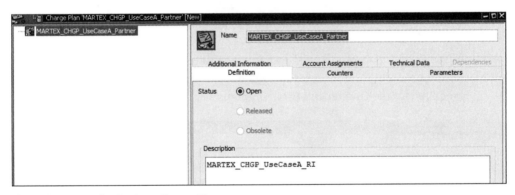

Figure 3.78 Creating Partner Charge Plan

2. Right-click the **Charge Plan** object in the tree structure on the left and select **Add Item** from the context menu. This setup enables the association betweeen charges and the charge plan, as shown in Figure 3.79.

3. On the **Account Assignment** tab on the charge plan level, define the default postpaid account by clicking the 📇 button, as shown in Figure 3.80.

187

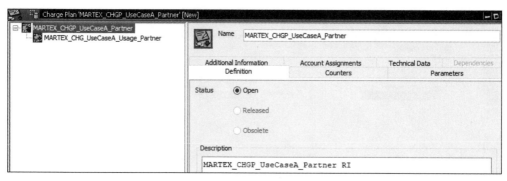

Figure 3.79 Adding Charge to Partner Charge Plan

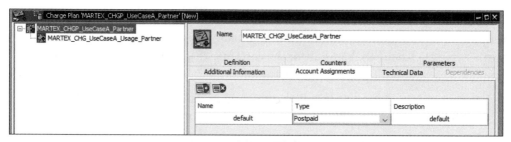

Figure 3.80 Adding Account Assignment to Partner Charge Plan

On the **Technical Data** tab on the charge plan level, add a user technical identifer called "subscriber id" by clicking the button (as shown in Figure 3.81). No action is required for the **Counter** and **Parameter** tabs.

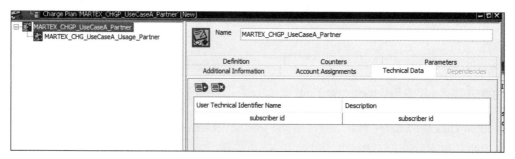

Figure 3.81 Technical Data Tab

Once the change plan level configuration is done, the next step is to configure the change level information on the charge plan:

1. On the **Tax** tab at the charge level, set the **Tax System** to **Disabled**, as shown in Figure 3.82.

Figure 3.82 Disable Tax Configuration for Partner Charge Plan

2. On the **Technical Data** tab, provide a service ID of HVRVSH and map it to the subscriber ID, as shown in Figure 3.83.

Figure 3.83 Linking Charge User Technical Identifier to Charge Plan User Technical Identifier

3. On the **Account Assignment** tab, set the charging reference **Type** as **Postpaid** and link it to the charge plan level. This allows the account information to be passed on from the charge plan to the charge level, as shown in Figure 3.84.

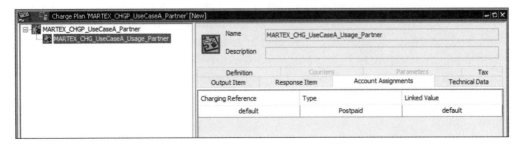

Figure 3.84 Linking Charge Account Assignments to Charge Plan Account Assignments

4. On the output item assignment by clicking on the Output Item, select **HCOS** as the output format (as shown in Figure 3.85).

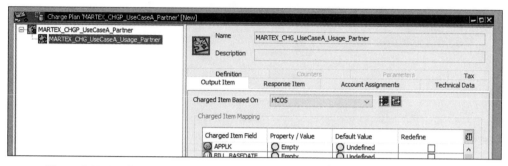

Figure 3.85 Configuring Charged Item for Partner Charge Plan

When the HCOS charged item class is picked, a list of of fields belonging to the item class will be populated. In an SAP BRIM integrated scenario, the fields BITTYPE and SUBPROCESS are mandatory. The values that need to be populated in the BITTYPE and SUBPROCESS fields will be communicated by the SAP Convergent Invoicing team because they will drive billing behavior.

For our example, the values in Table 3.3 need to be populated for each charge.

MARTEX_CHG_UseCaseA_Usage Partner	
BITTYPE	ZBC1
SUBPROCESS	ZHC1

Table 3.3 Partner Charge Plan Values

Finally, release the charge plan for SAP BRIM subscription order management to perform cross-catalog mapping by saving the charge plan via menu path **File · Save · In the Database**. SAP Convergent Charging will display a prompt for catalog selection and subsequently save the charge plan in go into display mode. Next, toggle to edit mode by selecting **File · Edit Mode** and select the **Released** radio button, then save again, as shown in Figure 3.86.

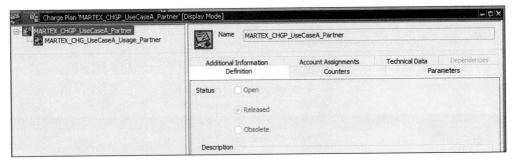

Figure 3.86 Partner Charge Plan in Released Mode

In Chapter 2, we saw how SAP BRIM, subscription order management behaves as the system of engagement. Martex Corp. employees can log in to create and maintain master data elements like the business partner (both customer and vendor), business agreements and products, as well as transactional data like provider contracts. We saw how entities like business partners, business agreements, products, and provider contract are distributed automatically to SAP Convergent Charging and SAP Convergent Invoicing.

Provider contracts in SAP Convergent Charging can be accessed by navigating to **File · Open · Provider Contract**. Figure 3.87 shows provider contract 10333 (created for reserved instance), contract 10335 (created for non-reserved instance), and contract 10337 (for partner charge plan).

> **Note**
> There is no provider agreement object in SAP Convergent Charging. Partner agreement are created as provider contracts in SAP Convergent Charging.

Once the provider contracts are created in SAP Convergent Charging, the provider contracts containing one-time and recurring charges will be rated, and billable items will be created in SAP Convergent Invoicing. In Chapter 4, we'll explore how usage charges for both accounts receivable and accounts payable items are triggered by the rating process of consumption items.

Figure 3.87 Martex Corp. Provider Contract

3.3   Summary

In this chapter, we discussed key SAP Convergent Charging components and how they interact with other SAP BRIM components like SAP BRIM, subscription order management and SAP Convergent Invoicing. In an integration scenario, SAP Convergent Charging is used primarily for modeling logic and performing charging. Objects such as subscriber accounts, external accounts, and provider contracts are replicated in SAP Convergent Charging and originate from the SAP BRIM, subscription order management system.

Chapter 4

Invoicing

This chapter explains how to setup and use SAP Convergent Invoicing. It also provides a brief overview of the master data and transactional data needed for the case study described in Chapter 1. We will also discuss billable items, consumption items, rating, billing, invoicing, partner settlement, and reporting.

4

SAP Convergent Invoicing is a component of SAP Billing and Revenue Innovation Management (SAP BRIM), which provides comprehensive capabilities to support business processes from inception and storage of usage/consumption records through to billing and invoicing. SAP Convergent Invoicing is thoroughly integrated with Contract Accounts Receivable and Payable (FI-CA).

Configuration nodes for SAP Convergent Invoicing are available in Transaction SPRO under **SAP Customizing Implementation Guide · Financial Accounting · Contract Accounts Receivable and Payable**. The business functions associated with SAP Convergent Invoicing, shown in Figure 4.1, must be activated to enable SAP Convergent Invoicing's functionalities.

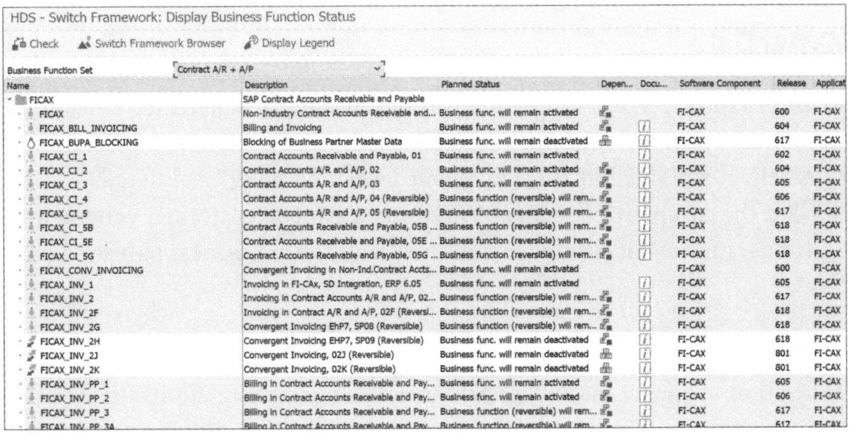

Figure 4.1 Business Functions

SAP Convergent Invoicing is part of the consume-to-cash process (as seen in Figure 4.2). It provides the capability to store and manage rated consumption data records from the SAP Convergent Charging system natively. Rated consumption data records are also known as billable items and undergo a billing and invoicing process with posting of receivables in FI-CA.

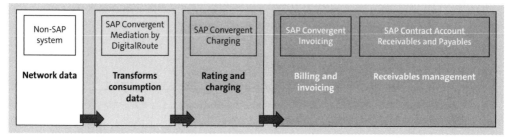

Figure 4.2 Consume-to-Cash Process

SAP Convergent Invoicing can perform grouping and aggregation at various stages of a transaction record, from rating of consumption data records to the invoicing process, which significantly reduces the storage of data. It can also be used to integrate with other non-SAP applications to receive billable transactions and perform grouping and aggregation as per business requirements and present a consolidated invoice to the customer. It provides the capability to invoice billing documents originating from multiple external systems, including sales and distribution and billing documents generated within SAP Convergent Invoicing.

4.1   Master Data

As part of this chapter, you will learn about various master data elements—including business partners, products, contract accounts, and prepaid accounts. Master data contains details maintained at the SAP client level, and additional details can be maintained at the company code level. With SAP S/4HANA, customer, vendor, and business partner master data is now maintained centrally as business partner data.

4.1.1   Business Partner

Any organization, group, or individual person with a business relationship with the company is represented as a business partner in SAP BRIM. Details like names, correspondence addresses, fax numbers, telephone numbers, email addresses, bank information, and payment card information are stored in business partner master data.

Configurations associated with business partner setup are maintained under **Cross-Application Components · SAP Business Partner · Business Partner**.

Business partner master data is created in FI-CA and can have various roles based on its usage. Business partner roles are assigned to specify their functions (as seen in Figure 4.3). These roles are defined in customizing and are assigned to a business partner at the time of its creation.

Dialog Structure		BP Roles		
🗑 BP Roles		🗋 BP Role	Title	Description
▼ 📁 BP Role Categories		MKK	Contract Partner	Contract Partner
📁 BP Role Category --> Business Transaction		PSSP01	Sponsor	Sponsor
		RCFAGY	Agency	Agency

Figure 4.3 Business Partner Roles

Business partner roles are maintained under **Cross-Application Components · SAP Business Partner · Business Partner · Basic Settings · Business Partner Roles · Define BP Roles**.

A business partner can have role FLCU000 to integrate SAP SD with FI-CA. A business partner must have role MKK (Contract Partner) to post business transactions to it.

Business partners either can be created internally within SAP S/4HANA and replicated to other SAP systems like SAP CRM or can be created externally from SAP CRM and replicated to SAP S/4HANA systems.

Each business partner receives a number on creation. The business partner number assignment is controlled by maintaining the number ranges for the business partner. Business partners created through an external system like SAP CRM will have number ranges created as external in SAP S/4HANA, and those created internally will have internal number ranges (as seen in Figure 4.4).

The number ranges created are assigned to the business partner grouping and are maintained under **Cross-Application Components · SAP Business Partner · Business Partner · Basic Settings · Number Ranges And Grouping** (as seen in Figure 4.5).

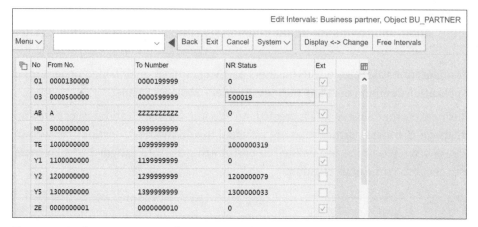

Figure 4.4 Business Partner Number Ranges with 01 as External and 03 as Internal Number Ranges

Grouping	Short name	Description	Number ran...	External	Int.Std.Grping	Ext.Std Grping	H
0001	Int. No.Assgnmt	Internal number assignment	TE	☐	⊙		
0002	Ext.No.Assgnmnt	External Number Assignment	AB	☑		⊙	

Figure 4.5 Business Partner Grouping and Number Range Assignment

During the time of creation of a business partner, the business partner **Grouping** field value is assigned. Based on the assigned number range for the business partner group, a business partner number is generated.

4.1.2   Product

Products are goods and services sold to the customers or subscribed to by customers, through which a company generates its revenue. Products can be tangible like cellphones or PlayStation machines or can be intangible like software subscriptions, maintenance services, or bandwidth usage.

Intangible products or subscription-based products are created in FI-CA and tangible products are maintained in materials management, with sales handled in sales and distribution.

4.1.3   Contract Account

A contract account is another component of business master data. It is used to group together the business partner postings. All accounting transaction data associated with subscription service, payments, returns, interest calculation, and dunning is recorded in the contract account.

The contract account contains the parameters that determine the business partner posting details, like payment terms, incoming/outgoing payment methods, taxes, and discounts.

The contract account provides a business partner's account management functionality. One business partner can hold multiple contract accounts according to business needs.

Configurations for contract accounts are maintained under **Contract Account Receivables and Payables • Basic Functions • Contract Accounts**.

Contract Account Number Ranges

Each contract account created receives a unique two-digit number based on the number ranges maintained in the configuration. Each number range is maintained as either internal or external. Contract account creation or business agreement creation from SAP CRM uses external number ranges for SAP S/4HANA, and direct creation of a contract account in SAP S/4HANA uses internal number ranges (see Figure 4.6).

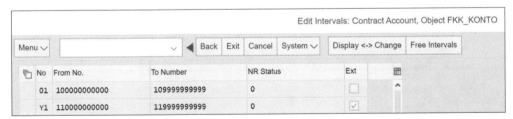

Figure 4.6 Number Ranges for Contract Account Creation

Contract Account Categories

Contract account categories are used to categorize the contract accounts. Each contract account created is assigned a contract account category. Number ranges created for the contract accounts are assigned to the contract account categories. Contract account categories control the number range assignment, specify whether the account is one time, determine if one or more business partners can be assigned, indicate whether the account is a collective account, denote whether it can hold one or more contracts, and mark if the account is a customer or vendor type (see Figure 4.7).

Figure 4.7 Contract Account Categories

Contract Account Relationship

A contract account relationship describes if the assigned business partner of the contract account is the account holder or not. The contract account relationship is assigned at the time of creation of the contract account (see Figure 4.8).

Partner Account Relationships			
Acct Rel.	Description	AH	
Z1	Account Holder	☑	

Figure 4.8 Contract Account Relationship

Account Determination Characteristics

Account determination IDs, along with company code, division, main transaction, and subtransactions, are used for general ledger account determination for FI-CA document postings (see Figure 4.9).

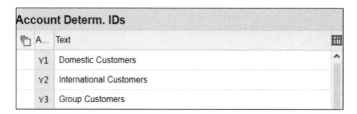

Figure 4.9 Account Determination IDs for Contract Account

4.1.4   Prepaid Account

A prepaid account is an account managed by the SAP Convergent Charging system internally. The prepaid account is preloaded with a minimum threshold amount to pay for the service when used. Prepaid accounts contain a monetary counter associated with a currency.

The agreed-upon amount is placed in the prepaid account before service can be provisioned. Based on the usage of the service provided by the service provider, a particular amount is deducted from the preloaded balance in real time.

When the threshold amount is reached, then further usage of service is declined. In certain scenarios, if debits beyond the threshold limit are allowed, then continued usage of service will be allowed, with the amount maintained in the prepaid account reduced.

Refilling the prepaid account increases the amount in the account and debiting the prepaid account on use of service decreases the amount in the account.

There are two type of alerts associated with the prepaid account:

- **Amount alert**
  The amount alert sends a notification to the associated system when the prepaid balance is less than or equal to the threshold amount value.

- **Expiration alert**
  The prepaid account has certain a validity maintained. When the expiration of the validity period approaches, an alert is sent to the associated system as a refilling reminder a certain number of days before expiration.

There are four statuses a prepaid account can obtain:

- **Active**
  An active status indicates that a prepaid account can be debited with the service usage amount up to the threshold limit maintained. If overspending is authorized for the account, then debits beyond the threshold limit can be made. An active account can be blocked, locked, or closed.

- **Blocked**
  The prepaid account cannot be debited in a blocked status; only free usage can happen. Overspending can happen if authorized. A blocked account cannot be refilled. It can be reactivated, locked, or closed.

- **Locked**
  A locked account cannot be debited, and free usages are not allowed. Locked accounts can be reactivated, blocked, or closed.

- **Closed**
  Debit and refill are not possible for closed accounts. Once closed, the account cannot be changed further.

We have covered master data details in this section and the associated configuration settings required. The next section will cover the details of the SAP Convergent Invoicing objects and their required configuration settings.

4.2   Configuring SAP Convergent Invoicing

This section will cover the concept of billable items, the configuration required for their setup, and the management of billable items. When you finish this section, you will understand the definition and use of the various objects of the billable items and will be able to configure SAP Convergent Invoicing's mappings to meet business requirements.

4.2.1   Billable Items

Billable items are rated consumption data records. Billable items hold the information for the sale of a product or service and are used to post the revenue generated by the service provider for the use of a service by a customer. These items can originate from SAP Convergent Charging, an external rating system, or even from within SAP Convergent Invoicing. Billable items can be recurring charges from SAP Convergent Charging, one-time charges originating from SAP BRIM, subscription order management, or rated usage consumption items.

Billable items record the details of the services used by a customer based on the contractual agreement. They are the input for the billing process for the generation of billing documents, which are inputs for the invoicing process.

Billable items hold information like product details, amount of usage, quantity, period of usage, and other details that determine the accounting posting during the invoicing process.

Billable items obtain different statuses, starting with creation and going to the invoicing process, as shown in Table 4.1

Billable Item Status	Description
0	Raw
1	Raw-excepted
2	Billable

Table 4.1 Billable Item Statuses

Billable Item Status	Description
3	Billable-excepted
4	Billed

Table 4.1 Billable Item Statuses (Cont.)

Let's take a deeper look at each status:

- The raw status indicates that the billable item does not contain complete information and values in the fields can be changed. Raw billable items (BIT) are not eligible for the billing process. Raw billable items should be transferred to status 2 (billable) to be considered for the billing process.

- Raw-excepted billable items are not considered during transfer or billing. Such items should be restored and then transferred to billable status to be considered for further processing.

- Billable status items only are considered for the billing process. The billable status indicates the information contained in the billable items is complete and consistent.

- The billable-excepted status is generally obtained by billable items when a billing document is reversed. Billable items then should be restored if they need to be considered in the billing process.

- The billed status is obtained by the billable items when the billing process is performed successfully on them.

Billable items based on their statuses are stored in separate database tables. There are four types:

- **Main items (IT)**
  Main items are mandatory and contain the basic data for billing. Other record types are dependent on the main items, without which the system will not process the other record types.

- **Payment data (PY)**
  Payment data record types contain the details associated with payments and are linked to the corresponding main item by the payment group field.

- **Tax item (TX)**
  Tax items contain data associated with taxes and are linked by the tax group field with the main item.

- **Text items (TT)**

  Text items contain the test fields for the main items and are linked by the text group field.

Different record types are stored in different database tables. While creating the billable item class, the interface components are selected for the class, and upon generation activation and generation of the interface for the billable item class, the database table is created for each record type and for each status of the billable items. The naming conventions for the tables are described in Figure 4.24.

Billable Item Class

The billable item class specifies the technical attributes for the Billable items. SAP does not provide standard classes; they are created based on your business requirements. Let's look at an example.

Martex Corp. sells SaaS and IaaS offerings to customers obtained from multiple vendors. The company provides two types of services, A and B, for SaaS for cloud computing. Martex provides a reserved instance option to its customers, in which they can pay a recurring charge in exchange for lower usage rates. The services details are as follows:

- Service A
  - $300/GB without reserved instance
  - $250/GB with reserved instance
- Service B
  - $20/hour without reserved instance
  - $10/hour with reserved instance

Let's set up the configuration for Martex to record the service usage to perform billing and invoicing for a customer.

To record the revenue from the sales of service and cost of products obtained from the vendors, let's create the billable item class HREV for revenue and billable item class HCOS for the product cost.

BIT classes are created under **Contract Account Receivables & Payables · Convergent Invoicing · Basic Functions · Billable Item Classes · Maintain Billable Item Classes** (as in Figure 4.10).

Figure 4.10 Billable Item Class Creation

SAP provides a set of standard interface components, which are assigned to a class at the time of its creation. Interface components contain technical attributes like fields; structure definitions, which upon class activation and generation create the associated function modules for receiving data and storing data; database tables according to record type and billable item statuses; and standard fields for storing data in the billable items of the associated class. Custom fields can also be added to the class and will be extended to the billable items of the class upon creation.

Interfaces can be viewed under **Contract Account Receivables & Payables • Convergent Invoicing • Basic Functions • Billable Item Classes • Define Interface Components**.

Interfaces selected for the billable item class, as shown in Figure 4.11, provide the fields for storing the data for the billable item class.

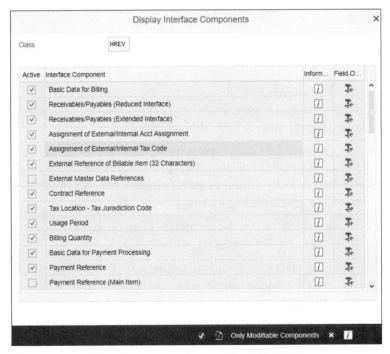

Figure 4.11 Interface Components Selected for HREV BIT Class

Upon creation of the billable item class and interface assignment, the billable item class needs to be activated, and then generation of the interface components of the class needs to be performed to generate the database tables, billable item creation API, and structures for the billable item class, which then can be used for storing the transactional data.

Billable item classes can be activated under **Contract Account Receivables & Payables · Convergent Invoicing · Basic Functions · Billable Item Classes · Maintain Billable Item Classes** (as in Figure 4.12).

Figure 4.12 Billable Item Class Activation

The generation of the interface components of the billable item class is performed under **Contract Account Receivables & Payables · Convergent Invoicing · Basic Functions · Billable Item Classes · Generate Interfaces For The Billable Item Classes** (as seen in Figure 4.13).

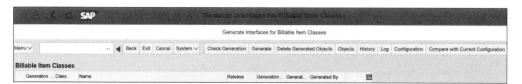

Figure 4.13 Billable Item Class Generation

Upon generation of the interfaces of the billable item class, the tables, function module, tables for billable items for each record type and status, and table for simulation records and structures will be generated (Figure 4.14).

Similarly, class HCOS is also created to store the cost details of products obtained from the vendors.

Different classes are generally created according to business requirements, keeping in mind that if the same class is used for several products and services, then billable items might end up with a very long list of fields that are not required for certain billable items for the products.

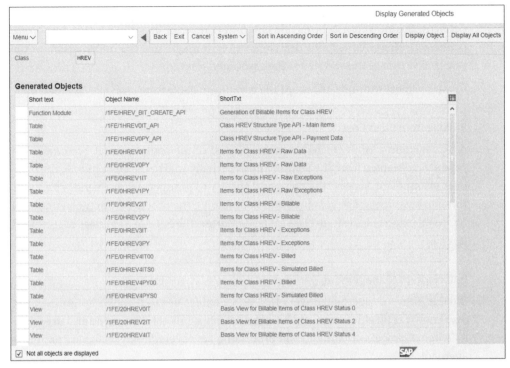

Figure 4.14 Objects Generated for HREV BIT Class

A billable item class can be created or modified under **Contract Account Receivables & Payables · Convergent Invoicing · Basic Functions · Billable Item Classes · Maintain Billable Item Classes** (as seen in Figure 4.15).

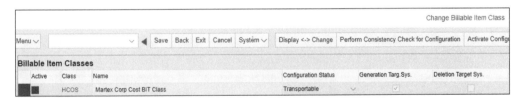

Figure 4.15 HCOS BIT Class for Cost

Billable Item Class Revenue

A billable item class is created to store the transaction details for the usage or sale of a service. The business requirement mapping determines the creation and use of a billable item class.

Billable item class revenue signifies that the created class will be used to record the details of business transactions relevant for the revenue generated by the sale or use of a service. The billable items described in Section 4.2.1 hold the information for the sale transaction of the service for the associated class.

In our business example, to record the revenue, billable item class HREV is created.

Billable Item Class Cost

A billable item class is created to store the cost to the company that occurs when a product is obtained from the vendor and eventually sold to the customer. In the business example for Martex, the company purchases products from a vendor and sells them to customers. The cost incurred in obtaining the product from the vendor can be stored in the billable item class cost. For Martex, the billable item class cost created is HCOS.

Billable Item Management

Billable item management covers the management of rated consumption records, also known as billable items, and how the billable items are configured and used. Billable item storage, enrichment, and processing are covered under billable item management.

Billable item types are configured in system to record the business transaction. Based on the type of transaction or charges, billable item types are created for a class.

After a class is activated and generated as mentioned earlier, the billable item types are created for the class. Billable item types hold business transaction details and differentiate business transactions like sales, returns, royalty sharing, and so on.

> **Business Example**
>
> Martex, as described in earlier, provides services A and B with and without a reserved instance. For Martex, in a reserved instance scenario, it receives the upfront charge, monthly recurring charge, and usage charge. These three different types of charges need to be stored separately. To achieve this, three different billable item types can be created.

Let's create the three different billable item types for the billable item class HREV. To record the up-front charge for the reserved instance scenario, billable item type ZBT1 will be created to record the one-time charge, billable item type ZBT2 to record the recurring charges, and ZBT3 for usage-based charges.

Billable item types created for the class receive the business transaction details, which will be used in billing and invoicing.

Before billable item types can be created, a subprocess is created. A subprocess is a self-contained processing operation for a billing process. Subprocesses are assigned to a billable item class, and billable item types, once created, are assigned to subprocesses, thus linking the billable item types to a billable item class. Subprocesses select the billable items during billing process execution. They are created based on the business requirements for how a charge, a billable item type, should be processed during billing.

> **Business Example**
> For Martex, create a subprocess ZHR1 and assign it to the billable item class HREV.

Subprocesses are maintained under **Contract Account Receivables & Payables · Convergent Invoicing · Basic Functions · Billable Item Billable Item Management · Define Subprocess for Billing** (as seen in Figure 4.16).

Figure 4.16 Subprocess Creation Screen

Once a subprocess is created, it is assigned to the billable item class. Assignment of a subprocess to a billable item class is done under **Contract Account Receivables & Payables · Convergent Invoicing · Basic Functions · Billable Item Billable Item Management · Assign Subprocesses to Classes** (as in Figure 4.17).

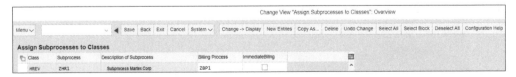

Figure 4.17 Subprocess Assignment to Billable Item Class

Once a subprocess is created and assigned to a billable item class, billable item types are created and assigned to the subprocess.

Billable items are created under **Contract Account Receivables & Payables · Convergent Invoicing · Basic Functions · Billable Item Billable Item Management · Define Item Types** (as in Figure 4.18).

Figure 4.18 Billable Item Types

Billable item type creation is followed by assignment of the billable items to the subprocess. Assignment of billable item types to a subprocess is done under **Contract Account Receivables & Payables · Convergent Invoicing · Basic Functions · Billable Item Billable Item Management · Assign Item Types to Subprocesses** (as in Figure 4.19).

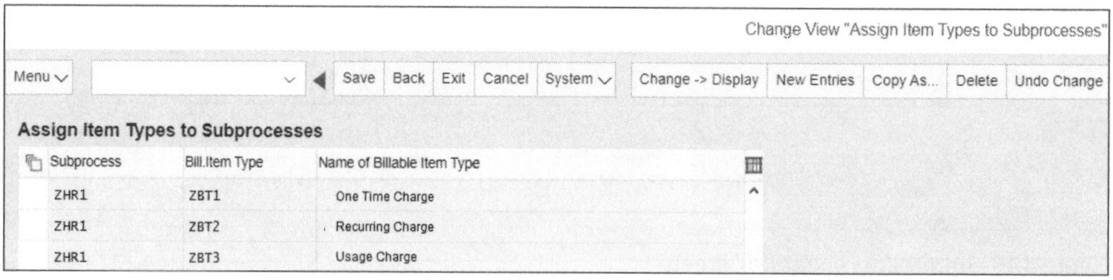

Figure 4.19 Billable Items Assignment to Subprocess

SAP Convergent Invoicing provides the functionality to receive the rated events from SAP Convergent Charging or from other external systems and store them in the form of billable items and perform billing and invoicing.

The API created at the time of generation of the billable item class is used to import data from the external systems and store it in the database tables generated as part of class generation.

Although interface components selected for the class generally provide all the necessary fields, to meet specific business needs you may need to create certain custom fields also. The class also provides the option to add these custom fields. To assign the custom fields to the class, fields must be added to the customizing includes before they can be added to the class (as in Figure 4.20). The custom includes need to be generated before they can be used (as seen in Table 4.2).

Figure 4.20 Custom Fields Option during Class Creation

Customizing Include	Description
CI_FKKBIXBIT_IT	Include for Main Items
CI_FKKBIXBIT_PY	Include for Payment Items
CI_FKKBIXBIT_TX	Include for Tax Items

Table 4.2 Customizing Includes for Billable Item Class

Billable item classes follow a sequence of creation, activation, and generation, but they cannot be used to store business transaction data until they are made active for use.

Activation of a billable item class for which billable items can be created is done via **Contract Account Receivables & Payables · Convergent Invoicing · Basic Functions · Billable Item · Billable Item Management · Assign Item Types to Subprocesses· Activate Billable Item Classes** (as in Figure 4.21).

Figure 4.21 Billable Item Class Activation for Use in Client

Billable items originating from SAP Convergent Charging or other external systems can be stored based on business needs. There are various upload options provided by

SAP to store the input billable items. Also, SAP provides various standard events that can be used to perform checks or even perform enrichment of billable items, from receiving to saving the billable items in SAP Convergent Invoicing.

Storing and processing of the input billable items is handled via **Contract Account Receivables & Payables · Convergent Invoicing · Basic Functions · Billable Item Classes · Billable Item Management · Define Processing Rules and Program Enhancements** (as in Figure 4.22).

Billable items received in SAP Convergent Invoicing can be stored based on the upload rule for the billable item class. The billable items can be stored as raw data, or items with errors can be stored as raw data else in billable status. Also, you can return the received data to the originating system if the data received is incomplete.

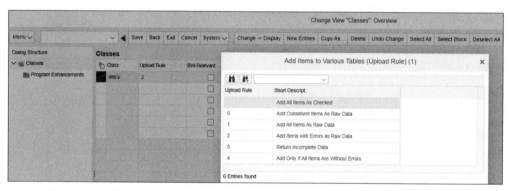

Figure 4.22 Billable Items, Processing Rules

In certain business scenarios you must put a check on the billable item's field for validation of data. There can be scenarios in which the billable item fields may require data to be populated at the time of storing because the data required in the fields can only be obtained within SAP Convergent Invoicing, and in such scenarios program enhancements come into play.

SAP has provided 17 events to handle the various steps of transferring, storing, reversal, and exceptions for billable items. For each associated event, standard sample function modules are provided that can be used to create the custom function modules to code the requirements (as in Figure 4.23).

For each billable item class activation and generation, database tables are created for the class for storing data. Tables are created for each record type, status, and simulation. The tables generated follow a pattern in their naming (as in Figure 4.24).

Figure 4.23 Billable Items Program Enrichment

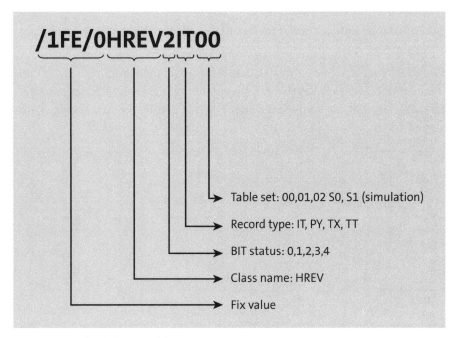

Figure 4.24 Billable Items Table Naming Convention

Billable items move from one table to another based on their status. Additional table sets can also be assigned for billed items and simulated items and will become applicable based on the validity period of each table. A table set should always be assigned for both simulated and actual billed items.

The additional tables are created in the billable item class in the creation screen. These tables are then further assigned to the billable item classes to be used based on the validity period (as in Figure 4.25).

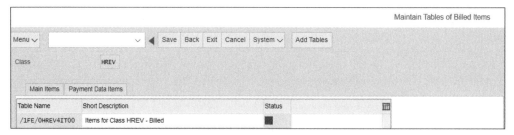

Figure 4.25 Additional Table Creation for Billable Item Class

Using the add tables option, further tables can be added to the class definition maintained at the node.

Additional tables created for the billable item class are set for data storage under **Contract Account Receivables & Payables · Convergent Invoicing · Basic Functions · Billable Item Classes · Billable Item Management · Make Setting For Data Storage** (as in Figure 4.26).

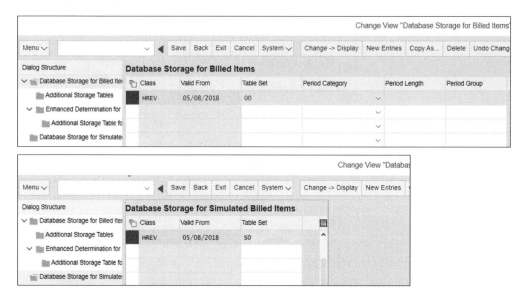

Figure 4.26 Additional Data Storage for Billed and Simulated Items

The default table set is OO for billed item tables and SO for simulated items. If additional tables are added, they follow the sequence O1 and S1 for billed and simulated items respectively. The date available on the storage screen marks the beginning validity date of the table set.

Billable Item Transfer

Billable items originating from SAP Convergent Charging or another external system populates the billable item fields with most of the details required for the processing, but there are certain fields required to be obtained within SAP CI during the transfer of the billable items from the various systems. Various fields for account assignment like company code, main and subtransactions for credit and debit posting, and the payment method assignment for the payment records types of the billable item are set during the billable items transfer. The configuration required for the account assignments is described the following sections.

Account Assignments

Account assignment is the process of obtaining information like company code, business area, profit center, main and subtransactions, and payments method, which will eventually help in the general ledger accounts determination during the invoicing process for posting of receivables in FI-CA. The account determination is essential for recording the sales, expenses, taxes, and payments in the SAP system.

Values for company code, division, business area, segment, and profit center are derived based on the value of the subprocess, billable item type, and set of four external key fields present on the billable items input to SAP Convergent Invoicing. The billable items received contain the information about the subprocess and billable item types, based on which the configuration maintained in the SAP posting areas will determine the account assignment values for those billable items.

The Assignment of External/Internal Account Assignment or Receivable/Payables interface component on the billable item class is responsible for the account assignment.

Posting area 8120 is maintained for the account assignment. In this posting area, you maintain the selection values for subprocess, billable item type, and, if required, four additional keys to derive account assignment values like company code, division, business area, segment, and profit center (as in Figure 4.27).

The posting area can be accessed using Transaction FQC0 or from menu path **Contract Account Receivables & Payables • Convergent Invoicing • Basic Functions • Billable Items • Billable Item Transfer • Define Account Assignments** (as in Figure 4.28).

Billable items during the transfer from an external system to SAP will fetch the value of account assignment fields from posting area 8120 based on the subprocess and billable item types. The values obtained will be used during the receivables posting in invoicing process execution.

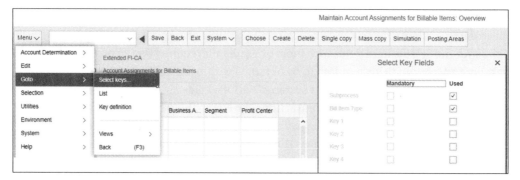

Figure 4.27 Selection Keys for Posting Area 8120

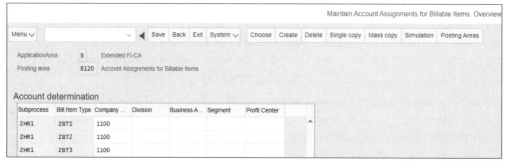

Figure 4.28 Posting Area 8120 for Account Assignment

Main and Subtransactions

Main and subtransactions are used to identify the general ledger accounts. The main transactions identify the subledger account and main and subtransactions together identify the revenue general ledger account for the revenue posting in FI-CA.

Business Example

In Martex Corp., for the different charges for the use of the service the billable items types ZBT1, ZBT2, and ZBT3 are received. The amount associated with the billable item types would need to be posted to the general ledger account for accounting. The subprocess ZHR1 and the billable item types will determine the main and subtransactions from posting 8121 and will identify the general ledger accounts during invoicing, and they will post the receivables with the general ledger account entries.

Main and subtransactions identify a transaction as a credit or debit posting, which also associates it with the general ledger account determination for financial postings. The general ledger accounts determined by the main and subtransactions are posted with the amount for the revenue and tax if applicable by the posting document created during the invoicing process. The posting document is an accounting document in the FI-CA component of SAP BRIM.

The main transaction is maintained under **Contract Account Receivables & Payables · Basic Functions · Postings and Documents · Document · Maintain Document Assignment · Maintain Main Transaction** (as in Figure 4.29).

Figure 4.29 Main Transaction Creation Screen

The subtransactions are maintained under **Contract Account Receivables & Payables · Basic Functions · Postings and Documents · Document · Maintain Document Assignment · Maintain Sub Transaction** (as in Figure 4.30).

FI-CA: Sub-transactions												
ApArea	MTrans	STrans	Description	Rev...	Rev...	Main ...	Subtr...	Due date	AddRecRule	Payment	Negativ...	Withholding tax
E...	ZM01	Z110	Sale Software DR			ZM01	Z110			☐	☐	
E...	ZM01	Z111	Sale Software CR			ZM01	Z111			☐	☐	

Figure 4.30 Subtransaction Creation Screen for Main Transaction

The main and subtransactions created are then parameterized to indicate a debit or credit transaction. The configuration is maintained under **Contract Account Receivables & Payables · Basic Functions · Postings and Documents · Document · Maintain Document Assignment · Maintain Transactions for Non-Ind Contract Account Receivables and Payables · Define and Parameterize External Transactions** (as in Figure 4.31).

The credit/debit indicator can be left blank, and the credit/debit posting can be controlled based on the sign of the amount received in the billable items. A negative sign (-) before an amount indicates a credit posting.

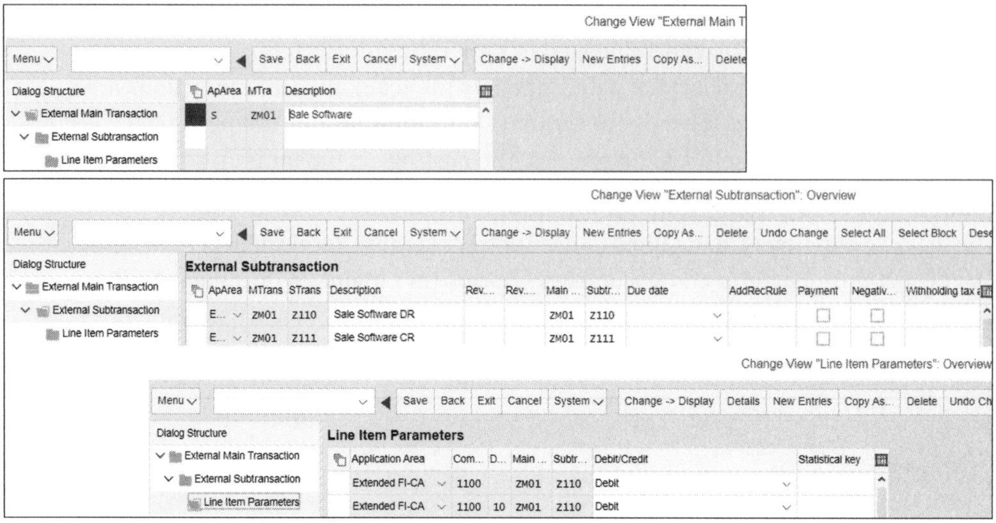

Figure 4.31 Parameterize Main and Subtransactions

The main and subtransactions thus created are then maintained in posting areas 8122 and 8121. These posting areas are maintained with and without product details respectively for determination of the main and subtransactions. Subprocess, billable item type, and four external key fields help derive the main and subtransaction details.

Posting areas 8122 and 8121 can be accessed using Transaction FQC0 or at the following menu paths. The associated configuration is maintained under **Contract Account Receivables & Payables · Convergent Invoicing · Basic Functions · Billable Items · Billable Item Transfer · Account Assignment Derivation · Define Main & Sub Transactions for Items With Product Account Assignment** (as in Figure 4.32).

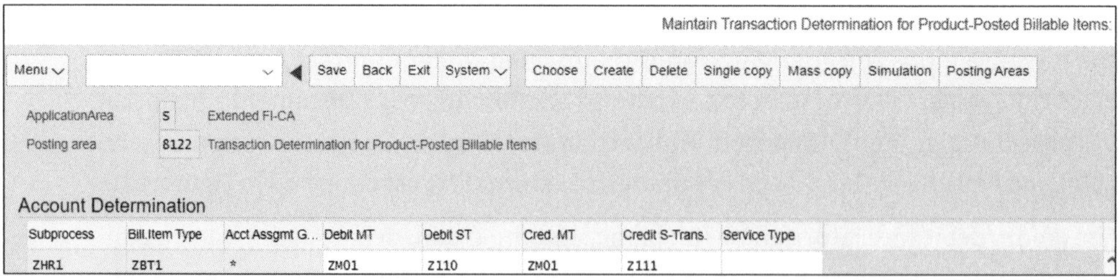

Figure 4.32 Posting Area 8122

To define the main and subtransactions for posting area 8121, navigate to **Contract Account Receivables & Payables · Convergent Invoicing · Basic Functions · Billable Items · Billable Item Transfer · Account Assignment Derivation · Define Main & Sub Transactions** (as in Figure 4.33).

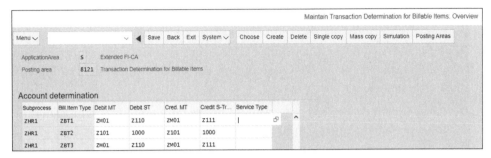

Figure 4.33 Posting Area 8121 for Main and Subtranasction Determination

Payment Method for Payment Processing

Billable items with record type payment items along with main items contain payment details like authorization number, card number, card type, and so on. These payment items require a payment method with a corresponding processing type to be updated in the fields of the payment items record type. This information is required at the time of invoicing to post the payment against the receivables posted in FI-CA.

Configuration is maintained under **Contract Account Receivables & Payables · Convergent Invoicing · Basic Functions · Billable Items · Billable Item Transfer · Define Payment Method for Payment Processing** (as in Figure 4.34).

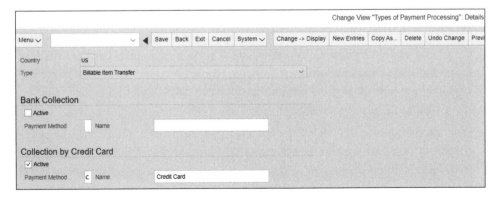

Figure 4.34 Payment Method Settings for Billable Item Type Payment Items

4.2.2   Consumption Items

Consumption items contains the details of the usage of the service, like type of service, units, duration of usage, amount per unit which are processed in rating process in SAP Convergent charging. Usage records are also called consumption data records which are processed to form the billable items which are then billed and invoiced.

Consumption data records are captured either by third-party software or using SAP Convergent Mediation by DigitalRoute. These consumption data records capture detailed information about the usage of services, which is required in rating and charging processes.

The consumption data records are triggered by the business events or usage of the service and are then either passed into the SAP Convergent Charging system and stored as consumption items in SAP Convergent Invoicing or can directly be entered into SAP Convergent Invoicing using the associated APIs and stored as consumption items. Then the rating process is performed to obtain the billable items.

Also, in a partner settlement functionality scenario in SAP Convergent Invoicing, the consumption items for the vendors are created automatically in SAP Convergent Invoicing using details of the billable items. This functionality will be discussed in detail in Section 4.2.6.

Consumption Item Class

Like billable items, consumption items also follow the class concept.

To store the consumption items in SAP Convergent Invoicing, a consumption item class is created. There are several interface components provided by the SAP that are used according to business requirements to make fields available to store information about the consumption records. A consumption item class specifies the technical attributes of the consumption items.

Configuration for consumption item classes is maintained under **Contract Account Receivables & Payables · Convergent Invoicing · Basic Functions · Consumption Items · Consumption Item Classes · Maintain Consumption Item Classes** (as in Figure 4.35).

Upon activation and generation of the class, interfaces create the structures, tables, function modules, and fields for the consumption item class. Standard fields for the consumption items are obtained based on the interfaces selected for the class, and custom fields can be assigned to the class. Creation, activation, and generation of class interfaces are explained in Section 4.2.1.

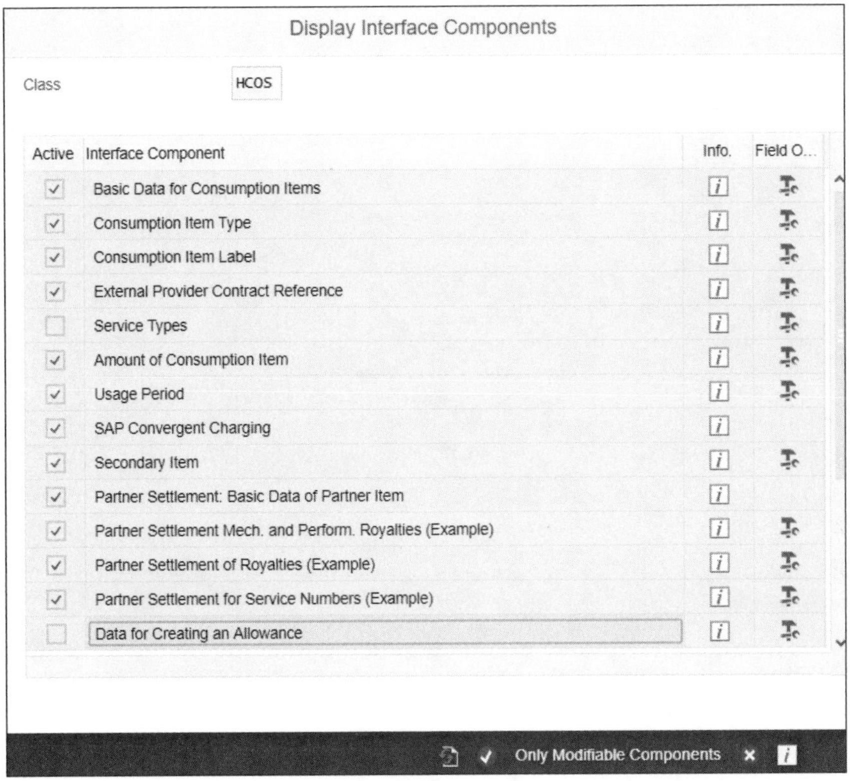

Figure 4.35 Interface Components for Consumption Item Class HCOS

There are separate tables created for each month for the rated items. Each status of the consumption items has separate tables for storing it (as in Figure 4.36 and Figure 4.37).

Business Example

For Martex Corp., consumption item class REVE is created for consumptions items that will be used to store the usage records consumption data records and consumption item class HCOS is created to store the consumption records for the cost of the products obtained from vendors. The HCOS class will be used in the partner settlement functionality to bill and invoice vendors.

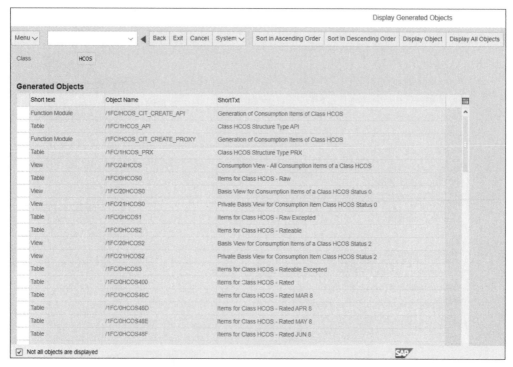

Figure 4.36 Objects Generated for HCOS Consumption Item Class

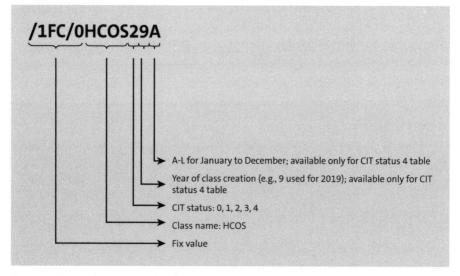

Figure 4.37 Naming Convention for Consumption Item Class Tables

Consumption items obtains various statuses during their lifecycle in the SAP Convergent Invoicing system (as in Table 4.3).

Consumption Item Status	Description
0	Raw
1	Raw-excepted
2	Unrated
3	Rated-excepted
4	Rated

Table 4.3 Statuses of Consumption Items

The raw status indicates that the consumption item does not contain complete information and values in the fields can be changed. Raw consumption items are not eligible for the rating process. Raw consumption items should be transferred to status 2 (unrated) to be considered for the rating process. Let's take a look at these statuses:

- **Raw**
  Excepted consumption items are not considered during transfer or rating. Such items should be restored and then transferred to unrated status to be considered for further processing.

- **Raw-excepted**
  The consumption items having this status are missing some fields value or value is incorrect. For such items to be considered for the rating the status should be restored to unrated.

- **Unrated**
  These items only are considered for the rating process. Unrated status indicates the information contained in the consumption items is complete and consistent.

- **Rated-excepted**
  The rated-excepted status is generally obtained by consumption items when the rating is reversed. Consumption items then should be restored if needed to be considered in the rating process.

- **Rated**
  The rated status is obtained by consumption items when the rating process is performed successfully on them.

Consumption Item Management

Consumption items contain the consumption item ID type and consumption item ID, which together uniquely identify the consumption items in the system. The consumption item ID type specifies the business significance of the consumption item from the rating perspective.

To store the consumption items in the SAP Convergent Invoicing system, it is essential to store a provider contract in the consumption item. The provider contract contains contract details like duration, associated business partner, contract account, product details, and billing cycle. The consumption date of the items is checked with the provider contract dates.

Processing Rules and Program Enhancements

Consumption items transferring from the SAP Convergent Charging system or the external usage recording system to SAP Convergent Invoicing based on business requirements can be enriched with certain values for the consumption item fields. The process of populating certain standard fields or custom fields based on certain conditions during the transfer of consumption items to SAP Convergent Invoicing is called consumption item enrichment. SAP provides sample function modules for each status of the consumption items, which can be modified according to your business requirements.

Also, SAP provides the facility to process the consumption items received in SAP Convergent Invoicing.

The configuration is maintained under **Contract Account Receivables & Payables · Convergent Invoicing · Basic Functions · Consumption Items · Consumption Item Management · Define Processing Rules and Enhancements** (as in Figure 4.38).

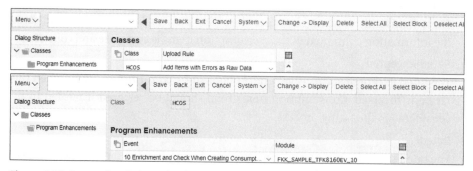

Figure 4.38 Processing Rule and Enhancement for HCOS Consumption Item Class

Reversal of Consumption items

Consumption items transferred to SAP Convergent Invoicing may sometimes have incorrect data and may require that such incorrect data not be processed. Such consumption item records can be reversed; reversed consumption items are not considered for the rating and are moved to an excepted status table. The reversal of consumption items requires an exception reason, which provides the following options for reversal of the consumption items:

- Reverse item (not possible to restore it)
- Except item (possible to restore it)

The first option reverses the consumption item, and the reversed item cannot be restored to rated status and cannot be processed further.

The second option lets you except the consumption items: fields of the items can be edited, and the consumption item can be restored back to unrated status by providing a restoration reason and can be further processed in rating.

Configuration for the reversal, exception reason, and restoration reason is maintained under **Contract Account Receivables & Payables · Convergent Invoicing · Basic Functions · Consumption Items · Consumption Item Management**. Here you will find the following options:

- **Activate Classes for Consumption Items**
- **Define Processing Rules and Program Enhancements**
- **Define Schema for Duplicate check**
- **Assign Schema for Duplicate Check**
- **Define Field Configuration for Consumption Items**
- **Define Changeable Fields for Consumption Items**
- **Enter Exception Reasons**
- **Enter Reasons for Restoration**
- **Make Standard Settings for Reversal**

Consumption items can be created directly in SAP Convergent Invoicing to test the system configuration using Transaction FKKBIXCIT_CWB. This transaction can also be accessed in SAP Menu under **Accounting · Financial Accounting · Contract Account Receivables & Payables · Convergent Invoicing · Consumption Items · Enter & Change Manually** (as in Figure 4.39).

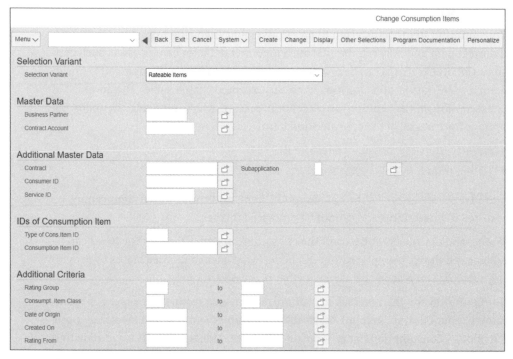

Figure 4.39 Consumption Item Creation Screen

Transaction FKKBIXCIT_CWB provides the option to create, change, and display consumption items. Using the create option, you can directly create consumption items within SAP Convergent Invoicing. Also, if certain consumption items present in system require any field value to be changed, that also can be done using this transaction if a field is made modifiable for the unrated status. For display of consumption items, various selection screen parameters are provided. By selecting a variant for the status, all the consumption items can be displayed at once for a particular status or for all status.

The created consumption items are stored in the tables based on the status in which they are created. These items can be viewed using Transaction FKKBIXCIT_MON, which also can be accessed in SAP Menu under **Accounting · Financial Accounting · Contract Account Receivables & Payables · Convergent Invoicing · Consumption Items · Display** (as in Figure 4.40).

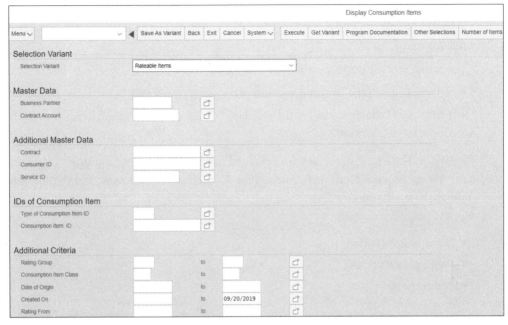

Figure 4.40 Consumption Item Display Screen

Consumption items can be viewed using Transaction FKKBIXCIT_MON. There are several selection parameters provided, using which consumption items can be viewed. A selection variant can be used to view all the consumption items at once based on their status. The other options available on the consumption item display screen are rating, restore, reverse, and except (as in Figure 4.41).

Figure 4.41 Consumption Item Processing Options

4.2.3   Rating and Rating Groups

Rating is a process that takes in the unrated consumption items, applies the associated calculations rule to obtain the amount for the usage, associates it to the contract, and creates the billable items for billing and invoicing.

The rating process is triggered in SAP Convergent Invoicing, which sends the consumption items to SAP Convergent Charging for rating and charging and receives the billable items.

The rating process performs the following tasks:

- Selection, grouping, and aggregation of consumption items
- Creation of billable items for the rated and charged consumption items from SAP Convergent Charging

Rating and charging processes are executed in SAP Convergent Charging. To trigger the rating process from SAP Convergent Invoicing, the following configurations should be maintained:

- Rating group
- Grouping variant
- Aggregation variant
- Billing process

The configuration for setting up the rating process is maintained under **Contract Account Receivables & Payables · Convergent Invoicing · Rating**.

Rating Group

A rating group is essential for the rating process to trigger. The rating group is used to set the parameters required for the rating execution. A rating group is used to group together the consumption items based on business requirements.

Rating groups specify parameters like the following:

- Parallel processing criteria for mass execution of the rating job
- Grouping variants for the creating the rating units
- Assignment of billing process to billable items from rating
- Whether aggregation of billable item should be performed

The configuration to maintain the rating group can be maintained under **Contract Account Receivables & Payables · Convergent Invoicing · Rating · Define Rating Groups** (as in Figure 4.42).

The rating group also provides the enhancement options for the rating process. In the rating group, based on business requirement rating units, billable items can be updated. You can also specify whether a rating is to be executed in SAP Convergent

Charging or within SAP Convergent Invoicing. For a rating to be performed in SAP Convergent Charging, in program enhancement a event rating is selected and function module FKK_BIX_RATING_EVENT_30_SAPCC is assigned (as in Figure 4.43).

Figure 4.42 Rating Group Creation Screen

Figure 4.43 Program Enhancement for Rating Group

Rating processing in SAP CI can be performed if the function module FKK_BIX_RATING_EVENT_30 is used for the rating in the program enhancement. Only simpler rating logic can be performed in SAP Convergent Invoicing; for more complex logic, SAP Convergent Charging is used.

Because we are using SAP Convergent Charging for rating and charging, we'll use function module FKK_BIX_RATING_EVENT_30_SAPCC.

Grouping and aggregation play a very important role in the rating process. Grouping is used for grouping the consumption items together, which are sent as a rating unit to SAP Convergent Charging for rating.

An aggregation variant summarizes the consumption items within a group to further consolidate them and sends them for rating, thus reducing the number of individual consumption items sent for rating. The consolidated consumption items contain a total quantity in the consumption item quantity field. Both grouping and aggregation variants are created and assigned with characteristics, based on which the grouping and aggregation are performed:

- **Grouping variant**
  The grouping variant assigned to the rating group is used to group together the consumption items that are required to be rated together based on business requirements. A grouping variant specifies the technical fields or attributes of the consumption item class that will be used to group together the items. Attributes like rate first date, product, usage period, and so on are used to group together the consumption items to be rated together. Items grouped together form the rating unit.

- **Aggregation variant**
  The aggregation variant is used to consolidate the consumption items within the rating unit based on the consumption item class attributes. This reduces the number of consumption items sent to SAP Convergent Charging for rating and subsequently reduces the billable items received from SAP Convergent Charging.

Business Example

Martex sells service A. A customer who has subscribed to the service with a reserved instance will generate consumption data or usage records for the use of the service for a month. These usages will be stored as consumption items. Martex's business requirement is to group those consumption items of Service A together that have same target rating date (RATE_FROM) and start of consumption period date (CIT_FROM), as well as aggregate the consumption items that have the same consumption item creation date (CITCRDATE).

Rating group YN001 is created for Martex. The grouping variant ZGRP is used with the RATING_FIRST and CIT FROM fields as the grouping criteria. Aggregation variant ZAGV is created with the CITCRDATE parameter for aggregation.

Before creating the grouping variant, the grouping characteristics are maintained. Grouping variants for the rating are maintained under **Contract Account Receivables & Payables · Convergent Invoicing · Rating · Define Grouping Variants** (as in Figure 4.44 and Figure 4.45).

Figure 4.44 Grouping Characteristics

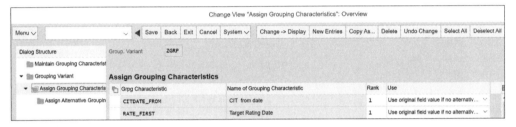

Figure 4.45 Grouping Variant for Rating Group

Aggregation variants are maintained under **Contract Account Receivables & Payables · Convergent Invoicing · Rating · Define Aggregation Variants**.

In the configuration node, the first aggregation variant is created, then the consumption item class is assigned, following which the aggregation characteristics are assigned (as in Figure 4.46).

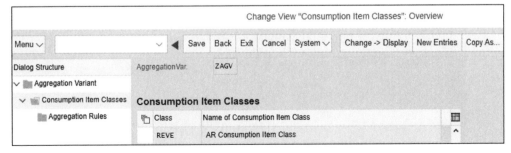

Figure 4.46 Aggregation Variant for Rating Group

The grouping variant and the aggregation variant created are assigned to the rating group. Posting area 8177 is maintained for the assignment. In the posting area, a new entry is created with the rating group as the selection key, and output values are assigned as grouping and aggregation variants. Three additional selection keys are also available and can be used based on business requirements. Selection keys can be obtained via **Menu · Goto**.

The configuration to maintain posting area 8177 is done under **Contract Account Receivables & Payables · Convergent Invoicing · Rating · Define Aggregation for Consumption Items** (as in Figure 4.47).

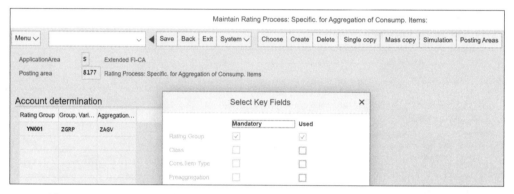

Figure 4.47 Grouping and Aggregation Variant Assignment for Rating Group

Note the following key points of the rating process:

- Consumption items that have the same business partner in the rating process are grouped together by default.

- Consumption items for which the rating first/target rating date is not reached will not be considered in the rating process.

- If an aggregation variant is not assigned to the rating group, then each consumption item selected will be rated individually.

Rating process maintenance can be seen in Figure 4.48.

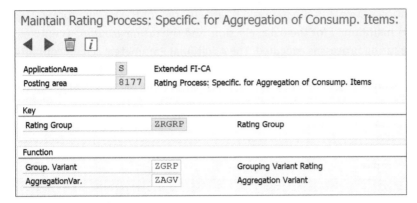

Figure 4.48 Maintain Rating Process

Ratings can be triggered from SAP Convergent Invoicing individually or en masse. For individual runs, use Transaction FKKBIX_RATE_S, and for mass runs, use Transaction FKKBIX_RATE_MA. These transactions can also be accessed through SAP Easy Access menu: **Accounting · Financial Accounting · Contract Account Receivables & Payables · Convergent Invoicing · Periodic Processing · Rating** (as in Figure 4.49).

		Rating

| Menu ∨ | ∨ | ◀ Back | Exit | Cancel | System ∨ | Display <-> Change | Copy | Delay run dates by n days |

Run ID		Run Status		Interval Status	
Date ID	*	🔁 Parameter:	Not Saved	Number:	1
Identification	*	Program Run:	Not Scheduled	Ready:	0

| General Selections | Add. Parameters | Technical Settings | Logs |

Rating Groups

| Rating Group | | to | | ↱ |

General Selections

| Business Partner | | to | | ↱ |
| Contract Account | | to | | ↱ |

Type of Run

☐ Simulation run

▤ Custom Selections   No Custom Selections Defined

Figure 4.49 FKKBIX_RATE_MA Mass Rating Transaction Screen

On the execution screen, the run date and ID are entered for the rating process. The **General** tab is maintained for the data selection, and the rating grouping is entered for which the rating process is executed. The **Additional Parameters** screen contains the target rating date for which rating will be performed. The **Technical Settings** tab contains the parallel processing object. Once the parameters are set, the job can be executed immediately in the background or can be scheduled to run at a later time based on business requirements.

> **Business Example**
>
> Martex uses consumption item class REVE created for usage records. The usage records from the customer for service A will be stored in the consumption item class REVE. Then the rating process will be executed using rating group YN001. The usage records will be sent to SAP Convergent Charging, which will rate and charge the consumption items and send them back to SAP Convergent Invoicing as a billable item of class REVE and billable item type ZBT3.

Once the rating process is executed it will send the consumption items to the SAP Convergent Charging system. SAP Convergent Charging will rate the usage records received from SAP Convergent Invoicing. Rated and charged consumption items in SAP Convergent Charging are sent to SAP Convergent Invoicing as billable items. The billable items received from SAP Convergent Charging assign a source transaction ID to the billable items, and the same is updated in the consumption items; this links the consumption item to the corresponding billable items.

Transaction FKKBIXCIT_MON, which is used to view the consumption items, also shows the link to the billable items. Also, the same transaction provides the option to trigger the rating process for the unrated consumption items. For more details, Section 4.2.2.

The transaction can be accessed in SAP Easy Access Menu: **Accounting** · **Financial Accounting** · **Contract Account Receivables & Payables** · **Convergent Invoicing** · **Consumption Items** (as in Figure 4.50).

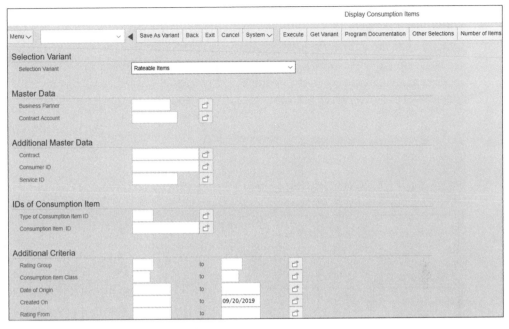

Figure 4.50 Consumption Items Display Screen

4.2.4   Billing

Billable items obtained from the sale of service, usage of service, refunds, cancellations, returns, and so on are processed in billing process to create the billing document.

The billing process creates the billing document by processing the billable items that have the same business significance. Billing groups aggregate the billable items.

Billing Process

Billing is performed using the billing process configured in the system. A billing process is a collection of billing subprocesses which are responsible for selection, grouping, and aggregation of the billable items (as in Figure 4.51).

Business Example

Martex has three different billable item types: ZBT1, ZBT2, and ZBT3, for up-front charges, monthly recurring fees, and usage charges. Billable items received for the different charges are processed by the billing process. For Martex's billing process, ZBP1 will be created, which will have subprocess ZHR1 assigned.

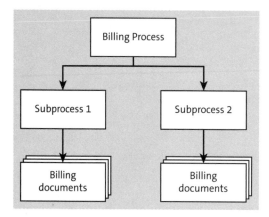

Figure 4.51 Billing Process and Subprocess

A billing process can have one or more subprocess assigned to it. Billing subprocess are assigned to billable item class, and the billable item types of the class are assigned to the subprocess, which will be considered during the billing process execution.

A billing process contains the subprocess, selection variant, grouping variant, and billing type, and aggregation variants are assigned (as in Figure 4.52).

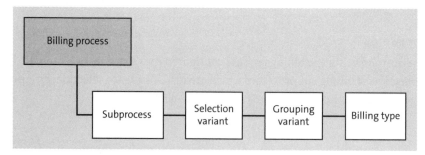

Figure 4.52 Billing Process

A billing process is created under **Contract Account Receivables & Payables · Convergent Invoicing · Billing · Billing Processes · Define Billing Processes** (as in Figure 4.53).

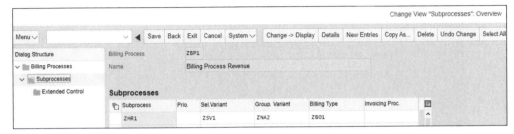

Figure 4.53 Billing Process Creation Screen

A billing subprocess is mandatory for a billing process to execute. Separate billing documents are created based on business partner, contract account, and billing subprocess. Each subprocess will lead to creation of a separate billing document. Billable items belonging to separate subprocesses cannot be processed together in a common billing document.

The billing subprocess controls the selection of billable items, grouping into billing units, and billing type specification.

Billing process assignment to a subprocess and billable item class was shown in Figure 4.17.

The selection variant specifies which billable items of which billable item class will be selected on the execution of the billing process. Billable items belonging to different subprocesses are processed separately in seperate billing documents.

> **Business Example**
>
> For Martex, there are three charges or billable item types generated. To bill and invoice the customer, these charges should be selected and processed. To select these charges in the billing process, a selection variant ZSV1 will be created then assigned to the billable item class HREV, and the billable item types ZBT1, ZBT2, and ZBT3 will be assigned. When the billing process ZBP1 is executed, all the billable items of type ZBT1, ZBT2, and ZBT3 will be selected (as in Figure 4.54).

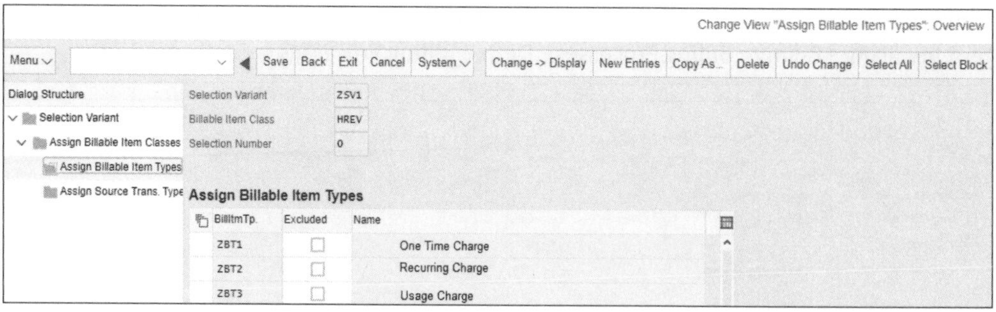

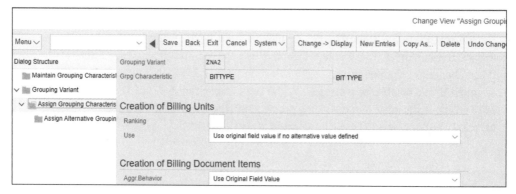

Figure 4.54 Selection Variant for HREV Class

Business Example

Martex has created billing selection variants for the charges to be selected during the billing process. Now it needs to group the similar charges together and aggregate the selected charges within a group. To achieve this, grouping variant ZNA2 will be created with grouping characteristic as billable item type and aggregation variant as ZNA1 with aggregation characteristic as billable item type.

A grouping variant is used for grouping selected billable items based on the grouping criteria. The billable items belonging to the same group will form the billing unit, which will create a billing document.

A grouping variant for a billing process is created under **Contract Account Receivables & Payables · Convergent Invoicing · Billing · Billing Processes · Define Grouping Variants** (as in Figure 4.55).

Figure 4.55 Grouping Variant for Billing Process

For creation of a grouping variant, first grouping characteristics are maintained, which can be assigned to the grouping variant once it is created. Next a grouping variant is created, then the grouping characteristics are assigned. In addition, alternate grouping characteristics can also be maintained.

Creation of the billing process also requires a billing assignment. Billing types specify the type of the billing process—for example, whether the billing process is for the termination of the service or a periodic billing run. For Martex, billing type ZB01 will be created.

The billing type is maintained under **Contract Account Receivables & Payables · Convergent Invoicing · Billing · Billing Processes · Define Billing Item Types** (as in Figure 4.56).

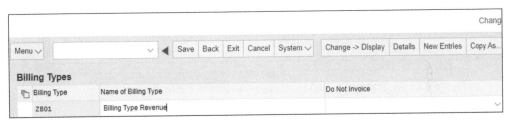

Figure 4.56 Billing Item Type

Assignment of a billing type to a billing process is shown in Figure 4.56).

An aggregation variant is used for aggregation of the billable items within the same billing unit. The aggregation variant is created in the same node in which a grouping variant is created, but the assignment of the variant happens as an aggregation variant in posting area 8115. The creation of an aggregation is done under **Contract Account Receivables & Payables · Convergent Invoicing · Billing · Billing Processes · Define Grouping Variants** (as in Figure 4.57).

Figure 4.57 Grouping Variant Created for Aggregation for Billable Items

An aggregation variant can be assigned to the combination of the billing process, subprocess, class, and billing type selection keys in posting area 8115.

The assignment is performed under **Contract Account Receivables & Payables · Convergent Invoicing · Billing · Billing Processes · Define Aggregation for Billable Items** (as in Figure 4.58).

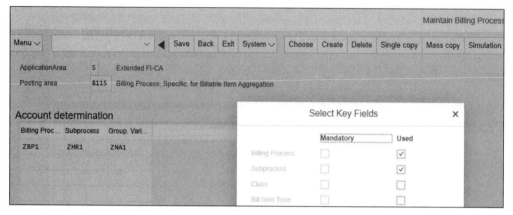

Figure 4.58 Assignment of Variant for Aggregation to Billing Process

Billable Item Types

Billable item types are used for storing business transaction details specific to transaction events like sales, refunds, recurring charges, and so on.

Billable item types created are assigned to the subprocess and the subprocess is assigned to a billable item class; therefore, each billable item of the respective class holds the same properties/fields as the class.

Billable items are maintained under **Contract Account Receivables & Payables · Convergent Invoicing · Billable Items · Billable Item Management · Define Item Types**.

Billable item types are created as per the business requirements associated with the different kinds of charges that will be recorded in SAP Convergent Invoicing as part of day-to-day business. It is essential to map the different kinds of charges originating from the various business transactions to the billable item types; this will help in processing the charges as required and also will be useful if reports must be generated based on billable item types for business transactions.

One Time

One-time billable items are created for charges that are levied once. These are generally for one-time sales of products or service activation charges. One-time charges can be received directly from sales order management. When a sale of a product is done through SAP CRM or SAP BRIM, subscription order management, the one-time price of the product is transferred to SAP Convergent Invoicing.

The configuration for one-time charges originating from SAP BRIM, subscription order management is maintained under **Contract Account Receivables & Payables • Convergent Invoicing • Integration • Customer Relationship Management • Transfer of One-Off Charges • Define Billable item Classes**.

In this node, the billable item class, subprocess, and billable item types are assigned for the one-time charges, which will flow from SAP BRIM, subscription order management to SAP Convergent Invoicing (as in Figure 4.59).

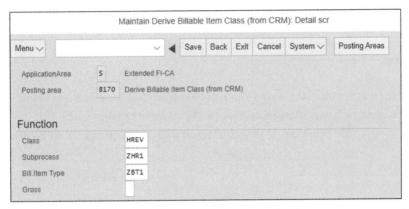

Figure 4.59 Billable Item Class, Subprocess, and Billable Item Type Assignment for One-Time Charge

The next step for the integration is the configuration of account assignment settings for the billable items for the one-time charge. The account assignment objects include company code, division, business area, and segment.

Account assignment configuration is maintained under **Contract Account Receivables & Payables • Convergent Invoicing • Integration • Customer Relationship Management • Transfer of One-Off Charges • Define Account Assignments** (as in Figure 4.60).

The next step for the configuration setting for the one-time charges from SAP BRIM, subscription order management is defining the main and subtransactions required to post the accounting entries in FI-CA during the invoicing process. Both main and subtransactions for credit and debit postings are assigned in posting area 8172 for one-time charges.

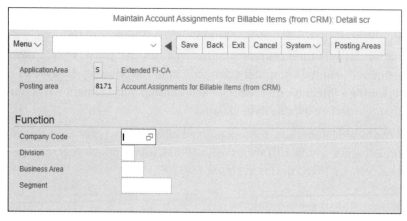

Figure 4.60 Account Assignment for One-Time Charges from SAP BRIM, Subscription Order Management/SAP CRM

The configuration is maintained under **Contract Account Receivables & Payables · Convergent Invoicing · Integration · Customer Relationship Management · Transfer of One-Off Charges · Define Main Transactions and Sub Transactions** (as in Figure 4.61).

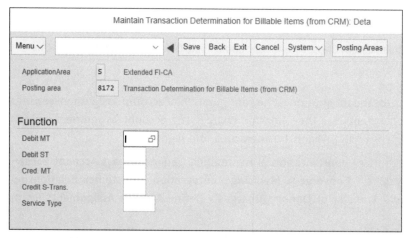

Figure 4.61 Main and SubTransaction Assignment for One-Time Charges from SAP BRIM, Subscription Order Management/SAP CRM

Recurring

Charges that are levied for the subscription term recursively for maintaining the subscription are referred to as recurring charges. Recurring charges are posted based on the subscription type: if it's a monthly subscription, then the recurring charges are posted monthly. These charges are usually posted either at the start of the subscription month/period or toward the end of the month/period. When an invoice is generated for the month/period, these charges along with the usage charge and other charges are invoiced and posted on the customer's account.

For Martex, billable item type ZBT2 is used for posting the recurring subscription charges.

Usage-Based

Usage-based charges are the charges levied for the use of services in the subscription plan by the customer. The usage-based charges are recorded in SAP Convergent Invoicing over a period—monthly, for example—and at the period end are sent for rating to SAP Convergent Charging, which sends the rated and charged items as billable items that are billed and invoiced in the regular periodic invoicing cycle. Receivables are posted to the customer's account.

For Martex, billable item type ZBT3 is used for the usage-based charges.

Pay-per-Use

These are the charges levied on the customer's account only for when they use the services. These kinds of charges are billed and invoiced as soon as they are received in the SAP Convergent Invoicing system. For example, highway tolls are levied on commuters who use the highway, and these toll charges are made per the use of the highway. A commuter can opt for a monthly pass/subscription instead and can receive the subsidized rate for tolls and be charged at the month end for usage throughout the month.

Refund

These are the charges posted in the system to refund an amount the customer has already paid in advance for purchasing the product or the service subscription. Considering a scenario in which a customer has paid up-front for a monthly subscription, as in the case of Martex, this is a reserved instance amount. If the customer later decides not to go ahead with the product or service purchased and asks for the contract to end, in such a scenario the prorated amount is generally refunded from the up-front charge paid if the contract allows. Separate billable item types are generally created to record the refund amount.

Trial

These are generally zero-amount charges or a certain amount of charges that are not billed and invoiced to the customer. These kinds of charges are used in scenarios of product trials or free subscription trial periods.

Cost

These kinds of charges are generally the cost of buying a product from a vendor or can be revenue sharing for selling services on behalf of a vendor. For Martex, which purchases the products it sells from different vendors, it uses partner settlement to post the purchases as outgoing charges to the vendors. The partner settlement is described in detail in Section 4.2.6.

Cancellation

Billable item type cancellation is used to create the billable items for the order/subscription cancellation. Cancellation billable items are triggered upon the cancellation of service. Upon the service cancellation, the contract with the service provider ends. The customer account is then invoiced with the final invoice and any charges applicable are posted to the customer's account upon invoicing.

Billing Documents

The billing process execution results in the creation of the billing documents. Billing documents contain the grouped and aggregated billable items. Billing process execution can generate several billing documents for the same business partner and contract account depending on the subprocess and grouping criteria.

Billing documents can be generated individually or in a mass run of the billing process. Transactions FKKBIX_S and FKKBIX_MA are used for billing process execution individually and en masse, respectively. These transactions can also be accessed through SAP Easy Access menu: **Accounting** · **Financial Accounting** · **Contract Account Receivables & Payables** · **Convergent Invoicing** · **Periodic Processing** · **Billing** (as in Figure 4.62).

Figure 4.62 Billing Process Mass Run

Business Example

Billable items created for ZBT1 (one-time charge), ZBT2 (recurring charge), and ZBT3 (usage charge) need to be billed on the billing cycle of the customer. To execute the billing, billing process ZBP1 will be executed. The execution will create the billing documents, which will then be invoiced.

The billing documents created by the billing process have the following sections:

- **Header data details**
  The header section of the billing documents contains details like posting date, customer master data details, start and end dates of the billing period, billing process, billing type, and, most importantly, the invoice from date, which indicates on what date the created billing documents can be invoiced.

- **Line item details**
  The line items section contains details like quantity, amount, and main and subtransactions. In the case of aggregated billable items, the **Quantity** field contains the total quantity and the **Amount** contains the total amount of all the aggregated billable items.

- **Tax items**

  If a tax is calculated on the billable items, then the tax amount and other tax-related information is displayed in this section.

- **Additional items**

  During the billing process, if additional billable items are created and billed together, then this section displays the additional billable items that are created and billed.

- **Payment data items**

  If the customer has paid up-front for the purchase, the details of payment are received in the PY record type along with sale billable item record type IT. During the billing process, the payment-related details are populated in the payment data section, which will be used during the invoicing of the billing documents.

- **Invoicing history**

  This section contains the details of the invoicing document when the billing documents are invoiced.

- **Source items**

  This section contains all the billable item links, which are grouped and billed together. This section also contains the database table names in which the billed items are stored and also has the field billing item group, which you can click to reach a list of all the billable items that are grouped and aggregated together.

Figure 4.63 shows a sample billing document.

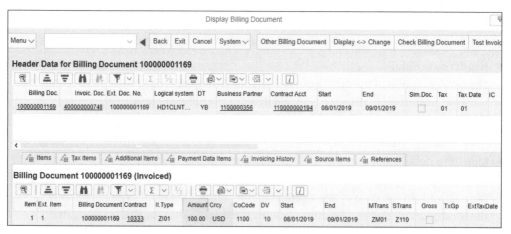

Figure 4.63 Sample Billing Document

We have the discussed billing process and generation of the billing document in detail. In the next section, the invoicing process will be explained in detail, including how billing documents are processed during invoicing.

4.2.5 Invoicing

The invoicing process is used to invoice the billing documents obtained from the billing process. These billing documents can be from the external system, Sales and Distribution, or from within SAP Convergent Invoicing. The billing documents obtained from the different systems can be invoiced together to provide a consolidated invoice to customers.

During the invoicing process, discounts can also be provided to the customers on the basis of a discount key maintained in the contract account.

Invoicing also provides options to calculate interest on open items and cash security deposits, plus account maintenance based on the invoicing functions.

Invoicing Process: Revenue/Cost

The invoicing process is set up for processing the billing documents created for the billable item to invoice the customer. The invoicing process creation leads to the creation of receivable posting documents in a scenario for revenue posting from a sale to a customer or a payable document in a scenario for cost posting for obtaining the product from the vendor.

> **Business Example**
>
> Martex generates revenue from the sale of services to its customers, selling services obtained from its vendors. To post the receivables for the revenue, an invoicing process ZI will be created.

The invoicing process has similar steps as the billing process, with the difference in the selection of billing documents instead of billable items. The following steps are required for setting up the invoicing process:

- Grouping variant setup
- Creation of invoicing process
- Selection control
- Invoicing functions assignment

Each of these steps are described in the following sections in detail.

Grouping Variant

A grouping variant is used to group together the selected billing documents based on grouping characteristics that can be selected from structure FKKINV_TRIG for the invoicing orders. Some of the fields include source document category, company code, and contract. Also, customer-specific fields can be used using a function module that can be assigned to the grouping characteristics.

Grouping variants created are assigned to invoicing processes while creating the invoicing processes. They are maintained under **Contract Account Receivables & Payables · Convergent Invoicing · Invoicing · Invoicing Process · Maintain Grouping Variants** (as in Figure 4.64).

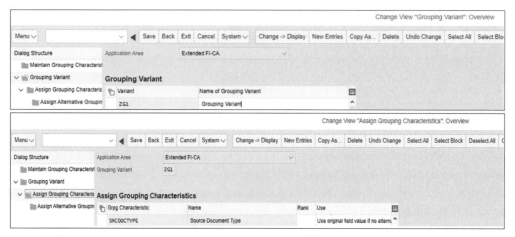

Figure 4.64 Invoicing Grouping Variant

Invoicing Process

To perform invoicing of the billing documents, an invoicing process is created. In the invoicing process, selection conditions are maintained that select the billing documents. A grouping variant is assigned to the invoicing process, which groups the selected billing documents for creation of invoicing units. The invoicing process is assigned invoicing functions that are used for performing the invoicing of billing documents.

The invoicing process is configured under **Contract Account Receivables & Payables · Convergent Invoicing · Invoicing · Invoicing Process · Define Invoicing Processes** (as in Figure 4.65).

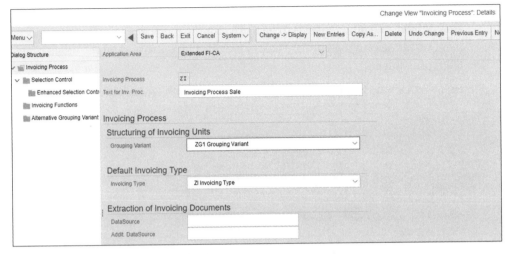

Figure 4.65 Invoicing Process Creation Screen

Selection Control

Selection control is maintained within the invoicing process creation screens. Selection parameters maintained in the selection control are used to control the selection of the billing documents for processing (as in Figure 4.66).

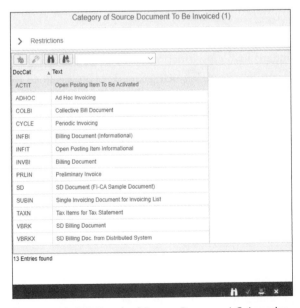

Figure 4.66 SAP Standard Source Document Categories

The source document category maintained in the selection control specifies which kind of billing document needs to be picked for the invoicing process. Source document categories are the standard values provided by SAP based on the origin of the billing documents.

Figure 4.67 shows the invoicing process selection control screen.

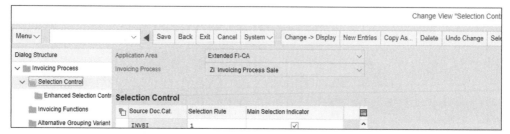

Figure 4.67 Invoicing Process Selection Control Screen

INVBI is the source document category for the billing documents generated within SAP Convergent Invoicing by the billing process executed on the billable items.

The VBRK source document category is used for Sales and Distribution billing documents, which are pushed to FI-CA for invoicing in SAP Convergent Invoicing.

Invoicing Functions

Invoicing functions indicate the various supported functionalities within an invoicing process. There is a set of standard invoicing functions provided by SAP that is assigned to the invoicing process configuration. Invoicing functions are assigned to the invoicing process at the time of its creation (as in Figure 4.68).

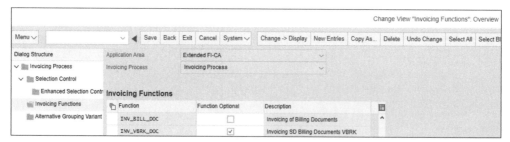

Figure 4.68 Invoicing Function Assignment to Invoicing Process

There are 51 standard functions provided by SAP (as in Table 4.4).

Invoicing Function	Description
ACCT_MAINT	Automatic Account Maintenance
ACCT_MAINT_D	Manual Account Maintenance (Dialog Call)
ACCT_MAINTX	Enhanced Automatic Account Maintenance
ACCT_MAINTXD	Enhanced Manual Account Maintenance
ACTIVATE_OI	Activation of Open Items
ACTIVATE_RDI	Activate Documents from Revenue Distribution
ADD_DOC	Creation of Additional (Customer-/Industry-Specific) Docs
BOLLO_CALC	Stamp Tax
BW_INTEGR	Integration in BW Sales Statistics
CHARGE_DISC	Charges and Discounts
CHARGE_DISC2	Individual Charges and Discounts
DEBIT_STAT_I	Debit Entry for Statistical Documents
DEBIT_REV_BY_E	Deferred Revenues - Event-Based
DEF_REVENUES	Deferred Revenues
DUNNING_PROP	Dunning
HIST_ITEMS	Subitems
INSTPLAN_DUE	Set Installment Plan to Due
INTEREST_DEB	Calculate Interest on Open Items
INTEREST_SEC	Calculation of Interest on Cash Security Deposit
INV_ADHOC	Ad Hoc Invoicing
INV_BILL_DOC	Invoicing of Billing Documents
INV_COLLBILL	Creation of Collective Invoicing Document
INV_CYCLE	Periodic Invoicing

Table 4.4 List of Invoicing Functions

Invoicing Function	Description
INV_OFFSET	Offsetting in Invoicing
INV_SD_DOC	Invoicing of SD Documents
INV_VBRK_DOC	Invoicing SD Billing Documents VBRK
OFFIC_DOC_NO	Official Document Number
PAYFORM	Payment Form
PAYM_HISTORY	Payment History
PAYM_METHOD	Payment Method Determination
PAYM_REF	Payment Reference
PCARD_PAYMET	Card Payment (Payment Method)
PCARD_PAYMNT	Card Payment with Immediate Clearing
PPACC_MAINT	Account Maintenance for Prepaid Account
SUBINV_LIST Create	Invoicing List
SUBINV_TRIG	Preselect Invoicing Document for Invoicing List
PPACC_MAINTD	Manual Account Maintenance for Prepaid Account (Dialog Call)
PPACC_REFILL	Balance Change of Prepaid Account
PRELIM_INV	Creation of Preliminary Invoices
REV_STAT_IT	Reversal of Statistical Line Items
REVERSAL	Invoicing Reversal
RND_INV_DOC	Rounding per Invoicing Document
RND_POST_DOC	Rounding per Posting Document
SECURITY_ADJ	Release/Adjust Cash Security Deposit
SECURITY_CRT	Create Cash Security Deposit
SEPA_PRENOT	SEPA: Direct Debit Pre-Notification
TAX_NOTIF	Create Tax Notification

Table 4.4 List of Invoicing Functions (Cont.)

Invoicing Function	Description
TRANSFER_IT	Transfer Open Item
VALIDAT_INV	Invoicing Document Plausibility Checks
VALIDAT_SRC	Source Document Plausibility Checks
WRITEOFF	Write Off

Table 4.4 List of Invoicing Functions (Cont.)

The invoicing functions are classified further into main/mandatory and additional/optional invoicing functions. The main invoicing functions are important for the generation of the invoicing documents. The additional invoicing functions are used for additional functions that could be performed along with invoice generation. The following are some of the mandatory and additional invoicing functions:

- **Main invoicing functions**
  - Invoicing of Billing documents (INV_BILL_DOC)
  - Invoicing of SD Billing documents (INV_VBRK_DOC)
  - Creation of collective invoicing documents (INV_COLLBILL)
  - Creation of Ad Hoc invoice (INV_ADHOC)
  - Periodic Invoice (INV_CYCLE)
  - Invoicing of SD Documents (INV_SD_DOC)
- **Additional invoicing functions**
  - Card Payment with Immediate Clearing (PCARD_PAYMNT)
  - Card Payment (Payment Method) (PCARD_PAYMET)
  - Payment History (PAYM_HISTORY)
  - Invoicing Reversal (REVERSAL)
  - Automatic Account Maintenance (ACCT_MAINT)

All main and additional functions were listed in Table 4.4.

Invoicing functions should be included for the document categories to be invoiced; for example, invoicing function INVBI should be used for invoicing billing documents created within SAP Convergent Invoicing by the billing process.

Invoicing function PCARD_PAYMNT is used in the scenario in which payment data details are received along with the main billable item record type. During the invoicing process, the receivable is posted in FI-CA and immediate clearing is performed for the receivable posted using the payment details received in the payment data of billable items.

Invoicing Type

Invoicing types are used to distinguish the invoicing process, like periodic invoices or final invoices for the customer. Invoicing types can be used to differentiate invoicing units. It is essential to assign an invoicing type to each invoicing process.

During the creation of the invoicing process, invoicing functions are assigned as shown in Figure 4.69, and the assigned functions can be marked as optional. Optional invoicing functions in the invoicing process can be performed based on the activation status maintained in the invoicing type.

There are three type of activation statuses available for the optional invoicing functions, which are available in the invoicing types. Based on the status, an invoicing function can be activated or deactivated when invoicing is performed in dialog mode. Those three include:

- **Active, cannot be deactivated in dialog**
  An invoicing function with this status would be executed and cannot be deactivated.

- **Active, can be deactivated in dialog**
  Such invoicing functions can be deactivated when invoicing is performed in dialog mode.

- **Not active, can be activated in dialog**
  Such invoicing functions are not active until activated during the dialog mode of invoice process execution.

Invoicing types are maintained under **Contract Account Receivables & Payables · Convergent Invoicing · Invoicing · Invoicing Process · Define Invoicing Types** (as in Figure 4.69).

The created invoicing type is assigned to the invoicing process. For Martex, invoicing type ZI is assigned to invoicing process ZI. Assignment to an invoicing process is done in the subnode of the invoice type creation node (as in Figure 4.70).

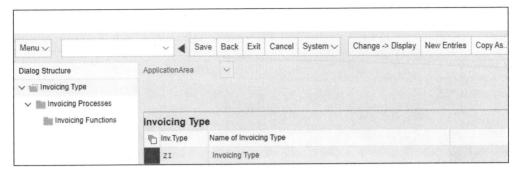

Figure 4.69 Invoicing Type Creation Screen

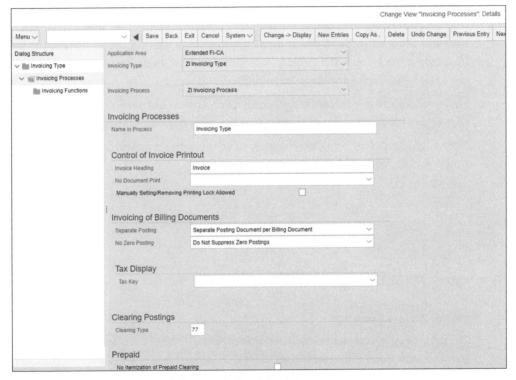

Figure 4.70 Assignment of Invoicing Type to Invoicing Process

The invoicing functions marked optional in the invoicing process, as shown in Figure 4.71, are assigned to the invoicing type and an activation type is mentioned.

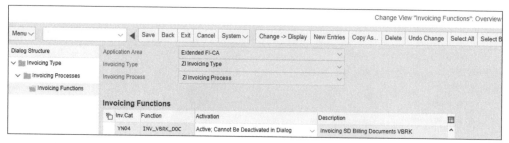

Figure 4.71 Optional Invoicing Function Assignment to Invoicing Type

Invoicing Category

An invoicing category is used for finer control of invoicing. It is assigned to the contract account under the **Convergent Invoicing** tab and is maintained under the invoicing type along with the optional invoicing functions. During the execution of the invoicing process, only the contract accounts with an invoicing category can have the optional invoicing functions executed.

The invoicing category is configured under **Contract Account Receivables & Payables · Convergent Invoicing · Invoicing · Invoicing Process · Define Invoicing Categories**.

The assignment of an invoicing category to an invoicing type and optional invoicing function is shown in Figure 4.72.

Figure 4.72 Invoicing Category Creation Screen

Invoice Process Execution

The invoicing process can be executed in individual or mass processing. Its execution requires selection parameters to be filled in. The business partner and contract are general selection parameters and can be used for parallel job execution. An invoicing run execution also requires an invoicing process to be maintained on the selection screen for execution. Based on the selection parameters and any customs selections, the billing documents are selected. Selected billing documents whose target invoicing dates are reached are processed in the invoicing process. Invoice process execution generates an invoicing document and posts the receivables documents in FI-CA on the customer account.

Transactions for invoice execution are FKKINV_S and FKKINV_MA, and the same can be accessed from SAP Easy Access menu **Accounting · Financial Accounting · Contract Account Receivables & Payables · Convergent Invoicing · Invoicing · Documents · Create** and from **Accounting · Financial Accounting · Contract Account Receivables & Payables · Convergent Invoicing · Invoicing · Periodic Processing · Invoicing · Execute Invoicing** (as in Figure 4.73).

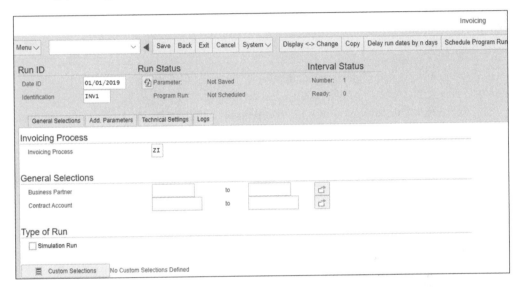

Figure 4.73 Mass Invoicing Run Screen

Invoice Documents

An invoice document is the invoice sent to customers for their use of a service. It contains the details of the amount, usage, previous unpaid receivables, payment details, and so on. Invoicing documents hold financial entries and are generated upon the successful execution of the invoicing process. The invoicing process generates the invoicing document along with the FI-CA posting documents, which post the accounting entries (as in Figure 4.74).

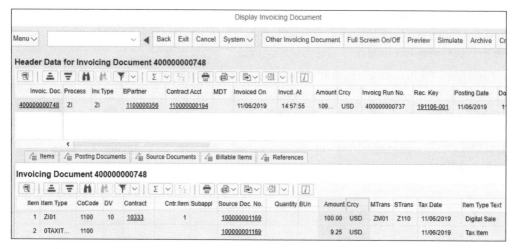

Figure 4.74 Sample Invoicing Document

An invoicing document contains several pieces of information, structured as follows:

- **Header section**

  Contains information like posting dates, due dates, master data, total invoiced amount, document type, invoicing process, invoicing type, reconciliation key, and reversal document information.

- **Items**

  Contains the details of invoice line items, including amounts, invoicing types, and account assignment details.

- **Posting documents**

  This section contains the details of the FI-CA posting document, which navigates to the document view in FI-CA upon clicking.

- **Source documents**

  This section contains the details of the billing documents invoiced together in the invoicing process. Upon selection, you will be taken to the billing document view.

- **Billable items**

  This section contains details of the billable items associated with the billing documents invoiced.

- **References**

  This section contains the reference information for the provider contract or provider agreement.

- **Invoicing document type**

  The document type is used to identify the postings. Document types are associated with number ranges for individual and mass processing. A posted document uses these ranges to assign document numbers to the document types. Document types, together with document numbers, uniquely identify the invoicing document posted by the invoicing process.

Customizing for the document type can be maintained under **Contract Account Receivables & Payables · Convergent Invoicing · Invoicing · Documents · Invoicing Documents · Maintain Document Types & Assign Number Ranges** (as in Figure 4.75).

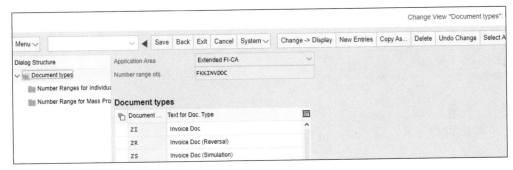

Figure 4.75 Document Type for Invoicing Documents

Separate document types can be assigned to the invoicing process. Simulation and reversal of invoicing also requires document number ranges to be maintained (as in Figure 4.76). The associated posting area is 2600.

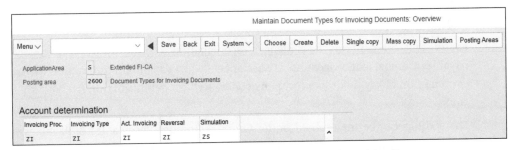

Figure 4.76 Document Type Assignment to Invoicing Process and Invoicing Type

Posting Documents

The invoicing process posts invoicing documents along with the posting documents in FI-CA. A document type also is assigned to the posting documents against each invoicing process and invoicing type. The associated posting area is 2605.

The associated settings can be maintained under **Contract Account Receivables & Payables · Convergent Invoicing · Invoicing · Documents · Posting Documents · Define Document Types for Posting Document for Invoicing** (as in Figure 4.77).

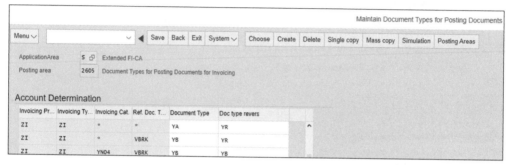

Figure 4.77 Posting Document Types Assignment for Invoicing

Account Assignment for Posting Documents

Posting documents associated with the invoicing document are posted in FI-CA for receivables management. The revenue, expense, tax, and subledger postings are required to be posted in the relevant general ledger accounts. The determination of the general ledger accounts is achieved by using posting areas.

Posting Area 2611 for Business Partner Items

Posting area 2611 contains the subledger/reconciliation accounts for the receivables/payables. General ledger accounts are assigned against each main transaction with a combination of key fields like company codes, account determination IDs, and divisions.

The settings can be maintained under **Contract Account Receivables & Payables · Convergent Invoicing · Invoicing · Documents · Posting Documents · Define Account Assignment for Business Partner Items** (as in Figure 4.78).

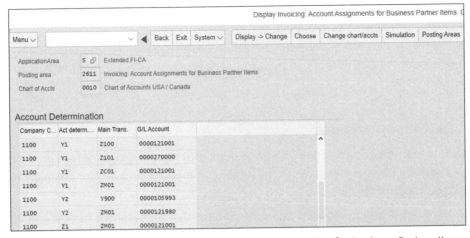

Figure 4.78 Posting Area 2611 for General Ledger Determination for Business Partner Items

Posting Area 2610 for General Ledger Items

Posting area 2610 contains the general ledger accounts for the revenue, expense, and tax determination. The general ledger accounts are maintained against each main and subtransaction combination using key parameters like company code, division, and account determination ID.

The settings can be maintained under **Contract Account Receivables & Payables · Convergent Invoicing · Invoicing · Documents · Posting Documents · Define Account Assignment for General Ledger Items** (as in Figure 4.79).

Display Invoicing: Account Assignments for General Ledger Items: Overv

Menu ∨		∨ ◀	Back	Exit	System ∨	Display -> Change	Choose	Change chart/accts	Simulation	Posting Areas

ApplicationArea   S 🗗 Extended FI-CA
Posting area   2610   Invoicing: Account Assignments for General Ledger Items
Chart of Accts   0010   Chart of Accounts USA / Canada

Account Determination

Company Code	Division	Act determ. ID	Main Trans.	Subtransaction	G/L Account	Tax Determina...	Business Area	CO acc. ass.	
1100		Y1	ZM01	Z110	0000410000	Y0			
1100		Y1	ZM01	Z111	0000410000	Y1			
1100		Y1	ZM01	Z510	0000270000	Y1			
1100		Y1	ZM01	Z511	0000270000	Y1			
1100		Y2	Y900	1010	0000672005	Y2			

Figure 4.79 Posting Area 2610 for General Ledger Items

259

As of SAP S/4HANA 1909, we are able to process intercompany settlement in SAP Convergent Invoicing by handling dual rates and tax account keys. Generating an invoice with the other processes in SAP Convergent Invoicing can significantly reduce delays caused by intercompany reconciliation with sales and distribution processing.

4.2.6   Partner Settlement

The process of sharing revenue with the vendor, generated from the sale of a product to a customer by the company for the product acquired from a vendor company is termed as partner settlement.

In scenarios in which products and subscriptions that are acquired from a vendor that owns the rights to the same are sold to end customers, vendors are entitled to revenue sharing, and in SAP Convergent Invoicing, this is achieved via partner settlement. Vendors in such scenarios are called partners with whom partner agreements are set up.

> **Business Example**
> Martex sells cloud products to customers on behalf of vendors from which it obtains products. For each sale of a product, Martex pays the vendor the cost of the product. This is achieved by partner settlement, as described in this section.

The details of the sales of a product are recorded in SAP Convergent Invoicing in the form of billable items. When billable items are created, based on the partner settlement category (PSCAT), type of user reference ID (PT_USERID_REFTY), and partner reference ID (PT_USERID_REF) fields, the consumption items are created for the vendor/partner in SAP Convergent Invoicing. The consumption items thus created contain the reference to the partner agreement and are sent for rating and charging to SAP Convergent Charging by the rating process. SAP Convergent Charging then sends billable items for the partner to be billed and invoiced. Upon invoicing, the payables are posted to the partner account in FI-CA.

Partner settlement functionality is activated in SAP Convergent Invoicing by selecting the associated interface component of the class. Upon activation and generation of the class, the fields for the partner settlement become available in the class structure.

The interface components for the class that are used for partner settlement functionality are as follows:

- **Partner settlement: basic data of customer items**
  This interface makes the PSCAT field (partner settlement) category available in the billable item class for the revenue posting for the customer items.

- **Partner settlement: basic data for partner items**
  This interface makes the PTSRL (partner settlement rule) and PTAMOUNT_ADJ (adjustment amount for partner settlement) fields available.

- **Partner settlement of royalties (example)**
  This interface makes the following fields available:

  - PT_USERID_REFTY: Type of reference for partner ID of consumption item
    A value of I means the value in PT_USERID_REF can be directly used as ACCESS_USERID. A value of E means that the value needs to be mapped using a table.

  - PT_USERID_REF: Partner ID of consumption item
    This is used for determining the consumer ID of the consumption item (partner ID) for the partner item.

  - PT_PRODUCT_CAT: Product category from partner viewpoint
    This is used for determining the price.

4.2.7   Partner Settlement Categories

The partner settlement category is used to categorize the different revenue-sharing scenarios for the generation of the partner settlement consumption items.

In conjunction with the settlement reason, the partner settlement category creates the consumption items. To activate the functionality, first the interface components are selected for the class. Then the partner settlement category is maintained. Categories basically describe the type of service that is used by the customer for partner settlement.

Configuration of partner settlement categories is maintained under **Contract Account Receivables & Payables · Convergent Invoicing · Partner Settlement · Define Categories of Transactions to be Billed** (as in Figure 4.80).

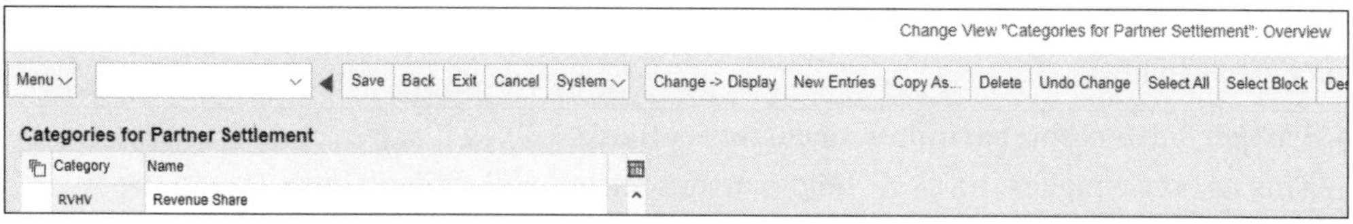

Figure 4.80 Partner Settlement Category

Reason for Partner Settlement

Settlement reasons are contractual agreements based on which the partner amount is decided. Settlement reasons are assigned with function modules, which creates the consumption items automatically when billable items are received with partner settlement categories.

After creation of the settlement category, the settlement reason is set up. SAP does not provide any standard reason. A settlement reason is created and assigned with a function module, which is used for creation of the consumption items for the partner settlement. SAP provides a sample function module that can be used and can be modified as needed for creation of the consumption items.

Configuration of partner settlement reasons is maintained under **Contract Account Receivables & Payables · Convergent Invoicing · Partner Settlement · Define Reason for Partner Settlement** (as in Figure 4.81).

Figure 4.81 Partner Settlement Reason

Reasons and Categories Assignment

The partner settlement category and settlement reason created are assigned to the consumption item class for the partner settlement. The partner settlement category populated on the billable item field triggers the function module associated with the assigned reason to category, which creates the consumption items of the assigned consumption item class.

Assignment of reasons and settlement categories to consumption item classes is done under **Contract Account Receivables & Payables · Convergent Invoicing · Partner Settlement · Assign Reasons to Categories** (as in Figure 4.82).

Figure 4.82 Consumption Item Class Assignment to Category and Reason

4.3 Using SAP Convergent Invoicing

So far, we have covered the various configurations required for setting up the SAP Convergent Invoicing objects and how to associate them with the business requirements. After setting up the configurations, you need to test them. To test the configurations for SAP Convergent Invoicing alone when a connection to a different SAP system is not in place, there are different ways that consumption and billable items can be created in SAP Convergent Invoicing directly. Let's discuss them in detail.

4.3.1 Creating a Consumption Item or Billable Item

Consumption items can be created using below mentioned options via Transaction FKKBIXCIT_CWB.

This transaction lets you display, change, and create consumption items. Consumption items can be displayed by the selecting the variant for the consumption item and providing the selection conditions (as in Figure 4.83). The displayed items can be rated, reversed, excepted, restored, and changed based on the action required to be performed (as in Figure 4.84).

Figure 4.83 Consumption Items Display

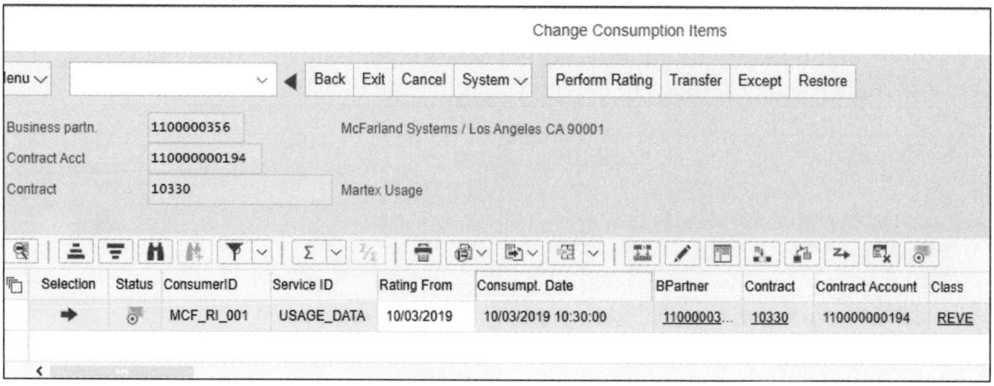

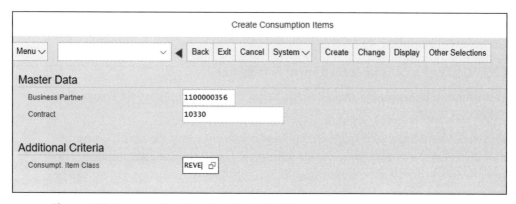

Figure 4.84 Consumption Item Change

Consumption items can be created directly by selecting the **Create** option from within Transaction FKKBIXCIT_CWB. The business partner, contract, and consumption item class can be entered on the consumption item creation screen, then the **Create** option selected (as in Figure 4.85).

Figure 4.85 Consumption Item Creation Initial Screen

After the **Create** option is selected, select the **Add Item** option. Once details are entered, the consumption item can be saved (as in Figure 4.86).

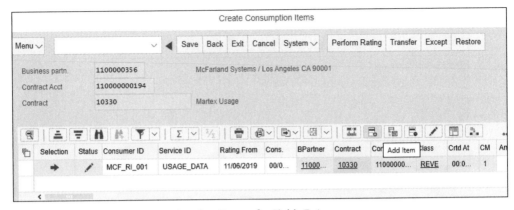

Figure 4.86 Consumption Item Creation Screen for Fields Entry

Report RFKKBIXCITSAMPLE

Report RFKKBIXCITSAMPLE is used for creation of consumption items for test data (as in Figure 4.87). The report is executed using Transaction SE38.

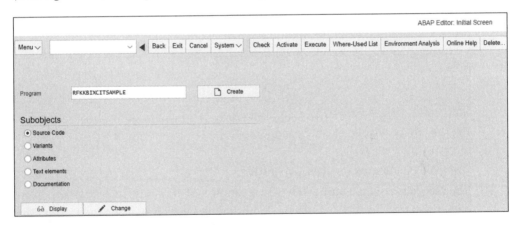

Figure 4.87 Report Program Execution Screen

In this report, enter consumption item details, then select the **Execute** option to store the consumption item (as in Figure 4.88).

This report also provides the option to simulate the consumption item creation before saving the consumption items. You can also debug the consumption item creation if required.

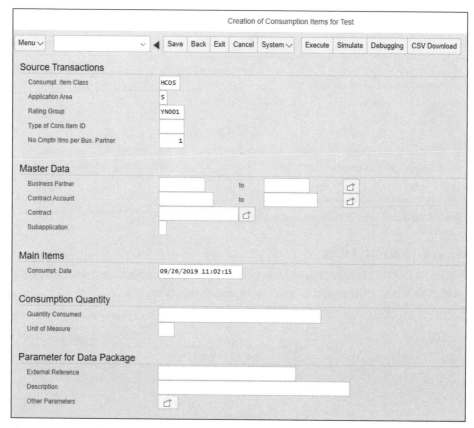

Figure 4.88 Consumption Item Creation Screen

Using APIs Generated on Class Generation

Interfaces are assigned during the class creation, and once class interfaces are generated, the tables, structures, and function modules are created for the classes. The function module generated for the consumption item class can be used for creating the consumption items.

The created function module can be obtained by selecting the consumption item class and then selecting the **Objects** option under menu path **Contract Account Receivables & Payables · Convergent Invoicing · Basic Functions · Consumption Items · Consumption Item Classes · Generate Interface for the Consumption Items Classes** (as in Figure 4.89).

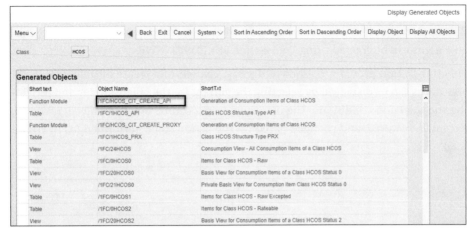

Figure 4.89 Objects for Consumption Item Classes

The function module can be executed in Transaction SE37 and you can enter details for the consumption items to be created. Once the function module is executed, the entries for the consumption items are created (as in Figure 4.90).

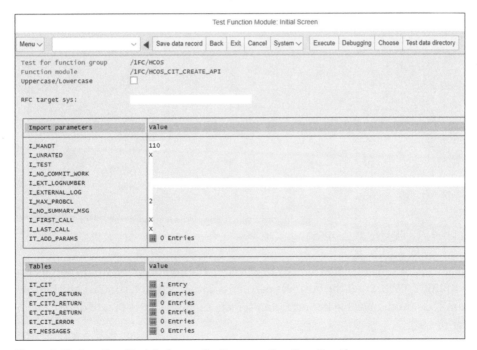

Figure 4.90 Function Module Screen for Consumption Item Creation

Billable Item Creation

Billable items for test data can be directly created in SAP Convergent Invoicing. Billable items can be created using Transaction FKKBIXBIT_CWB.

This transaction provides options to display, change, and create billable items. Billable items can be displayed by selecting the variant for the billable items and providing the selection conditions. The displayed items can be billed, invoiced, reversed, excepted, restored, and changed based on the action to be performed (as in Figure 4.91).

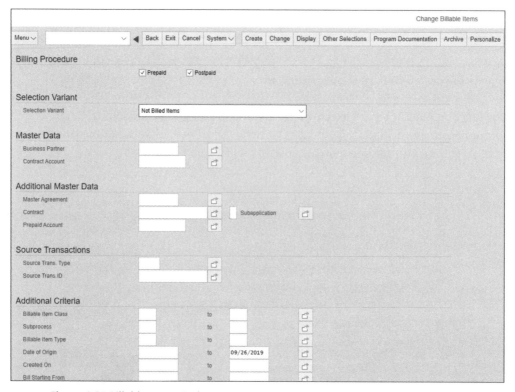

Figure 4.91 Billable Item Display

Billable items can be created directly by selecting the **Create** option from Transaction FKKBIXBIT_CWB. Enter the business partner, contract account, contract and billable item class on the billable item creation screen, then select the **Create** option (as in Figure 4.92).

Figure 4.92 Billable Item Creation Initial Screen

After the **Create** option is selected, select the **Add Item** option. Once details are entered, the billable item can be saved (as in Figure 4.93).

Figure 4.93 Billable Item Creation Screen for Fields Entry

Report RFKKBIXBITSAMPLE

Report RFKKBIXBITSAMPLE is used for creation of billable items for test data (as in Figure 4.94). The report is executed using Transaction SE38.

Figure 4.94 Report Program Execution Screen

After executing the report, enter billable item details, then select the **Save** option to store the billable item (as in Figure 4.95).

This report also provides the option to simulate the billable item creation before executing the billable item creation. The **Execute** option will create the billable item, but the limitation if that it does provide the option to input the value for the custom fields.

The **Create Manually** option lets you enter custom fields. The **Create + Postprocess** option creates the billable items and also sets the billable items in change mode for any field modifications (as in Figure 4.96).

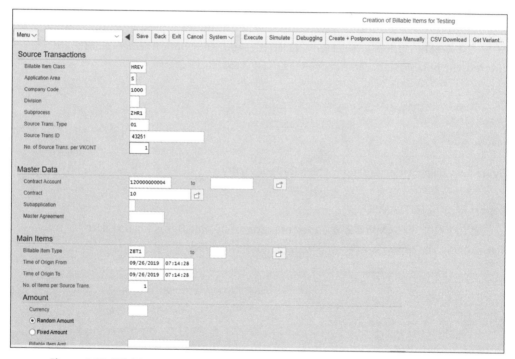

Figure 4.95 Billable Item Creation Screen

Figure 4.96 Create+Postprocess Option Screen for Billable Item Change

Sample File Download and Uploading Updated Sample File

Report RFKKBIXBITUPLOADSAMPLEFILE (Sample File Download) and RFKKBIXBIT-UPLOAD (Uploading Updated Sample File) together are used for billable item creation by uploading the billable item creation file (as in Figure 4.97).

Report RFKKBIXBITUPLOADSAMPLEFILE lets you download the sample file that can be updated with the values of fields for the billable item creation. On the selection screen, enter the billable item class for which the sample/test file needs to be generated. On execution, the program asks for the storage location. When you provide the same, a CSV file will be downloaded, which is used for the billable item data creation.

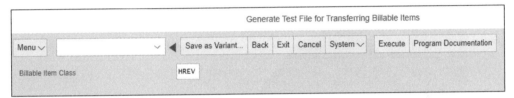

Figure 4.97 Billable Item Test File Creation Screen

The updated file for billable item creation is then uploaded to create the billable item items (as in Figure 4.98). Report RFKKBIXBITUPLOAD is used to upload the file. On execution, it creates the billable items in the SAP Convergent Invoicing system. The **Load Local File** option loads a file from the local system.

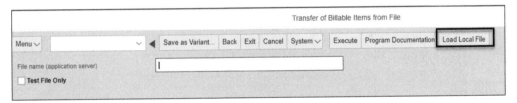

Figure 4.98 Billable Item File Upload Screen

Using API Created on Class Generation

Interfaces are assigned during the class creation, and once class interfaces are generated, the tables, structures, and function modules are created for the classes. The function module generated for the billable item class can be used for creating billable items.

The created function module can be obtained by selecting the billable item class and then the **Objects** option under the path **Contract Account Receivables & Payables · Convergent Invoicing · Basic Functions · Billable Items · Billable Item Classes · Generate Interface for the Billable Items Classes** (as in Figure 4.99).

The function module can be executed in Transaction SE37, where details for the billable items to be created are entered (as in Figure 4.100). Once the function module is executed, the entries for the billable items are created.

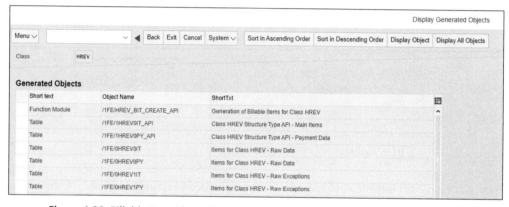

Figure 4.99 Billable Item Class Objects

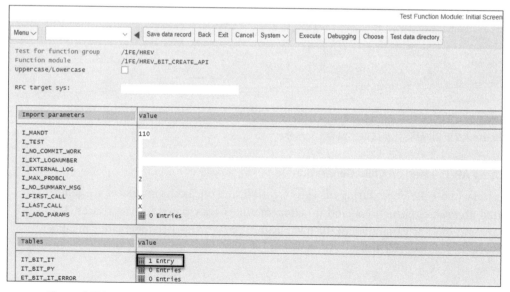

Figure 4.100 Function Module Screen for Billable Item Creation

4.3.2 Modifying Consumption Items or Billable Items

This section will describe the options available in SAP Convergent Invoicing for modification of consumption and billable items created in the system.

Consumption Item Changes

Fields of consumption items created in the system can be changed. The fields that need to be changed need to be made modifiable in the system. The consumption item fields can be made modifiable for each status type. The standard fields available for consumption item status 4 (rated) cannot be changed.

The fields can be made modifiable under **Contract Account Receivables & Payables · Convergent Invoicing · Basic Functions · Consumption Items · Consumption Item Management · Define Changeable Fields for Consumption Items** (as in Figure 4.101).

Figure 4.101 Modifiable Consumption Item Field

The consumption item class and status for which the consumption item field is to be assigned are input on creation. Using the **New Entries** option, the field that is to be made modifiable can be entered on the screen.

Transaction FKKBIXCIT_CWB or FKKBIXCIT_MON can be used to modify the consumption item fields.

The consumption item whose field is to be modified is selected, and the **Process Item** option is selected (as in Figure 4.102).

After changing the field value, the **Apply New Values** option is selected, which updates the field. On selecting the **Save** option, the new value for the consumption item is saved in the system (as in Figure 4.103).

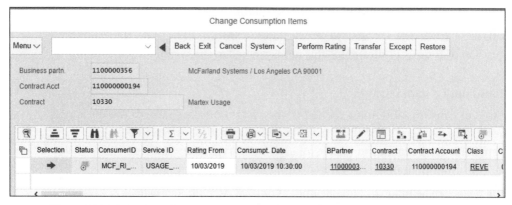

Figure 4.102 Selection of Consumption Item for Modification

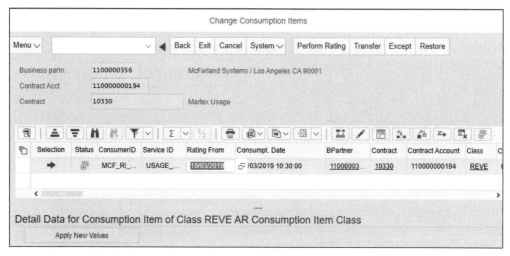

Figure 4.103 Field Modification for Consumption Items

Billable Items Change

Fields of billable items created in the system can be changed. The fields that need to be changed need be made modifiable in the system. The billable item fields can be made modifiable for each status and record type. The standard fields available for billable item status 4 (billed) cannot be changed.

The fields can be made modifiable under **Contract Account Receivables & Payables · Convergent Invoicing · Basic Functions · Billable Items · Billable Item Management · Define Changeable Fields for Billable Items** (as in Figure 4.104).

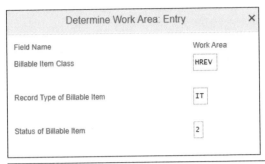

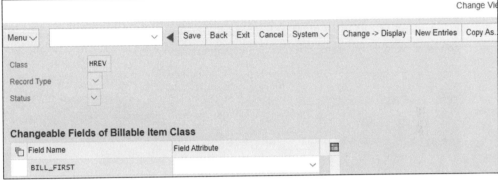

Figure 4.104 Modifiable Field for Billable Item Class Record Type IT

The billable item class, record type, and status for which the billable item field is to be assigned are input on the creation. Using the **New Entries** option, the field to be made modifiable can be entered on the screen.

Transaction FKKBIXBIT_CWB or FKKBIXBIT_MON can be used to modify the billable items fields (as in Figure 4.105).

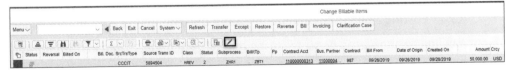

Figure 4.105 Billable Item Selection for Field Modification

The billable item whose field is to be modified is selected, and the **Process Item** option is selected.

After changing the field value, the **Save** option is selected, which saves the new value for the billable item in the system (as in Figure 4.106).

Figure 4.106 Field Modification for Billable Items

4.3.3   Viewing Provider Contract

A provider contract represents the agreement or contractual details with the service provider company. A provider contract is created in FI-CA when a provider order is released in SAP CRM/SAP BRIM, subscription order management. Provider contracts can be viewed using Transaction FP_VT3 (as in Figure 4.107).

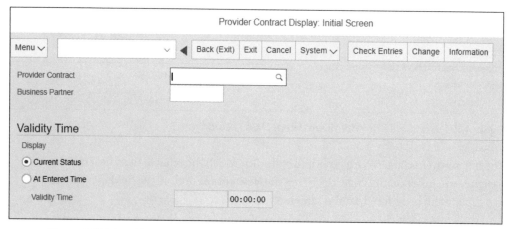

Figure 4.107 Provider Contract Display Screen

4.3.4   Posting a Billing Document, Invoicing Document, and Posting Document

A billing document can be posted using the transactions discussed in the following sections.

Using Billable Item Monitoring Screen

Transaction FKKBIXBIT_MON is used for billable items monitoring. This transaction also provides the options to bill and invoice the billable items. When a billable item is selected and the **Bill** option is selected, the billing process is triggered for the billable items, thus creating a billing document (as in Figure 4.108).

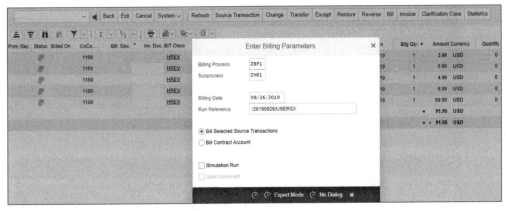

Figure 4.108 Billing Process Execution from Transaction FKKBIXBIT_MON

Individual Billing

The billing process can directly be triggered with Transaction FKKBIX_S for the individual business partner and contract account. The billing process, subprocess, business partner, and contract account are entered on the selection screen for the billing process execution. Billing document simulation is also provided on the screen (as in Figure 4.109).

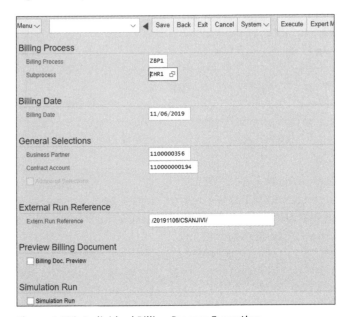

Figure 4.109 Individual Billing Process Execution

Mass Billing Parallel Run

The billing process in an actual production environment is executed as a mass job, via Transaction FKKBIX_MA. Mass jobs are generally set up as batch jobs that execute daily at a desired time and generate the billing documents. Mass jobs are executed in parallel processing with the contract account as a parallel processing parameter. The parallel processing parameter is mentioned in the **Technical Settings** tab of the mass processing screen. The details of the billing process, subprocess, and contract account range are maintained in the **General Selections** tab (as in Figure 4.110).

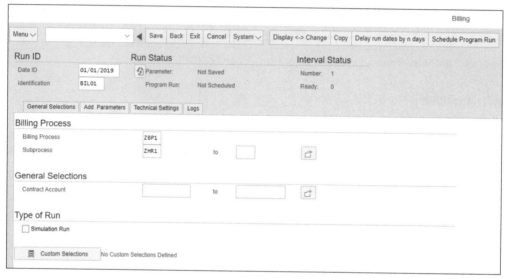

Figure 4.110 Mass Billing Parallel Run Screen

The mass job is scheduled in the background for execution. The job logs of the execution can be seen in the **Logs** tab of the screen.

Mass Billing

Transaction FKKBIX_M also creates the billing documents in mass, but the sequential run is performed and not the parallel run. This job's execution time for similar data is greater than that of Transaction FKKBIX_MA (as in Figure 4.111).

An invoicing document can be posted using the transactions discussed in the following sections.

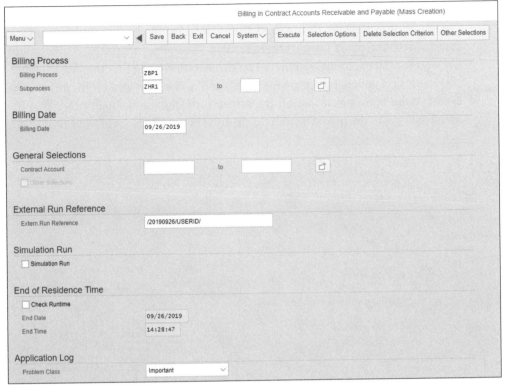

Figure 4.111 Mass Execution Screen for Billing Process

Using Billable Item Monitoring Screen

Transaction FKKBIXBIT_MON is used for billable items monitoring. This transaction also provides an option to invoice the billable items that are already billed. When billable items for which a billing document is posted are selected and the **Invoice** option is selected, the invoicing process is triggered, creating an invoicing document (as in Figure 4.112).

Figure 4.112 Billable Item Monitoring Screen

Individual Invoicing

The invoicing process can be triggered directly for an individual business partner and contract account, or via Transaction FKKINV_S. The invoicing process, business partner, and contract account are entered on the selection screen for the invoicing process execution. Invoicing document simulation is also provided on the screen. The **Expert Mode** option available on the screen provides the flexibility to assign the invoicing type to the invoicing units at the time of execution (as in Figure 4.113).

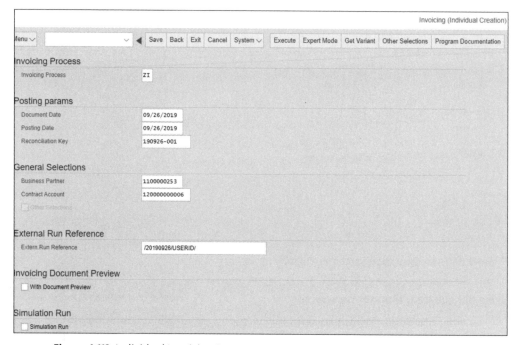

Figure 4.113 Individual Invoicing Run

Mass Invoicing Parallel Run

The invoicing process in an actual production environment is executed as a mass job, via Transaction FKKINV_MA. Mass jobs are generally set up as batch jobs that execute daily at a desired time and generate the invoicing documents. Mass jobs are executed in parallel processing with the business partner or contract account as a parallel processing parameter. The parallel processing parameter is mentioned in the **Technical**

Settings tab of the mass processing screen. The details of the invoicing process, business process, and contract account range are maintained in the **General Selections** tab (as in Figure 4.114).

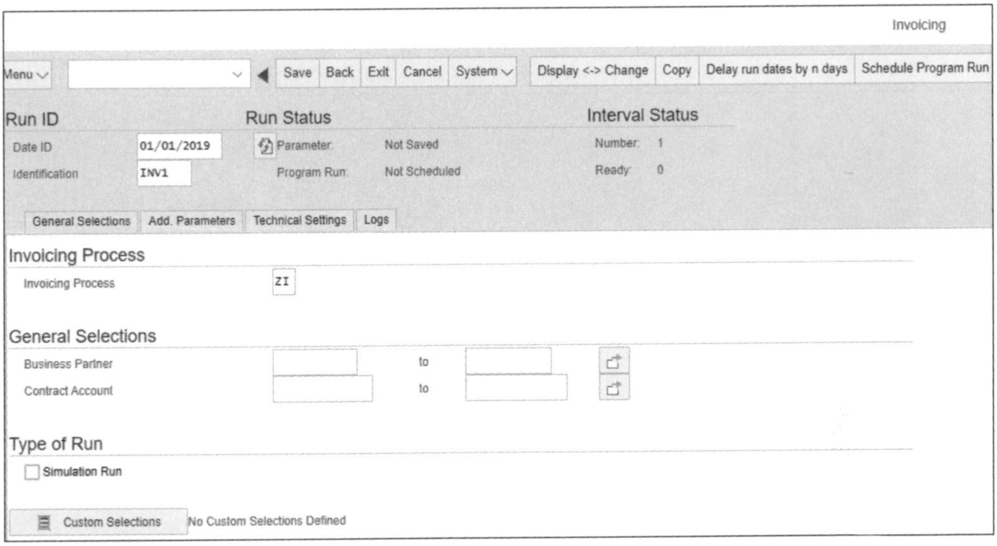

Figure 4.114 Mass Invoicing Run

The mass job is scheduled in the background for execution. The job logs of the execution can be seen in the **Logs** tab of the screen.

Mass Invoicing

Transaction FKKINV_M creates the invoicing documents in mass, but the sequential run is performed and not the parallel run. This job's execution time for similar data is greater than that of Transaction FKKINV_MA (as in Figure 4.115).

Posting documents are posted using the invoicing functions. When invoicing is performed, the invoicing function posts the posting document or FI-CA receivables document automatically.

Posting documents can be viewed by selecting the document number under the **Posting Document** tab of the invoicing document display (as in Figure 4.116).

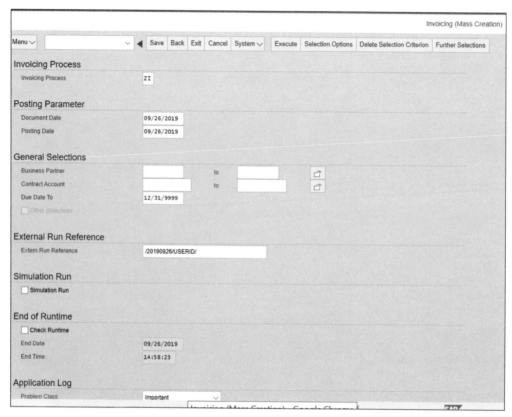

Figure 4.115 Mass Invoicing Sequential Run

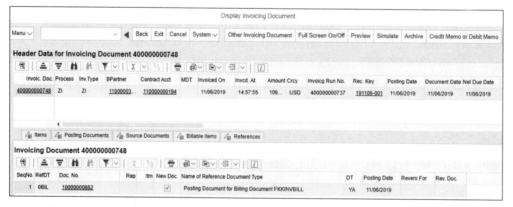

Figure 4.116 Posting Document Number under Posting Documents Tab in Invoicing Document

In addition, if a posting document number is known, then it can be viewed directly using Transaction FPE3 (as in Figure 4.117).

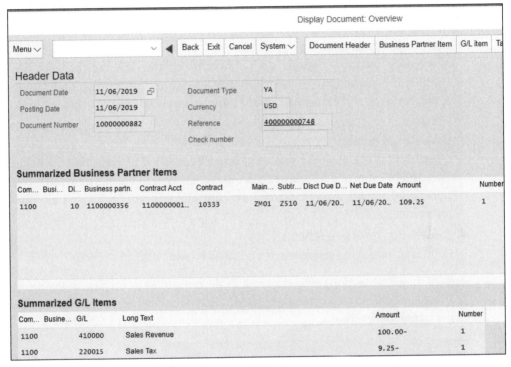

Figure 4.117 Posting Document/FI-CA Document Display

Having demonstrated how the billable items can be created directly within SAP Convergent Invoicing and having covered the concepts of provider contract, billing, and invoicing, let us now look at how the billable items have been created for the Martex Corp. use case within the integrated SAP BRIM solution.

For the use case, we have created the following provider contract scenarios:

- Provider contract 10333 for the reserved instance
- Provider contract 10335 for the non-reserved instance

We have also created a partner agreement that references the contract with the vendor since the vendor does not sell its software directly to customers, but rather through multiple distributors in different regions. Distributors like Martex Corp.

invoice the customers. In return, the vendor gives Martex Corp. a 10% discount off the MSRP based off partner agreement 10337.

For the first scenario, provider contract 10333 (reserved instance), we'll walk through the following transactions:

- **Recurring billable item**
  A monthly recurring billable item for $100 for the sale for the customer 1100000356, McFarland Systems, will be triggered from SAP Convergent Charging. A billable item will be created in SAP Convergent Invoicing for this recurring charge.

- **Usage-based charges**
  Usage records are created in SAP Convergent Invoicing as consumption items. They will be rated at a discounted price and converted to billable items. The customers are eligible for a better rate per unit of consumption, as they are on a reserved instance.

- **Cancellation (prorated refund)**
  Contract cancellation will result in a prorated refund to the customer.

Each of these transactions will result in billable items in SAP Convergent Invoicing, indicated in Table 4.5 with a unique billable item type configured to indicate the type of the transaction.

Billable Item	Use for Martex Corp.
ZBT2	Recurring charges
ZBT3	Usage-based charges
ZBT6	Cancellation (prorated refund)
ZBC3	Partner charges (partner settlement)

Table 4.5 Billable Items for Martex Corp.

For the second scenario, provider contract 10335 (non-reserved instance), we'll walk through the following transactions:

- **Usage-based charges**
  Usage records are created in SAP Convergent Invoicing as consumption items. They will be rated at a non-discounted price and converted to billable items. The

customers are *not* eligible for a discounted rate per unit of consumption, as they are on a non-reserved instance.

- **Partner settlement**
  Vendor payable component will be calculated by SAP Convergent Charging and a billable item for the vendor payable amount will be created in SAP Convergent Invoicing.

So let's examine at the transaction flow for provider contract 10333, beginning with the recurring billable item.

As shown in Figure 4.118, the billable item for the recurring charge for product MRTX_ RI referenced in the provider contract 10333 is triggered from SAP Convergent Charging on first day of every month.

Figure 4.118 Billable Item for Recurring Charge for Provider Contract 10333

Once created successfully in SAP Convergent Invoicing, the billable item is now eligible to be billed and invoiced. Figure 4.119 shows the billing document created for the recurring charge for provider contract 10333.

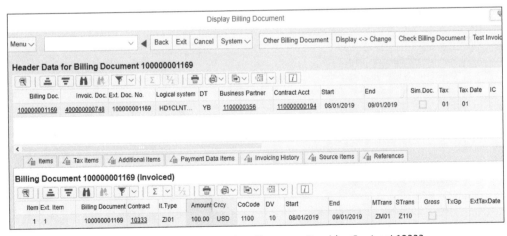

Figure 4.119 Billing Document for the Recurring Charge on Provider Contract 10333

Once the invoicing run for the billing document is performed, the invoicing document shown in Figure 4.120 and the corresponding FI-CA posting document are created shown in Figure 4.121 (along with any applicable taxes).

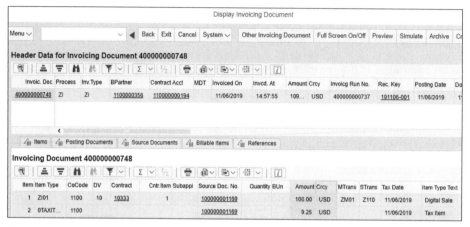

Figure 4.120 Invoicing Document for the Recurring Charge on Provider Contract 10333

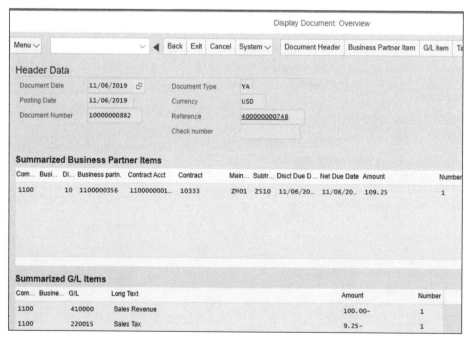

Figure 4.121 Posting Document FI-CA Document Display on Provider Contract 10333

Let's move to provider contract 10333's usage-based charges. The metered usage records are created in SAP Convergent Invoicing as consumption items are shown in Figure 4.122. Next, the rating request for these usage records are initiated from SAP Convergent Invoicing and rated in SAP Convergent Charging. As a result, a billable item is created in SAP Convergent Invoicing for this transaction.

Figure 4.122 Usage Records Created as Consumption Items in SAP Convergent Invoicing on Provider Contract 10333

The billable item resulting from the rating process is shown in Figure 4.123. The total quantity of **3** units has been rated at a rate of **$250** per unit, as defined in SAP Convergent Charging; this is a discounted rate since the customer has a reserved instance.

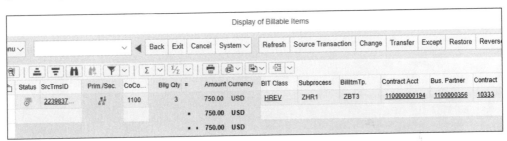

Figure 4.123 Billable Items for Rated Consumption Items on Provider Contract 10333

Once created successfully in SAP Convergent Invoicing, the billable item is now eligible to be billed and invoiced. Figure 4.124 shows the billing document created for the usage charge for provider contract 10333.

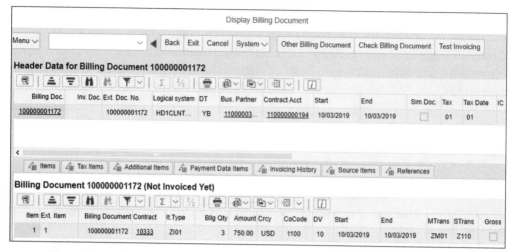

Figure 4.124 Billing Document for Usage Charges on Provider Contract 10333

Subsequently, once the invoicing run for the billing document is performed, the invoicing document shown in Figure 4.125 and the corresponding FI-CA posting document shown in Figure 4.126 are created (along with any applicable taxes).

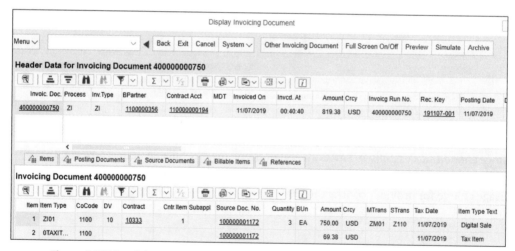

Figure 4.125 Invoicing Document for Usage Charges on Provider Contract 10333

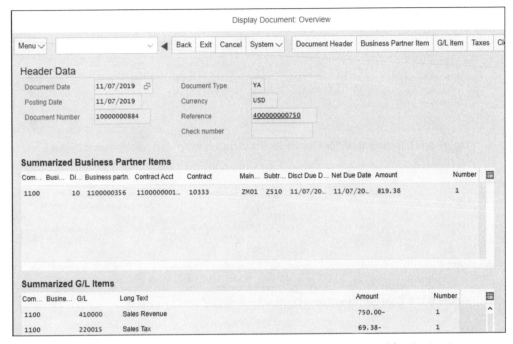

Figure 4.126 Posting Document FI-CA Document for Usage Charge on Provider Contract 10333

Finally, when a customer decides to cancel the contract, the contract cancellation process is initiated in subscription order management as a result of a change order process. A prorated refund amount for the recurring charge is calculated in SAP Convergent Charging, and a prorated refund billable item is sent to SAP Convergent Invoicing, as shown in Figure 4.127.

Let us now look at the transaction flow for the second scenario (provider contract 10335), beginning with usage-based charges.

Similar to the previous scenario for the reserved instance, the metered usage records for the non-reserved instance are created in SAP Convergent Invoicing as consumption items, as shown in Figure 4.128.

Figure 4.127 Billable Item for Prorated Refund for Contract Cancellation on Provider Contract 10333

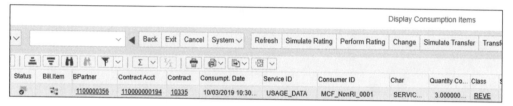

Figure 4.128 Consumption Items Display for Provider Contract 10335

Let's consider the partner settlement. The rating request for the usage record is initiated from SAP Convergent Invoicing and is rated in SAP Convergent Charging. As a result, the following items are created in SAP Convergent Invoicing for this scenario, which is relevant for partner settlement:

- An AR billable item
- An AP consumption item associated with the usage record

In our example, the AR billable item AR for $900 resulted from the rating process is shown in Figure 4.129. (The total quantity of **3** units has been rated at a rate of **$300** per unit, as defined in SAP Convergent Charging; this is a non-discounted rate since the customer has a non-reserved instance.) Clicking the icon in the **Prim./Sec.** column navigates to the AP partner consumption item, which is shown in Figure 4.130.

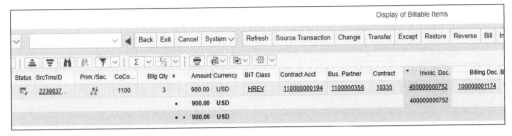

Figure 4.129 Billable Items for Rated Consumption Items for Provider Contract 10335

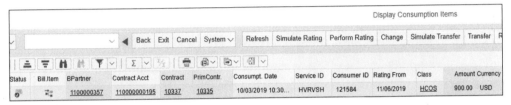

Figure 4.130 Consumption Items Display for Partner Agreement 10337

As shown in Figure 4.131, the vendor payable amount calculated for the vendor **Loren Systems** is **$675**, as the vendor provides a 10% discount off MSRP for Martex Corp.

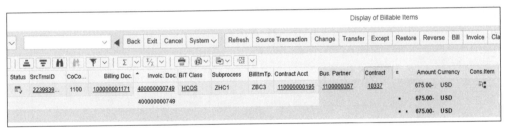

Figure 4.131 Billable Items for Rated Consumption Items for Partner Agreement 10337

4.4   Reporting and Analytics

Now we'll explore the reporting and analytics functionality with SAP Convergent Invoicing, from viewing and processing billable items and consumption items, to document analysis.

4.4.1 All Billable Items View/Processing

Billable items created in the system can be viewed using Transaction FKKBIXBIT_ MON or using the SAP Easy Access menu: **Accounting · Financial Accounting · Contract Account Receivables & Payables · Convergent Invoicing · Billable Items** (as in Figure 4.132).

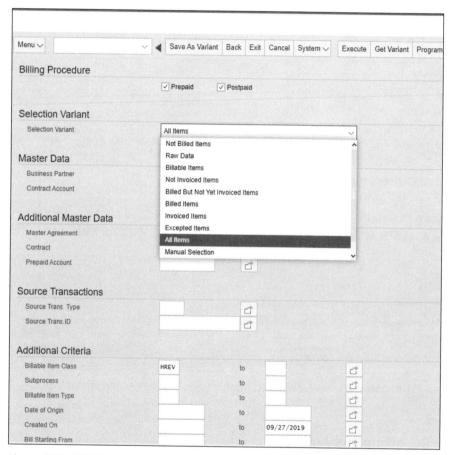

Figure 4.132 Billable Item Display Selection Screen

This transaction provides a view of billable items based on their statuses, among other selection parameters. Status 'ALL STATUSES' is used to display billable items of all status on a single screen (as in Figure 4.133).

Figure 4.133 Billable Item Display

The options available on the screen for processing billable items are as follows:

- **Change**
  Used for modifying the fields of the billable items.

- **Transfer**
  Used for transferring raw status billable items to billable status.

- **Except**
  Used for changing the status of billable item from billable to billable-excepted to exclude them from the billing process. Excepting billable items requires an exception reason.

- **Restore**
  Used for restoring a billable-excepted status billable item to billable status to be considered for billing. Restoration of billable items requires a restoration reason.

- **Reverse**
  Used for reversing the billable item moving to excepted status and reversing the rating of associated consumption items, changing them to either unrated or excepted status based on exception reason settings.

- **Bill**
  Billable items in status billable are considered for billing. The billing process can be executed on the selected billable items.

- **Invoice**
  Billed billable items can be processed in invoicing using this option.

- **Clarification Case**
  Billing documents and even invoice documents of the billable items can be put in clarification case status for further processing based on clarification rules based on amount or quantity.

4.4.2   Consumption Items View/Processing

Consumption items in the system can be viewed using Transaction FKKBIXCIT_ MON, which also can be accessed under the SAP Easy Access menu: **Accounting · Financial Accounting · Contract Account Receivables & Payables · Convergent Invoicing · Consumption Items** (as in Figure 4.134).

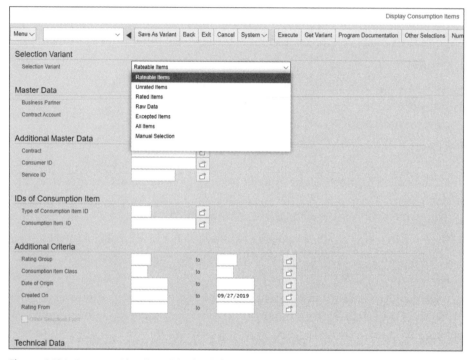

Figure 4.134 Consumption Item Display Selection Screen

The transaction provides the option to view the consumption items sorted by status or all together. This is controlled by the selection variant provided on the screen as one of the selection parameters (as in Figure 4.135).

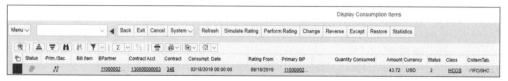

Figure 4.135 Consumption Item Display Screen

There are several processing options available on the display screen that can be performed on consumption items based on requirements:

- **Perform Rating**
  The rating process is described in detail in Section 4.2.3. The unrated consumption items can be sent to the SAP Convergent Charging system for rating through this option.

- **Change**
  The consumption item fields can be modified using this option. The consumption item fields that are made modifiable in the configuration can be modified. The configuration is shown in Figure 4.101.

- **Reverse**
  The consumption items that are not to be used for rating or are created in error can be reversed using this option. The reversing will require a reversal reason.

- **Except**
  Erroneous unrated consumption items can be moved to an excepted status using this option by providing an exception reason.

- **Restore**
  The excepted unrated consumption items can be moved to an unrated status using this option. Erroneous consumption items that are modified can be restored.

4.4.3   Raw Data View of Billable Items

Billable items of raw status can be viewed using Transaction FKKBIXBIT_MON by selecting **Raw Data** as the **Selection Variant** (as in Figure 4.136).

Figure 4.136 Raw Data Selection for Billable Items

Also, Transaction FKKBIXBITR_MON can be used directly to view raw and raw excepted status billable items (as in Figure 4.137).

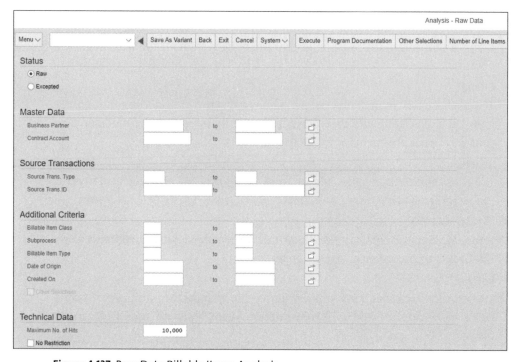

Figure 4.137 Raw Data Billable Items Analysis

4.4.4   Display Invoicing Orders

Billing documents that are eligible for invoicing or for which invoicing orders are present in table DFKKINV_TRIG can be viewed using Transaction FKKINV_MON, which also can be accessed under the SAP Easy Access menu: **Accounting · Financial Accounting · Contract Account Receivables & Payables · Convergent Invoicing · Invoicing Documents** (as in Figure 4.138).

The billing documents that originate from different processes or billing systems are differentiated by the source document category. To view the invoicing order, the source document category is provided as the selection criterion, among other selection parameters (as in Figure 4.139).

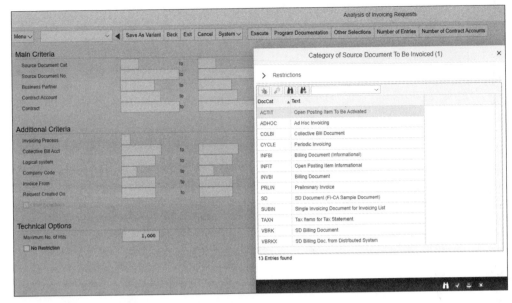

Figure 4.138 Invoice Order Monitoring Screen

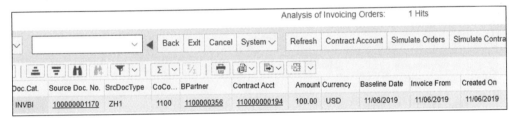

Figure 4.139 Invoicing Order Display Screen

4.4.5   Display Accrual/Deferral Items

Revenue recognition in the standard, the revenue posting takes place at the time of invoicing itself. Revenue accrual/deferral in SAP Convergent Invoicing is related to the revenue recognition of the billable items that are not invoiced. For a class to have billable items for the accrual or deferral, the interface components for accrual/deferral should be selected, and during the creation/transfer of billable items, the accrual/deferral posting type should be assigned.

The accrual/deferral of billable items created in SAP Convergent Invoicing can be viewed using Transaction FKKBIX_REVREC_MON (as in Figure 4.140).

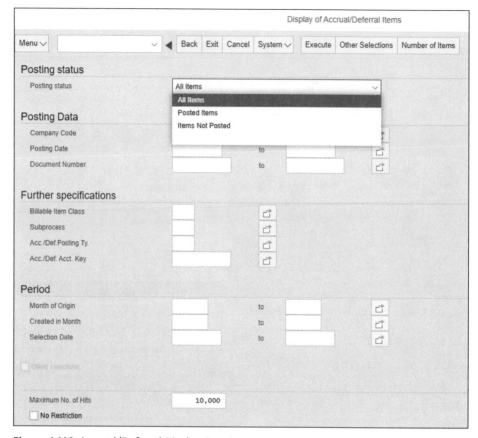

Figure 4.140 Accural/Deferral Display Screen

4.4.6   Billable Items View/Processing

The billable items can be viewed using Transaction FKKBIXBIT_MON by selecting the **Billable Items** variant. The view and processing details are described in Section 4.4.1.

In addition, the billable items also can be viewed using Transaction FKKBIXBITB_ MON, which also can be accessed under the SAP Easy Access menu: **Accounting · Financial Accounting · Contract Account Receivables & Payables · Convergent Invoicing · Billing Documents** (as in Figure 4.141).

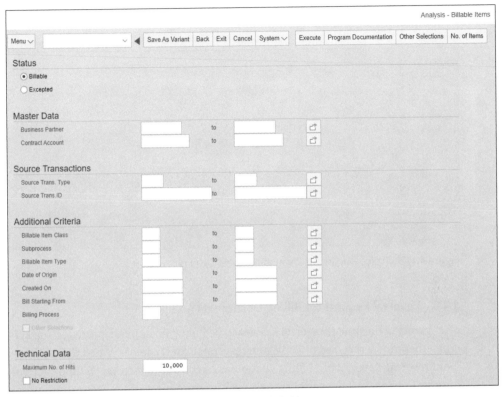

Figure 4.141 Billable Items Display Screen for Status Billable

4.4.7   Reversal Request for Invoicing Documents Analysis

The invoicing documents posted in the system either can be reversed directly, or a reversal request can be created for the document reversal. Reversal of an invoicing document can be due to incorrect invoicing data or a customer request. For reversal to happen, the reversal request/task is created.

The reversal request for the invoicing documents can be viewed using Transaction FKKINV_REV_MON, which also can be accessed under the SAP Easy Access menu: **Accounting · Financial Accounting · Contract Account Receivables & Payables · Convergent Invoicing · Invoicing Documents** (as in Figure 4.142).

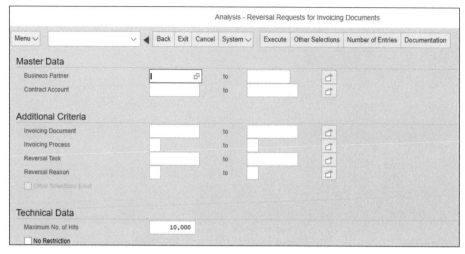

Figure 4.142 Invoice Document Reversal Request Display Screen

4.4.8   Reversal Request for Billing Documents Analysis

Like invoicing document reversal requests, the billing documents posted in the system either can be reversed directly, or a reversal request can be created for the document reversal. Reversal of a billing document can be due to incorrect billing data. For reversal to happen, the reversal request/task is created.

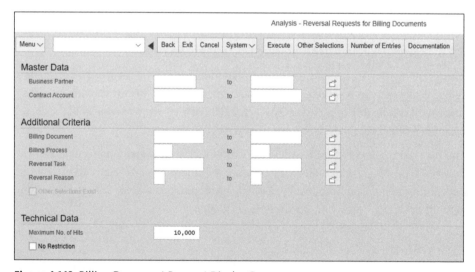

Figure 4.143 Billing Document Request Display Screen

The reversal request for the billing documents can be viewed using Transaction FKK-INVBILL_REV_MON, which also can be accessed under the SAP Easy Access menu: **Accounting · Financial Accounting · Contract Account Receivables & Payables · Convergent Invoicing · Billing Documents** (as in Figure 4.143).

4.5 Summary

You should now understand the consume-to-cash process and the system architecture and various terminology used in SAP Convergent Invoicing.

You also should be able to set up the system with SAP Convergent Invoicing configurations and be able to map your business requirements.

Chapter 5

Contract Accounts Receivable and Payable

This chapter explains how to set up and use Contract Accounts Receivable and Payable (FI-CA). It provides a brief overview of master data and transactional data, some key concepts like account determination, open item management, account balance display, and integration with FI-GL, as well as some of the standard out-of-the-box reporting capabilities and relevant transaction codes for FI-CA.

Contract Accounts Receivable and Payasble (FI-CA) enables subledger accounting for receivables and payables, typically in industries that require processing of huge volumes of business transactions and business partners. It also enables necessary capabilities to manage accounts receivable and payable (e.g., open item management and account balance display) along with capabilities like dunning and interest calculation. Figure 5.1 shows some of the relevant industry applications for the FI-CA solution.

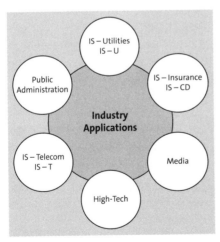

Figure 5.1 Relevant Industry Applications for FI-CA

This chapter describes the relevant master data for posting documents (e.g., business partners, contract accounts, and general ledger accounts) and then shows how to configure and use FI-CA with step-by-step instructions. The chapter concludes with a description of core FI-CA reporting and analytics capabilities.

> **Martex Corp.**
>
> As a quick refresher of our example case study, Martex Corp., a company that distributes software, has transformed itself into a company that distributes cloud products with infrastructure-as-a-service (IaaS) and software-as-a-service (SaaS) offerings. With its new strategy, it obtains products from multiple vendors and sells them to its customers on behalf of those vendors. Each of the products are sold in different types of offerings, such as recurring, usage consumption, one-off, and pay per use. There are two use cases, which were explained in Chapter 1, related to SaaS combo charges and SaaS prorated charges. In this chapter, we will work through the setup and concepts primarily related to account determination, open item management, and account balance display.

SAP Convergent Invoicing, which we discussed in Chapter 4, is a submodule of FI-CA. All the necessary master data attributes that SAP Convergent Invoicing uses for transaction processing is primarily defined in FI-CA. Let's take a look at the following key functionalities carried out in each of the modules within the SAP BRIM solution:

- **Non-SAP system**
  Captures network data usages and sends payload

- **SAP Convergent Mediation by DigitalRoute**
  Transforms raw consumption data into SAP Convergent Charging–readable CSV file

- **SAP Convergent Charging**
  Performs rating and charging on the usage items and creates billable items in SAP Convergent Invoicing

- **SAP Convergent Invoicing**
  Stores rated usage items and performs billing and invoicing

- **Contract Accounts Receivable and Payable**
  Posts receivables from invoicing, process payments, collections, dunning, and more

The steps of the consume-to-cash process are as follows:

1. **Capture of consumption data**

   The usage of a service is captured in a non-SAP system. The usage is the consumption of the service provided by the service provider. The consumption data records details like the time of usage, quantity consumed, and master data of the customer for which consumption is tracked. This consumption data is in a raw format and needs to be formatted before rating can be performed on it.

2. **Transformation of consumption data**

   The consumption data recorded outside of SAP needs to be transformed into an SAP format before it can be used for the rating process. SAP provides SAP Convergent Mediation by DigitalRoute to transform the raw data captured in the non-SAP system and transform it into a format that can be fed into SAP Convergent Charging.

3. **Rating and charging**

   The consumption data record transformed by SAP Convergent Mediation by DigitalRoute is fed into SAP Convergent Charging for the rating and charging process. The rating and charging process calculates the amount of the consumed quantity based on the pricing rules maintained in the SAP Convergent Charging system. The calculated amount is then associated with the business partner account that has consumed the service in the charging process. The rated and charged consumption items, which are known as billable items, are sent to the SAP Convergent Invoicing system for the billing and invoicing process.

4. **Billing and invoicing**

   The billable items received from SAP Convergent Charging act as an input to the billing process. The billing process groups and aggregates the billable items and creates the billing documents, which are used as an input to the invoicing process. The invoicing process groups and aggregates the billing documents and creates the invoicing document that is sent to the customer.

5. **Receivables management**

   The invoicing process creates a posting document for the receivables posting in FI-CA. The posting document posts the accounting entries to the customer account, against which payment is received from the customer.

As described in Chapter 4, the receivables created by the invoicing process finally gets posted in FI-CA as a subledger posting. The payment is later realized in FI-CA, and the customer open items and the account balance is managed. The general ledger postings are transferred to financials as a result of general ledger integration from FI-CA.

Figure 5.2 shows the configuration node for Contract Accounts Receivable and Payable.

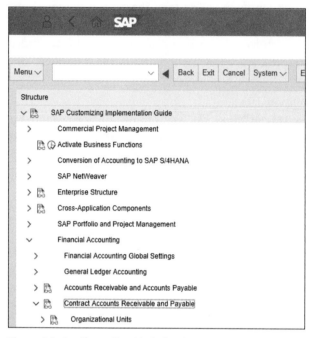

Figure 5.2 Configuration Node for Contract Accounts Receivable and Payable

5.1   Master Data

In this section, we will look at the master data elements in FI-CA relevant to the Martex case study established in Chapter 1. The master data elements will be required to create and process transactions using FI-CA. We will discuss business partners, business agreements, products, contract accounts, provider contracts, and partner agreements.

The following master data objects will be explained in detail in this chapter:

- Business partner
- Contract account
- Provider contract
- Partner agreement

The following master data objects have been explained in detail in other chapters, so in this chapter we will only call out their significance for transaction postings from a FI-CA perspective:

- Business agreement (SAP BRIM, subscription order management)
- Product (SAP BRIM, subscription order management)

5.1.1   Business Partner

This section will explain the concept of the business partner master data object from a FI-CA perspective. We will go through the configuration set up for the business partner in FI-CA and discuss why we need a business partner object as a prerequisite for account determination, open item management, and account balance display.

In this chapter, we will be referencing a customer or a vendor in FI-CA as a business partner. A business partner can be an organization, a person, or a group of persons or organizations that have a business relationship with a company.

A business partner can also be extended to various partner roles (e.g., general business partner, contract partner, customer, or vendor).

Figure 5.3 shows the business partner view in FI-CA under the business partner general role.

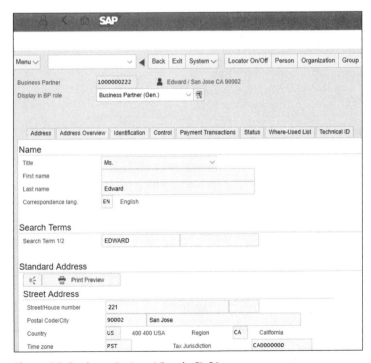

Figure 5.3 Business Partner View in FI-CA

Use Transaction BP to view a business partner in FI-CA.

Next, let's extend the business partner to the contract partner role to ensure that a corresponding contract account is created for the business partner.

Figure 5.4 shows some of the business partner roles in the **Display in BP Role** drop-down that the business partner can be extended to, including the **Business Partner (Gen.)** (general business partner) and **Contract Partner** roles, which are particularly relevant for our case study.

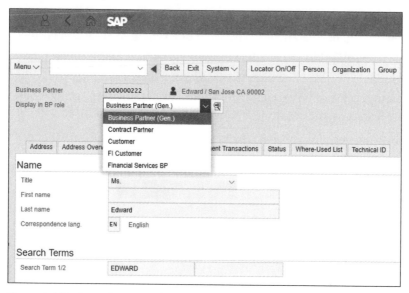

Figure 5.4 Business Partner Roles

The general business partner role enables maintenance of business partner general data such as name, address, and payment data (bank details, payment card information, etc.). In FI-CA, it is necessary to create a business partner and a contract account to be able to record a transaction in the system.

We will walk through the key integration points and setup needed to create a business partner in FI-CA. Similar set up is also needed in SAP CRM to enable business partner setup and replication to FI-CA.

Figure 5.5 shows the master data flow across SAP systems.

Now let's configure a business partner. To configure a business partner in SAP ERP or SAP S/4HANA, navigate to **SAP Customizing Implementation Guide · Cross Application Components · SAP Business Partner · Activation Status for Functions**.

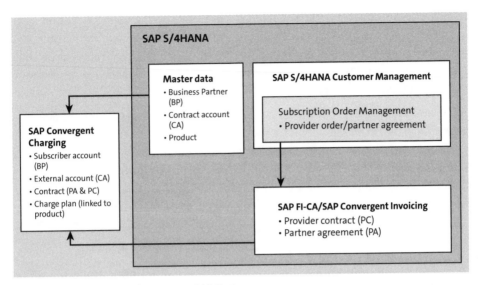

Figure 5.5 Master Data Flow across SAP Systems

Figure 5.6 shows the functions necessary to be activated for business partners. Activate the functions as shown. There are quite a few other functions that are available and can be activated as needed.

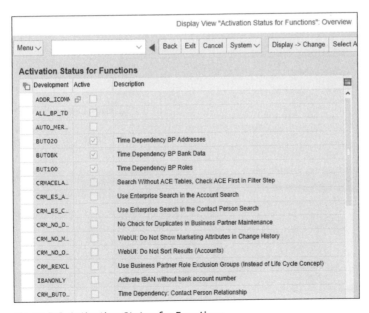

Figure 5.6 Activation Status for Functions

Several standard business partner roles are delivered by the application, and each role determines the functions that can be carried out with the business partner. The business partner is the highest level, equivalent to a customer in accounts receivable. The contract account is the next level. A contract account cannot be created without a corresponding business partner.

To create a contract account for a business partner, the prerequisite is to extend the business partner to an MKK contract partner role. To create the contract partner role, navigate to **SAP Customizing Implementation Guide · Cross Application Components · SAP Business Partner · Business Partner · Basic Settings · Business Partner Roles · Define BP Roles**. Then, click **New Entries** and create the MKK role. Once the MKK role has been created and saved, the new entry is visible under the list of business partner roles, as shown in Figure 5.7.

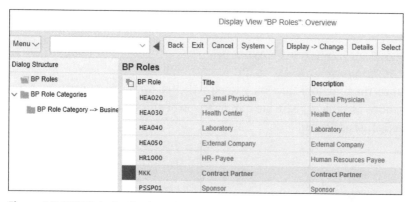

Figure 5.7 MKK Role for Contract Partner Created as New Business Partner Role

Now, let's assign the business transactions, such as Business Partner Usage (BPUS) and Change Business Partner (CHAN), functions needed for the MKK role. Click **New Entries** as shown in Figure 5.8, then assign BPUS and CHAN as shown in Figure 5.9.

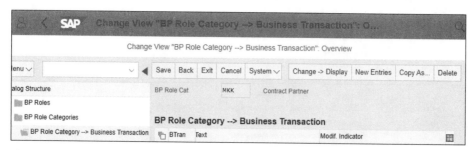

Figure 5.8 Business Partner Role Category to Business Transaction Assignment

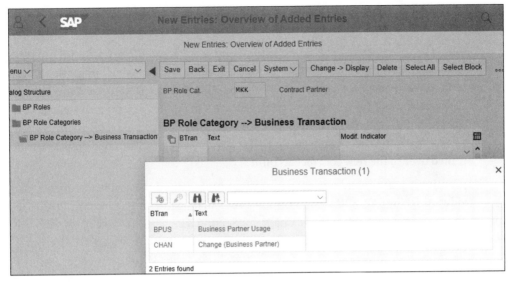

Figure 5.9 Business Transaction Selection

What we have seen thus far, is creation of the MKK 'Contract Partner' Role relevant for Contract Accounts Receivable and Payable as shown in Figure 5.10.

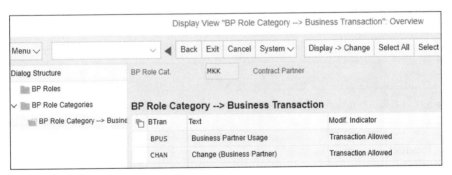

Figure 5.10 Business Transactions Assigned to MKK Contract Partner Business Partner Role

5.1.2   Business Agreement

A business agreement is a master data object that is the equivalent of a contract account in FI-CA. One business partner can have several business agreements associated with it. Business agreements house data that controls processes in billing and invoicing in SAP Convergent Invoicing, payments, correspondences, and tax calculations.

A business agreement created in SAP BRIM, subscription order management is replicated to FI-CA as a contract account with SAP-standard replications.

Navigate to the following SAP Customizing Implementation Guide menu path **Financial Accounting · Contract Accounts Receivable and Payable · Integration · Customer Relationship Management · Business Agreement · Determine Template for Contract Account for Replication**. Next, as shown in Figure 5.11, enter a reference contract account, which will be used as a template when a business agreement is replicated as a contract account in FI-CA. All the attributes available in the template will be copied over to the new contract account.

A business partner and business agreement are required to be able to create a provider order in SAP BRIM, subscription order management. For more information about business agreements, see Chapter 2, Section 2.1.2.

With SAP S/4HANA release 1809 release, SAP has moved SAP BRIM, subscription order management to customer management within the SAP S/4HANA system.

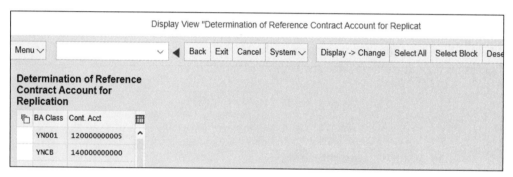

Figure 5.11 FI-CA Integration with SAP CRM for Business Agreement Replication

5.1.3   Product

A product is another component necessary to create a provider order. The product can either be a tangible product defined within materials management that contains all the relevant information required for purchasing, sales, accounting, and so on, or a subscription product defined within FI-CA as a FI-CA product that contains a lean product structure required for subscription processing (as explained in Chapter 4, Section 4.1.2). As illustrated in Figure 5.12, the FI-CA subscription product is a lean structure containing the description of the product and the sales area data. Once created in SAP BRIM, subscription order management, the product will be replicated to FI-CA.

Use Transaction FPPRD3 to view the FI-CA product in FI-CA.

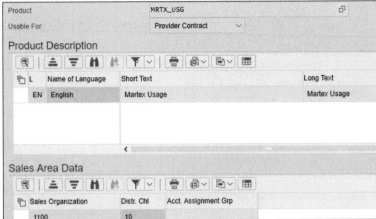

Figure 5.12 FI-CA Product in Contract Accounts Receivable and Payable

The next step is to define the type of product to be used for a provider contract.

5.1.4   Contract Account

A contract account is an essential master data object in FI-CA that stores payment/ tax, dunning/correspondence, and SAP Convergent Invoicing attributes that will be applicable for the contract items created for the contract account. It is a mandatory object required to create billable items in SAP Convergent Invoicing. The billable items are created for a business partner and contract account combination. A contract account will be extended to a company code, and all the attributes stored in the contract account will be at the company code level.

Figure 5.13 illustrates the relationship between a business partner and a contract account. As shown, the business partner is extended to one or more sales organizations. A contract account is extended to a company code. A 1:N relationship exists between a business partner and a contract account.

For Martex Corp., a business partner and a contract account will need to be created to create billable items for the business partner and contract account combination.

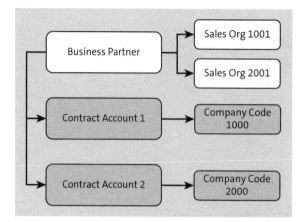

Figure 5.13 Business Partner and Contract Account Relationship

A contract account category categorizes contract accounts that require similar controls or reporting for a specific business. Now that you understand what a contract account is and its relationship with the business partner, let's configure the number ranges and the contract account categories.

First, navigate to menu path **SAP Customizing Implementation Guide · Financial Accounting · Contract Accounts Receivable and Payable · Basic Functions · Contract Accounts · Number Ranges and Contract Account Categories · Define Number Ranges**. Here you can define the number ranges for the contract account, as shown in Figure 5.14.

No	From No.	To Number	NR Status	Ext	
01	100000000000	109999999999	0	☐	
Y1	110000000000	119999999999	0	☑	
Y2	120000000000	129999999999	120000000799	☐	

Edit Intervals: Contract Account, Object FKK_KONTO

Menu ∨ · Save · Back · Exit · Cancel · System ∨ · Display <-> Change

Figure 5.14 Number Ranges for Contract Account

Next, navigate to menu path **SAP Customizing Implementation Guide · Financial Accounting · Contract Accounts Receivable and Payable · Basic Functions · Contract Accounts · Number Ranges and Contract Account Categories · Configure Contract**

Acct Categories and Assign Number Ranges. Here you can configure the contract account categories and assign the number ranges.

Figure 5.15 illustrates the definition of contract account categories and number range assignments for contract account creation.

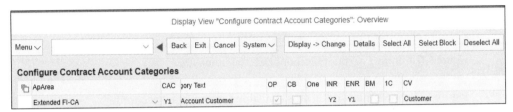

Figure 5.15 Configure Contract Account Categories

Contract account relationships are required to determine the relationship that the business partner holds with the contract account. If there are multiple business partners for a contract account, the account relationship differentiates the relations that each business partner holds for a contract account.

Navigate to menu path **SAP Customizing Implementation Guide · Financial Accounting · Contract Accounts Receivable and Payable · Basic Functions · Contract Accounts · Contract Account Relationships · Define Contract Account/Business Partner Relationships**. Here, assign **Account Holder** as the account relationship (**Acct Rel.**).

As shown in Figure 5.16, the account relationship is defined to determine the relation between the business partner and the contract account.

Partner Account Relationships		
Acct Rel.	Description	AH
Z1	Account Holder	☑

Figure 5.16 Definition of Partner Account Relationship

Now, navigate to **SAP Customizing Implementation Guide · Financial Accounting · Contract Accounts Receivable and Payable · Basic Functions · Contract Accounts · Define Account Determination Characteristics**. Here you can configure the account determination ID, a key characteristic that will be used in subsequent configurations to automatically determine the general ledger accounts for posting a document in FI-CA (see Figure 5.17).

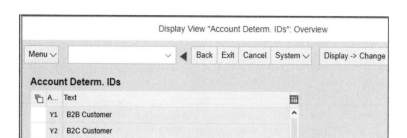

Figure 5.17 Contract Account: Account Determination IDs

Figure 5.18 shows the various tabs available for a contract account.

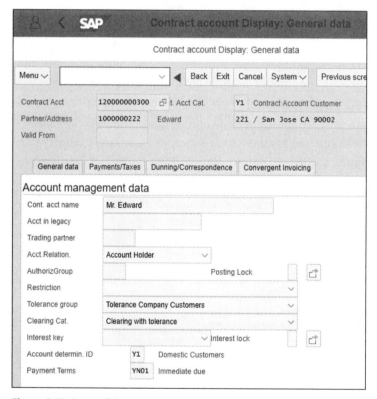

Figure 5.18 General Data

The business agreement 120000000300 created in SAP BRIM, subscription order management for the Martex Corp. case study has been replicated as a contract account. The tabs for the contract account are as follows:

- **General Data**

  As shown in Figure 5.18, the **General Data** tab contains some key information, such as contract account name, account reference from legacy, account relationship with the business partner, tolerance group, account determination ID, payment terms, and so on.

  The values updated in this object will be common for all the billable items created for this contract account.

- **Payments/Taxes**

  As shown in Figure 5.19, the **Payments/Taxes** tab contains some key information related to the group: standard company code information, incoming and outgoing payment methods, and more.

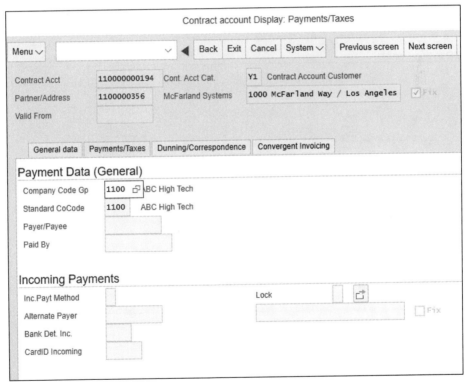

Figure 5.19 Contract Account: Payment/Taxes Tab

- **Dunning/Correspondence**

  As shown in Figure 5.20, the **Dunning/Correspondence** tab contains key information such as alternative dunning recipient, dunning procedure, dunning lock, correspondence controls, and so on. We will not be using this tab for the Martex case study.

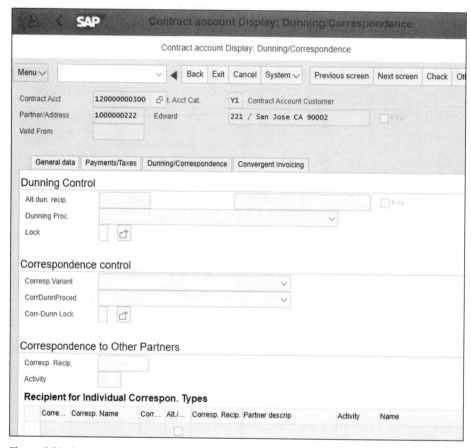

Figure 5.20 Contract Account: Dunning/Correspondence Tab

- **Convergent Invoicing**

  As shown in Figure 5.21, the **Convergent Invoicing** tab contains some of the key billing/invoicing attributes that will be used to determine the selection criteria for the accounts for billing/invoicing, as well as for determination of the billing cycles for the periodic bills.

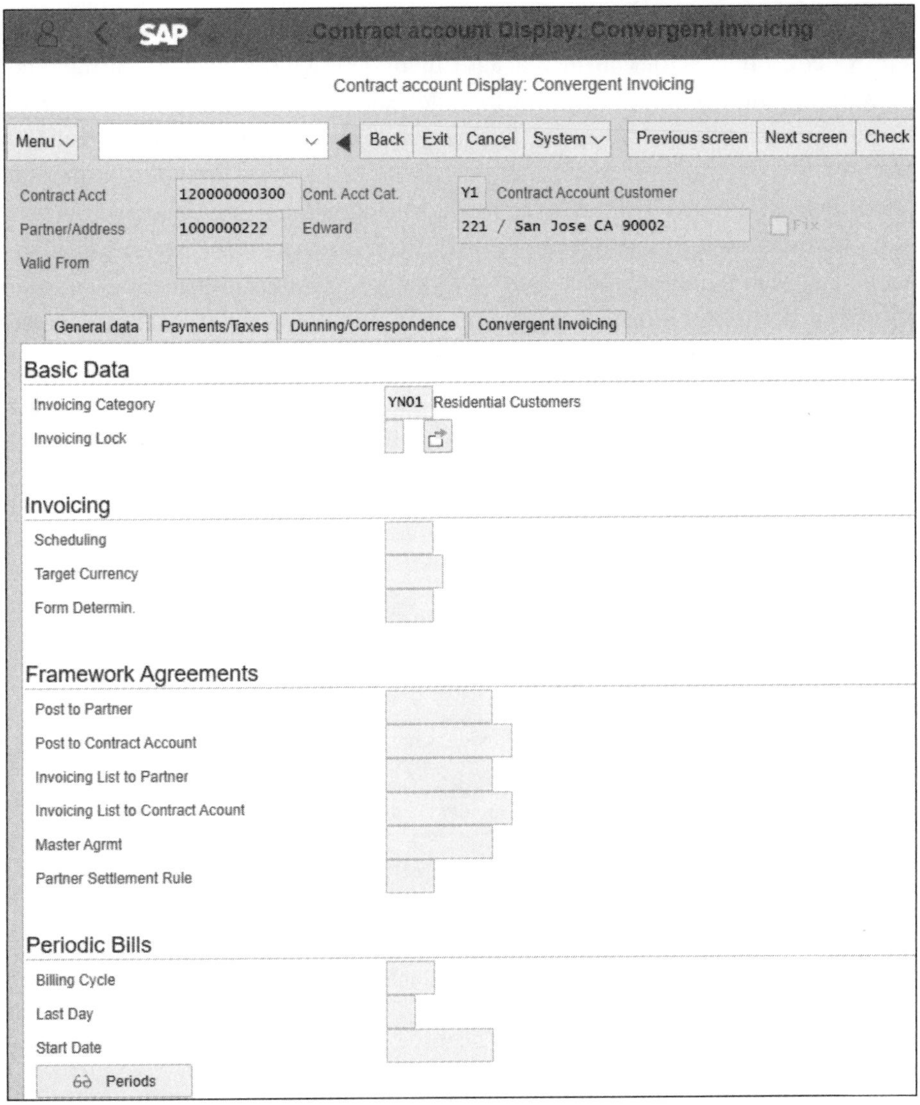

Figure 5.21 Contract Account: Convergent Invoicing Tab

The business agreement created in SAP BRIM, subscription order management is replicated in FI-CA as a contract account. This is defined in FI-CA as part of FI-CA integration with SAP CRM. See Section 5.1.2 for FI-CA integration with SAP CRM in order to replicate the business agreement as a contract account in FI-CA.

5.1.5   Provider Contract

A provider contract is the contractual agreement between the business partner and the provider offering the contract. The provider contract contains a header section to capture general data such as name, business partner, and contract header validity dates. It also contains an item section in which some key item level details are captured, such as item text; contract account; master agreement (see Chapter 2, Section 2.1.4); organizational data determining which sales organization, distribution channel, and division combination the contract belongs to; product information; and billing cycle and discount information. There can be multiple provider contracts created for a business partner and contract account combination.

Figure 5.22 illustrates the relationship between the business partner, contract account, and provider contract. As seen above, the provider contract is a lower-level item that represents the contract. A provider contract can also contain multiple items pertaining to different contract accounts.

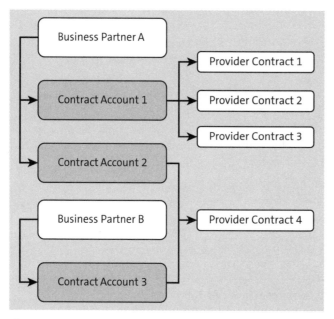

Figure 5.22 Business Partner, Contract Account, and Provider Contract Relationship

The configuration for provider contract setup in FI-CA is found under **Contract Account Receivables & Payable • Basic Functions • Provider Contract • Activate Provider Contract**.

Now let's define the central settings for the provider contract, as shown in Figure 5.23.

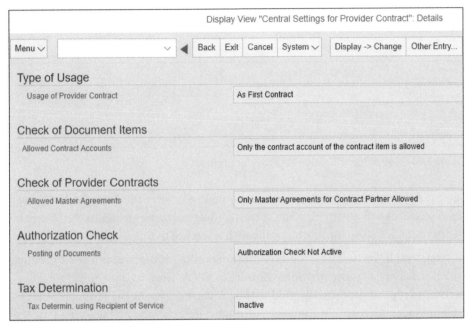

Figure 5.23 Defining Provider Contract in FI-CA

In addition to this setup, it is necessary to define identification types for the provider contract. For the Martex example, a customer ID has been defined to uniquely identify the provider contract in FI-CA.

The configuration to define types of IDs for the provider contract setup in FI-CA is found under **Contract Account Receivables & Payables • Basic Functions • Provider Contract • Define the Type of ID**.

As shown in Figure 5.24, Customer ID **CN** has been configured as a unique identifier for the contract. A contract created for a customer will have a unique identifier (e.g., a mobile number).

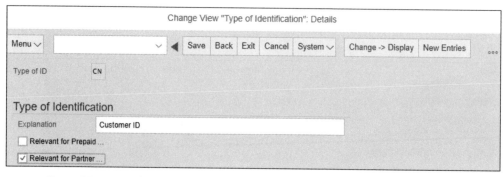

Figure 5.24 Type of Identification for Provider Contract

Once the type of identification has been configured, select the **Relevant for Partner** checkbox. This will ensure that the corresponding partner agreement (for any partner payouts) is looked up automatically with reference to this unique ID.

As explained in Section 5.1.3, the subscription product is defined as a FI-CA product, which is assigned to the provider contract in FI-CA. Now, as shown in Figure 5.25, define the type of product assigned to the provider contract. The FI-CA product is a lean product structure that contains the product description and sales area data. The menu path to maintain the central settings for a product is **SAP Customizing Implementation Guide · Financial Accounting · Contract Accounts Receivable and Payable · Basic Functions · Provider Contract · Make Central Settings for Products**.

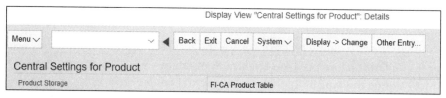

Figure 5.25 Product Storage Definition Indicating Product Used for Provider Contract Is FI-CA Product

The setup explained above was focused on the key configuration elements required to create and replicate a provider contract in FI-CA.

Now, use Transaction FP_VT3 to view the provider contract in FI-CA, which has been created for the Martex example case study. Figure 5.26 shows the details of the general data stored in the provider contract. This represents the header section of the contract. Here you see key attributes like **Contract Start Date**, **Contract End Date**, and **Company Code**.

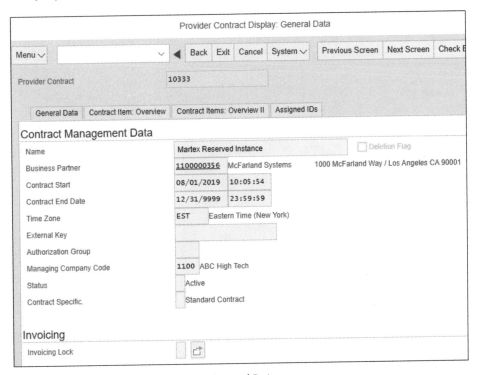

Figure 5.26 Provider Contract in FI-CA: General Data

Figure 5.27 and Figure 5.28 show the contract item view of the provider contract. The item-level details—**Valid From**, **Valid To**, **Contract Account**, **Sales Organization Data**, **Company Code**, and **Product**—are stored in this section.

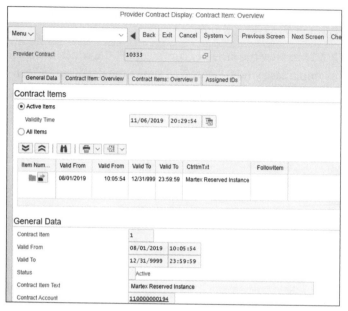

Figure 5.27 Provider Contract in FI-CA: Contract Item: Overview 1

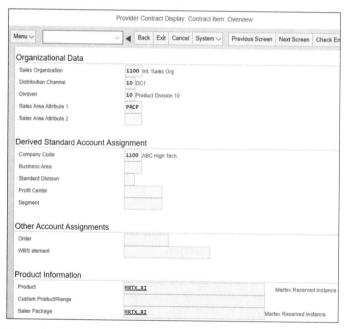

Figure 5.28 Provider Contract in FI-CA: Contract Item: Overview 2

As shown in Figure 5.29, the **Customer ID** configured to uniquely identify the contract, **CN**, is stored in this section of the provider contract.

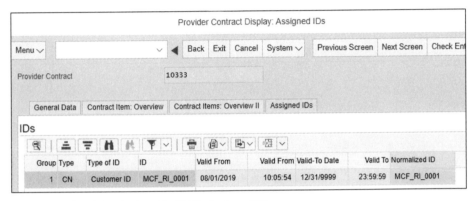

Figure 5.29 Provider Contract in FI-CA: Assigned IDs

Billable items created for the provider contract inherit the attributes stored in the provider contract. For example, the billing cycle stored in the provider contract will be used to determine the billing date for the billable item. If the billing cycle is not stored in the provider contract, the billing cycle at the contract account level will be picked up for processing. The values for the attributes maintained at the provider contract level precede the values maintained for the attributes at the contract account level.

5.1.6   Partner Agreement

A partner agreement is the contractual agreement between the business partner and the provider offering the contract. The partner agreement contains a header section to capture general data such as name, business partner, and contract header validity dates. It also contains an item section in which some key item-level details are captured, such as item text; contract account; master agreement (see Chapter 2, Section 2.1.4); organizational data determining which sales organization, distribution channel, and division combination the contract belongs to; product information; and billing cycle and discount information. There can be multiple provider contracts created for a business partner and contract account combination.

Now use Transaction FP_PV3 to view the partner agreement object in FI-CA. Figure 5.30 illustrates the partner agreement object in FI-CA representing the vendor agreement.

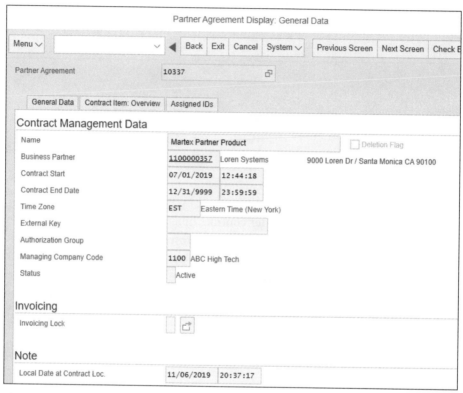

Figure 5.30 Partner Agreement in FI-CA: General Data

This object has been replicated in FI-CA from SAP BRIM, subscription order management. The **General Data** tab contains some key attributes like the business partner (representing a vendor, Loren Systems), contract start date, contract end date, and company code.

Figure 5.31 shows the contract item view of the partner agreement. Note the key fields like **Valid From**, **Valid To**, **Contract Account**, and **Partner Settlement Rule** that are stored in this section.

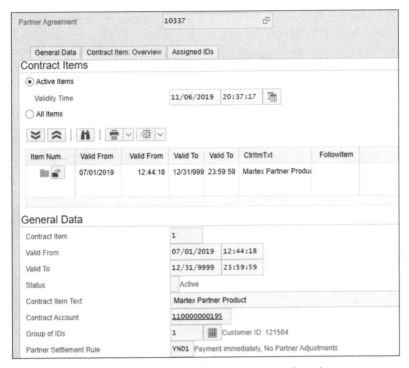

Figure 5.31 Partner Agreement in FI-CA: Contract Item: Overview

Chapter 4, Section 4.2.6 explains the partner settlement setup and the partner settlement rule definition in detail. The partner settlement rule is referenced in the partner agreement.

Figure 5.32 shows customer ID CN, which is referenced in the partner agreement.

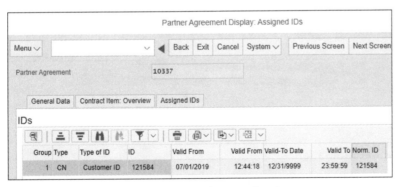

Figure 5.32 Partner Agreement in FI-CA (Assigned IDs)

As explained in Chapter 4, Section 4.2.6, this ID will be referenced in the revenue bill-able item, based on which the partner agreement will automatically be determined for any given transaction relevant for partner payouts.

5.2 Configuring Contracts Accounts Receivable and Payable

In this section, we will continue to look at some of key configuration elements for posting a document, viewing the account balance display, and open item manage-ment in FI-CA. We will explain key concepts like main transactions and subtransac-tions, needed to determine accounts for posting a FI-CA document. Figure 5.33 shows how the general ledger account for receivables and revenue and expense is derived based on the combination of key transaction attributes like company code, division, account determination, main transaction, and subtransaction.

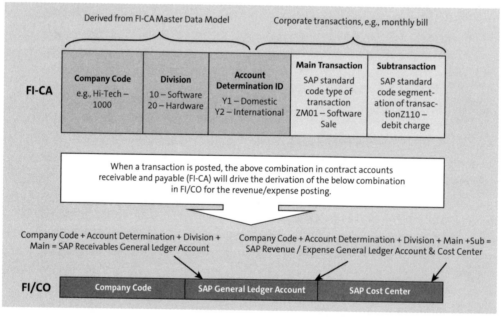

Figure 5.33 General Ledger Account Determination for Financial Posting

5.2.1 Account Determination

In this section, we will explain basic concepts like the account determination ID, main transactions, and subtransactions related to FI-CA document postings and will configure the same in FI-CA. The account determination ID helps automatically determine the general ledger account for a business transaction. See Section 5.1.4 for more details on account determination ID setup. When an invoicing document in SAP Convergent Invoicing is posted, a financial posting can be automatically enabled in FI-CA. The subledger posting and a general ledger posting is possible with a combination of company code, account determination, division, and main and subtransactions.

Main Transaction

The main transaction is a key element used to determine the receivables and payables account, along with a combination of other document posting characteristics, as shown in Figure 5.33. Each main transaction has a description associated with the definition, which is printed on the customer's invoice.

The configuration setup for main transactions is found under **Contract Account Receivables & Payables · Basic Functions · Postings and Documents · Document · Maintain Document Assignments · Maintain Main Transaction**. Now, create a main transaction as shown in Figure 5.34. This will be the main transaction used to determine the account assignment for the Martex example case study.

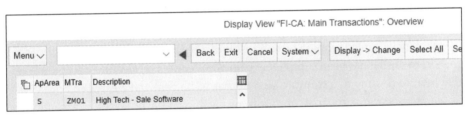

Figure 5.34 FI-CA Main Transaction

Subtransactions

The subtransactions are key elements used to determine the revenue and expense accounts, along with a combination of other document posting characteristics, as shown in Figure 5.33. See Section 5.2.5 for further details. Subtransactions also control the following:

- Tax determination
- Debit/credit posting for a transaction
- Additional account assignments (company account assignment and business area)

The configuration setup for subtransactions is found under **Contract Account Receivables & Payables · Basic Functions · Postings and Documents · Document · Maintain Document Assignments · Maintain Sub Transaction**. Now, create a subtransaction as shown in Figure 5.35 to determine the account assignment for the Martex example.

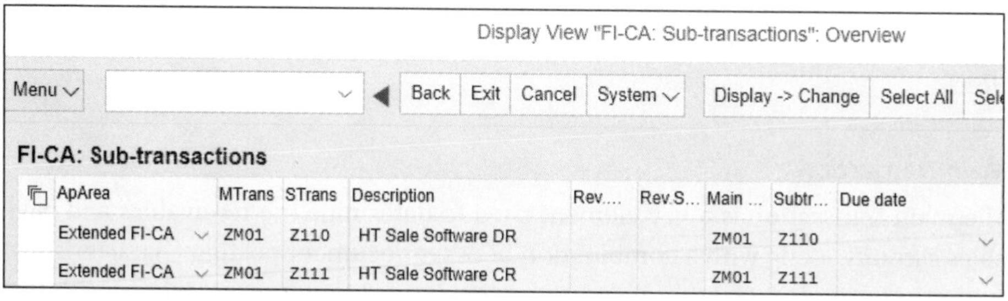

Display View "FI-CA: Sub-transactions": Overview									
Menu ∨		∨ ◀	Back	Exit	Cancel	System ∨	Display -> Change	Select All	Sel

FI-CA: Sub-transactions

	ApArea	MTrans	STrans	Description	Rev....	Rev.S...	Main ...	Subtr...	Due date
	Extended FI-CA ∨	ZM01	Z110	HT Sale Software DR			ZM01	Z110	∨
	Extended FI-CA ∨	ZM01	Z111	HT Sale Software CR			ZM01	Z111	∨

Figure 5.35 FI-CA: Subtransactions

Once the main and subtransactions are defined, the combination of these can be configured to determine the financial postings for any given transaction. See Section 5.2.5 for more on posting area 2610 (account assignment for general ledger items) and posting area 2611 (general ledger determination for business partner items).

5.2.2   Open Item Management

Every financial subledger posting as a result of a business transaction remains as an open item until it has been completely paid. An accounts receivable or accounts payable invoice posting to a contract account has to be paid and cleared to appear as a closed transaction. Similar to accounts receivable, FI-CA provides a capability for users to manage such open accounts receivable or accounts payable transactions.

Every open subledger posting can be tracked under the FI-CA subledger as an open item against which an incoming payment can be received or an outgoing payment can be posted. Various screen layouts can be configured to ensure that select fields relevant to the business process are available for display as part of an open item report. The report provides a view of open invoices as well as unapplied payments (if any), which aids accounts receivable in carrying out cash application.

Let's now look at some of the key steps involved in configuring open item management in FI-CA. To start, navigate to menu path **Contract Account Receivables & Payables · Basic Functions · Open Item Management · Define Line Layout Variants for Open Item Processing**.

Next, configure a line layout YN1 with the variant fields as shown in Figure 5.36. Some of the fields configured are GPART (Business Partner), VKONT (Contract Account), OBPEL (Document Number), FAEDN (Net Due Date), and TXTU1 (Text). You can choose any field available in the FI-CA open item management table FKKCLIT as required.

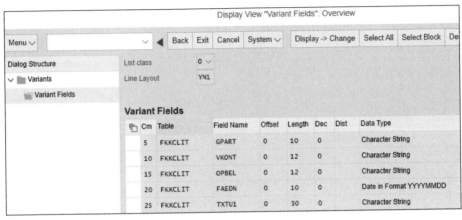

Figure 5.36 Line Layout Variants for Open Item Processing

Next, use Transaction FP06 (Account Maintenance: Process Open Items) to view the layout you have defined. As shown in Figure 5.37, enter the business partner ID, then press ⟨Enter⟩.

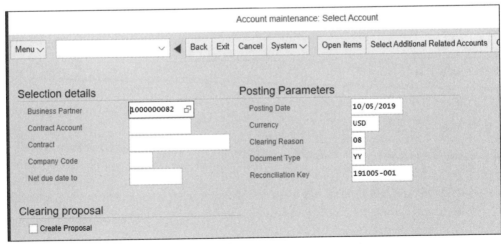

Figure 5.37 Open Item Management: Transaction FP06, Account Maintenance: Process Open Items

As shown in Figure 5.38, the fields visible are as configured in the line layout variants for open item management.

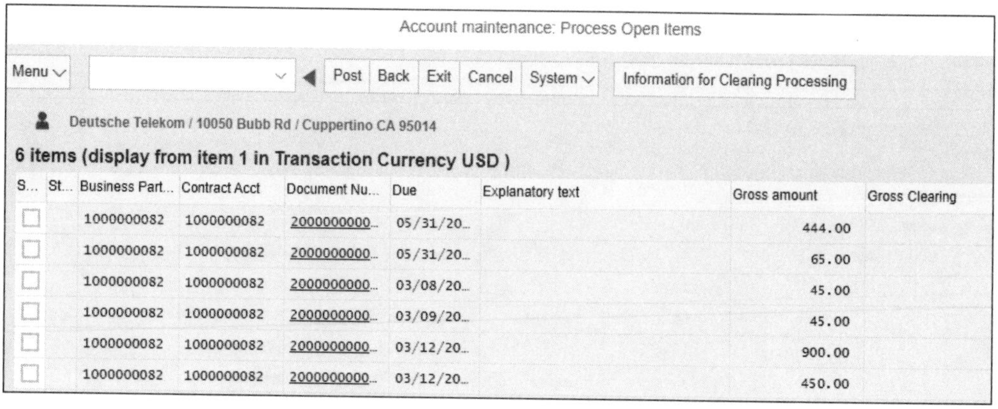

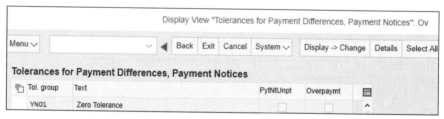

Figure 5.38 Account Maintenance: Process Open Items

Appropriate tolerance groups can also be defined if needed to accept any minor payment differences. The tolerance group is primarily defined in FI-AR and can be invoked as a configuration item within FI-CA.

The configuration setup for open item management is found under **Contract Account Receivables & Payables** • **Basic Functions** • **Open Item Management** • **Maintain Tolerance Groups**. The next step is to configure the tolerance group as shown in Figure 5.39.

Figure 5.39 Tolerance Group for Payment Differences in FI-CA

Once the tolerance group has been defined, next step is to determine the dollar or percentage of tolerance allowed, which in this case has been set to zero (**Zero Tolerance**) as shown in Figure 5.40.

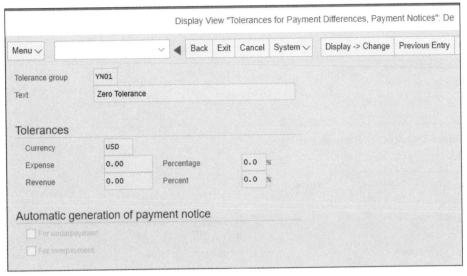

Figure 5.40 Tolerance Amount for Payment Differences during Open Item Clearing

5.2.3   Account Balance Display

The account balance display provides a detailed view of the account transactional information, including any open, cleared, or statistical transactions for a business partner. The account balance can be viewed for a given business partner and contract account relation or for all the contract accounts for a business partner. The report also can be executed for a group of business partners. Various screen layouts can be configured to ensure that selection fields relevant to the business process are available for display as part of the report output.

The configuration setup for account balance display is found under **Contract Account Receivables & Payables • Basic Functions • Account Balance Display • Define List Category**. Now, create an account balance list type as the first step. As shown in Figure 5.41, create your own **List Type** (in this case, enter "ALLES" for *all items*) definition for the account balance.

Once the list type has been created, refer to Figure 5.42 to configure further selections to display **Open Items**, **Cleared Items**, and **Nonstatistical Items**. The list type will need to be selected on the account balance display screen to execute the report.

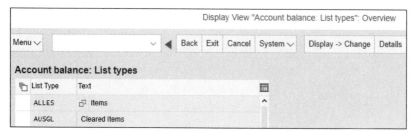

Figure 5.41 Account Balance: List Type

List Type	ALLES	All Items

Item Selection
- ☑ Open items
- ☑ Cleared items
- ☐ With other partners' postings
- ☑ Non-stat. items

Selection by Installment Plans
- ◉ Inst. Plan Items
- ○ Source Items

Statistical Items
- ☑ All
- ☐ Dwn pyt request
- ☐ Quotation
- ☐ Outstndng charges
- ☐ BB Plan
- ☐ Install. Plan Itm
- ☐ Collective Bill
- ☐ Payment request
- ☐ Cash security deposit requests
- ☐ Down Pmt Requests- Invoicing
- ☐ Payment Requests- Invoicing

Further Settings
- ☐ Determine Payment Status

Figure 5.42 Account Balance: List Type: Selection

Once the account balance list type has been configured, the next step is to configure the line layout variants for the account balance display. Navigate to menu path **Contract account receivables & Payables · Basic Functions · Account Balance Display · Define Line Layout Variants for Account Balance**. Now configure the line layout as shown in Figure 5.43. FI-CA provides the capability of defining your own line layout for the account balance display. This configuration screen contains two main sections. Enter the header of the layout with the desired spacing in the **Text** section.

Next select the **Fields of the Variant** that need to be displayed on the account balance report. See Figure 5.43 for the field selections.

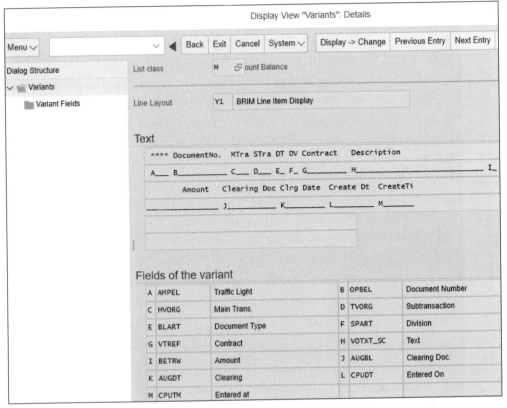

Figure 5.43 Account Balance Display: Line Layout Variant

For further details on how to use the account balance display, Section 5.4.5.

5.2.4   Payments and Returns

Similar to accounts recievable, FI-CA also provides standard out-of-the-box capabilities to handle incoming payments to clear open accounts receivable and outgoing payments to clear open accounts payable invoices. FI-CA also supports the returns process in case of payment returns from the bank.

This section highlights the capabilities of incoming and outgoing payments that can be enabled within FI-CA, including payment lot, check lot, credit card lot, and more.

Clarification account postings, which are a key feature of FI-CA, enables posting to a clarification account in case a corresponding open item or contract account is not determined automatically for payment posting.

This book does not dwell on the specifics of enabling incoming payments and clearing the open accounts receivable posted for our running example. Our primary focus is on the integration aspects of FI-CA within the SAP BRIM solution.

The automatic payment program within FI-CA enables payment postings and clearing of open accounts receivable and accounts payable transactions, in addition to creating a payment medium output with payment instructions to carry out bank transfers, check payments, and so on.

Electronic bank statement postings within FI-CA enable bank statement reconciliation and clearing of open accounts receivable postings in case of bank transfers. The bank statement setup includes integration aspects of the electronic bank statement setup between FI and FI-CA.

As of SAP S/4HANA 1909, FI-CA also provides a feature to receive and automate payment clearing by receiving bank files that contain a customer's check information.

5.2.5   Integration with SAP Convergent Charging

Replication of business partners (as external accounts in SAP Convergent Charging) and contract accounts (as subscriber accounts in SAP Convergent Charging) is enabled via integration between FI-CA and SAP Convergent Charging. Similarly, provider contracts are also replicated from SAP BRIM, subscription order management to SAP Convergent Invoicing/FI-CA and then to SAP Convergent Charging.

Some of the key integration aspects of contract accounts receivable and payable with SAP Convergent Charging are as follows:

- **Activate joint replication of all master data**
  This option ensures that the business partner, contract account and provider contract is replicated from FI-CA to SAP Convergent Charing at the same time. The business partner is created first, followed by the contract account, and finally the provider contract. If this option is selected, the business partner and the contract

account remain in FI-CA and are not replicated to SAP Convergent Charging until the provider contract is created in FI-CA.

Navigate to menu path **Contract Accounts Receivable and Payable · Integration · Convergent Charging · Activate Joint Replication of All Master Data**. Select the **Joint Replication of All Master Data to SAP CC** checkbox, as shown in Figure 5.44.

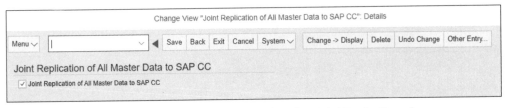

Figure 5.44 FI-CA Integration with SAP Convergent Charging: Joint Replication of Master Data

- **Make specifications for connecting multiple FI-CA systems to an SAP Convergent Charging system**
  It is possible to connect multiple FI-CA systems to an SAP Convergent Charging System. This a feature provided by SAP BRIM. We are not using this feature for our example case study, so we will not be activating it.

- **Specifications for connecting multiple SAP CC systems to a FI-CA system**
  It is also possible to connect multiple SAP Convergent Charging systems to a FI-CA system. We are not using this feature for our example case study, so we will not be activating it.

Master data replication between SAP BRIM, subscription order management, SAP Convergent Charging, and SAP Convergent Invoicing can be seen in Figure 5.45.

In addition to this integration setup, SOAMANAGER settings are needed to enable replication of data and transactions between SAP BRIM, subscription order management, SAP Convergent Charging, and SAP Convergent Invoicing. As discussed in Chapter 3, SAP Convergent Charging is a Java-based application, and web service settings are required for SAP BRIM, subscription order management and SAP Convergent Invoicing to communicate with SAP Convergent Charging.

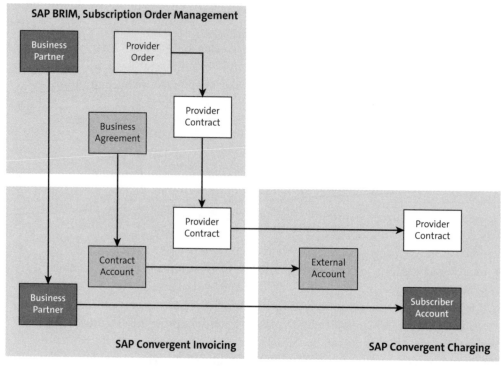

Figure 5.45 Master Data Replication

5.2.6   Integration with General Ledger

This section explains the capability of transferring general ledger summary records from FI-CA to general ledger. All of the financial documents posted in FI-CA are eventually transferred to general ledger for reporting.

Let's discuss the reconciliation key (as in Figure 5.46). It's a key that stores a summary of all the line items resulting from the FI-CA posting. This key is stored in the **Document Headers** section of the documents transferred. The reconciliation key is used to reconcile the FI-CA document postings with the corresponding general ledger postings. The reconciliation key can be determined automatically by background system batch runs, as well as manually during any foreground execution of a transaction.

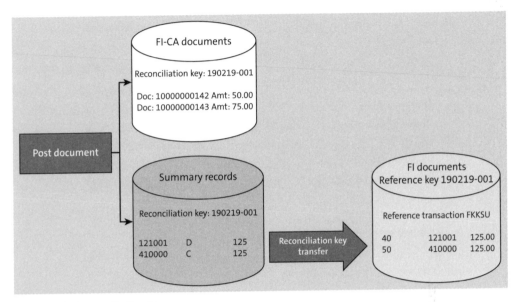

Figure 5.46 Reconciliation Key

Reconciliation key statuses are described in Table 5.1.

Status	Description
Created/open	Postings can be made under the key
Closed	No further postings can be made under the key and key is ready for transfer
Transferred	Indicates whether the key is transferred to general ledger and profitability analysis

Table 5.1 Reconciliation Key Status

Now that you have learned about the reconciliation key, let's use Transaction FPF3 to display the reconciliation key in FI-CA (as in Figure 5.47).

Click on **Totals Records** to view all of the documents tied to the reconciliation key that are related to the general ledger account. As shown in Figure 5.48, a detailed list of multiple records tied to the reconciliation key is displayed.

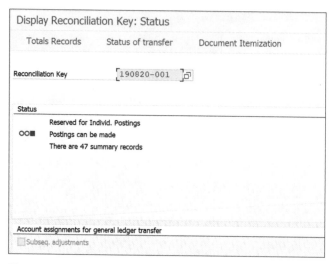

Figure 5.47 Reconciliation Key Display Screen

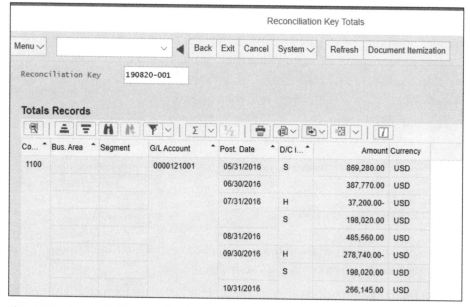

Figure 5.48 Reconciliation Key: Totals

Double-click a line item to view the documents tied to that line item. As shown in Figure 5.49, here you can view the document itemization of the posting totals.

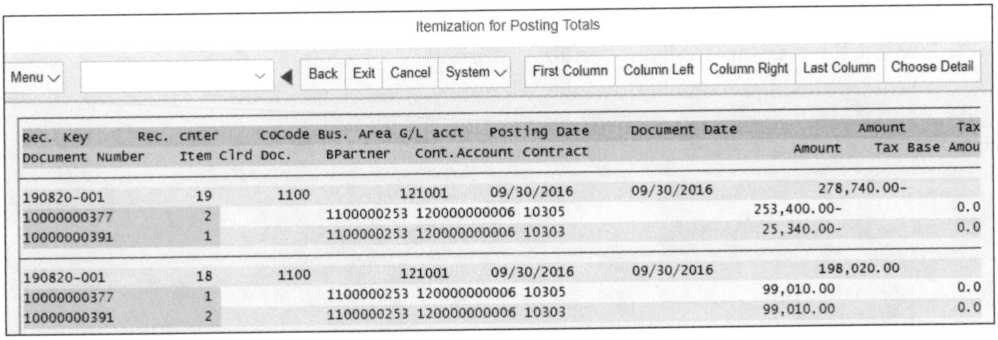

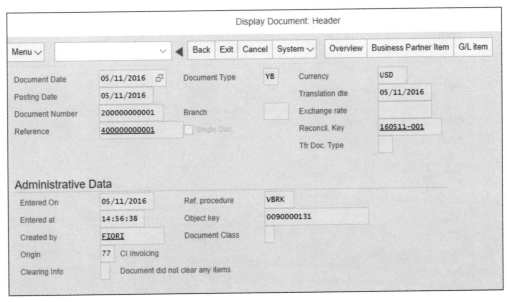

Figure 5.49 Reconciliation Key: Itemization for Posting Totals

Next, use Transaction FPE3 to view a FI-CA document and view the reconciliation key, which is present in the document header of every FI-CA document regardless of its origin. As shown in Figure 5.50, reconciliation key (**Reconcil. Key**) 160511-001 is listed in the document header.

Figure 5.50 Document Header: Reconciliation Key

The reconciliation key holds information about all the postings done on the general ledger accounts. Once closed and transferred to FI, it updates the general ledger accounts.

Reconciliation keys for most of the mass processes are closed automatically as soon as the job is completed, but certain processes in which individual postings are done require closing reconciliation keys manually. A reconciliation key can be closed via Transaction FPG4 (as in Figure 5.51).

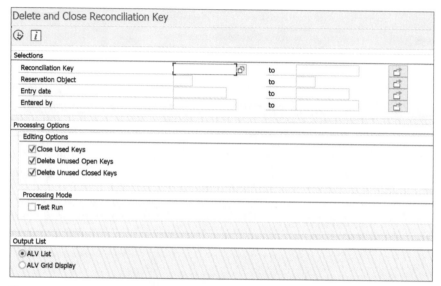

Figure 5.51 Reconciliation Key Close Transaction Screen

The closed reconciliation keys are then transferred using the Transaction FPG1M for mass transfer (as in Figure 5.52).

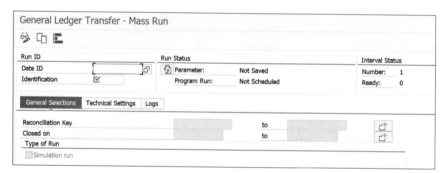

Figure 5.52 Reconciliation Key Mass Transfer Screen

As of SAP S/4HANA 1909, manually posted and reversed FI-CA documents can be updated directly to the general ledger.

5.3 Using Contract Accounts Receivable and Payable

This section explains how to use key transaction codes in FI-CA, including creating a business partner or contract account, viewing or editing a document, viewing the customer's balance, and using open item management. After learning to configure account determination, account balance display, and open item management in the previous sections, it is now time to run a few transaction codes and view the output.

5.3.1 Creating a Business Partner

The business partner can be created directly in SAP BRIM, subscription order management and replicated to FI-CA or directly created in FI-CA. For our example, the business partner is created in SAP BRIM, subscription order management and replicated to FI-CA and to SAP Convergent Charging.

The main definition of a business partner within the SAP ERP or SAP S/4HANA system resides at menu path **SAP Customizing Implementation Guide · Cross-Application Components · SAP Business Partner**. The definition of business partner roles, number ranges, business partner types, and so on is performed in this node.

In this section, we'll focus on the master data elements needed for the case study. Business partner 1100000356 (McFarland Systems) has been created for the Martex Corp. example.

First, use Transaction BP to view business partner 1100000356. As shown in Figure 5.53, enter the **Business Partner** number and click **Start**. This will return the business partner replicated in FI-CA from SAP BRIM, subscription order management.

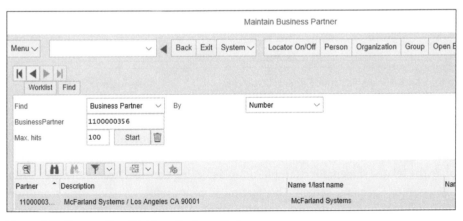

Figure 5.53 Transaction BP: View Business Partner

Next, double-click the business partner. As shown in Figure 5.54, the **General Data** view of the business partner contains key attributes such as the name, search term, and address information of the customer.

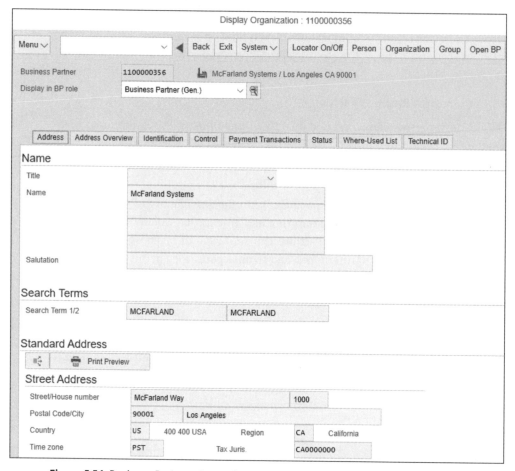

Figure 5.54 Business Partner: General Data View

Now, click the **Where-Used List** tab for the business partner, as shown in Figure 5.55. You will be able to see the references of the contract accounts and the provider contracts created for the business partner. Double-clicking any of the references will take you to the related screen; for example, double-clicking **Contract Account** will lead you to the contract account screen. This feature is very useful for navigating from one screen to another and is very prevalent across all FI-CA screens.

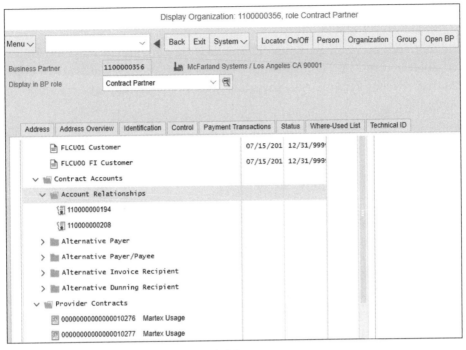

Figure 5.55 Business Partner: Where-Used List

To create a business partner directly in FI-CA, use Transaction BP. The business partner will need to be extended to the MKK contract partner role to create a corresponding contract account.

5.3.2   Creating a Contract Account

A contract account holds the transactional data for the business partner. All FI-CA document postings done for a business partner, whether payments, receivables, or interest, are recorded under the contract account. The contract account master data contain various details associated with mode payments, dunning, account determination, and billing cycles. This info is available under various tabs on the contract account display screen.

The contract account can be created directly in SAP BRIM, subscription order management (as a business agreement linked to the business partner) and replicated to FI-CA or can be created directly in FI-CA and replicated to SAP Convergent Charging (as subscriber account).

The basic settings required for the creation of the contract account are described in detail in Chapter 4, Section 4.1.3.

The contract account can be directly created in FI-CA using Transaction CAA1, which can also be accessed via the SAP Easy Access menu: **Accounting · Financial Accounting · Contract Account Receivables & Payables · Master Data · Contract Account** (as in Figure 5.56).

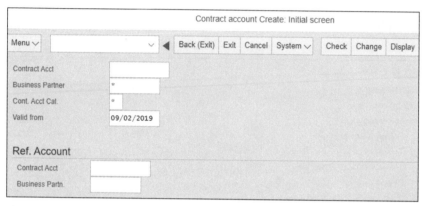

Figure 5.56 Contract Account Creation: Initial Screen

The contract account can be created in reference to the existing contract account by providing the reference contract account on the creation screen. Certain details like contract account category, account relationship, tolerance group, clearing category, account determination ID, payment terms, and company code are mandatory values for creating a contract account.

Contract Account 110000000194 for McFarland Systems has been created for the Martex example.

Now let's use Transaction CAA3 to view the contract account. It can also be accessed via the SAP Easy Access menu: **Accounting · Financial Accounting · Contract Account Receivables & Payables · Master Data · Contract Account** (as in Figure 5.57).

Figure 5.57 Contract Account Display Screen

5.3.3 Viewing or Editing a Posting Document

A posting document in FI-CA is an accounting document that gets posted during the invoicing process execution. The posting document contains both master data details of the customer, like business partner, contract account, and contract, and also the transaction data for the business transaction, like sale of service, tax data, and other payment-related details. FI-CA documents can originate directly within FI-CA via processes like interest calculation, dunning charges, installment plans, and payment lot postings.

The documents in FI-CA can be viewed using Transaction FPE3, which also can be accessed via the SAP Easy Access menu: **Accounting · Financial Accounting · Contract Account Receivables & Payables · Document** (as in Figure 5.58).

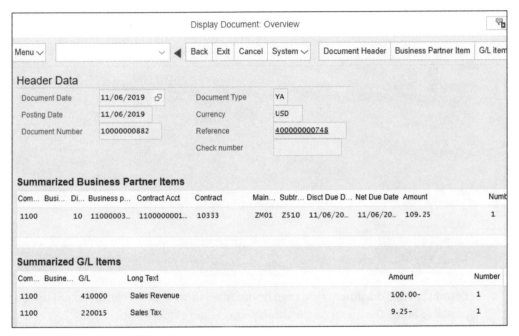

Figure 5.58 Document Display Screen

The screen provides the option to directly view the business partner items, general ledger items, and document header details. Upon execution, the header, summarized business partner items, and summarized general ledger items are displayed (as in Figure 5.59).

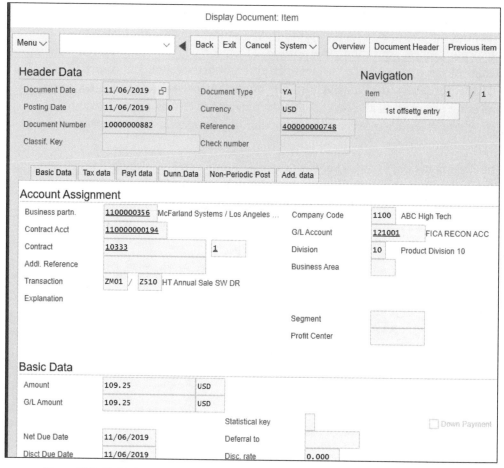

Figure 5.59 FI-CA Document View

Certain posting document fields can be modified using the change document option available under the menu on the display screen (as in Figure 5.60).

A document can also be modified using Transaction FPE2, which can be accessed via the SAP Easy Access menu: **Accounting** · **Financial Accounting** · **Contract Account Receivables & Payables** · **Document** (as in Figure 5.61).

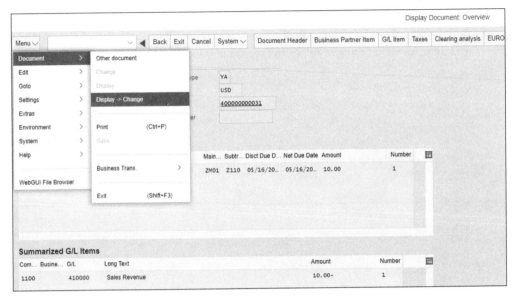

Figure 5.60 Menu Option for Document Change

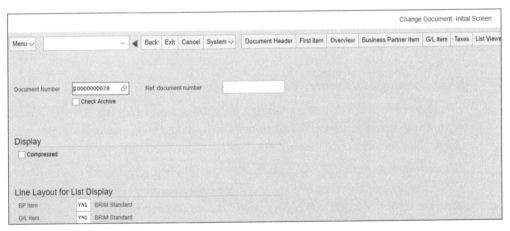

Figure 5.61 Change Document Screen

The fields that are made changeable via configuration are available to change in the change document screen.

Fields can be made changeable under the **SPRO** node at **Contract Account Receivables & Payables · Basic Functions · Postings & Documents · Basic Settings · Define Authorizations for Field Changes** (as see in Figure 5.62).

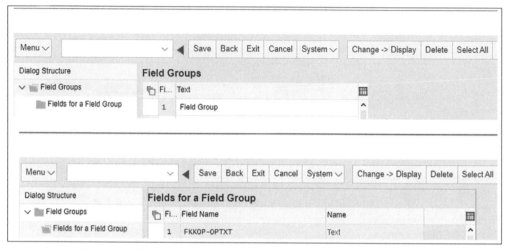

Figure 5.62 Field Group for Modifiable Document Fields

For the created group, change authorization can be given to users.

5.3.4   Viewing a Customer's Balance on Account

The customer's account balance display provides a view of all the transactions or accounting entries posted to the customer's account and even provides other details, like receivable item status (open, cleared, or overdue) or dunning level.

The customer account balance can be viewed in FI-CA using Transaction FPL9, which also can be accessed via the SAP Easy Access menu: **Accounting · Financial Accounting · Contract Account Receivables & Payables · Account** (as seen in Figure 5.63 and Figure 5.64).

Figure 5.63 Account Balance Initial Screen

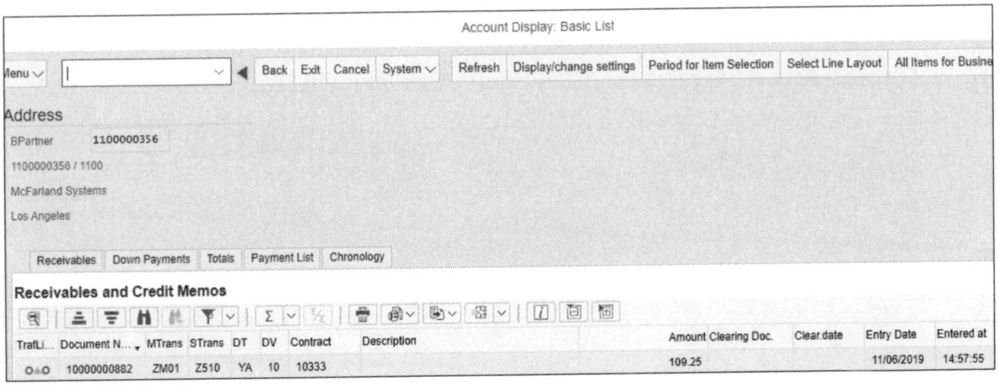

Figure 5.64 Account Balance Screen

The receivables and payment postings are displayed under the **Receivables** tab. The **Down Payment** tab contains the released security deposit payment or down payment items, the **Totals** tab shows the total amount, the **Payment List** tab shows only the payments posted on the account, and the **Chronology** tab displays the receivables and associated posted payments.

Further details of each posted document can be seen by double-clicking the document. The various columns shown in the account balance screen are controlled using the line item layout. The account balance display is described in detail in Section 5.2.3.

5.3.5   Using Open Item Management

This section explains the various FI-CA functionalities for managing the open items on the customer/vendor account. Functionalities like clearing, account maintenance, clearing control, and clearing restrictions are covered here.

Account Maintenance

Account maintenance is used to set off a credit balance with a debit balance present on a customer's account. This is key in scenarios in which there is a credit balance originating from a credit posting or the release of a security deposit and the credit amount needs to be adjusted with the monthly or the final invoice.

Account maintenance can be performed explicitly by manually executing the account maintenance transaction or in a mass batch job each day at the end of business hours, or it can be done implicitly during the process like clearing during payments or invoicing.

To execute manual account maintenance, use Transaction FPO6, which also can be accessed through the SAP Easy Access menu: **Accounting** · **Financial Accounting** · **Contract Account Receivables & Payables** · **Account** (as in Figure 5.65).

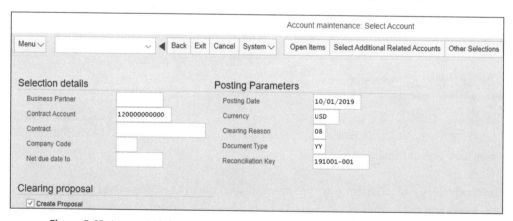

Figure 5.65 Account Maintenance Screen

On the account maintenance screen, the selection parameters are entered to determine account for which account maintenance needs to be performed. On execution, the list of open items and payment or credit on an account is displayed. The following steps should performed for account maintenance:

1. **Selection and activation**

   The items that are to be set off are selected and activated. Upon activation, the items are marked for account maintenance. Under the processing status the difference becomes green if the difference amount is zero; otherwise it is red. If difference amount is not zero, then a debit balance amount is made equal to the credit item in the **Gross Clearing** field (as in Figure 5.66).

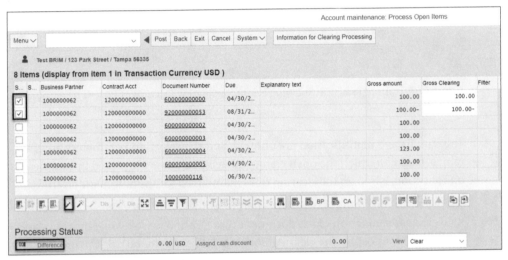

Figure 5.66 Selection and Activation of Account Items

2. **Posting**

   Selecting the **Post** option posts the clearing document, and the credit and debit items are set off (as in Figure 5.67).

The account maintenance in the production system is done using a mass batch job. When account maintenance must be done on multiple accounts and in parallel, the mass run is executed. The mass run is executed to set off the credit balance on the customer's account with the debit balance. Use Transaction FPMA for this task, which also can be accessed through the SAP Easy Access menu: **Accounting · Financial Accounting · Contract Account Receivables & Payables · Periodic Processing · For Contract Accounts**.

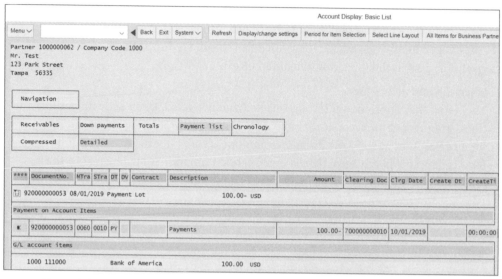

Figure 5.67 Transaction FPL9, Showing a Sample Clearing Document Posted by Account Maintenance

The date ID and identification are entered, and the selection parameters are maintained, based on which the open credit and debit balances are picked up and cleared on execution, based on the clearing rules maintained for the automatic clearing.

There are certain configurations required to be maintained for the account maintenance for determination of the document type clearing reason while the transaction is executed for posting the clearing document. Posting area 1020 is maintained for these entries.

Posting Area 1020

Default settings associated with the account maintenance like document type, clearing reason, and whether a clearing proposal should be created during account maintenance are maintained in posting area 1020 (as in Figure 5.68).

SAP provides a set of standard clearing reasons for the type of process the clearing is originating from. Clearing reason 08 is used for the account maintenance performed using Transaction FP06 or manually.

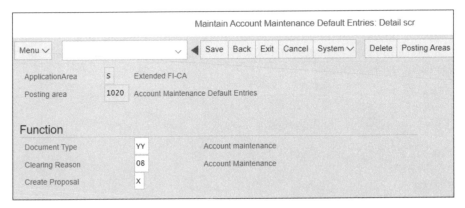

Figure 5.68 Posting Area 1020

Posting Area 1025

Automatic clearing also requires values like document type and clearing reason to be determined during the posting of the automatic clearing or mass clearing. These parameters are maintained in posting area 1025 (as in Figure 5.69).

Figure 5.69 Posting Area 1025 for Default Values for Automatic Clearing

Reset Clearing

A document can be cleared by the incoming payment, account maintenance, or during the invoicing process. When there is a need to separate the clearing document from the cleared item to either reverse the receivable item or to make the incoming payment a payment on account, in such scenarios the clearing document is reset. Resetting the clearing document makes the receivable document an open item again, and the payment document becomes the payment on account.

Transaction FP07 is used to perform the clearing reset and it can also be accessed through the SAP Easy Access menu: **Accounting · Financial Accounting · Contract Account Receivables & Payables · Periodic Processing · For Contract Accounts · Documents** (as in Figure 5.70).

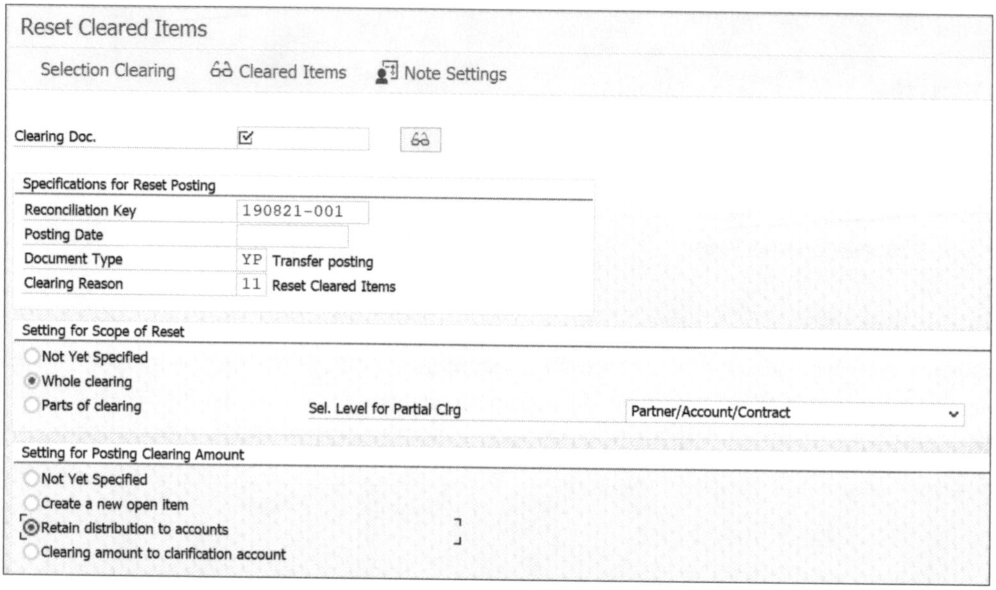

Reset Cleared Items

Selection Clearing   🔍 Cleared Items   📇 Note Settings

| Clearing Doc. | ☑ | | 🔍 |

Specifications for Reset Posting

Reconciliation Key	190821-001
Posting Date	
Document Type	YP Transfer posting
Clearing Reason	11 Reset Cleared Items

Setting for Scope of Reset
- ○ Not Yet Specified
- ● Whole clearing
- ○ Parts of clearing   Sel. Level for Partial Clrg   Partner/Account/Contract ⌄

Setting for Posting Clearing Amount
- ○ Not Yet Specified
- ○ Create a new open item
- ● Retain distribution to accounts
- ○ Clearing amount to clarification account

Figure 5.70 Reset Clearing Screen

The clearing document that needs to be reset is entered in the **Clearing Document** field of the reset clearing screen.

Then the setting for the scope of the reset is selected. If a full reset of the clearing document is required, which makes the receivable item fully open (not partially cleared), the **Whole Clearing** option is selected.

Then the setting for the posting clearing amount is selected. To retain the original accounting entries of the receivable item, the **Retain Distribution to Accounts** option is selected. If the **Create a New Option Item** option is selected, the original receivable remains cleared and the new receivable is posted. In this scenario, the original receivable cannot be reversed.

On selecting the **Post** option, you reset the clearing and the payment, and the receivable item becomes open on the customer account.

On the reset clearing screen, parameters like document type and clearing reason are required for posting the reset clearing document.

Posting Area 1060

A clearing reason and document type for the reset clearing document are maintained in posting area 1060. These values are automatically populated on the reset clearing screen and are used for posting the reset clearing document (as in Figure 5.71).

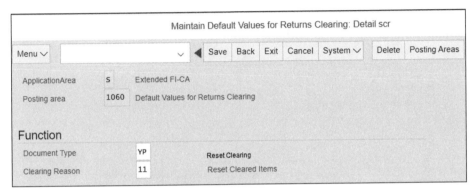

Figure 5.71 Default Parameters for Reset Clearing

Posting Area 1090

While posting the reset clearing, if the **Create New Open Items** option is selected in the settings for the posting clearing amount, a new receivable item is created. The creation of a new receivable item requires the main and subtransactions for the posting. Posting area 1090 is used to assign the main and subtransactions for creation of new items during the reset clearing (as in Figure 5.72).

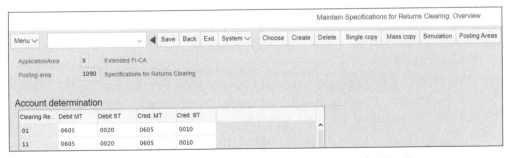

Figure 5.72 Main and Subtransactions Assignment to Clearing Reason for New Item Creation

Clearing Restrictions

Clearing restrictions are generally applied on the open items that should be ignored during the automatic clearing process. Based on business requirements, these restrictions can be removed and the account items can be considered for clearing.

Clearing restrictions can be created under the **Contract Account Receivables & Payables · Basic Functions · Open Item Management · Define Modifiable Clearing Restrictions** node (as in Figure 5.73).

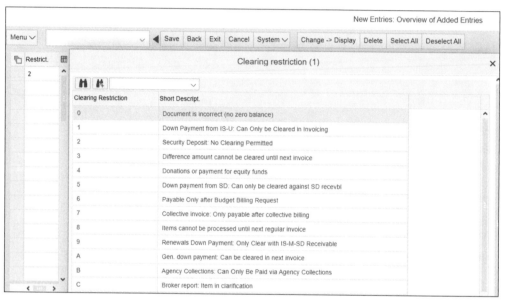

Figure 5.73 Modifiable Clearing Restrictions

The clearing restrictions applied on the documents can be removed manually using the change document functionality described in Section 5.3.3.

Clearing Control

This is a very important functionality when it comes to the clearing of the open items. Product or service provider companies have different rules or laws based on which the clearing of different kinds of receivables should be cleared.

Clearing control provides a set of configuration nodes in which you can set up rules for how the clearing of open items takes place. Different rules can be assigned to different payment originating processes, like payment lot, payment run, account maintenance, invoicing, and so on.

These rules guide the selection, grouping, and sorting of the open items for the payment or clearing to be applied.

The configuration for the clearing control is maintained under **Contract Account Receivables & Payables · Basic Functions · Open Item Management · Clearing Control · Clearing Variants**.

5

> **Clearing Variant**
>
> A clearing variant is created for different processes and the steps are maintained which are basically rules for selection, grouping and sorting for the clearing process. These variants are assigned to the standard processes.

The various steps involved in setting up clearing variants are as follows:

1. **Defining grouping and sorting features**

   SAP provides a set of standard fields that can be used for grouping and sorting the open items. These fields are from the FKKOP structure. Standard function module FSC_SAMPLE_TFK116 can also be used to create a custom function module based on requirements for the grouping fields (as in Figure 5.74).

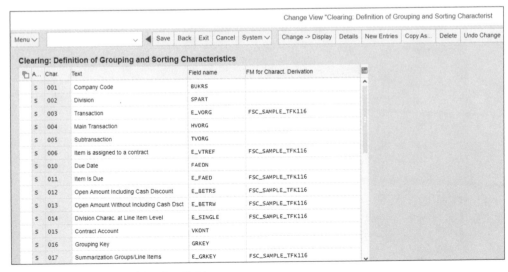

Figure 5.74 Grouping and Sorting Fields

359

2. **Defining a clearing variant and the clearing steps**

A clearing variant is created that is specific to the processes through which the clearing process is executed, like account maintenance, invoicing, and incoming payments (as in Figure 5.75).

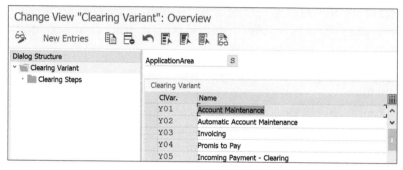

Figure 5.75 Clearing Variants

Clearing steps are created next for the clearing variants created. Clearing steps use the grouping and sorting fields defined for grouping the items and sorting them (as in Figure 5.76).

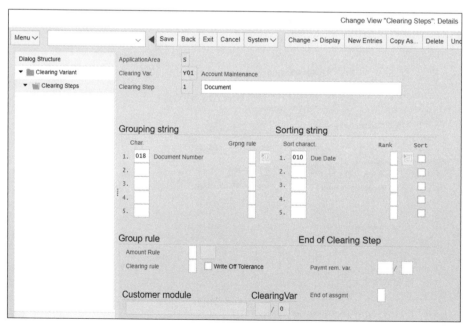

Figure 5.76 Clearing Steps

After the clearing variants are created and clearing steps are defined, the clearing variants are assigned to the clearing types. The clearing types are the processes through which clearing is triggered upon execution.

The assignment of the clearing variant to the clearing type is done under **Contract Account Receivables & Payables · Basic Functions · Open Item Management · Clearing Control · Define Clearing Specifications for Clearing Types** (as in Figure 5.77).

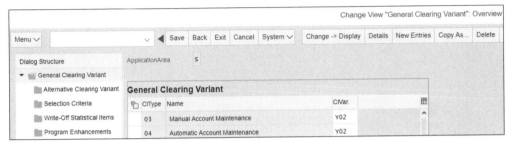

Figure 5.77 Clearing Variant Assignment to Clearing Type

5.4   Reporting and Analytics

SAP provides several reporting options for the account postings performed in FI-CA. The reports provided are useful for extracting the details of the business partner/customer items based on their status—that is, whether items are cleared or open—using several parameters like dunning, document type, and so on. Reports can also be used to obtain the entries for the general ledger account postings in FI-CA. The reports obtained provide a view of the data and help in analysis. This section will cover several report options available in FI-CA.

5.4.1   FI-CA Items List: Open/All Items

SAP has provided Transaction FPO4 to obtain the details or a report of the receivable and payable items on an account. This report can be extracted based on the master data details and even the general ledger accounts.

These reports specifically can get the open items on a key date and extract the details of all items (as in Figure 5.78).

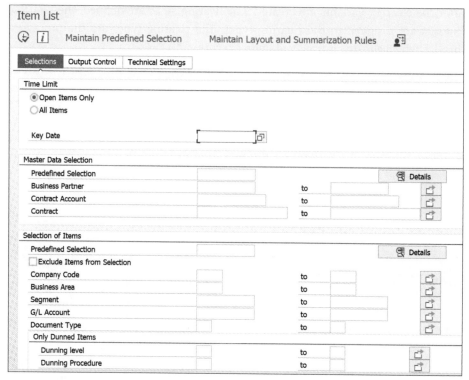

Figure 5.78 Report for Open/All Items

In the **Output Control** tab, the output of the report can be controlled and obtained on the desired format.

5.4.2   List of Open Items at Key Date

The FI-CA documents that are not cleared in the system by invoicing, account maintenance, reversal, or payments are called open items. Transaction FPO1P is used to obtain the list of open items on a key date.

This transaction can also be accessed through the SAP Easy Access menu: **Accounting · Financial Accounting · Contract Account Receivables & Payables · Periodic Processing · Closing Preparation** (as in Figure 5.79).

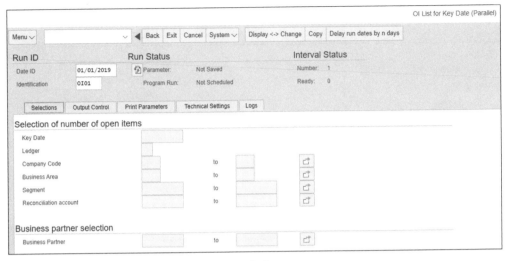

Figure 5.79 Report to Obtain Open Items at Key Date

This transaction is a parallel mass job that generates the spool, and the display of the spool is controlled by the parameters maintained in the output control of the job settings.

5.4.3   Reconciliation of Open Items and General Ledger

All FI-CA documents are posted under a reconciliation key. The reconciliation key at close of business hours for the day is then closed and transferred to SAP FI system. The reconciliation key transfer posts a finance document and updates the general ledger accounts with the accounting entries. To reconcile the accounting entries transferred to the Finance system and those that have yet to be transferred, SAP has provided a report. Transaction FPO2 is used for an individual run to obtain the details of the amounts present in the general ledger accounts, the amount under the reconciliation key, and the total amount of open items (as in Figure 5.80). The report provides the data per reconciliation general ledger account. Transaction FPO2P is used for a mass run (as in Figure 5.81).

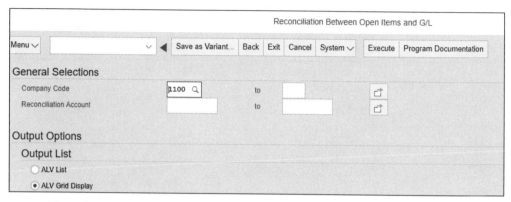

Figure 5.80 FPO2 Reconciliation Report: Initial Screen

Figure 5.81 FPO2 Reconciliation Report Data

The report provides a status for the reconciliation. The red status indicates that the reconciliation has a difference. The yellow status indicates that there is no difference amount: the amounts in the general ledger accounts and the reconciliation key match with the open item balance, but the reconciliation key is not yet transferred. The green status indicates that the reconciliation keys are transferred and the reconciliation is successful.

5.4.4   List of Open Items for Business Partner on Key Date

The posting documents that are not cleared are called open items. A business partner can have several contract accounts, and each contract account can have multiple open items posted on the account. This report provides a list of all the open items on a key date for the business partner, extracting open items from all the contract accounts under the business partner.

Transaction FPO1_ACC is available to extract the details of the open items on a key date specific to the business partners (see Figure 5.82).

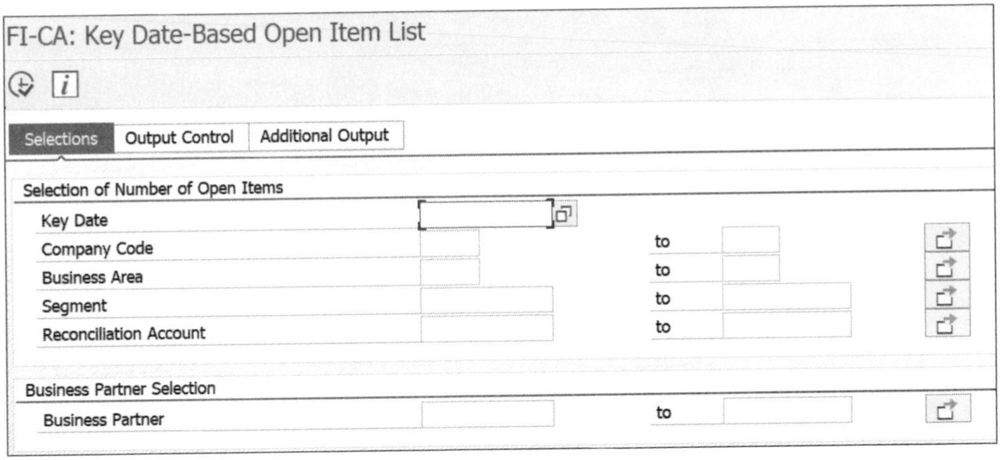

Figure 5.82 Report for Extracting Open Items for Business Partner on Key Date

In the **Selection Screen** tab, input is maintained for the data selection; the **Output Control** tab controls the output data display; and **Additional Output** controls the data format.

5.4.5   Customer Account Balance Display

All receivables, payables, payments, charges, interest, and several other transactions are posted on the contract accounts. The customer account balance display provides the detailed information about the various documents posted on the contract account, as well as the details of the amount of each posting and the total amount for the complete account.

Transaction FPL9 is available to display the customer account balance details. The output is controlled by the list type and line layout, discussed in Section 5.2.3. The items/documents—receivables, cleared items, open items, overdue items, statistical postings like installment plans, security deposit request, down payments, and son on—can be displayed here. The layout contains several fields that can be set up easily based on business needs.

The transaction can also be accessed via SAP Easy Access menu: **Accounting • Financial Accounting • Contract Account Receivables & Payables • Account** (as in Figure 5.83).

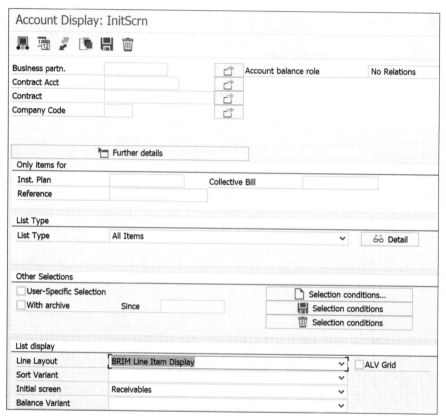

Figure 5.83 Account Balance Display Screen

The account items can be obtained by master data like the business partner, contract account, and contract. Information like clearing documents, reversal documents, details related to a document, posting dates, and so on can be seen easily in a single place in the account balance display.

5.5   Summary

This chapter has described in detail the various objects of FI-CA, the various configurations required for setting up the FI-CA processes, and the various reports available for data reconciliation and analysis.

You should now be able to configure your system to meet your business requirements and perform various FI-CA processes.

5

Chapter 6
Integration with Other Solutions

This chapter will provide an overall picture of the integration points for all SAP BRIM components. These points include the integrations between each of the applications within SAP BRIM and those between SAP BRIM and other solutions.

SAP BRIM is a full solution suite, but there are rare cases in which companies will only implement some SAP BRIM components. As the best practice across industries, SAP BRIM works best when all or most of the components are implemented together and with other additional applications. As a result, companies typically implement SAP BRIM in conjunction with other applications to create an SAP CRM ecosystem that provides an end-to-end solution.

This chapter will first highlight the integrations between core SAP BRIM components and how they interact with each other. The chapter will not go in depth into the step-by-step setup of the technical activities, but rather will describe how data and information flow between these components. Once this is done, we will branch out to additional applications. This is where we will explore how SAP BRIM is integrated with other auxiliary applications, such as SAP Convergent Mediation by DigitalRoute, SAP Customer Financial Management, and more.

6.1 Integration between SAP BRIM Core Components

SAP BRIM is implemented to streamline high-volume revenue management processes. There are two implementation paths: SAP S/4HANA and SAP ERP. Each path includes an SAP Convergent Charging system and an SAP CRM system. The SAP CRM component can be implemented via the add-on or run externally, depending on the version of SAP S/4HANA. SAP BRIM has solutions based on the following industries: SAP for Telecommunications, SAP Utilities Customer Engagement, and SAP Public Sector Collection and Disbursement (SAP PSCD). SAP BRIM is modular, so you have the option of deploying one or more elements depending on your requirements.

A key step in SAP BRIM integration is activation of the business functions in your SAP S/4HANA system. The set of business functions is based on your industry. If you want to use any integration of the business processes between SAP S/4HANA and SAP CRM, you will need to activate those business functions in SAP CRM as well.

For SAP BRIM integration, products are defined. A product is the tangible item for which you are building the revenue management process. They are divided into three logical views: commercial, charging, and technical. Let's discuss each view.

A commercial view of products is within SAP CRM. It contains what can be defined as the master of the commercial view of all products. It contains the definition of the available options for customer selection, the bundling of different services, and the one-off charges.

The charging view is within SAP Convergent Charging, which is where you define the charge plans for the consumption of services. This system receives chargeable items or consumption data records. Chargeable items are real-time consumption data, whereas consumption data records are in batch mode. The charge plans and the refill plans are defined here and used to perform the rating, charging, and refilling processes for consumption and refill data.

The technical view is within SAP CRM. It is where you activate the services to which your customers subscribe.

Also note that for each product you define in SAP CRM, the system creates a mapping table in SAP Convergent Charging. The mapping table contains the price conditions for recurring charges within the product.

Prices are maintained accordingly:

- You maintain usage prices in SAP Convergent Charging.
- You maintain one-off prices in SAP CRM.
- You maintain recurring prices in SAP CRM as pricing condition records.

Prices are replicated to SAP Convergent Charging, which applies the recurring charges during each billing cycle. SAP CRM specifies prices for complete billing periods. SAP Convergent Charging can prorate prices if services have only been consumed during part of a billing cycle. To distribute prices from SAP CRM to SAP Convergent Charging, you must configure the consumer proxy. This configuration is done in SAP CRM via Transaction SOAMANAGER.

The product definition is shown in Figure 6.1.

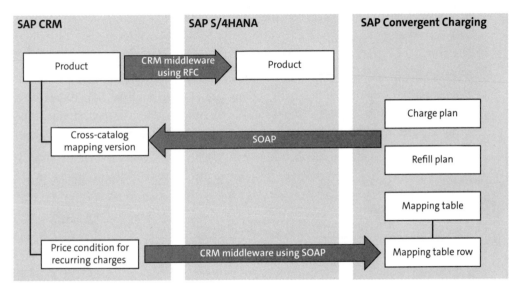

Figure 6.1 Product Definitions

Business partner master data is managed in both SAP CRM and SAP S/4HANA or SAP ERP. Similar configuration is done in SAP S/4 HANA and SAP ERP; both systems contain the Contract Accounts Receivable and Payable (FI-CA) functions. The rest of the chapter will mention SAP ERP only if it differs from SAP S/4HANA.

The SAP CRM system is where customer and contract data is entered and managed. The data required in FI-CA and SAP Convergent Invoicing is transferred to the SAP S/4HANA system. In addition, the prepaid account data of the business agreement is maintained in SAP CRM. The account and business agreement and the master agreement in SAP CRM are replicated to SAP S/4HANA. The SAP CRM system also replicates the provider contract to SAP S/4HANA via the SAP CRM middleware. The middleware ensures that as soon as prepaid-relevant data is maintained in the business agreement, the data is transmitted to the prepaid account in the SAP S/4HANA system.

The SAP S/4HANA system is where the business partner, contract account, and prepaid account data is transferred to the SAP Convergent Charging system via a web service using the simple object access protocol (SOAP). The corresponding subscriber account, external account, and prepaid account are created in SAP Convergent Charging. The complete provider contract message is stored SAP S/4HANA. When the contract is created in SAP S/4HANA or SAP Convergent Charging, each component only stores those attributes relevant for further processing within that component.

The business partner, contract accounts, and prepaid accounts are distributed to the SAP Convergent Charging system from the SAP S/4HANA system when the data of the provider contract they belong to is received in SAP S/4HANA.

The transactional flow of data begins in SAP CRM, where the order type is created. SAP Convergent Invoicing contains the billing and invoicing. The SAP Convergent Charging system creates the changeable item for refilling, the chargeable item, or the refilling item and sends it to SAP Convergent Invoicing for billing and invoicing (as in Figure 6.2).

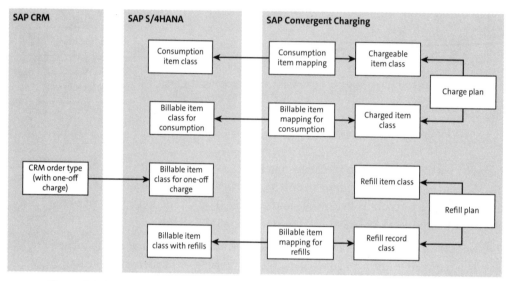

Figure 6.2 Transactional Data Flow from Master Guide

6.1.1   Consumption Data

The original consumption data is stored in SAP Convergent Invoicing in the SAP S/4HANA system. It is stored in the form of consumption items both before and after rating. The benefits of storing consumption data in SAP S/4HANA are as follows:

- It enables you to work with scaled prices.
- It triggers rerating in SAP Convergent Invoicing.
- You can use partner settlement.
- You can correct consumption items in SAP S/4HANA.

Flow of Consumption Data

Charging data such as charged items, refill records, ABM notifications, and unrated chargeable items is created from rated or unrated chargeable items or refill requests in SAP Convergent Charging. SAP Convergent Charging then reads and maps these files to the format of the associated billable item class or consumption item class in SAP S/4HANA. Then the SAP Convergent Charging bulk loader loads the data as billable items and consumption items into SAP S/4HANA.

Rating of Consumption Data

SAP Convergent Charging receives unrated consumption items and enriches them with information related to provider contracts or subscriptions. SAP Convergent Charging then transfers the unrated consumption items to SAP Convergent Invoicing, which stores and manages the unrated consumption items. SAP Convergent Invoicing then sends them back to SAP Convergent Charging for rating.

6.1.2   One-Off Charges

The SAP CRM systems transfer the one-off charges to SAP S/4HANA automatically using the SAP CRM middleware and based on the configuration of the order item type. One-off charges are processed in SAP S/4HANA using a billable item class that is configured for one-off charges and using the CRM Order interface component.

6.1.3   Prepaid Data

Billing in SAP Convergent Invoicing receives prepaid data for refills as billable items from SAP Convergent Charging. It stores, manages, and groups the data together with the existing consumption of the customer. SAP Convergent Invoicing then summarizes the data into a billing document. One or more billing documents are merged into an invoice. SAP Convergent Invoicing is a module within the SAP S/4HANA system.

6.1.4   Billing and Invoicing

Billable items originate in SAP Convergent Charging as consumption and refill data and in SAP CRM as one-off charges. SAP Convergent Charging triggers periodic or event-based charges and creates billable items in the SAP S/4HANA system.

The billing component in SAP S/4HANA receives billable items from SAP Convergent Charging. The billable items are charged consumption and refill data in SAP Convergent Charging and charges from SAP CRM and SAP Convergent Charging. During invoicing, one or more billing documents can then be merged into one invoice.

Invoicing creates an invoice for the customer based on the billing document and on additional source documents from other systems if available. Invoicing posts this total amount to the contract account of the business partner as a receivable.

6.1.5   Contract Data

When configuring SAP BRIM, you work with the following types of contracts and agreements:

- A *provider contract* comprises all legally binding agreements regarding the provision and billing of services that are entered by a customer and a company for a specified period.

- A *master agreement* is a contractual agreement between a service provider and a business customer.

- *Partner agreements* are used to share revenue with a content provider or to pay royalties. With end customers, you have provider contracts; with partners, you have partner agreements.

- A *sharing contract* specifies services, such as shared minutes or data on a phone plan. The contract applies to all individual contracts assigned to a sharing contract and can be used by all contract partners.

Discount keys are configured in SAP S/4HANA. They are replicated to the SAP CRM system. SAP CRM replicates the discount assignment to the provider contract when the provider contract is replicated in SAP S/4HANA.

6.1.6   Disputes

A dispute is created from the bill stored in SAP Convergent Invoicing. It is replicated to FI-CA in a FI-CA dispute case. The FI-CA dispute case contains information on the receivables related to the bill and the disputed object. A dispute can be created for bills, bill line items, or billing detail records. All data relating to and used for processing the dispute is stored in SAP S/4HANA FI-CA system. Adjustment requests can be created from a bill or as a subitem of a dispute. Adjustments are posted directly in SAP S/4HANA FI-CA as credit items.

6.1.7   Communication between Systems

SAP S/4HANA, SAP ERP, and SAP CRM communicate with SAP Convergent Charging via web services. These web services use the SOAP protocol and are configured in each respective system using Transaction SOMANAGER. SAP Convergent Charging communicates with SAP S/4HANA, SAP ERP, or SAP CRM via a JCo communication. SAP CRM and SAP S/4HANA or SAP CRM and SAP ERP communicate with each other via RFC communication.

6.1.8   Additional Integration

The SAP Revenue Accounting and Reporting add-on can be integrated with the offer-to-cash SAP BRIM integration. SAP Revenue Accounting and Reporting provides functions to manage revenue recognition regulations. The add-on is used for managing regulations in countries subject to both US GAAP and IFRS.

The integrations between SAP CRM, SAP S/4HANA or SAP ERP, and SAP Convergent Charging require some activation of business functions, configuration of products, and connections between systems. Configuring these integrations is core to implementing the SAP BRIM solution.

6.2   SAP Convergent Mediation by DigitalRoute

As discussed in previous chapters, consumption data can be passed directly into SAP BRIM systems as consumption items. However, there are some scenarios in which a mediation layer is required to aggregate consumption data or to enrich consumption data with additional information.

SAP Convergent Mediation by DigitalRoute provides out-of-the-box connectivity with SAP Convergent Charging. It can be accessed using the desktop launcher provided as part of the installation file. This section highlights the out-of-the-box integration component provided by SAP Convergent Mediation by DigitalRoute for SAP Convergent Charging, but it does not include in-depth information about installation and set up, such as platform and execution containers.

Mediation logic or rules for SAP Convergent Mediation by DigitalRoute are defined in the workflow object. Figure 6.3 illustrates a sample of how the desktop launcher is used for modeling workflows.

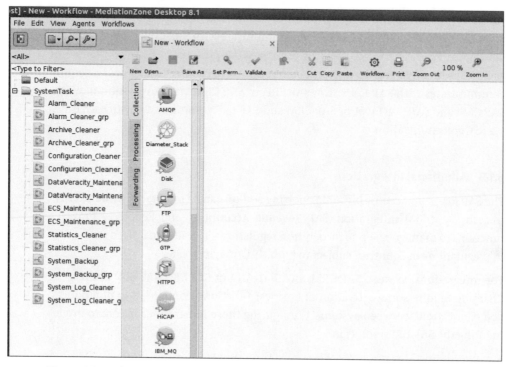

Figure 6.3 Desktop Launcher

SAP Convergent Mediation by DigitalRoute supports connectivity with any rating and charging API, but has out-of-the-box integration with SAP Convergent Charging. In Figure 6.4, within the **Processing** tab, you can see two agents for SAP Convergent Charging: **SAP_CC_Batch** and **SAP_CC_Online**.

SAP Convergent Mediation by DigitalRoute has three types of agents: collection, processing, and forwarding. When integrated with SAP Convergent Charging, the collection agent is typically used to read files or incoming streams from a source location. SAP Convergent Mediation by DigitalRoute supports receiving from multiple source types, such as FTP, direct disk reads, or message queues. In Figure 6.5, a disk agent is being used as the collection agent. In the collection agent, there are areas to specify the directory and filename to process.

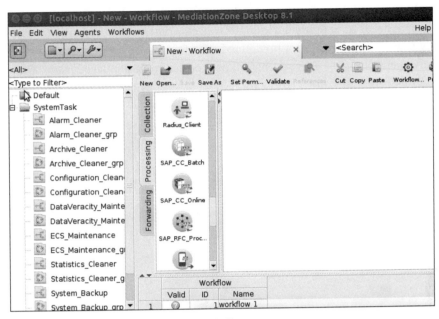

Figure 6.4 SAP_CC_Batch and SAP_CC_Online

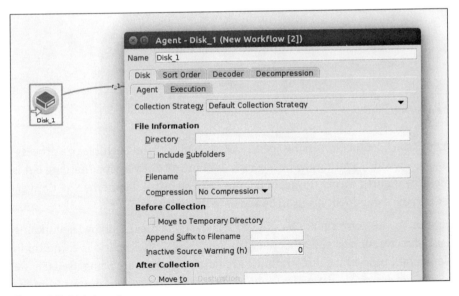

Figure 6.5 Disk Agent

To be able to pass the correct data to the processing agent, the user detail record (UDR) format needs to be defined within the collection agent. SAP Convergent Mediation by DigitalRoute provides a predefined UDR format for communication with SAP Convergent Charging. This setting can be accessed from the **Decoder** tab of the collection agent (Figure 6.6).

Figure 6.6 Decoder

Next, let's consider the processing agent. SAP_CC_Online is an example of a processing agent, via which a rating can be triggered within SAP Convergent Charging if it is correctly configured within the agent (Figure 6.7). The dispatcher of the SAP Convergent Charging component needs to be added to the hostname/port.

In addition to SAP Convergent Charging, SAP Convergent Mediation by DigitalRoute can also directly connect to SAP Convergent Invoicing. This scenario is common in implementations in which other rating and charging systems are being used (Figure 6.8). SAP Convergent Mediation by DigitalRoute can be used to read output from the rating system, enrich rating results, and create billable items directly in SAP Convergent Invoicing. The SAP RFC processor can be used in the workflow after setting up the RFC profile (Figure 6.9).

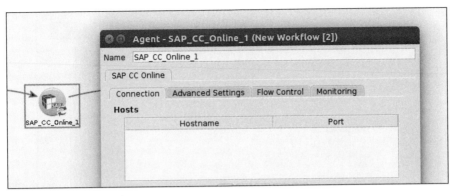

Figure 6.7 SAP_CC_Online

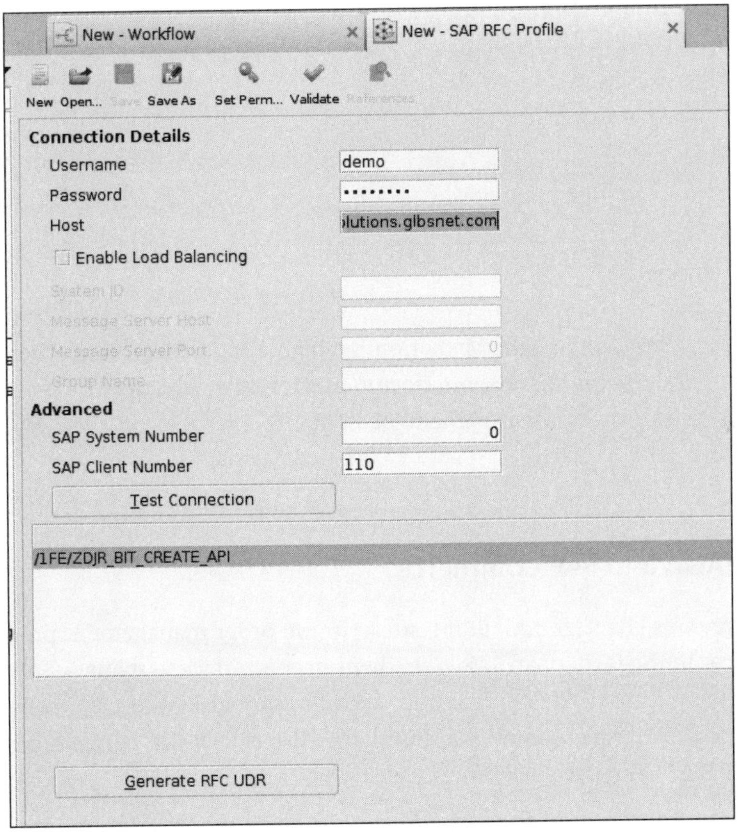

Figure 6.8 New SAP RFC Profile

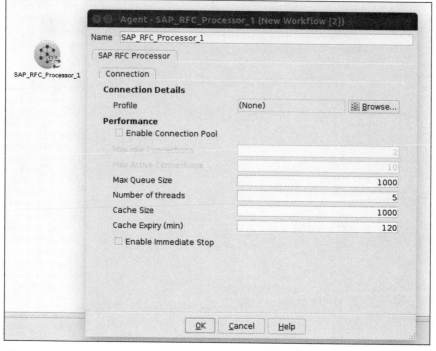

Figure 6.9 SAP RFC Processor

As mentioned earlier, SAP Convergent Mediation by DigitalRoute has many other features that are out of scope for this chapter. Documents for other advanced capabilities, such as aggregation or data enrichment of UDR, are available on the DigitalRoute wiki website.

6.3   SAP C/4HANA and SAP Commerce

As discussed in previous chapters, SAP BRIM, subscription order management provides user interfaces in the form of an SAP Web Client user interface to manage SAP BRIM objects such as business partner, contract account, provider order, and contracts. However, for most implementations, companies (especially B2C companies) implementing SAP BRIM also have e-commerce systems.

For integration with an e-commerce system, the only module required for integration is usually SAP BRIM, subscription order management. SAP has provided several

APIs in the form of remote function calls to integrate with the SAP C/4HANA Commerce systems (Figure 6.10).

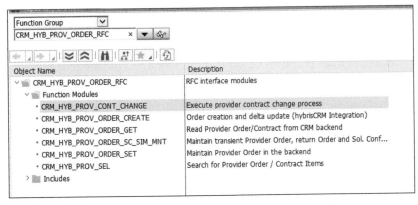

Figure 6.10 APIs for Integration with SAP C/4HANA Commerce Systems

When integrating with a commerce system, there are two type of approaches: asynchronous and synchronous. An asynchronous scenario is usually applicable in a B2C scenario, in which transaction volumes are high and real-time pricing is not required. In this approach, the e-commerce system will pass in the orders to SAP BRIM, subscription order management using a message queue service, such as IDocs or any message bus system.

Synchronous scenarios are usually applicable for B2B scenarios in which transaction volumes are low and real-time pricing information is required. In such a scenario, the RFC discussed earlier can be called directly or wrapped in OData or web services.

6.4   SAP Revenue Accounting and Reporting

This section provides key considerations for the integration of SAP Revenue Accounting and Reporting and SAP BRIM. We will discuss the nuances of revenue recognition from a process perspective. The other chapters discussed earlier focused on describing the episode-related key components and linking them back to the configuration setup needed for the Martex case study.

6.4.1 SAP Revenue Accounting and Reporting and SAP BRIM Integration Architecture

SAP S/4HANA offers standard compatibility between SAP BRIM and SAP Revenue Accounting and Reporting. The architecture provides direct integration to the Sales and Distribution (SD) system, SAP Convergent Invoicing billable items, and FI-CA provider contracts. For the purposes of SAP BRIM integration, the focus of this section will be on FI-CA and SAP Revenue Accounting and Reporting integration.

SAP Revenue Accounting and Reporting is driven by three main data types, types of revenue accounting items: order items (CAO1), fulfillment items (CAO2), and invoice items (CAO3). FI-CA supplies SAP Revenue Accounting and Reporting with these revenue accounting items in the SAP BRIM framework. Initial setup for settings needs to be completed for activating the standard revenue item classes and interfaces for CAO1, CAO2, and CAO3. These general activations, assigning logic systems, BRFplus application maintenance, and other general SAP Revenue Accounting and Reporting–specific configurations, will not be covered in detail here to keep our focus on the SAP BRIM and SAP Revenue Accounting and Reporting integration.

Figure 6.11 shows the business function that must be activated to enable SAP Revenue Accounting and Reporting integration with FI-CA.

| FICA_EHP7_RA | Integration with Revenue Accounting | Business func. will remain activated | [i] | S4CORE | 618 | FI-CA |
| FICA_EHP7_RA2 | Integration of Revenue Accounting 2 (Reversible) | Business func. will remain deactivate | [i] | S4CORE | 801 | FI-CA |

Figure 6.11 Business Functions for SAP Revenue Accounting and Reporting and FI-CA Integration

Once these business functions are activated, the configuration nodes shown in Figure 6.12 for SAP Convergent Invoicing and FI-CA integration with SAP Revenue Accounting and Reporting will be available under **Financial Accounting · Contract Accounts Receivable and Payable · Integration · Revenue Accounting**.

Once the configuration nodes are available, as a starting step the interface components relevant to SAP Revenue Accounting and Reporting based on the business use case will need to be activated for the billable item class. The interface components that are SAP Revenue Accounting and Reporting–relevant are **Service Types for Revenue Account Assignment** and **Integration with Revenue Accounting** (Figure 6.13).

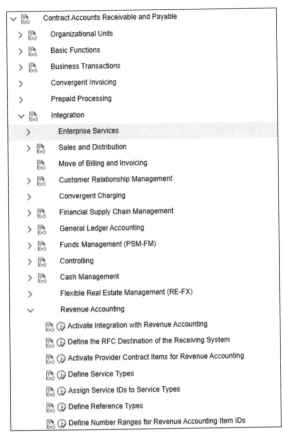

Figure 6.12 Configuration Nodes for SAP RAR Integration with FI-CA

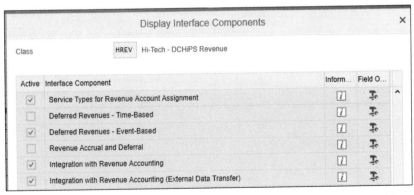

Figure 6.13 Interface Components Relevant to SAP Revenue Accounting and Reporting

6.4.2   Five-Step Model in Relation to SAP BRIM and SAP Revenue Accounting and Reporting Integration for Martex Case Study

Accounting standard ASC606 defines a five-step model to recognize revenue for multielement arrangements, which led to the development of SAP Revenue Accounting and Reporting. This section will break down the ASC606 five-step model with relevant integration with SAP Revenue Accounting and Reporting steps, key configurations, and examples from the Martex case study.

The ASC606 revenue recognition five-step model is as follows:

1. Identify a contract with a customer.
2. Identify the separate performance obligations in the contract.
3. Determine the transaction price.
4. Allocate the transaction price to the performance obligations of the contract.
5. Recognize revenue when (or as) the entity satisfies a performance obligation.

Let's look at each step in more detail.

Step 1: Identify a Contract with a Customer

In the SAP BRIM integration with SAP Revenue Accounting and Reporting, a provider contract or multiple provider contracts can be combined to create a single holistic SAP Revenue Accounting and Reporting contract for a business partner. In the Martex case study, there is a one-to-one relationship between the provider contract and SAP Revenue Accounting and Reporting contract. Once the SAP Revenue Accounting and Reporting-relevant integration business functions and interface components are activated, nominating provider contracts and service types for SAP Revenue Accounting and Reporting processing can be configured.

The RFC destination and activating provider contract items for SAP Revenue Accounting and Reporting relevance are configured with selections and indicators (Figure 6.14 and Figure 6.15).

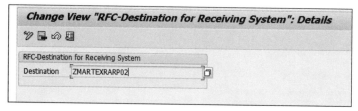

Figure 6.14 RFC Destination for Receiving System

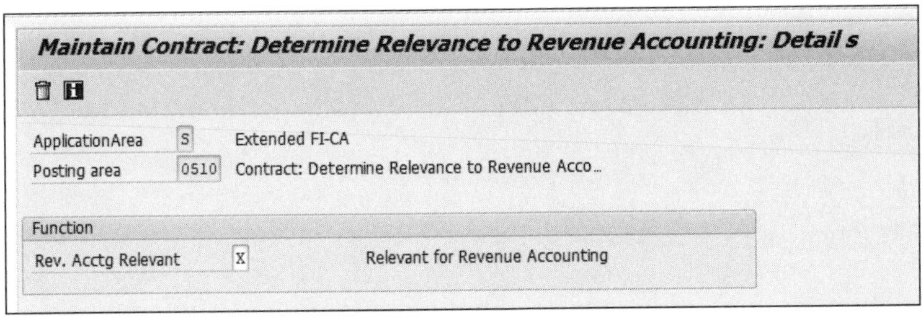

Figure 6.15 Determine Provider Contract Relevance for SAP Revenue Accounting and Reporting

These configurations will make available a separate SAP Revenue Accounting and Reporting–specific tab in the provider contract. This enrichment will include line items with service types which will be described in step 2 of the five-step model. Transaction price and standalone selling price details will also be available to receive relevant details from upstream applications.

Step 2: Identify the Separate Performance Obligations in the Contract

The performance obligation data object in SAP Revenue Accounting and Reporting holds attributes in relation to revenue recognition, including but not limited to general data, revenue recognition fulfillment attributes, allocation data, status, and account assignments. Performance obligation attributes are defined by a combination of the operational document (provider contract) configuration and BRFplus decision tables (Figure 6.16).

For Martex, the performance obligation would be related to line items in the Martex Usage and/or Martex Partner Product provider contracts. The definition of service types drives the creation of SAP Revenue Accounting and Reporting order items, fulfillment items, invoice items, and one-off charges. Via configuration, service types are mapped to SAP BRIM, subscription order management service IDs, save for the recurring charge service type. After a service type is indicated as an order item, a provider contract creation with a recurring charge (Figure 6.17) and/or a usage service type will generate an order item revenue accounting item to subsequently create a SAP Revenue Accounting and Reporting contract and relevant performance obligations.

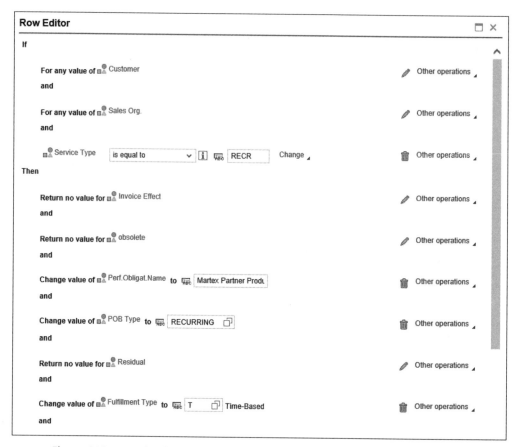

Figure 6.16 Example of Decision Table Entry for Performance Obligation Determination via BRFplus

Service Types for Revenue Accounting Items					
Service Type	Service Type Text	Order Item	One-Time Charge	Fulfill. Item	Invoice Item
RECR	Martex Partner Product	✔	☐	☐	✔
ZUSG	Martex Usage	✔	☐	✔	✔

Figure 6.17 Define Service Types

The integration of SAP Convergent Invoicing billable items and provider contracts to create revenue accounting order items sets the table for SAP BRIM transactions to supply SAP Revenue Accounting and Reporting with fulfillment items and invoice items. The decoupling of the ordering and billing systems supports transactional integrity, auditable end-to-end document referencing, automated adherence to the timing of revenue, and accuracy of balance sheet postings.

Step 3: Determine the Transaction Price

The transaction price in an SAP Revenue Accounting and Reporting contract is relevant for the amount to be invoiced and fulfilled for the duration of an agreement with a customer. As a part of the business functions shown in Figure 6.11, SAP delivers extensions to the provider contract replication from SAP CRM to SAP ERP. The enhanced structure includes a selection of the relevant fields described in Table 6.1.

Field	Contents	Example
REVACC_REFID	Revenue accounting reference ID	Default is provider order number
REVACC_REFTYPE	Revenue accounting reference type	Standard value PO
TRANS_PRICE	Revenue accounting transactional price	100.00
TP_CURRENCY	Transactional price currency	USD
TP_REC_DURATION	Duration of a recurrence period	1
TP_REC_UNIT	Time unit of a recurrence period	Month
STANDALONE_PRICE	Revenue accounting standalone selling price	85.00
SP_CURRENCY	SSP currency	USD
SP_REC_DURATION	Duration of a recurrence period	1
SP_REC_UNIT	Time unit of a recurrence period	Month
VALIDTO_RT	Valid to time stamp	End of duration of contract: 06/30/2019

Table 6.1 Transaction Price Fields

SAP Revenue Accounting and Reporting calculates the total transaction price for a recurring charge as follows:

*Revenue Accounting Transactional Price / Days in Recurrence Period * Days in Valid From to End of Duration*

In the case of Martex, the revenue accounting transactional price is 100.00 USD (as noted in Table 6.2). The number of days in the recurrence period is set to 30 as the recurring charge is once a month; although days in a month can vary, SAP uses 30 to derive a per-day transactional price. The valid from date is 07/01/2019. An end of duration date is to be provided in a provider contract to calculate the SAP Revenue Accounting and Reporting transaction price, although this agreement may not have a specified end date. For Martex, the end of duration is 06/30/2020, for a total of 365 days between the valid from and end of duration dates. The total transaction price of the performance obligation is calculated as USD1,216.67 (as in Table 6.3). Similarly, the standalone selling price (SSP) can be sent as an optional field from the provider contract replication and would derive a total SSP for the performance obligation of USD1,034.17. The standalone selling price can also be determined via BRFplus decision tables.

SAP Revenue Accounting and Reporting Contract					
Performance Obligation	Performance Obligation Type	Contractual Price	SSP	Frequency	Quantity
Martex partner product subscription	Subscription	$100.00	$85.00	Per month	1
Martex usage	Usage	$10.00	$10.00	Per unit	200

Table 6.2 Martex SAP Revenue Accounting and Reporting Contract 1

SAP Revenue Accounting and Reporting Contract					
Performance Obligation	Start Date	End Date	Fulfillment Type	TP Total	SSP Total
Martex partner product subscription	7/1/2019	6/30/2020	Time-based	$1,216.67	$1,034.17
Martex usage			Event-based consumption	$2,000.00	$2,000.00

Table 6.3 Martex SAP Revenue Accounting and Reporting Contract 2

Default condition types for standalone selling price and transaction price must be defined, as well as a default service type for recurring charges. The default service type is defined for SAP Revenue Accounting and Reporting because service IDs from SAP BRIM, subscription order management are not maintained for recurring charges (see Figure 6.18).

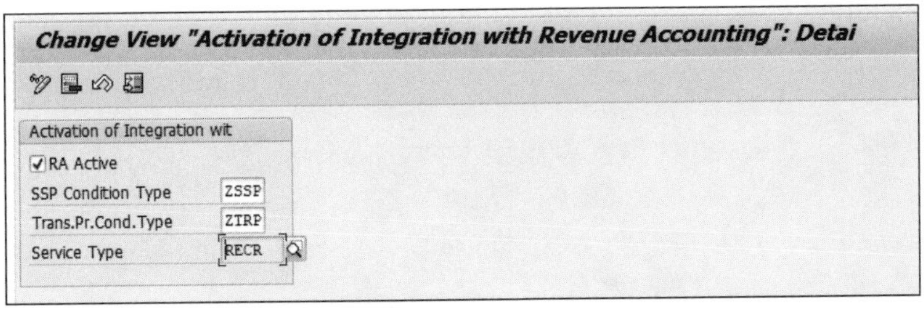

Figure 6.18 Activation of Integration with SAP Revenue Accounting and Reporting

At the time of provider order creation, service type ZUSG for usage/consumption-based charges would not be available for performance obligation creation; at this time, there is no quantity or transaction price for these items. It may be deemed valuable to estimate consumption at usage-based performance obligation inception. For this, SAP Revenue Accounting and Reporting has provided BRFplus decision tables to provide SAP Revenue Accounting and Reporting estimated usage quantity, transactional price, and standalone selling price per unit. Such estimates are based on quantitative evaluations that are calculated outside the framework of SAP BRIM and SAP Revenue Accounting and Reporting. An **Estimate Quantity** indicator in the order item revenue accounting item (usage-based) must be set to utilize BRFplus for estimating consumption. For Martex, a usage estimation has been determined for this contract of 200 units at a $10 transaction and standalone selling price per unit.

This SAP Revenue Accounting and Reporting contract now has two performance obligations, one recurring and one usage-based with transaction price and standalone selling prices maintained. We will see how allocation, fulfillment, and invoicing affect the revenue recognition in the next steps.

Step 4: Allocate the Transaction Price to the Performance Obligations of the Contract

Allocating the transaction price is done based on the standalone selling price of the performance obligations in the contract. The overall objective is to obtain an allocation of the amount of consideration that the organization considers to be entitled to pass the good or service promised. The calculation of the allocated transaction price is handled by SAP Revenue Accounting and Reporting and is calculated as follows:

*(Total SSP of the Performance Obligation / Total SSP of the RAR Contract) * (Total Transaction Price of the Contract) = Allocated Transaction Price of the POB*

For Martex, the allocated amounts are $1,096.37 and $2,120.30 for the two performance obligations, as noted in Table 6.4.

Revenue Allocation			
Performance Obligation	Transaction Price Total	SSP Total	Allocation to Performance Obligations
Martex partner product subscription	$1,216.67	$1,034.17	$1,096.37
Martex usage	$2,000.00	$2,000.00	$2,120.30
Total contract value	$3,216.67	$3,034.17	$3,216.67

Table 6.4 Revenue Allocation

SAP Revenue Accounting and Reporting automatically calculates the allocation of performance obligations at SAP Revenue Accounting and Reporting contract creation. In the next step, you will see how the fulfillments and invoices from SAP BRIM allow SAP Revenue Accounting and Reporting to calculate revenue, contract asset/unbilled receivables and contract liabilities, and deferred revenue.

Step 5: Recognize Revenue when (or as) the Entity Satisfies a Performance Obligation

In the final step of the five-step model, SAP Revenue Accounting and Reporting will receive fulfillments and invoice data from SAP BRIM to subsequently adjust the general ledger based on calculations for revenue and balance sheet items. In SAP Revenue Accounting and Reporting, a *fulfillment* is defined as the point in time to recognize revenue and any related cost of goods sold. In this step, we will expand on consumption fulfillments, time-based fulfillments, and invoice transfers from FI-CA. Briefly, we will touch on general ledger account determination and SAP Revenue Accounting and Reporting subledger general ledger transfer.

SAP Revenue Accounting and Reporting defines and provides various standard fulfillment methods for revenue recognition, including but not limited to event-based—customer invoice, shipping, or consumption; percentage of completion; and time-based with various deferral methods. In the SAP BRIM integration with SAP Revenue Accounting and Reporting, the fulfillment methods generally used are time-based, event-consumption, and event-customer invoice.

Referring to service types, an indicator with a fulfillment item is set for billable items related to usage in configuration, as shown in Figure 6.19. This configuration enables billable items to be evaluated and transferred periodically to be processed by SAP Revenue Accounting and Reporting to fulfill usage-based performance.

Service Types for Revenue Accounting Items						
Service Type	Service Type Text	Order Item	One-Time Charge	Fulfill. Item	Invoice Item	
RECR	Martex Partner Product	☑	☐	☐	☑	
ZUSG	Martex Usage	☑	☐	☑	☑	

Figure 6.19 Define Service Types

SAP Revenue Accounting and Reporting–specific fields are enabled in the billable items from convergent invoicing to support the consumption values to RAR. Usage billable items can rise in data volume because organizational units of consumption can be at a low level, such as minutes used or GB consumed. An aggregation occurs of the billable items as fulfillments in batches based on organizational need of frequency, corresponding revenue is realized. Transaction FP_RAI_TRANSF transfers revenue accounting fulfillment items from SAP Convergent Invoicing/FI-CA to SAP Revenue Accounting and Reporting en masse and can be set up as a recurring batch process.

Because SAP Revenue Accounting and Reporting relies on SAP BRIM to provide consumption events via billable items on a periodic basis to appropriately recognize revenue, for recurring charges the relevant fulfillment details are available at provider contract inception. For recurring charges, or subscription-based billing, related performance obligations receive the transaction price and the start and end dates from the provider contract. The start and end dates are received from the **Valid To** and **End of Duration** fields in the provider contract. SAP Revenue Accounting and Reporting will automatically generate a revenue schedule of amounts to be recognized over financial periods based on the start and end dates and deferral method. A deferral method defines how revenue will be amortized; there are several to choose from in standard SAP Revenue Accounting and Reporting based on business requirements.

For the purposes of Martex, we will be *1: Linear Distribution, Day-Specific, 365/366 Basis*. SAP Revenue Accounting and Reporting will calculate and spread the allocated transaction price for the performance obligations over financial periods based on how many days are in the period.

Figure 6.19 also displays the invoice item indicator, allowing the transfer of invoicing from FI-CA to SAP Revenue Accounting and Reporting. As invoices are processed in FI-CA, the relevant details are transferred to SAP Revenue Accounting and Reporting in batches periodically via Transaction FP_RAI_TRANSF as revenue accounting invoice items. Revenue accounting invoicing items contain main and condition items in parallel to revenue accounting order items. These attributes, as well as the source item ID of the original order item, will support referencing the performance obligation to enrich invoicing values. The difference between the recognized revenue and invoiced amount for the performance obligation is calculated and is posted to the balance sheet. This adjustment will post to contract asset/unbilled receivable and contract liability/deferred revenue respectively based on account determination and whether the difference is positive or negative.

For the Martex case study, we will consider consumption for usage charges (Martex Usage) and time-based for recurring charges (Martex Partner Product Subscription) scenarios.

In Table 6.5 and Table 6.6, a depiction of the SAP Revenue Accounting and Reporting contract allocation and revenue recognition for the first period of contract inception is displayed. As discussed in step 4, the allocation to the performance obligations has occurred. The usage and time-based fulfillments occur for July 2019 for these performance obligations, and revenue is recognized accordingly. The revenue calculated for the usage-based performance obligation is calculated as 20 units at $2,120.30/200=$10.6 each, for a total of $212.03 recognized revenue for the period. The Martex partner product subscription is calculated for 31 days in July 2019. The allocated transaction price ($1,096.37) is recognized for 31 days out of 365 for a total of $93.12 in recognized revenue for the July financial period. As a result of receiving a total invoice amount of $300 for the contract in the July period, there is a difference between the total recognized amount and invoiced amount. Because this difference realizes a recognized amount greater than the invoiced/billed amount, a net amount of $5.15 will be posted to the unbilled receivables balance sheet general ledger account.

SAP Revenue Accounting and Reporting Revenue Recognition for July 2019			
Performance Obligation	Performance Obligation Type	Transaction Price Total	Allocation to Performance Obligations
Martex partner product subscription	Subscription	$1,216.67	$1,096.37
Martex usage	Usage	$2,000.00	$ 2,120.30

Table 6.5 Martex SAP Revenue Accounting and Reporting Contract July 2019: Part 1

RAR Revenue Recognition for July, 2019				
Performance Obligation	Effective Quantity	Fulfilled Quantity	Recognized Amount	Invoiced Amount
Martex Partner Product Subscription	1	N/A	$93.12	$100.00
Martex Usage	200	20	$212.03	$200.00
			$305.15	$300.00

Table 6.6 Martex SAP Revenue Accounting and Reporting Contract July 2019: Part 2

There are two ledgers SAP Revenue Accounting and Reporting interacts with: the revenue accounting subledger and the financial general ledger. The SAP Revenue Accounting and Reporting subledger defines more details to support external disclosure reporting, analysis, and reconciliation. The transfer from the SAP Revenue Accounting and Reporting subledger to the FI general ledger occurs in batches and generally has summarized details, based on configuration. The postings are not in the scope of this documentation, but understand that SAP Revenue Accounting and Reporting derives accounts to be posted to via BRFplus configuration. SAP Revenue Accounting and Reporting account determination can derive the general ledger account to post to if a reference general ledger account is provided. A reference general ledger account is provided by the sender system. In the case of SAP BRIM, the provider contract will not provide reference accounts. BRFplus has the capability to use other attributes from the provider contract, such as service type, company code, business partner and others, to determine the general ledger accounts for SAP Revenue Accounting and Reporting to post to. Revenue, deferred revenue, unbilled receivables, contract assets, and contract liabilities, among others outside the scope of this chapter, can be determined.

6.5   SAP Customer Financial Management

This section will explain how to set up SAP Customer Financial Management, also known as SAP Financial Supply Chain Management, which includes collections management, dispute management, and credit management. SAP Customer Financial Management is an integrated solution within SAP BRIM that provides the capability of tracking, monitoring, and taking proactive action to get ahead of the financials of your customers.

SAP Customer Financial Management is an integrated solution suite alongside SAP BRIM. SAP Customer Financial Management is also available as part of the separate SAP FSCM suite or the full SAP S/4HANA solution suite. With SAP Customer Financial Management, companies can effectively record and manage their accounts receivable data for all customers, which leads to an increase in automation and reduction in manual effort and eventual costs. Additional benefits also include the availability of integrated data for dispute, collections, and credit management applications.

6.5.1   Collection Management

The collection management component integrates with the FI-CA, accounts receivable, and dispute management components of the SAP S/4HANA suite to support the processes of receivables management. As part of SAP S/4HANA, the following business functions are delivered by SAP as activated:

- FSCM, Enablement of Financial Shared Services (`FIN_FSCM_SSC_AIC_1`)
- FSCM Functions 3 (`FIN_FSCM_CCD_3`)
- FSCM Functions 2 (`FIN_FSCM_CCD_2`)
- FSCM Function (`FIN_FSCM_CCD`)

Collection management works in conjunction with accounts receivable to proactively collect outstanding payments from customers and allow companies to effectively manage their collections operations. There are three main processes supported by collection management:

- Collecting receivables
- Controlling the collection of receivables
- Data synchronization and creation of worklist

These processes are supported by various organizational data, master data, and configurations.

6.5.2 Organizational Structure

There are three components of the SAP ERP solution: organizational structure, master data, and transactional data. The organizational structure is the foundation of SAP ERP and reflects the structure of your company or business group.

Collection management's foundational structure is represented by collection profiles, collection segments, and collection groups. The collection profile is the highest level node in the organizational structure. Collection profiles are assigned with collection segments, and each collection segment can be assigned to multiple company codes to group the receivables from the respective company codes. Collection segments assigned to company codes represent lines of business.

In some firms, the accounts receivable team and collections team are the same; in others, they are separate. Depending on the client requirements and collections team structure, you can define the equivalent node in collection Management, called a collection group. A collection group represents the collections team. You can assign collection group to one or multiple collection segments depending on which company codes these collection groups will be performing receivables collection activities for.

6.5.3 Master Data

Collection activities are performed by collection segments and for business partners. Business partners need to be set up for collection management. A collection profile, collection segment, and collection group need to be assigned to a business partner along with the collection specialist. When the collection specialist or collection group is assigned to a business partner, all the receivables related to that business partner goes to the worklist of the specialist that's assigned to the business partner. If the business partner is not assigned with a specialist, then the receivables for all the business partners should be randomly distributed among specialists that are present in the collection group in the business partner master data. Based on who will handle the collection activity for the business partner, collection specialists are assigned to collection groups and the collection groups are assigned to business partners in the business partner master data.

One more important components of the master data/configuration is the collection strategy that allows a supervisor to define the rules for your worklist prioritization and display of items.

For a look at the organizational structure for collection management, see Figure 6.20.

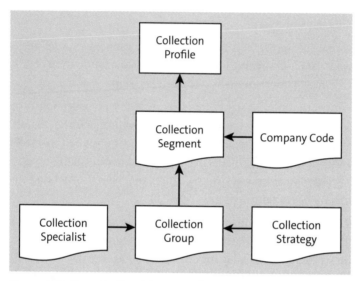

Figure 6.20 Organizational Structure for Collection Management

6.5.4   Collection Strategies

The worklist of a collection specialist is prepared automatically based on the settings maintained in the collection strategy. The collection strategy allows you to define the currency for the worklist, and usually it should be consistent with the document currency.

The collection strategy allows you to configure the following aspects of the worklist:

1. Overdue receivables aging bucket
2. Due receivables aging bucket
3. Prioritizing business partners for collection activity based on the collection rules
4. Receivables processing before due date
5. Excluding items that are legally dunned or defining tolerance days after dunning

SAP delivers standard basic rules that serve as conditions for prioritization of work-list items for each business partner. It also determines if the business partner is supposed to be included in the worklist or not.

For example, Rule BR00000016 Customer is not a direct payer. If this rule is part of the strategy as an exit rule, then any business partner that satisfies this rule will not be included in the worklist.

One or more basic rules are assigned to a collection rule, and along with preconditions defined in the collection rule for the basic rules, they allow you to prioritize and filter the worklist based on business partners. At the time of worklist generation, the business partners go through the check of collection rules and in turn basic rules. Collection rules are configured in collection strategies, a collection strategy is assigned to a collection group, and a collection group is assigned to a business partner.

6.5.5 Promise to Pay

One of the main activities of collection specialists is to keep track of customers who have promised to pay certain invoices/amounts by certain dates and make sure they are being followed through with in a timely manner.

Promise-to-pay functionality of collection management allows you to execute this function of a collection specialist by allowing you to create a promise to pay for each open item for a business partner.

Promise-to-pay functionality allows you to keep track of the promises to pay that are created for an invoice:

- Open (no payment exists)
- Open (payment exists, not applied)
- Broken
- Partially kept
- Kept

Withdrawal of the promise to pay is allowed in case a customer gives another promise to pay with a new date. Each promise to pay received for a business partner receives a level so that collection specialists can keep track of the number of promises to pay issued.

The installment plan function of the promise to pay allows a customer to define the number of installments for the amount that is being promised.

6.5.6   Customer Contact

In day-to-day collection activity performed by collection specialists, they will record multiple pieces of information based on follow-ups with customers. These follow-ups, whether successful or unsuccessful, can be recorded in a customer contact with a reason, date/time, contact type, result, user, and contact person.

Actions like promise to pay, dispute cases, resubmissions, or notes create a customer contact automatically.

6.5.7   Resubmission and Note

Resubmission works as reminder for the collection specialist to carry out any activity for a customer or invoice. Resubmission can also be used as a criterion in generating the worklist.

6.5.8   Integration with SAP Dispute Management

The SAP S/4HANA financial supply chain management suite provides a comprehensive solution for receivables management by seamlessly integrating collection management, dispute management, and credit management.

In collection management, you can activate the integration component of dispute management. You can also define a dispute case status code that you want to consider not collectible.

6.5.9   Dispute Management

In the world of providing products or services to a customer and charging them for those products and services, there will always be scenarios in which customers dispute a charge for various reasons. SAP provides the dispute management component to address this process and make sure that the complaints lodged by customers are recorded properly until they have reached their logical conclusions.

The dispute management component can be configured to integrate with the FI-CA component of SAP BRIM. In most FI-CA processes, a customer is on a recurring autodebit, so a customer usually raises a complaint rather than an automatic dispute case being created based on an underpayment.

Integration of Dispute Management and FI-CA

Dispute management can be integrated with FI-CA by activating the `FICA_FSCM_CRM_DISPUTE` business function. In addition, the `FIN_FSCM_CCD` and `FIN_FSCM_INTEGRATION` business functions also need to be activated to ensure the prerequisites are complete. Once these business functions are activated, they all are available for integration and configuration.

Configuring Dispute Management

The dispute management component is integrated with the FI-CA system at the company code level to determine which legal entity's receivables and customers are going to be part of the dispute management process. Figure 6.21 and the following configuration path show how to set up this configuration: **Financial Accounting · Contract Accounts Receivable and Payable · Organizational Units · Set Up Company Code for Contract Accounts Receivable and Payable**.

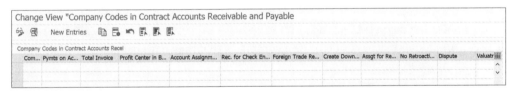

Figure 6.21 Company Codes in FI-CA

Assuming the company code for FI-CA contract receivables and payable is already done, you need to select the company for dispute cases in dispute management.

The next step in the process is to configure the integration of the both components (as shown in Figure 6.22). Go to **Financial Accounting · Contract Accounts Receivable and Payable · Integration · Financial Supply Chain Management · Dispute Management · Make Basic Settings for Dispute Management**.

As you can see, you need to set the **Active** field to tell the FI-CA system that in this instance dispute management is active.

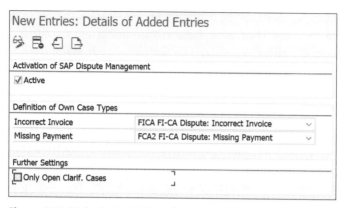

New Entries: Details of Added Entries

Activation of SAP Dispute Management
✓ Active

Definition of Own Case Types
| Incorrect Invoice | FICA FI-CA Dispute: Incorrect Invoice |
| Missing Payment | FCA2 FI-CA Dispute: Missing Payment |

Further Settings
☐ Only Open Clarif. Cases

Figure 6.22 Make Basic Settings for Dispute Management

Dispute cases are created by case types that act as containers for the dispute case that holds all the attributes for the dispute case. There are two scenarios—(1) incorrect invoices or incorrect credits or missing credits and (2) missing payments—for which SAP provides two standard case types: FICA and FCA2. You can create your own case types if there is a client-specific requirement to add more fields or change the case attribute profile, search profile, and so on. These standard case types contain attributes like priority, disputed amount, reason for the complaint, clerk responsible for resolution, and contact data of the business partner. Let's take a deeper look:

- **Missing payment**
  Customer reaches out to raise a complaint that they have paid but are still receiving a dunning notice

- **Incorrect invoice**
  Customer complaining about an incorrect amount on the invoice or an incorrect invoice in its entirety

6.5.10   Dispute Management for FI-CA

In this section, we'll cover dispute management. First, we'll start with the records management system.

Records Management System

The records management system is the instance in which you want to create dispute cases and store. You can create multiple record management systems or use the standard one provided by SAP, UDM _DISPUTE. Change the record management system ID to UDM_FICA_DISPUTE to process cases from FI-CA (as shown in Figure 6.23).

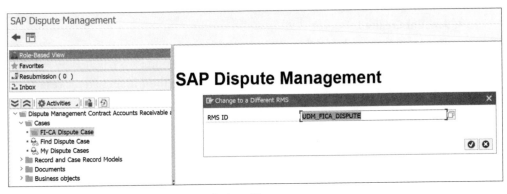

Figure 6.23 Select Record Management System ID

The UDM _DISPUTE record management system ID delivers standard element types in the dispute case processing system. Element types like dispute cases, business object include contact account/business partner, invoice or credits, and more, as in Figure 6.24.

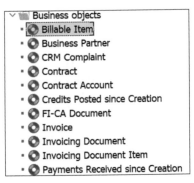

Figure 6.24 Element Types in Dispute Case

There are some important amount fields that need to be taken into consideration when looking at the case attributes:

- **Total Amount**
  This field is not updated automatically; it is total of all items for a business partner within a dispute case.

- **Disputed Amount**
  This is the amount in dispute raised by the customer. This does not change automatically if postings are made.

- **Amount Credited**
  This is automatically if the credit is posted against an invoice for an open dispute case using Transaction FPE1. Non-invoice-related credits are handled by the system to link them with the dispute cases based on the missing credit case type, business partner, and event 1251.

- **Amount Paid**
  Based on the missing payment category, the system determines the total amount paid for the total payment received for dispute cases.

- **Amount Written Off**
  If you write off a certain amount from a dispute case, the system will move that amount to this field.

Note that the creation of a dispute case is not supported from dispute management. Dispute cases can only be created in the FI-CA system.

Account Balance Display

There are two scenarios in which you can create a dispute case:

- **Dispute case with reference to an invoice**
  In SAP Easy Access menu, choose **Account · Account Balance**. Display the balances for a business partner (contract account) and then select one of the open documents to create a dispute case in reference to it.

  The dispute case type will be either incorrect invoice or incorrect credit. The scenario here shows that customer has determined that the invoice in question is open incorrectly even though they have made the payment, or a credit should be applied.

- **Dispute case without reference to an invoice**
  Inside the **Account Balance** menu, choose **Environment · Account · Dispute Cases · Create**.

  If you create a dispute case without selecting any document, then the system creates a dispute case without reference to an invoice or credit. This type of dispute case is defined as a missing payment case type. The scenario is that the customer has called in to report that they have made the payment, but it's not applied to an invoice.

Dispute Cases in Dispute Management

Once you access Transaction UDM_DISPUTE, it calls dispute case processing. You will need to expand the **Case** folder to find the dispute case or select **My Dispute Case** in order to find the dispute cases that are assigned to you as a person responsible or coordinator.

You can change the dispute case in Transaction UDM_DISPUTE by going to dispute case change mode. Only lot payments are assigned to the dispute case in the case of a missing payment because none of the payment-program-related payments are missing. Statistical amount, down payment, payment posted in the payment program, and payment posted in posting area 0113 are not considered as amounts of credits.

Attribute Profile

SAP delivers standard attribute profiles that are assigned to the standard case types that we talked about earlier (FICA, FCA2), as shown in Figure 6.25.

FICADIS2	FI-CA Dispute: Missed Payment	UDMCASEATTR10
FICADISP	FI-CA Dispute: Incorrect Invoice	UDMCASEATTR10

Figure 6.25 Standard Case Types

The attribute profile determines the field in the dispute case; if the standard attribute is insufficient or is too detailed, you can change the profile.

Status Profile

The status determines the lifecycle of the dispute case and allows you to identify the stage the dispute case currently is in. SAP delivers standard status profiles that provide statuses like new, being processed, closed, confirmed, and voided.

If you want to implement additional statuses by connecting to central status management, then you need to use BAdI SCMG_SET_STATUS_S for the initial status and BAdI SCMG_INIT_STATUS_S for a status change. To change the status, use the CRM_STATUS_CHANGE_FOR_ACTIVITY function module.

For the list of system statuses, see Table 6.7.

Status code	Description
003	External processing
007	Completed
008	Confirmed
009	Canceled

Table 6.7 System Statuses

Transfer to External Application

There are scenarios in which your FI-CA system and dispute management system in separate system for that you can configure the external application that you want to transfer the dispute case.

6.5.11   Credit Management

Managing credit in today's complicated marketplace is very important, including managing the risk associated with the customer. The credit management component is seamlessly integrated with FI-CA in SAP BRIM and allows you to manage credit for contract accounts.

Activate credit management under FI-CA in the integration section (as shown in Figure 6.26).

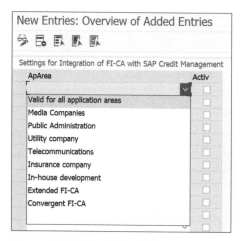

Figure 6.26 Activate Credit Management

Navigate to **Financial Accounting · Contract Accounts Receivable and Payable · Integration · Financial Supply Chain Management · Credit Management · Activate Credit Management**.

This configuration allows you to configure above listed application area. You need to activate Credit Management for the application areas that we will be using.

Maintain Credit Segment

 Accounts receivable credit management or sales and distribution credit management uses a credit control area for maintaining the credit limit at the credit control area level, but in credit management you can define a credit segment that allows you to store more than one credit limit and exposure for a business partner. You can also define the currency for the credit segment, which behaves as document currency for the credit segment.

Assign a credit segment to a difference posting area that uses the parameters, posting area, division, account determination ID, and business area.

Credit Worthiness

In FI-CA, integrated credit management is stored in an external credit rating procedure. This credit worthiness information is included in calculating the score for the business partner (contract account). The rating procedure for FI-CA with the function rating in the formula is configured in the following location: **Financial Supply Chain Management · Credit Management · Credit Risk Monitoring · Master Data · Define Rating Procedure**. To check credit limits, navigate to **Financial Supply Chain Management · Credit Management · Credit Risk Monitoring · Credit Limit Check**.

To determine credit worthiness, consider the following formula:

Score = FI-CA creditworthiness + Further items from SAP Credit Management

For a commitment query to work, you must define the check rule at the following location: **Financial Supply Chain Management · Credit Management · Credit Risk Monitoring · Credit Limit Check · Define Check Rules**.

Credit exposure update from contract accounts receivables and payable, all the business partners are transferred from SAP Credit Management. There are some mass activities for FI-CA:

- Business partner exposure data is sent to SAP Credit Management.
- Business partner payment behavior is sent to SAP Credit Management.
- The credit worthiness value is replicated.

6.6 Tax Engine

Countries like the United States and Canada have specific tax calculation requirements that are generally addressed by third-party tax engines. These tax engines provide a tax calculation outside of SAP systems, but they are flexible and seamlessly integrated with SAP systems.

Indirect tax calculation for the sale of hardware or software is addressed by using external tax engines.

Indirect taxes are levied by the service provider company against the customers, and then the tax collected is paid to the government by the service provider company.

During the sale of a product, the estimated tax is provided to the customers, and upon invoicing the actual tax is calculated and posted to the customer's account (see Figure 6.27).

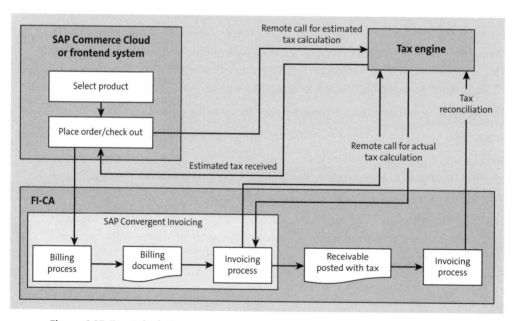

Figure 6.27 Tax Calculation Process

When SAP Commerce is used for frontend sales of a service, a remote call is made to the external tax engine for the estimated tax calculation, following which the billable items for the sale of the service are received in SAP Convergent Invoicing which undergoes a billing process and subsequently an invoicing process.

During the invoicing process, a remote call is made to an external tax engine and the data for tax calculation is passed to the tax system, in which the actual tax is calculated. The tax system then passes the tax data back to the SAP Convergent Invoicing system, and then receivables are posted with the tax amounts posted to the tax account.

SAP provides FQEVENTS as enhancement points, which can be used for coding custom logic if required.

FQEVENT 1110 is used for enhancing the invoicing process and for making a remote call for actual tax calculation. The data associated with the tax calculated externally is stored in database table DFKKEXTTAX.

Transaction FPTX is used for a tax audit for the tax calculation made by the external tax engine. Successful execution of this transaction updates the flag in table DFKKEXT-TAX (shown in Figure 6.28).

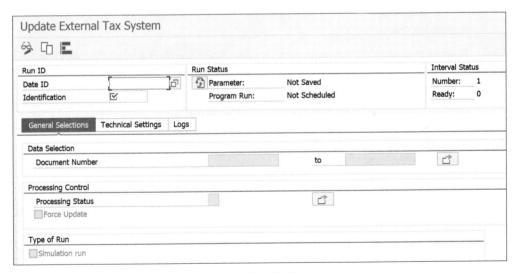

Figure 6.28 Transaction FPTX: Update External Tax System

In SAP Convergent Invoicing, during the invoicing process the RFC call is made to the tax engine for calculation of the final tax amount. The calculated tax is represented as a separate line item in the invoicing document, and the total amount is available in the invoice header.

There are different SAP-standard invoice item types that represent the line item types within the invoicing document. OTAXITEM is an item type for tax items. Tax items forms a separate line item within the invoice (as shown in Figure 6.29).

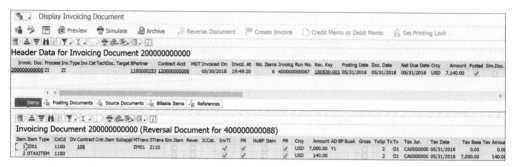

Figure 6.29 Invoice Document with Tax Item

The general ledger account determination for the tax posting is based on the tax determination code.

Posting area 2610 can be maintained at SPRO node **Contract Account Receivables and Payables · Convergent Invoicing · Invoicing · Documents · Posting Documents · Define Account Assignment for General Ledger Items** and contains the details of the revenue account determination and the tax determination code. This tax determination code linked to a tax code leads to the determination of a tax general ledger account for tax amount posting.

During the invoicing process, the tax calculated is shown in the line item of the invoicing document and the posting document, which is the FI-CA receivable document that contains the posting details of both the revenue and tax items (as in Figure 6.30).

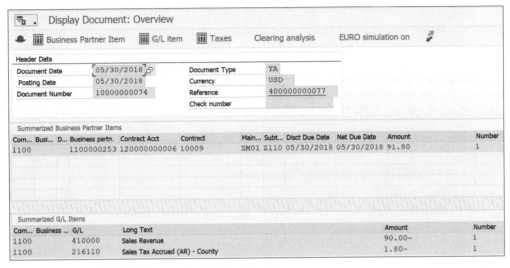

Figure 6.30 Sample FI-CA Document with Tax Line Item

6.7   Payment Gateway

In this section, we will explain the integration aspects of SAP BRIM with external payment gateways. This chapter generally focuses on options available within SAP BRIM, in which FI-CA can be integrated with the payment gateway for credit card settlements.

Let's start with some key terminology:

- **Payment gateway**
  Enables a payment transaction by transferring payment information like credit card details, transaction amount, and so on securely between the merchant and the payment processor.

- **Payment processor**
  Processes the payment transactions from various channels, like credit/debit cards, to the acquiring bank.

- **Acquiring bank**
  Processes the credit/debit card payments on behalf of the merchant. The payments from the issuing bank are transferred eventually to the acquiring bank.

In a scenario in which a customer makes a purchase with their credit card from any customer portal, the credit card details are validated and processed by the payment gateway. Once the payment is authorized, the credit card is charged and the payment details are sent to FI-CA as a payment billable items along with the revenue transaction in an integrated SAP BRIM solution. As explained in Chapter 4, every transaction is passed to FI-CA as a billable item—in this case, a revenue billable item and a payment billable item. The accounting entries after billing and invoicing are as follows:

- Revenue Posting (Revenue Billable Item):
  - Dr. Customer
  - Cr. Sales
- Payment Posting (Payment Billable Item):
  - Dr. Credit Card Clr. A/C
  - Cr. Customer

The payment received as part of the credit card charge has been captured in the credit card clearing A/C and the customer account has been cleared; that is, no open items remain on the customer account.

The next step is for the payment processor to settle the funds with the bank of the company providing the services. This can be automated from FI-CA as part of a credit card settlement run. As a result of the credit card settlement run, the following accounting entries are posted:

- Dr. Bank
- Cr. Credit Card Clr. A/C

The credit card settlement run is executed by running Transaction FPCS in FI-CA. As part of the settlement run, an integration can be built with the payment gateway to help enable the automated credit card settlement.

6.8   Summary

The SAP BRIM integration with SAP Revenue Accounting and Reporting has been important for organizations that have been affected by accounting standard ASC606. Many of the same organizations that leverage SAP BRIM for subscription and usage-based models are in the technology, media, and entertainment industries. These industries are the most affected by the transition to ASC606 due to the multielement nature of their agreements with customers.

A standard integration to handle large volumes of transactions from SAP BRIM in SAP Revenue Accounting and Reporting provides benefits for automated revenue recognition, flexible disclosure, and adherence accounting standards. For accounting organizations, the automation and reconciliation functionality provided by SAP Revenue Accounting and Reporting will reduce critical month-end close activities, as well as provide external auditors with a clear end-to-end order to revenue view to provide detailed support for reported financials.

6

Chapter 7
First Steps to SAP BRIM

Similar to other software implementation projects, getting SAP BRIM up and running requires planning, evaluation, and thoughtful consideration of current and future states. This chapter offers best practices for planning and considering SAP BRIM as a solution. You will learn how to avoid common pitfalls and gain insights into key decision points.

In this chapter, we will evaluate the leading thought principles you should consider for an implementation of SAP BRIM. There are many key decision points to consider when implementing SAP BRIM, including but certainly not limited to deployment options, product types, master data considerations, and more. Throughout this chapter, we will highlight key concepts to consider when implementing SAP BRIM and provide insights into how to successfully deploy this tool.

Each and every SAP implementation is filled with unique experiences driven by many factors, such as business scenarios, customer requirements, system landscapes, scope of the project, transactional volume, and company policy in regards to security, to name a few. Other factors that impact the implementation are the types of deployment, such as on-premise versus cloud. These factors drive the implementation approach, hardware size, type of software to install, and project duration.

In every SAP project, or any IT project, for that matter, initial planning is required. The planning phase is a critical step, and it can take weeks or even months. Depending on the project, it may require a full-time commitment from different groups such IT and business stakeholders, as well as time committed in multiple working sessions.

In this phase, team members gather information about current systems and business processes, discuss the deliverables of the project, and determining any dependencies to identify gaps.

7.1   Why Do Businesses Move into Subscription-Based Business?

In today's digital economy, most businesses transform their operating models into subscription-based business models. This move is driven by several factors, such as the following:

- The need to grow the business by expanding their offering portfolio horizontally and vertically via ambition and acquisition
- A need for a new path to market found by transforming the current product offerings from delivery-based into service-based ones

This business model also lets customers access, consume, and pay for services or products based on need and usage. From a financial standpoint, subscription-based business enables companies to have a more predictable and continuous revenue stream.

There are multiple flavors of subscription-based business models to support different types of revenue streams. The following provides some of the common ones:

- **Recurring fee and on-demand subscription**
  This offer allows customer to consume services with or without limits, according to the contract (such as video streaming, on-demand and fixed monthly fee, like cable TV and internet services)

- **Usage based subscription**
  This offer is based on services consumed by customers such as telecommunications data plan, cloud storage

- **One-off charge fee**
  This type of charges is usually triggered by new contract activation, contract renewal, and early termination of a contract

- **Predefined subscription**
  This offer provides access to specific resources (like a SaaS, PaaS, or XaaS)

- **Brokerage/transaction fees**
  This type of subscription is based on per transaction fee (such as Ameritrade and E-Trade)

To implement a flexible consumption and subscription business model, you need to build a landscape to support your desired model. In building your landscape, you can decide to leverage what you have in the cloud or on premise. The next step is to evaluate your landscape.

7.2   Evaluating Your Current Landscape

There are several different scenarios when implementing SAP BRIM. Before starting with an SAP BRIM project, you need to evaluate your current system landscape to determine what components of SAP BRIM to install.

SAP BRIM consists of three different application components: SAP BRIM, subscription order management; SAP Convergent Charging; SAP Convergent Invoicing; and Contract Accounts Receivable and Payable. Prior to SAP S/4HANA 1809, SAP BRIM, subscription order management was part of the SAP CRM system. With SAP S/4HANA 1809, it is included with SAP BRIM.

7.2.1   Company Currently Running SAP

If your company is already using SAP, use the following checks to help you determine what can be used for SAP BRIM:

- Check if your company has SAP CRM and SAP ERP. Determine if the versions are compatible:
    - Configuration would be SAP CRM 7.0, EHP 4; SAP ERP 6.0, EHP 8; and SAP Convergent Charging 5.0.
    - You may need to activate some additional business functions.
    - Configuration of SAP Financial Supply Chain Management/SAP Convergent Invoicing is also required.
- Check if your company only uses SAP ERP or SAP S/4HANA prior to 1809, and no SAP CRM:
    - For this scenario, you need to check if an upgrade to 1809 is planned in the near future.
    - If no upgrade is planned, then SAP S/4HANA version 1709, 1610, or 1511 can be used.
    - You will also need to install SAP CRM 7.0, EHP 4, as well as SAP Convergent Charging 5.0.
- Check if your company plans to upgrade to 1809. This scenario does not require SAP CRM. This scenario will be simple as it will only require an upgrade to SAP S/4HANA 1809 and installation of SAP Convergent Charging 5.0.
- Check if your company plans to install SAP BRIM from the ground up. This would be a greenfield installation. For this scenario, it would be best to install SAP S/4HANA 1809 or later and SAP Convergent Charging 5.0 with the latest support pack.

The recommended database is SAP HANA 2.0, but other databases are supported. Check the product availability matrix for compatibility.

Best practice recommends the installation of the latest support packs for all components.

7.2.2   Communication between Systems in the SAP BRIM Landscape

In addition, consider the communication between SAP CRM, SAP ERP, and SAP Convergent Charging. Depending on your security policies, you may need to secure RFC and web service calls. The communication to SAP Convergent Charging is through web service calls configured in Transaction SOAMANAGER. The connection can use an HTTP or HTTPS protocol depending on requirements. Systems spanning networks may require more secure communications like HTTPS, while systems in the same network may not have that requirement. The communication from SAP Convergent Charging and SAP ERP and SAP CRM leverages a JCO connection. This should also use load balancing if SAP CRM and/or SAP ERP have multiple application servers. RFC and JCO connections must be authenticated with a username/password. This user should be created as a system user. A system user will not be able to log on to your systems directly. You can also configure SAP CRM and SAP ERP to support SSL. A good practice is to use RFC load balancing to connect ABAP systems.

Once you have agreement on a deployment scenario, you may need to decide to update or upgrade some of your products.

SAP BRIM integration usually consists of the following products:

- SAP Convergent Mediation by DigitalRoute
- SAP BRIM, subscription order management
- SAP Convergent Charging
- SAP ERP (SAP Financial Supply Chain Management/SAP Convergent Invoicing) or SAP S/4HANA

7.2.3   Verify Landscape Selection with PAM

A good tool to check when deciding on product updates or upgrades is SAP's Product Availability Matrix. The PAM provides the technical information for all SAP product versions. It has upgrade paths, release dates, and support end dates. It should be the starting point for planning your environment. You also can check system landscape directory (SLD) and landscape management database (LMDB). This can be done in

SAP Solution Manager either directly in Transaction LMDB, or with the **Landscape Management** tile in the SAP Solution Manager. Figure 7.1 shows the **Landscape Management** tile in SAP Solution Manager.

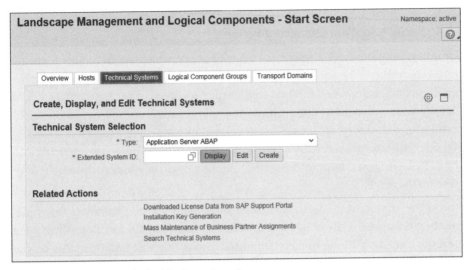

Figure 7.1 SAP LMDB Technical Systems Search

Once you have decided on products and versions, you can plan landscape changes with the maintenance planner, another tool offered by SAP for planning (as in Figure 7.2). This tool should contain information about all the products in your landscape.

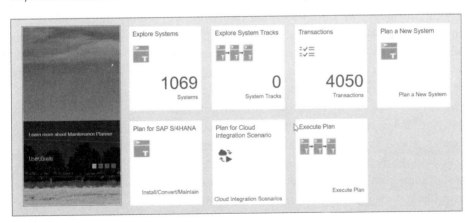

Figure 7.2 Maintenance Planner

From here, you can select a system and the planned upgrade. This will help determine the upgrade path. Follow-up steps include planning and executing the upgrade throughout your landscape.

7.2.4   Security for Your Connected Systems

Some organizations have a restrictive security policy, which would require securing the systems in your SAP BRIM landscape. Securing SAP Convergent Charging requires configuring SSL/TLS. When configuring, you need to generate certificates to identify your systems. Depending on your policy, you can use self-signed or signed certificates. Self-signed certificates are generated by open-source tools like OpenSSL. Signed certificates are signed by a certificate authority. Certificates are imported into the SAP Convergent Charging core server and should also be added to the default keystore on the server.

One of the important things to remember when using signed certificates for implementing enhanced security is that the root and intermediate certificates provided with the signed certificate must be imported into the default Java truststore on the server.

7.2.5   Load Balancing

Performance of the solution is always essential to its success. To increase the responsiveness of the SAP BRIM solution, consider implementing load balancing. Load balancing distributes the application load across multiple servers, thereby increasing the responsiveness of the solution. Load balancing can be in a round-robin style in which you let the application decide, or you can determine how the load is distributed by design. One of the great features of SAP Convergent Charging is that it has internal load balancing. When multiple dispatcher instances are installed, one dispatcher instance, the master dispatcher, controls where requests are directed. You can further decide on the robustness of your load balancing solution by the distribution of instances over multiple servers. For example, you can install dispatcher, guider, rater, bulkloader, and updater instances on multiple servers, or you can install some combination of the instances on a dispatcher/guider, rater/bulkloader, and updater on separate servers. The distribution and number of servers can be determined by performing a sizing exercise. There are multiple options for databases, for all systems in the landscape. SAP is encouraging moving to the SAP HANA database for SAP products. SAP HANA is an in-memory database that has faster transaction speeds. When processing, speed is a critical factor. SAP HANA also is scalable. You can scale by adding additional resources on a single hardware element or by adding additional hardware. You can start with a single node and add additional nodes later. With SAP HANA, you can also implement a high-availability solution, which is a requirement for most production systems. The goal for any production system is to *not* have a single point of failure. With SAP HANA 2.0, multitenancy is a default. Multitenancy provides multiple isolated databases per SAP HANA system. For instance, there can be one development SAP HANA system with multiple SAP HANA databases with their own system IDs.

For one specific client, the SAP CRM system was already on-premise, as well as FSCM/SAP Convergent Invoicing. SAP Convergent Charging was to be installed. Two instances were required to limit latency. The systems were built in the US and EMEA regions. For using the SAP Convergent Charging client applications, enhanced security was required for communicating across regions. Communication between SAP CRM and SAP Convergent Charging was through web service calls. Because there was an SAP CRM and FSCM system in each region, this communication was in the same region and thus enhanced security was not required.

If hardware is not available, it is possible to install on temporary hardware and migrate to newer hardware later. This is possible using virtual machines. This is seamless for the application and can be done by moving a virtual machine from one physical host to another. This can take place during a downtime period and usually takes a few hours.

7.2.6   Migrating Changes

How do you move changes throughout the landscape? For ABAP-based systems, this is not an issue: you can use a domain controller and add systems and transport routes. Because SAP Convergent Charging is Java-based, change and transport system (CTS+) is an option. For CTS+, you need to agree on the ABAP system to use for attaching SAP Convergent Charging. SAP Solution Manager is most often used because it has an ABAP and a Java stack. CTS+ requires both. Additional roles may be needed to be built so that developers/configurators can attach the work developed in SAP Convergent Charging to a transport. Usually, with segregation of duties, the creator of a transport cannot import a transport. If you have secured your landscape by enabling the HTTPS protocol, additional steps must be done in CTS+ configuration to connect to the core server for importing transports. If you choose not to duse CTS+ to migrate your changes through the landscape, you can use the client tool, called core_tool, to export and import your changes.

7.2.7   Monitoring

You will need to have a monitoring and alerting strategy. SAP Solution Manager is required for ABAP monitoring. There is alerting available, as well as notifications that can be triggered. In addition, there are tools for monitoring SAP HANA (as in Figure 7.3). The SAP HANA cockpit lets you monitor all your SAP HANA systems in one location. The cockpit runs on SAP HANA, and there is usually a separate SAP HANA instance solely for it. For SAP Convergent Charging root-cause analysis, use Wily Introscope Agent, which is part of SAP Solution Manager.

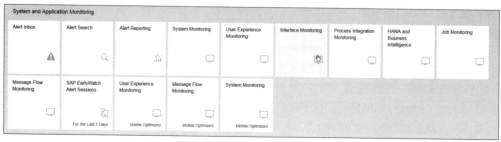

Figure 7.3 SAP Solution Manager Monitoring

7.2.8   Data Protection

Data protection involves protecting your data using a backup/recovery strategy. Most clients use a third-party tool such as Tivoli for backing up their entire landscape. Best practice is to have some automated backup strategy. Furthermore, you should decide when to backup and when to have a full backup or a delta backup. For SAP HANA, online backup is possible; other databases have online or offline options. It is possible to backup to disk, then to tape. Best practice is to test the system recovery to ensure your strategy is working.

7.2.9   Sizing

In addition to determining a production version, operating system, and database, you need to decide on hardware to determine if the current hardware is robust enough to handle additional functionality. A sizing exercise is a good approach to answer this question. SAP has defined three types of sizing, greenfield, production, and expert:

- Greenfield sizing is usually for new implementations. The tool to use for this is SAP Quick Sizer, which uses several metrics of your environment to produce recommendations for CPU, memory, database space, and disk I/O (as in Figure 7.4). With these results, you can work with your hardware vendor or you can check the benchmark table, all found on the SAP Quick Sizer site.

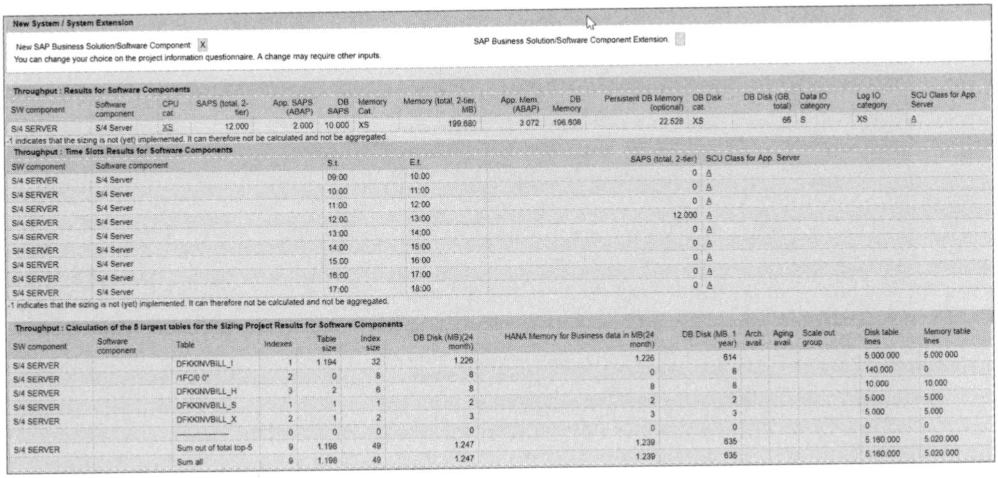

New System / System Extension

New SAP Business Solution/Software Component X   SAP Business Solution/Software Component Extension

You can change your choice on the project information questionnaire. A change may require other inputs.

Throughput : Results for Software Components

SW component	Software component	CPU cat	SAPS (total, 2-tier)	App. SAPS (ABAP)	DB SAPS	Memory Cat.	Memory (total, 2-tier, MB)	App. Mem. (ABAP)	DB Memory	Persistent DB Memory (optional)	DB Disk cat.	DB Disk (GB, total)	Data IO category	Log IO category	SCU Class for App. Server
S/4 SERVER	S/4 Server	XS	12.000	2.000	10.000	XS	199.680	3.072	196.608	22.528	XS	66	S	XS	A

-1 indicates that the sizing is not (yet) implemented. It can therefore not be calculated and not be aggregated.

Throughput : Time Slots Results for Software Components

SW component	Software component	S.t.	E.t.	SAPS (total, 2-tier)	SCU Class for App. Server
S/4 SERVER	S/4 Server	09:00	10:00	0	A
S/4 SERVER	S/4 Server	10:00	11:00	0	A
S/4 SERVER	S/4 Server	11:00	12:00	0	A
S/4 SERVER	S/4 Server	12:00	13:00	12.000	A
S/4 SERVER	S/4 Server	13:00	14:00	0	A
S/4 SERVER	S/4 Server	14:00	15:00	0	A
S/4 SERVER	S/4 Server	15:00	16:00	0	A
S/4 SERVER	S/4 Server	16:00	17:00	0	A
S/4 SERVER	S/4 Server	17:00	18:00	0	A

-1 indicates that the sizing is not (yet) implemented. It can therefore not be calculated and not be aggregated.

Throughput : Calculation of the 5 largest tables for the Sizing Project Results for Software Components

SW component	Software component	Table	Indexes	Table size	Index size	DB Disk (MB)(24 month)	HANA Memory for Business data in MB(24 month)	DB Disk (MB, 1 year)	Arch. avail.	Aging avail.	Scale out group	Disk table lines	Memory table lines
S/4 SERVER		DFKKINVBILL_I	1	1.194	32	1.226	1.226	614				5.000.000	5.000.000
S/4 SERVER		/1FC/0 0*	2	0	8	8	0	8				140.000	0
S/4 SERVER		DFKKINVBILL_H	3	2	6	8	8	8				10.000	10.000
S/4 SERVER		DFKKINVBILL_S	1	1	1	2	2	2				5.000	5.000
S/4 SERVER		DFKKINVBILL_X	2	1	2	3	3	3				5.000	5.000
		————————	0	0	0	0	0	0				0	0
S/4 SERVER		Sum out of total top-5	9	1.198	49	1.247	1.239	635				5.160.000	5.020.000
		Sum all	9	1.198	49	1.247	1.239	635				5.160.000	5.020.000

Figure 7.4 SAP Quick Sizer

- Productive sizing is done when you have already gone live and wish to add new functionality. For this, you can look at past performance and extrapolate. You can check transactions like ST03 and STAD as part of that process. In addition, reports like SAP EarlyWatch can provide further details. SAP has provided Report /SDF/HDB_SIZING to assist with sizing SAP HANA (as in Figure 7.5).

- Expert sizing for SAP Convergent Charging is done by SAP; it is not on the SAP Quick Sizer site. SAP will analyze your environment based on data such as number of contracts, growth rate, recurring charges, and charge plan complexity. With that input, SAP will determine the required throughput. A sizing recommendation is provided for the number of servers, number of CPUs, and amount of memory. This is provided to a hardware vendor to provision the required servers.

```
RESULTS OF SUITE ON HANA SIZING IN GB

Based on the selected table(s),the anticipated memory requirement is:

  Column store data                                              11,3
+ Row store data                                                 15,0
+ Work space                                                     26,3
+ Hybrid LOB stored on disk                                      13,3
+ Fixed size for code, stack and other services                 50,0

= Anticipated total memory requirement considering 20% records stored
    on disk are cached in memory                                105,3

Sizing report:                                           /SDF/HDB_SIZING
SID                                                                  HTP
NW release:                                                     740 SP 7
Date of analysis:                                             08.07.2019
Version of the report:                                                44
Selected accuracy:                                                     L
Number of work processes used:                                        01
Type of analyzed database:                                         MSSQL

Number of tables successfully analyzed:                          103.674
Number of tables partially analyzed:                                   0
Number of tables with error:                                           3
Error estimation in % due to tables with errors:                       0
```

Figure 7.5 Sample Report from SAP Quick Sizer

Expert sizing for the SAP HANA database for SAP Convergent Charging is also not available via the SAP Quick Sizer tool, and there is no official documentation. It is done by SAP based on SAP's internal testing and other clients running SAP Convergent Charging on SAP HANA. To provide a recommendation, several factors are taken into consideration, such as if the application is more geared toward real-time or batch-based processing. Also, SAP requires the hardware be certified to run SAP HANA. A list of certified vendors is provided in the certified and supported SAP HANA Hardware Directory.

Let's take a look at a sample SAP Convergent Charging SAP HANA sizing recommendation report (as in Table 7.1):

- Deploy six server hosts for SAP Convergent Charging core server instances:
    - Two servers to host dispatcher and guider instances (one each)
    - Two servers to host rater and bulkloader instances (one each)
    - Two servers to host updater instances (one each)

- Deploy a minimum-sized SAP HANA database node (RAM), 192 GB, based on certified hardware and deployment model
- Load test before go-live to assess suitability and to verify that the CPU sizing is sufficient

2M Contracts	SAPS	Memory (GB)	Storage (GB)
Server (dispatcher and guider)	1000	10	128
Server (rater and bulkloader)	7500	22	750
Server (updater)	7500	15	128
Database server (SAP HANA)	-	192	711

Table 7.1 Sample SAP Convergent Charging SAP HANA Sizing Recommendation Report

Whether you choose greenfield, production, or expert sizing, a sizing exercise should
be performed for all products that make up SAP BRIM. Your approach may be a mix-
ture of types depending on what is already installed on your landscape.

When evaluating your landscape, there are multiple factors to consider. Consider
hardware, software, security, and performance, as well as the other factors discussed
in this section. Appraise your landscape and how you want to deploy SAP BRIM.
Defining your landscape and deployment options is a building block for defining
your SAP BRIM solution.

There are multiple factors to evaluate when deciding to implement SAP BRIM. First,
decide what products to implement and determine what needs to be installed or
updated or upgraded. Second, what additional configuration needs to be done on
existing products? Determine where servers will be located to reduce latency if you
require global access. It is also important to decide on infrastructure—that is, physical versus virtual. Also, you should consider security, error reporting, and data protection.

7.3   Evaluating Your Deployment Options

There are several deployment options available according to different business
requirements. Every project has its own unique requirements and needs to be ana-
lyzed carefully while evaluating the deployment options. In one good example of

such a scenario, say that after the generation of invoices in SAP Convergent Invoicing, the process is extended for the billing process in Sales and Distribution. Another business requirement could be related to the billing of bundled products with hardware sales through Sales and Distribution and digital sales through SAP BRIM, subscription order management, SAP Convergent Charging, and SAP Convergent Invoicing in a single invoice. There are requirements for FI-CA postings as well, in which invoiced items in SAP Convergent Invoicing can be further processed for account postings either using the standard FI-CA integration or via FI with custom developments.

The following sections discuss a few deployment options.

7.3.1   Deployment Option with SAP Flexible Solution Billing

In this option, billing data from SAP Convergent Invoicing and other legacy systems can be integrated in Sales and Distribution for a unified billing process in SAP Flexible Solution Billing. This option is best suited for billing the bundled products having hardware sales through Sales and Distribution and digital sales through SAP BRIM (subscription order management, SAP Convergent Charging, and SAP Convergent Invoicing) in a single invoice.

7.3.2   Deployment Option with Sales and Distribution Integration

In this option, Sales and Distribution billing data from the legacy system can be integrated with SAP Convergent Invoicing to consolidate different streams of revenue. This option is best suited for billing the bundled products with hardware sales through Sales and Distribution and digital sales through SAP BRIM, subscription order management, SAP Convergent Charging, and SAP Convergent Invoicing in a single invoice. Evaluation is to be made between option one and two, based on future solution architecture, deployment effort, and more.

7.3.3   Deployment Options with FI-CA Posting

In this option, invoiced items in SAP Convergent Invoicing can be further processed for account postings, either using the standard FI-CA integration or via FI with custom developments. FI-CA includes all the standard features of FI, such as open item management, payments processing, dunning, and so on. In addition, FI-CA provides additional capabilities, such as mass parallel processing, summarized postings, and standard integration with the general ledger.

7.4   Reviewing Rapid Deployment Solutions and Implementation Best Practices

Rapid deployment solutions (RDS) are preconfigured applications that allow companies to deploy software in weeks or months for a set price. RDS are designed to address one area of an SAP enterprise application and address a specific function or need. They are designed to meet about 60% to 70% of what a customer needs, beyond which the customer can customize and tailor as needed to address unique requirements. Rapid deployment solutions are not just toolkits, but solutions that have configuration templates (customized settings) with supporting consulting services. They also provide best practices to customers who use SAP software. Licensed customers get an added advantage because the content is free, and this helps them to reduce implementation costs and speed up deployment, which in turn adds benefits to their investment in SAP products.

Rapid deployment solutions use the concept of assemble-to-order (A2O), which helps to create one project from different SAP rapid deployment solutions to address any critical business challenges. With the help of rapid deployment solutions, you can innovate and extend your technology to provide business solutions, provide mobile user experiences, and get help from the cloud. Rapid deployment solutions work with the ASAP methodology, which provides a framework for SAP projects for implementation and enhancements and customizations needed for postproduction support.

While deploying rapid deployment solutions, it can be done individually or can be combined. But combining solutions will take extra integration steps and testing. For installing a solution, one or more software products will be needed, and RDS come with an SAP Solution Manager template, which can be used individually or can be combined. A solution can be either implemented or configured using manual configuration or automated configuration. Once the configuration is done and activation is completed, you can test your solutions using the template test scripts provided along with the scope items.

RDS provide a complete configuration and master data setup, including business partners, products, pricing, and business agreements/contracts. The following sections provide basic information about master data and how to setup for SAP BRIM implementation.

7.5   Master Data

Master data is one of the most important objects in the SAP application framework and is used across almost all processes in every area of SAP and SAP BRIM.

The following master data needs to be considered while implementing the SAP BRIM:

- Business partner
- Business agreement (SAP CRM)/contract account (SAP ERP and SAP S/4HANA)
- Product
- Pricing

7.5.1   Business Partner

Business partner is a generic term used for parties involved in a business scenario and can represent anyone involved in the business or who shows interest in the business or project. The business transactions or scenarios they can access depend on the roles assigned to them. The business partner record holds vital information like name, address, bank details, communication details, and more. It is always best practice to create a business partner in SAP CRM first (if SAP CRM is deployed as a standalone application); once created, it can be replicated to SAP Convergent Invoicing (SAP ERP and SAP S/4HANA [prior to version 1809]) as a business partner and to SAP Convergent Charging as a subscriber account.

Each business partner is identified using a unique business partner number. A business partner is created in SAP CRM as a sold-to party role and it will be replicated to SAP Convergent Invoicing in either SAP ERP or SAP S/4HANA (prior to version 1809). The replicated business partner in SAP Convergent Invoicing will automatically create a business partner role MKK (Contract Partner). This role is mandatory for creating transactional data (provider contract) in SAP Convergent Invoicing (Figure 7.6). The business partner number range can be external or internal depending on the business scenario. For example, if business partner creation is being handled by a third-party system, then the external number range should be configured in SAP to accept the business partner ID. If SAP CRM is the leading system for maintaining master data, then an internal number range needs to be configured in SAP and SAP will generate business partner IDs when new business partners are created. An external or internal number range should be assigned to a business partner grouping. Starting from SAP S/4HANA, version 1809, a business partner is created directly in SAP S/4HANA. In addition, subscription order management is embedded as part of SAP S/4HANA in customer management.

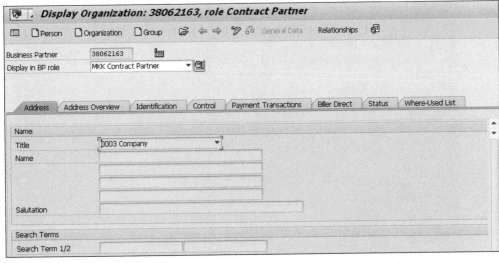

Figure 7.6 Business Partner in MKK Role in SAP ERP (SAP Convergent Invoicing)

7.5.2 Business Agreement (SAP CRM)/Contract Management (SAP ERP and SAP S/4HANA)

A business agreement is an object used to store controlling data for a long-term business relationship with a business partner. A business agreement is also used to store financial data details like the following:

- Payment scheduling
- Payment terms
- Tax
- Invoice creation

- Correspondence
- Dunning control
- Bank details/payment card details

These values control processes in open item accounting and invoicing.

A business agreement is used to handle both prepaid and postpaid products. In prepaid products, there is a prepaid account involved, which is a subset of the business agreement. Prepaid accounts have additional details like a minimum balance and are widely used in telecommunication and tollway solutions.

Once a business agreement is successfully created in the SAP system, the agreement will be replicated to SAP ERP or SAP S/4HANA (prior to version 1809) as a contract account via SAP CRM middleware (Figure 7.7).

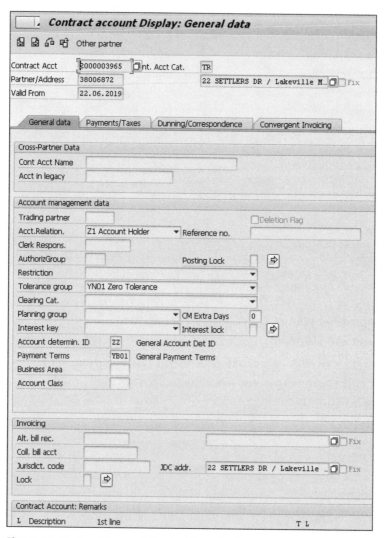

Figure 7.7 Contract Account Created from Business Agreement

A business agreement is always attached to a business partner, and a business partner can have one or more business agreements or contract accounts. When processing a business transaction (contract creation), you can always make sure that the system determines a suitable business agreement.

7.5.3 Products

SAP BRIM requires a product as part of the master data setup. The type of the product is a subscription product. You create a subscription product in SAP BRIM, subscription order management. A subscription product provides attributes and settings required to create a provider order and provider contract. Once the business requirements of the client are obtained, you can start planning what attributes and settings are required to create the products. Product setup starts with a product hierarchy and product category. Product master data is bundled into a product model, which is a container for modeling data. If your implementation requires configurable products, you need to perform additional setup, such as setting up classifications, dependencies, characteristics, and characteristic values.

For configurable products, a customer can choose from multiple given options. They can contain many characteristics, and a customer can select values for any characteristic while ordering the product. According to the value of each of the characteristics of each attribute/value, product components will be determined automatically by the rules configured during product modeling.

There are different types of products based on business usage:

- Rate plan products (recurring and usage)
- One-off product
- Hardware/physical products
- Configurable products

A subscription product must be assigned to a charge plan through cross-catalog mapping, which will be discussed in the next section. You need to create a charge plan in SAP Convergent Charging before you can perform cross-catalog mapping. A charge plan represents the charging part of a service that a service provider offers to its customers or partners via the product catalog and service provisioning. A charge plan must have one or more charge objects in the same catalog. A charge has three types of price plans: recurring, one-time, and usage-based types.

Cross-Catalog Mapping

Cross-catalog mapping is a process to assign a subscription product in SAP BRIM, subscription order management to a charge plan in SAP Convergent Charging. Cross-catalog mapping is done during product setup in SAP BRIM, subscription order management (see Figure 7.8). During this process, SAP BRIM, subscription order management calls a web service of SAP Convergent Charging to show the list of available charge plans. After the mapping process is completed, a mapping version will be automatically created in the SAP CRM product. The mapping version should be in released status for the cross-catalog mapping to be activated. The information stored in this mapping is then used during replication of contracts to SAP Convergent Invoicing and SAP Convergent Charging. Information needed in billing, provisioning, or other systems is gathered using the mapping rules defined in cross-catalog mapping. Cross-catalog mapping versions and details are available in the **Cross-Catalog Mapping** assignment block in the SAP CRM web UI.

Figure 7.8 Cross Catalog Mapping of SAP CRM Product in SAP BRIM, Subscription Order Management

Once the products are successfully created in SAP CRM and attached to the charge plan using cross-catalog mapping, they should be uploaded/replicated to FI-CA. There are two different product types available to replicate these products to FI-CA:

- FI-CA product
- Material master product

A FI-CA product is a lightweight entity that holds only language-dependent texts and sales-area-dependent data. If your implementation only involves either accounts receivable or accounts payable transactions, you can use either a FI-CA product or an material master product because it will be used only in provider contracts and partner agreements. However, if your implementation involves partner settlements or revenue shares, which will create account payable transactions along with the accounts receivable ones, you have the options to use either material master product or FI-CA product. Using an material master product for a partner settlement or revenue-share scenario allows both the provider contract and partner agreement to use the same product. On the other hand, if you choose to use a FI-CA product in SAP ERP, it only allows you to create a provider contract. For a partner agreement, you need to create a new product because SAP does not allow you to use the same product for both the provider contract (accounts receivable) and partner agreement (accounts payable).

7.5.4   Pricing

In a typical SAP BRIM implementation, as mentioned previously, there are different types of pricing:

- Pricing for a one-time charge
- Pricing for a recurring charge
- Pricing for a usage-based charge

Customers will be charged a one-time, recurring, or usage-based subscription charge based on the service they subscribe to and consume. This offers more flexibility in settlement of charges. For example, a mobile service provider offers services for customers such as a data plan based on usage consumption and voice and text messaging with a fixed monthly recurring charge; in addition, a one-time charge is usually applied for a new customer to activate services.

SAP BRIM, subscription order management has provided a standard pricing procedure, OPROV1, and this standard pricing procedure has the following condition types provided by SAP:

- OPRT, one-time fee
- OPMR, monthly fee (recurring)

For usage subscription, prices are maintained in a mapping table in SAP Convergent Charging.

7.6   Transactional Data

Let's take a look at some of the transactional data considerations, from provider order to provider contracts.

7.6.1   Provider Order

In a traditional SAP implementation, sales are usually captured in the sales order object. However, SAP BRIM has its own version of a sales order, called the provider order (Figure 7.9). The provider order differs from a typical sales order because it has special handling built-in to support both hardware and subscription-based products. For example, consider the technical resource ID, which is used by telecommunication companies to store a phone number that acts as a unique identifier for a customer order. Because SAP BRIM contains three distinctive modules, the data model of a provider order is designed to integrate with other SAP BRIM modules (e.g., placeholders for business agreements for SAP Convergent Invoicing/FI-CA integration and triggering of the order distribution infrastructure).

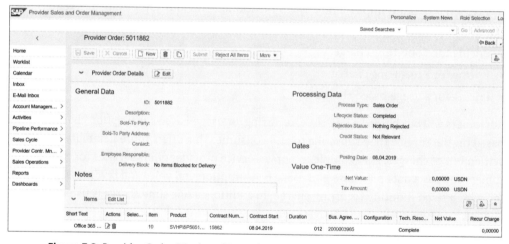

Figure 7.9 Provider Order Displayed in Web UI in SAP BRIM, Subscription Order Management

As part of SAP's standard delivery, a baseline provider order configuration is provided as transaction type PRVO. While that allows for end-to-end SAP BRIM integration, business processes specific to certain companies are not part of the flow (e.g., approvals or integration with different payment gateways/tax engines). Therefore, during SAP BRIM project implementation, making copies of the standard transaction is recommended.

7.6.2   Provider Contracts

A provider contract is an agreement placed between a customer and a service provider for the services rendered to the customer over an arc of time. A provider contract is generated as a subsequent document when a provider order that contains a rate plan product is released. During the release process, contract-relevant data from line items containing the rate plan product will be copied to the provider contract. Each line item containing a rate plan product will generate a new contract; therefore, it is not uncommon to see a provider order generating multiple provider contracts as a subsequent document.

Over the lifecycle of a provider contract, changes to the contract (e.g., cancellation or product change) are managed using a change process framework (Figure 7.10). Changes to a contract will first generate a new object called a change order. Change orders are temporary documents that hold contract changes for review or approval before merging the changes back to the provider contract.

As part of SAP's standard delivery, a baseline provider contract configuration is provided as transaction type PRVC, but it is often recommended to make a copy to support company-specific flows during implementation.

Figure 7.10 Contract History in Provider Contract Displayed in Web UI in SAP BRIM, Subscription Order Management

7.7   Replication of Provider Contract to SAP Convergent Invoicing and SAP Convergent Charging

Once the provider contract is successfully created in SAP CRM, it will be replicated to SAP ERP or SAP S/4HANA using the Order Distribution Infrastructure (ODI). The ODI uses Common Object Layer framework to distribute the provider contracts to SAP ERP or SAP S/4HANA and SAP Convergent Charging. This distribution of contract data to SAP ERP is applicable for create, change, and cancel scenarios/processes. ODI steps can be configured in SAP CRM under **SPRO • CRM • Cross Industry Functions • Provider Order and Contract Management • Transactions • Document Distribution**. You need to define the step types and schema here. The step types will be assigned to the schema based on the replication scenario.

Distribution of these contracts through ODI can be monitored using the distribution monitor. Using this monitor, contract replication can be reprocessed (displayed, rescheduled, and rerun). To access the distribution monitor, use Transaction CRM_ISX_DMON. In the SAP CRM web UI, there is an assignment block labeled **Fulfillment Status** (Figure 7.11), which will display the distribution status of the contracts, and this is applicable for provider contracts only. Once the provider contract is successfully replicated to SAP Convergent Invoicing and SAP Convergent Charging, the status of the contract in SAP CRM will be **Technically Active**.

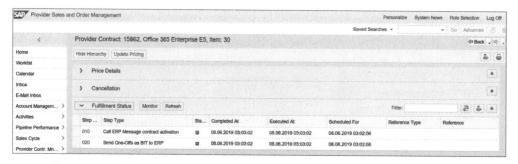

Figure 7.11 Fulfillment Status of Provider Contract

Let's take a deeper look at these pieces:

- **Partner Provider Order**

  To track the accounts payable part of the transaction, you need to create the partner agreement in SAP CRM. Similar to the provider order, there is a partner provider order that can be used to create the partner agreement. SAP has provided standard transaction type PRPO to create the partner provider order.

- **Partner Agreement**
  Once the partner provider order is released and submitted, it will create the partner agreement in SAP CRM. Once the partner agreement is successfully created in SAP CRM, it will be replicated to SAP Convergent Invoicing and SAP Convergent Charging through ODI. SAP has provided the standard transaction type PRPA for creation of a partner agreement.

- **Change Order**
  If further changes need to be executed on active provider contracts, SAP has provided the Change Process Framework to accomplish this.

The following are the preconfigured change processes provided by SAP to make changes to a provider contract:

- Product change
- Cancellation
- Change technical resources
- Contract extensions
- Change business agreement assignment

If any more additional change processes are to be configured, that can be done under **SPRO · CRM · Cross Industry Functions · Provider Order and Contract Management · Transactions · Provider Contract Specific Process Profiles**.

When a change process is executed on a provider contract, the system creates a change order by making an exact replica of the provider contract. This change order can be modified and released, and all the new changes will be updated in the provider contract.

The advantage of using the change process framework in updating the provider contract is that all changes are recorded, and the contract history is maintained correctly.

Just like the provider order being connected to the provider contract, change orders are also linked to the provider contract and will be visible under the **Contract History** assignment block. The change process can be executed on the provider contracts only if the contracts are technically active in the SAP CRM system.

7.8   Integration Points

Let's take a look at the integration between SAP CRM and SAP Convergent Invoicing (SAP ERP and SAP S/4HANA). The replication of transactional data (provider contract and contract change) from SAP CRM to SAP Convergent Invoicing happens through ODI.

For integration between SAP CRM and SAP Convergent Charging, the communication between SAP CRM and SAP Convergent Charging is through predefined web services provided by SAP Convergent Charging. These web services need to be activated during implementation.

For the integration between SAP Convergent Invoicing and SAP Convergent Charging, the communication between SAP Convergent Invoicing and SAP Convergent Charging is through the predefined web services provided by SAP Convergent Charging.

7.9   Summary

The first step toward SAP BRIM is deciding to transition to a subscription-based business model. Team members then need to gather information on the current systems and business processes and understand the deliverables and dependencies. As our customers' needs and requirements rapidly evolve, it is imperative that we continue to demonstrate a willingness to adapt and change our standard business practices. Implementing SAP BRIM is one of the first steps one can take to make this transition easier and smoother. As a reminder, the key steps to consider in the transition to SAP BRIM include the following:

- Considering the different subscription-based business models
- Evaluating your landscape to determine the best deployment scenario
- Choosing deployment options based on your product types
- Reviewing RDS and implementation best practices
- Master data considerations for implementing SAP BRIM
- Standard versus custom transaction types for provider orders or provider contracts

- Understanding the replication of provider contracts to SAP Convergent Invoicing or SAP Convergent Charging

- Considering the integration points between SAP CRM, SAP Convergent Invoicing, and SAP Convergent Charging

With the tools and knowledge provided, SAP BRIM can be leveraged as a solution in your journey toward a subscription-based business model.

7

Conclusion

Now, we'll quickly revisit the contents of these previous chapters, namely the SAP components and their benefits and how they integrate with each other. Then, we'll discuss the changing business models and the need for organizations to evolve their business processes to meet the customer expectations.

In **Chapter 1, Introduction to SAP BRIM**, we talked about the primary business drivers that motivate companies to follow a new platform for their order-to-cash process. The chapter explains the opportunities and risk for companies in the new economy model—the subscription economy. Then, readers are introduced to the key SAP BRIM components and its supporting add-ons. Finally, to prepare everyone for the subsequent chapters, a case-study which focusses on how Martex Corp.—a fictious company is trying to renovate its billing processes to stay competitive. Martex served as the baseline for the next several chapters master data and configuration set up.

In **Chapter 2, Subscription Order Management**, we discovered how to setup and enable SAP BRIM, subscription order management, including the configuration steps to build the use case and the integration with SAP Convergent Charging and SAP Convergent Invoicing.

In **Chapter 3, Rating and Charging**, we showed you how to setup and use SAP Convergent Charging and its modeling process based on Martex Corp. We went through the charge creation process by explaining the core tool, the charge types (recurring, one time, usage), and interface objects such as chargeable item classes and charged item classes.

In **Chapter 4, Invoicing**, we learned how to setup and use SAP Convergent Invoicing. We discuss billable items, consumption items, rating, billing, invoicing, and partner settlement, as well as some of the standard out-of-the-box reporting capabilities that SAP Convergent Invoicing offers.

In **Chapter 5, Contract Accounts Receivable and Payable**, we saw how to setup and use FI-CA, along with key concepts like account determination, open item management, account balance display, and integration with the general ledger, as well as some of the standard out-of-the-box reporting capabilities and relevant transaction codes for FI-CA.

In **Chapter 6, Integration with Other Solutions**, we learned how SAP BRIM is implemented in a heterogenous SAP CRM landscape and with other ancillary systems such as SAP Convergent Mediation by DigitalRoute, SAP Revenue Accounting and Reporting, SAP C/4HANA, CFM, entitlement management systems, tax engines, and payment gateways.

Chapter 7, First Steps to BRIM, explores leading practices for planning, evaluating, and considering SAP BRIM as a solution for the future. This chapter offered best practices for planning and considering SAP BRIM as a solution. You will learn how to avoid common pitfalls and gain insights into key decision points.

To thrive and succeed, companies should be able to see around corners, make quick course corrections, and harness technology to reimagine business models and reinvent how to deliver value to their customers. These strategies ensure companies maintain their competitive advantage and stay ahead of the curve.

With those principles in mind, many companies are looking beyond traditional infrastructure by migrating up the value chain—from products to platforms, software, and services. At the same time, many customers are demanding more control over what they consume and how they pay for it. Consequently, companies are shifting to the flexible consumption or everything-as-a-service (XaaS) model for their enterprise. Flexible consumption models can present XaaS providers with substantial potential benefits. These range from predictable, recurring revenue streams and improved margins to higher customer retention (driven by stickier, long-term relationships with those customers). Perhaps the biggest reason for some companies to consider transitioning to an XaaS model is that they can't afford not to.

There's a gigantic wave of companies shifting toward this new XaaS model. The first and most noticeable shift to the new flexible consumption model is with the technology industry, and most exciting is with the entertainment industry. The success of Netflix and Hulu have motivated many other companies to rethink their content delivery approaches. The traditional model, where the relationship ends with the final sale, is outdated. Many companies are doing everything they can to catch up or to further strengthen their position as the leaders.

To illustrate this point, let's look at an example. As of the time of writing this book (October 2019), Disney is preparing and about to release their first subscription model for their streaming services, which is giant step toward the future for the creator of Mickey Mouse.

Disney is not the only company trying to renovate their services. Apple is actively participating in this shift with their subscription offerings spanning from streaming services (Apple TV), to news (Apple News), and even gaming services (Apple Arcade).

Let's take another look into the wave of companies are shifting into the new flexible consumption model. If you are reading this book, that means you're familiar with the publisher of this book, SAP PRESS. This could mean two things: you have bought the book directly, or perhaps you have acquired this book by using the SAP PRESS subscription service.

This is not meant as a sales pitch for the SAP PRESS subscription service (even though they earn every right to have that). The paragraph serves as a clear example of how the companies across industries are getting into the new paradigm–the subscription economy where XaaS will be the new norm.

The Authors

Maniprakash Balasubramanian is a manager at Deloitte. He helps clients transform their business processes through flexible consumption models using SAP BRIM.

Chai Desai is a senior technology leader in Deloitte's SAP practice. He has more than 12 years of experience in implementing complex transformations in SAP BRIM and digital supply chain for Fortune 100 clients across various industries including technology, media, and telecommunication.

Sheikna Kulam is an experienced consultant working in the area of SAP BRIM. He is primarily focused in the area of subscription order management, and has been involved in multiple projects with other areas of SAP BRIM.

Chun Wei Ooi is a manager within the SAP BRIM practice in Deloitte. With his expertise in multiple SAP BRIM modules, he is a trusted advisor who helps clients from high-tech, media, and utilities industries embrace the new subscription economy.

Rakesh Rajagopal is a senior consultant within the SAP BRIM practice in Deloitte. He specializes in subscription and order Management in SAP CRM and SAP S/4HANA customer management.

Clement Sanjivi is a manager within the SAP BRIM practice in Deloitte who specializes in SAP Convergent Invoicing and FI-CA areas of SAP BRIM. He is a multiskilled SAP professional with all-around functional and technical expertise, and has played a key role in SAP implementations in the high-tech, transportation, and services sectors in the USA and UK.

Andreas Tan is a senior manager at Deloitte. He has more than 20 years of experience implementing large-scale projects, architecting anything-as-a-service (XaaS) solutions, and facilitating business transformation within the high-tech and software industries. He has in-depth, cross-module functional and technical knowledge of SAP BRIM and its integration with other SAP solutions.

Contributors

Denise Carew is an SAP NetWeaver administrator with extensive experience managing SAP HANA installations, upgrades, and migrations. She has a demonstrated ability to utilize SAP tools, services, methodologies, and best practices to design and implement solutions focused on elevating performance. She currently applying SAP best practices and methodologies to build SAP BRIM landscapes.

Swapnil Mehta is an experienced technologist working in the area of SAP accounts receivable and financial supply chain management. He primarily focuses on implementing order-to-cash processes for clients in the consumer product goods and automobile industries.

Dan Nguyen is an experienced technologist who focuses on SAP S/4HANA supply chain and order-to-cash capabilities and their integration with peripheral solutions such as SAP BRIM and SAP Service Cloud. Dan has participated in implementation projects associated with SAP BRIM and SAP S/4HANA across industries, but especially in the telecommunications and high-tech industries.

Bhargav Nutakki is an experienced supply chain consultant who helped design and implement industry standard business processes on large and complex projects. His main focus is on SAP products such as SAP S/4HANA, SAP Ariba, and order-to-cash solutions.

Neel Patel is a certified public accountant and a manager in the SAP practice at Deloitte. He specializes in SAP Revenue Accounting and Reporting and SAP S/4HANA Finance, and has experience with multiple implementations across varying industries.

Jyoti Prakash is a senior consultant focused on SAP BRIM solutions and an expert in its Contract Accounts Receivable and Payable and SAP Convergent Invoicing modules. He has more than eight years of SAP experience in the telecommunications, utilities, and consumer products industries. Jyoti has worked extensively in the meter-to-cash and consume-to-cash cycles.

Akshar Ved is a consultant in Deloitte's enterprise operations practice, where he supports the delivery of SAP embedded solutions. Akshar has participated in implementation projects in association with SAP BRIM and SAP S/4HANA in the telecommunications, high-tech, life sciences, and consumer goods industries. Akshar has experience with SAP BRIM, subscription order management, SAP Convergent Charging, and SAP Convergent Invoicing, and he looks forward to seeing how the capabilities enabled by SAP continue to expand in the future.

Index

R

S

- Implement SAP Commerce or SAP Commerce Cloud as your e-commerce platform

- Manage orders, content, catalogs, customer experience, and more

- Explore the SAP Commerce platform and the cloud portal

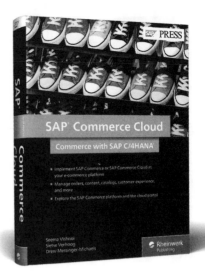

Seema Vishnoi, Sietse Verhoog, Drew Messinger-Michaels

SAP Commerce Cloud

Commerce with SAP C/4HANA

Connect and integrate your commercial channels with SAP Commerce and SAP Commerce Cloud! Learn to handle content, catalogs, and orders, configure essential components, and perform support and service tasks with step-by-step instructions. Get more from your implementation by improving your customer-facing search functionality and tweaking language and currency settings. Finally, integrate SAP Commerce with your backend system and see how successful organizations apply best practices.

531 pages, pub. 11/2018

E-Book: $79.99 | **Print:** $89.95 | **Bundle:** $99.99

www.sap-press.com/4621

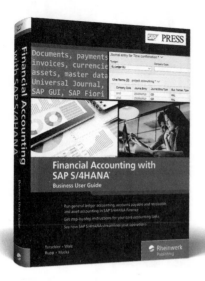

- Run general ledger accounting, accounts payable and receivable, and asset accounting in SAP S/4HANA Finance

- Get step-by-step instructions for your core accounting tasks

- See how SAP S/4HANA streamlines your operations

Jonas Tritschler, Stefan Walz, Reinhard Rupp, Nertila Mucka

Financial Accounting with SAP S/4HANA: Business User Guide

Finance professionals, it's time to simplify your day-to-day. This book walks through your financial accounting tasks, whether you're using SAP GUI transactions or SAP Fiori apps in your SAP S/4HANA system. For each of your core FI business processes—general ledger accounting, accounts payable, accounts receivable, and fixed asset accounting—learn how to complete key tasks, click by click. Complete your FI operations smoothly and efficiently!

604 pages, pub. 12/2019
E-Book: $69.99 | **Print:** $79.95 | **Bundle:** $89.99

www.sap-press.com/4938

Interested in reading more?

Please visit our website for all new book
and e-book releases from SAP PRESS.

www.sap-press.com